MEXICO

MEXICO

Narco-Violence and
a Failed State?

George W. Grayson

Transaction Publishers
New Brunswick (U.S.A.) and London (U.K.)

Third printing 2010
Copyright © 2010 by Transaction Publishers, New Brunswick, New Jersey.

This book is printed on acid-free paper that meets the American National Standard for Permanence of Paper for Printed Library Materials.

Library of Congress Catalog Number: 2009029164
ISBN: 978-1-4128-1151-4
Printed in the United States of America

Library of Congress Cataloging-in-Publication Data

Grayson, George W., 1938-
  Mexico : narco-violence and a failed state? / George W. Grayson.
       p. cm.
  Includes bibliographical references and index.
  ISBN 978-1-4128-1151-4
    1. Drug traffic--Mexico. 2. Narco terrorism--Mexico. 3. Drug control--Mexico. 4. Mexico--Politics and government. 5. Mexico--Economic conditions. I. Title.

HV5840.M4G73 2009
363.450972--dc22

                                                              2009029164

Dedication

To José Raúl Vera López, O.P., Bishop of Saltillo, Coahuila, and to Héctor González Martínez, Metropolitan Archbishop of Durango, for your courage in the face of personal danger, your readiness to condemn supposedly "untouchable" criminals and their enablers, and your inspirational commitment to uplifting the downtrodden.

Contents

Acknowledgments

Upon embarking upon this project, I had no idea of the spider web-like complexity of the drug world. Time constraints and scanty information force television news programs to simplify coverage: "Sinaloa Cartel May Resort to Deadly Force in U.S.," "Mexico Captures Powerful Gulf Cartel Hit Man," and "Suspected Cop Killer May Be in Zeta Gang,"—"Details to Follow."

Take, for example, Los Zetas. Trained with U.S. assistance as members of the Mexican Army's Special Forces Airmobile Groups (GAFES), several of these elite soldiers defected to protect the top dog in the Gulf Cartel, headquartered in the Matamoros area, south of Brownsville, Texas; after the incarceration of cartel leader Osiel Cárdenas Guillén. The paramilitaries gradually began acting on their own, eventually forging an independent, cellular structure. Yet it is unlikely that the separation is complete. The Gulf Cartel still controls 20 or 30 percent of Tamaulipas—with Los Zetas commanding the rest. The relatively low death toll in this coastal state attests not only to the coziness between local politicians with the narco-barons, but to the probability that Los Zetas and the Gulf Cartel have hammered out a modus vivendi and cooperate occasionally when it serves the interests of both. In southern Guerrero, a Hobbesian state of violence and misery, Los Zetas have cast their lot with the Beltrán Leyva family (former allies of the Sinaloa Cartel) and appear to have done the same in various municipalities of Mexico State, the nation's most populous jurisdiction. For a while, the ex-soldiers and their recruits made common cause with one of four segments of the shadowy, messianic La Familia. The syndicate is centered in bloodstained Michoacan state where the Milenio and Jalisco Cartels, comrades of the Sinaloans, long have operated.

Middle East scholar par excellence and a valued colleague at the College of William and Mary, James Bill, analogizes Mexico's drug world to Afghanistan, Pakistan, and Iraq. Political parties and their armies may dominate the headlines. A closer look, however, finds religious,

ethr   ng these organizations. Then there
are   ings within which exist tribes and
wa   ak for extended families that have
the   of *matryoshki*, the Russian nesting
do   l inside the other.

The challenge   earch on Mexico's underground also
springs from cartel members' employing multiple names; their readiness
either to take credit for operations they did not commit or to blame rivals
for those that they did; and the obvious barrier to talking with culprits and
suspects. Moreover, President Felipe Calderón Hinojosa's local version
of the war on drugs had produced the arrest of hundreds of narco-traffickers in 2009, often sparking changes in the leadership and structures
of criminal syndicates. A moving picture would be more useful, but the
author can present only his snapshot of the syndicates, *cartelitos*, gangs,
and freelance thugs.

For this reason, I admire authors of articles, reports, and books
that have brought clarity, insights, and a framework to the subject at
hand.

Among these astute individuals are Sigrid Arzt Colunga, Luis Astorga,
Bruce M. Bagley, Abel Barajas, John J. Bailey, Charles Bowden, William
Booth, Edgardo Buscaglia, Mark Bowden, Hal Brands, Tracy Carl and
her colleagues at the Associated Press in Mexico City, Jorge Chabat,
James H. Cheechan, Ron Chepesiuk, Hugh Collins, A.J. Corchado, Sam
Dillon, Ken Ellingwood, Jesús Esquivel, Samuel González Ruiz, José
Gil Olmos, Tim Golden, Dan Gretch, Ion Grillo, Alejandro Gutiérrez,
Enrique Krauze, Mark Lacey, and Sam Logan.

Other experts include Peter A. and Kip Schegel Lupsha, Adela Navaro
Bello and her colleagues at the *Zeta* news weekly, Terrence Popper, Julia
Preston, Sam Quiñones, Ricardo Revalo, Luis Rubio, Julio Scherer García, Diana Washington Valdez, Casey Wian, and scores of other careful
observers. Although I have talked directly with more than half of these
analysts, none of these individuals bears responsibility for the contents
of this book.

Only late in my work did I grasp the increasing importance of women
in Mexico's subterranean drug world. Although references to female
players appear throughout the text, Appendix 3 offers preliminary and
roughly-hewn generalizations about their role. Rather than leave out this
admittedly cursory view, I inserted it in hopes that it may prove helpful
to another researcher planning to prepare a comprehensive study of this
neglected subject.

Another mea culpa is in order for Appendix 1. The list of drug lords, traffickers, and hit men is far from complete and it was impossible to find complete information about all the individuals mentioned. Oh for a platoon of graduate students!

I enthusiastically thank Karen Rohan, managing editor at the Foreign Policy Association for allowing me to incorporate in this text segments of *Mexico's Struggle with Drugs and Thugs*, which the FPA published in early 2009. Ms. Rohan and Associate Editor Agnieshka—"St. Agnes"— Burke turned heaven and earth to ensure that the monograph saw the light of day. Debt is also due to Al Luxenburg (Foreign Policy Research Institute), Peter DeShazo (Center for Strategic and International Studies), and Mark Krikorian (Center for Immigration Studies) for allowing me to draw on material that I had originally prepared for their prestigious think tanks. Doug McVey, chief executive officer of Common Sense for Drug Policy, kindly approved my use of a meticulously documented analysis that his organization prepared on the causes of death in the United States. This table appears as Appendix 5.

The Reference and Inter-Library Loan Department at William & Mary's Swem Library performed miracles in locating "impossible-to-find" data, books, and articles.

Equally amazing was the College's Information Technology Department—and in particular, its unfailingly accommodating Technical Support Center. Lance Richardson, Technology Support Engineer, and his colleague Kitty Smith saved the life of the manuscript when an intruder—no doubt a cartel thug—infected the text with a mysterious disease.

For the maps (and I wish there were more), I am indebted to Joseph Gilley, graphic design manager, at William & Mary's Publications Office. Without the lead offered by Suzanne Seurattan, news marketing director of University Relations, I would not have learned of Joe's talents.

E.J. and Larry Storrs made invaluable comments on portions of the manuscript, and Mark Sullivan and June Beitiel, current staff members at the Library of Congress' Congressional Research Service, directed me to helpful CRS publications.

James Creehan, a Toronto-based sociologist and criminologist at the University of Toronto and University of Guelph continuously sent me articles, reports, and analyses. At the same time, he spent countless hours meticulous, intelligently, and patiently answering questions, proof-reading the entire manuscript, and offering incredibly lucid advice on content and style. In addition, Professor Creechan assisted in compiling the glossary of terms related to the drug underworld. Jim, please excuse the cliché, but you are "a gentleman and a scholar."

I would be remiss if I failed to thank Michael C. Andrews, Louis I. Jaffe Professor emeritus at Old Dominion University. He not only reviewed carefully and substantially enhanced the chapter on drug cartels, but informed me that not everyone knows Spanish and the nicknames used by narco-traffickers were often confusing. Many of these cognomens derive from Mexico's rich and unique rendition of Spanish, and I was reluctant to translate them, lest I lose original meanings. However, I have taken Michael's advice to heart and when possible employed dual translations or only the English version. Suffice to say that many of the sobriquets are diminutives of first names—that is El Chuy (Jesús), El Teo (Teodoro), El Efra (Efraín), El Kike (Enrique), and so forth. Anyone who remains baffled should consult Francisco J. Santamaría's incomparable *Diccionario de Mejicanismos.*

Similarly, my close friend, colleague, athlete *extraordinaire*, and Renaissance scholar, English professor John W. Conlee took time from practicing for Wimbledon competition to examine thoroughly more than fifty pages of the manuscript. Even though I was an undergraduate English major, John improved my roughly-hewn prose, while pointing out punctuation errors and inconsistencies in names, dates, and places. No wonder he is among the most admired faculty members on our campus.

Experts on Mexican security issues graciously allowed me to pick their fertile minds: Fred Álvarez Palafox, Peter K. Núñez, Leonardo Ffrench, Jon French, Steve Ordal, Roderic Ai Camp, Bruce G. Bagley, and Armand Peschard-Svedrup. Longtime friend and retired U.S. Foreign Service Officer Daniel L. Dolan made trenchant suggestions about the configuration and rituals of the Roman Catholic Church; and three über-experts—Guillermo Flores Velasco, Carlos Heredia Díaz, and Juan Gabriel Valencia Benavides—endeavored to enlighten me on Mexican politics over delicious meals.

I also interviewed scores of Mexican and American military officers, intelligence agents, diplomats, and other civilian public servants, who are familiar with, and often involved in making, anti-narcotics' policy. They went out of their way to provide unclassified information in off-the-record conversations and other communications.

I wish to recognize the financial contribution of William & Mary's Class of 1938, which endowed the academic chair that I am honored to hold.

Gabriela Regina Arias, a William & Mary undergraduate and my research assistant, who assiduously searched the Internet, ransacked libraries, proofread, and helped prepare tables. "Gabi" is a remarkable young person—intelligent, hard working, and thoroughly dependable. Luanna D. Martins, administrative assistant for International Relations and Global Studies at the College, came to my rescue when I needed fresh eyes to review the final version of the text. Whenever I required scanning, photocopying, safe-keeping of drafts, and other services, the Government Department's Administrative Office Manager Valerie S. Trovato and Budget Office Manager E.R. Leland came through with flying colors. Tessa Vinson and Elizabeth Wedding also provided critical help.

Above all, I wish to express appreciation to Professor Irving Louis Horowitz, founder, chairman of the board, and editorial director of Transaction Publishers at Rutgers—The State University of New Jersey. His faith in my ability to complete the venture, his encouraging letters and e-mails, and his infectious sense of humor applied balm to my soul.

Meanwhile, if a Croix de Guerre for editors were established, its first recipient would be Transaction Publishers' Andrew McIntosh. He demonstrated understanding, helpfulness, and professionalism when a medley of factors—a lost computer file, unexpected receipt of new material, minor eye surgery, and a substantial change in Mexico's prosecuting its drug war—delayed submission of the manuscript by a month. I explained these trials and tribulations to Professor Horowitz; praised Mr. McIntosh's forbearance; and suggested he should have had me taken out a week or two before. To this communiqué, Transaction's venerable chairman shot back: "He [McIntosh] is a very important part of Transaction, and an entirely decent person—and friend. However, he has poor judgment on hit men. The one that he sent to get you must have gotten lost bathing in Acapulco!"

Words fail to convey the gratitude deserved by my incredible wife, Bryan Holt Grayson. She became a writer's widow—literally a "Window's widow"—for at least two months, observing mainly the back of my head framed in the glow of a computer screen. It is testimony to her angelic qualities that she extended only support, succor, sustenance, and sweetness. Phone calls and visits by daughter Gisèle Ruth Artura Grayson Hamilton, Aunt Margaret Grayson Saunders, and belle mère Mary Bryan Holt also pepped me up. Son T. Keller Grayson III graciously shared his skill as a wordsmith when scrutinizing the Introduction and Chapter 1.

With all of the assistance rendered, it is clear that any shortcomings of this study rest with our 9-year-old white cat Lily. My protestations aside, no matter the day or hour she insisted on lying next to the word processor and, no doubt, made questionable entries that neither I nor the publisher discovered.

George W. Grayson
Williamsburg, Virginia
September 2009

Map of Mexico

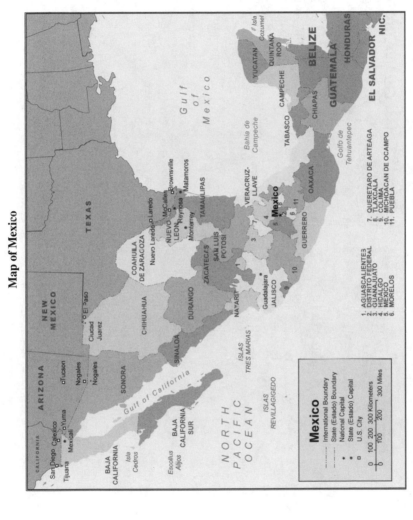

Source: Congressional Research Service, Mark P. Sullivan and June S. Beittel, *Mexico-U.S. Relations: Issues for Congress*, April 14, 2009.

Map of Michoacán

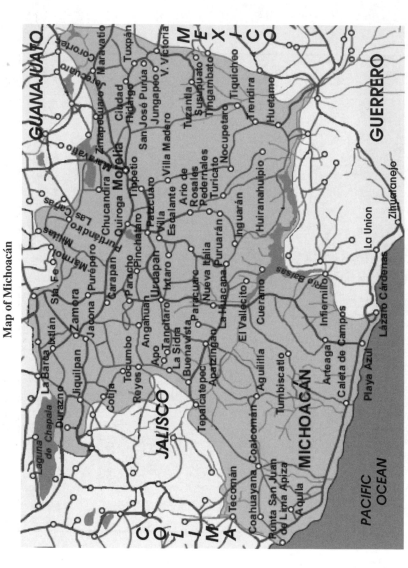

Source: GNU Operating System.

Introduction

Savage drug-related murders have incited nightmares in Tijuana, a city of 1.4 million inhabitants lying fifteen miles south of San Diego. American day-trippers now shun the blemished sidewalks of Avenida Revolución, the main tourist thoroughfare where strip-joints, table-dance bars, and aromatic restaurants beckon visitors with flashing neon signs and muscle-bound doormen doubling as bouncers. Nevertheless, one sector continues to flourish, the funeral industry—to the point that parlors are short of morticians. Once again on November 1, 2009, Mexicans will celebrate the annual Day of the Dead by placing marigolds, candy skulls, and candles on tombs. In accord with this practice, family members and friends leave toys for dead children ("the little angels" or "*los angelitos*"), and bottles of tequila, mescal, or pulque for adults. But death now means much more in Tijuana than the observance of a pre-Hispanic ritual.

The murder of approximately 160 people during 2008 overwhelmed local funeral homes. "We've seen a big increase in the number of clients because of the drug war, especially since September. It's gone from a few [bodies] a week to one or two every day," said Fernando, a funeral home owner. Once a wide-open town where Americans came to buy medicine, tequila, and sex, Tijuana now suffers from plummeting tourism, even while its mortuaries thrive because of shootouts and gangland mutilations.

Families must pay $1,000 or more to have their dead loved ones made presentable for wakes. In light of a surge in decapitations, undertakers now offer to hold a body until its head is found before proceeding with the obsequies. In fact, morticians from other states have seen a business opportunity and are opening branches in Tijuana. "We'll do the make-up on the body for free," said one employee as he distributed brochures outside a rival funeral home in Tijuana. This grisly phenomenon is also taking place in Ciudad Juárez, Nogales, Nuevo Laredo, and other smaller cities scattered like tarnished ornaments along the 2,000-mile-long U.S.-Mexican frontier.

The increase in funerals spurred the demand for caskets. The Sonora-based Grupo RI, which supplies coffins to the main funeral homes in Tijuana, reported that company sales doubled during the third quarter of 2008. "We used to sell around 49 caskets a month. Since August, we've been selling that number every 15 days," stated a distributor for the company.[1]

The exploding brutality sparked by drug cartels contrasts sharply with pre-1980s Mexico when a regime headed by a strong leader and a dominant political machine—the Institutional Revolutionary Party (PRI)—maintained order and stability, through both explicit and implicit arrangements understood by the government and its antagonists.

Indeed, this top-down flow of power evoked comparisons with the Roman Catholic Church, an analogy that will be developed in subsequent chapters. Lest I confuse readers, please know that I am not seeking to denigrate the Roman Catholic Church, many of whose leaders I esteem. Rather, I am drawing parallels between authoritarian, secular institutions in Mexico—notably, the PRI/government tandem and the Godless drug cartels—and the hierarchical structures of the Roman Catholic papacy. With few exceptions, the latter has resolutely condemned the criminal organizations, which evince values that are diametrically opposed to the teachings of Christ. Consequently, I have dedicated this book to José Raúl Vera López, O.P., bishop of Saltillo, Coahuila, and to Archbishop Héctor González Martínez, Metropolitan Archbishop of Durango. Regrettably, I know neither of these men. However, their courage in the face of personal danger, their readiness to condemn supposedly "untouchable" criminals and their enablers, and their commitment to uplifting the downtrodden have inspired me in more ways than they could ever know.

During the last twenty-five to thirty years, however, the influence of the PRI's "Revolutionary Church" has steadily dwindled, although its top figures are intent on recovering Mexico's Vatican, Los Pinos presidential residence, in 2012. At the same time, Mexico's chief executives—once as powerful as exalted popes—have suffered a diminishment of their public status.

As never before, eminent opinion-leaders lament that the country—characterized by strong men and weak institutions in the modern era—risks becoming a "failed state." For scholar Francis Fukuyama, this condition involves two dimensions of state powers—namely, its (1) "scope" or the different functions and goals taken on by governments and (2) "strength" or the ability of administrations to plan and execute policies.[2] Among other things, strong states guarantee security, law enforcement, access to high-quality schools and health-care, sound fiscal and monetary policies, responsive political systems, opportunities for employment and social mobility, retirement benefits, and transparency. In Fukuyama's dichotomy, Mexico's government boasts an extensive "scope" evidenced by its monopolistic control over the petroleum industry, its role as the principal supplier of electricity, its financing of and nominal control over public education, its diverse retirement and health-care programs, its administration of public universities, and its dominance over the armed forces and law enforcement agencies.

Meanwhile, a medley of factors—the population's growth and increasing diversity, the emergence of new political actors, tensions between the private and public sectors, a more assertive media, the rise of civic groups, and the impact of globalization—diminished the strength of the traditional state-PRI alliance in terms its "ability ... to plan and execute policies, and to enforce laws cleanly and transparently." In other words, the "institutional capacity" of the Mexican state has plunged in recent years.[3] "Weak" states fall short in these areas; "failed" states receive "Fs." We will return to the failed state issue in Chapter 10 and the Conclusions.

Indictment of the Mexican State

Respected analysts bemoan the surging debility of a Mexican state whose fragmentation is concomitant with increasing opportunities for drug lords to go about their nefarious trade with impunity. The pessimism extends even to those who had voiced high hopes for Felipe Calderón Hinojosa, an experienced politician, a social-Christian, and a moderate within the center-right National Action Party (PAN), who assumed the presidency on December 1, 2006.

Luis Rubio, the internationally acclaimed director general of the Center of Research for Development, argued that "our weaknesses as a society are formidable not only in the police and judicial domains, but also in the growing erosion of the social fabric and the absence of a sense of good and bad...."[4]

In the same vein, Luis F. Aguilar, an astute and veteran observer, stated the following with respect to the ubiquitous violence: "The public insecurity exhibits the impotence of its branches of government, the futility of its laws and the incompetence of its leaders.... The tragedy is that the decomposition of the State comes from within, largely from its policy whose responsibility is to apply the law fairly without exceptions ... but the situation of political paralysis and institutional weakness has made us recognize that we are really: a society searching for a State."[5]

Meanwhile, Javier Hurtado, a distinguished professor at the University of Guadalajara, addressed the despair of his countrymen who took part in a massive "Light up Mexico" march on August 30, 2008, in opposition to the horrendous criminality and precariousness: "In the face of this situation, citizens find themselves completely vulnerable. It is neither desirable to take justice into their own hands, nor is it possible to continue putting up with inept leaders."[6]

For his part, prize-winning journalist René Delgado averred that: "The people are fed up and disenchanted with institutions. They wish to reclaim the territory lost to the State [to narco-traffickers] with or without the government and [political] parties. And the [current official] gibberish will inevitably crystallize into disaster."[7]

Among factors that uphold the "weak" and "failed state" arguments are: a soaring murder rate, a jump in sadistic executions, increased kidnappings, prison escapes, the venality of local, state, and federal police, a failure of policy makers to enforce safety codes, and disenchantment with institutions occupied by officials who often live like princes even as 35 percent of Mexico's 110 million people eek out a living in hardscrabble poverty. Evidence of a failed state becomes apparent in efforts to immigrate to the United States.

Atrocities may have exacerbated the rate of northbound flows, which—contrary to conventional expectations—skyrocketed during Calderón's first year in office. Relying on U.S. Census data, Mexico's National Population Council reported that the number of Mexican migrants living north of the Rio Grande grew 679,611 in 2007—a five-fold jump over the increase in 2006 (105,347)—before a 25 percent decline took place in the year ending in August 2008.[8] Mexicans are prepared to risk life and limb to leave their country, even as the U.S. economy faces contraction, the employment outlook appears grim for Americans, and state legislatures are amplifying their crackdown on lawbreakers. It comes down to a wrenching choice to remain in a country suffering criminality and joblessness or migrate to a nation characterized by the rule of law and high unemployment.

Today, unremitting violence plagues Mexico—sensationalized by decapitations, torture, castrations, kidnappings, plunging victims in vats of acid, and burning them alive carried out by drug-cartel hit men and run-of-the-mill thugs. These heinous acts are driven by money, revenge, ransom, extortion, access to drugs, turf battles, propaganda, and the cartels' determination to spark fear in rivals, the police, the military, and the population.

On September 15, 2008, a possible act of terrorism took place for the first time since the revolutionary period. Around 11 p.m., as thousands of revelers celebrated Independence Day in Morelia, a city in southwest Mexico, miscreants heaved two fragmentation grenades into the crowd. When the smoke had cleared, eight people lay dead and more than 110 men, women, and children had been injured. TV networks beamed video footage of the gory scene to incredulous viewers across the country.

President Calderón waited a day before visiting disaster victims, while hundreds of military personnel and federal police immediately flooded into Morelia to provide security to shocked citizens. The Attorney General's Office (PGR) offered $1 million (then 10 million pesos) for information leading to the capture of the masterminds and perpetrators of the carnage. But Deputy Emilio Gamboa Patrón, with his own supersized closet of skeletons and a big shot in the once-dominant Institutional Revolutionary Party, admitted that citizens were afraid to file complaints. Only one of every five crimes is reported; only 13 percent of these crimes are investigated; and in only 5 percent of the cases are the accused brought before a judge.[9]

For their part, Calderón and other dumbfounded politicians speculated about who had inflicted this wanton slaughter amid an iconic fête in that picturesque colonial city, located in the chief executive's home state of Michoacán.

Were the perpetrators members of the powerful Gulf Cartel—headquartered just below Texas in Tamaulipas state—whose erstwhile leader had recruited ruthless paramilitaries known as Los Zetas? Were the miscreants members of the Gulf Cartel's chief rival, the Sinaloa Federation, centered in Sinaloa state, which nestles between the Sierra Madre Mountains and the Pacific Ocean? Might they be affiliated with The Michoacán Family (*La Familia Michoacana or La Familia*), a shadowy, segmented Bible-pounding gang that took credit for hanging seven banners blaming the bloodbath on Los Zetas, three of whom were subsequently taken into custody? Could they have been guerrillas from the *Insurgent People's Revolutionary Army* (ERPI) hoping either to impress drug mafias or launch a freelance strike?

Apart from the instigators' identity was an ominous possibility that the attack foreshadowed an escalation in strife: from homing in on targeted enemies to relying on indiscriminate terrorism. The "Morelia Massacre" occurred barely a week after sadists had carried out twenty-four executions in Mexico State alone. And a prisón riot on September 14 and 17, 2008, at Tijuana's La Mesa penitentiary took the lives of at least twenty-three inmates and injured scores of convicts and guards.

This volume (1) discusses the attributes of the once-almighty "revolutionary church"—the PRI, (2) focuses on wars, Prohibition, and other antecedents of the Narco Churches that sprang to life in Mexico during PRI rule, (3) explores the emergence of two "narco denominations" embodied by the Sinaloa and Gulf Cartels, (4) examines the deterioration of the revolutionary church, (5) illuminates the Diaspora of the drug denominations and their fragmentation, (6) lays out Calderón's evolving strategy against the narco-infidels, (7) analyzes the government's holy war against its evil adversaries, (8) casts light on the multiplication of narco-sects complicating this anti-drug crusade—with particular emphasis on the heretical Los Zetas and pious La Familia Michoacana, (9) reviews how drug issues changed U.S.-Mexican relations and led the 2008 Mérida Initiative and subsequent programs, and (10) evaluates the prospects of Mexico's becoming a failed state as it pursues its costly campaign against drugs.

Notes

1.   Lizbeth Diaz, "Mexico Death Industry Thrives on Drug War Killings," *Reuters*, November 1, 2008. http://wap.alertnet.org/thenews/newsdesk/N01349201.htm; and Omar Millán González, "Funeral Homes See Big Rise in Business," *San Diego Union-Tribune*, November 16, 2008. *www.signonesandiego.com.*
2.   Francis Fukuyama, "The Imperative of State-Building," *Journal of Democracy* 14 (April 2004): 17-31.
3.   Fukuyama, "The Imperative of State-Building."
4.   Quoted in Luis Rubio, "Violencia," *Reforma*, June 8, 2008.
5.   Quoted in Luis F. Aguilar, "En busca del Estado," *Reforma*, August 13, 2008.
6.   Quoted in Javier Hurtado, "México secuestrado," *Reforma*, August 14, 2008.
7.   René Delgado quoted in "Un país inseguro," *El Siglo de Torreón*, August 30, 2008. *www.elsiglodetorreon.com.mx.*
8.   Silvia Garduño, "Crece con Calderón la migración a EU," *Reforma*, September 21, 2008; and Julia Preston, "Mexico Data Say Migration to the U.S. has plummeted, *New York Times*, May 15, 2009.
9.   Testimony of Joy Olson, executive director of the Washington Office on Latin America, before the Subcommittee on State, Foreign Operations and Related Programs of the U.S. House of Representatives Appropriations Committee, March 10, 2009. *www.appropriations.house.gov/Witness_testimony/SFOPS/Joy_Olson_03_10_09.pdf.*

1

The Revolutionary Church

For much of the twentieth century, Mexico's chief executives presided over the nation in the manner of secular popes who regarded the average citizen as belonging to their flock. They came to this exalted position after the overthrow of dictator Porfirio Díaz (1876-1911) in the bloody, protracted revolution that drove out the *ancien régime*, and legitimated the new order by a 1917 Constitution. This fundamental law infused the presidency with sweeping powers, and—above all—made it the center-piece of the Mexican state reinforced by a hegemonic revolutionary party. This organization later became the PRI, which institutionalized these trappings into a revolutionary church.[1]

This secular church derived its inspiration and legitimacy from such sainted notables as Fathers Miguel Hidalgo and José María Morelos who had ignited the independence movement from Spain in the early nineteenth century, from Benito Juárez who championed the separation of the state from the Roman Catholic Church, from Francisco I. Madero who unfurled the banner of "effective suffrage, no re-election" to cata-lyze the upheaval that drove Díaz from office, from the Flores Magón brothers who fought for workers' rights, and from Emiliano Zapata and Francisco "Pancho" Villa who battled for land reform.

In the aftermath of the assassination of the chief executive-elect Ál-varo Obregón (1928) and a Cristero Rebellion pitting fervent Catholics against an anti-clerical state (1926-29), President Plutarco Elías Calles created the first incarnation of the revolutionary party. He conceived of it as a confederal organization composed of military caudillos, labor chiefs, small-party honchos, peasant organizations, and local power brokers—complemented by a silent but ever-present musculature of the armed forces, which could function as crusading knights when activated. Now remembered as the Maximum Chief (*Jefe Máximo*), Calles sought to stabilize an unsteady, fledgling regime that had been buffeted by revolution, assassination, and civil uprising for two decades. Although suppos-edly *primus enter pares* as each element of the confederation preserved its own identity, Calles served as de facto leader of the new party, gave visibility to its worthies at official events, strengthened its finances with tithes in the form of one day's annual salary by public employees, and marshaled government resources and the media to magnify his image and that of three successors who served as his proxies.

In 1938 Calles' choice for the presidency, General Lázaro Cárdenas del Río, enhanced his own standing and that of the new secular church by reconfiguring the powerful fledgling institution; specifically, he con-verted its nominally collegial framework into a corporatist body—with believers bound to the revolutionary party in an authoritarian fashion through components organized by occupations.

Members of *officially* recognized trade unions affiliated with the party's "labor sector," headed by the Confederation of Mexican Workers (CTM). In a similar fashion, residents of communal farms or *ejidos* were gathered into a "peasant sector" or National Confederation of Campesinos (CNC). Average citizens, white-collar state and federal bureaucrats, pro-fessionals, intellectuals, and owners of small businesses could join the catch-all "popular sector" formally known as the National Confederation of Popular Organizations (CNOP)—with the Federation of Government Employees' Unions and the National Syndicate of Educational Workers (SNTE) constituting its strongest components. A "military sector" existed briefly, but was dissolved in December 1940 when politicians acted to prevent the armed forces' becoming the ultimate mediator of disputes and the moral legitimator of new administrations. And interestingly, senior officers retreated gladly from the glare of public participation; those who sought or held political office wound up in the CNOP.

The tradition has remained potent, and eventually resulted in a number of religious "orders" and "sects." For example, since the late 1980s Elba Esther Gordillo Morales, the immensely wealthy and mighty "moral leader" of SNTE—has behaved as a kind of Mother Superior over an assemlage of 1.2-million teachers. Sometimes she backs the secular revolutionary church; at other times she confronts it. She is an ally of Carlos Romero Deschamps, the rich and venal superior general of another formidable order—the Mexi-can Oil Workers' Union (STPRM), renowned not for good works but for featherbedding, theft, sweetheart contracts, and costly subterfuges with the state oil monopoly, Petróleos Mexicanos (PEMEX).

As shrewd as a renaissance pope, Cárdenas divided and controlled his followers, obviating any challenge to his supreme power. He shrewdly separated trade unionists from peasants, placed white-collar and blue-collar union members in different sectors, and compartmentalized the CNOP into ten units. In addition, he created virtual cardinals of the bosses of these corporatist dioceses, all the while emphasizing that decision-making would flow from the top down.

Even though they were not fully invested in the revolutionary church, other associations formed to "represent" bankers, lawyers, large farmers, livestock producers, insurance interests, stockbrokers, and industrialists; they were required to register with the state—a de facto obligation to genuflect before, if not overtly kiss the ring of, the supreme secular pontiff who could exert life-or-death control over their economic fate.

Besides his formal attributes as chief executive and commander-in-chief of the armed forces, Lázaro Cárdenas relied on meta-constitutional rituals: above all, he formalized "*el dedazo*" and the anointment of a successor through a "big finger." He was faithfully served by syco-phantic princes of this secular church, such as CTM secretary general Fidel Velázquez Sánchez (1900-1997), and he often ritually circulated a short list of acceptable candidates to measure their popularity among his appointed potentates and cardinals. Before his death, the Roman Vicar of Christ may influence the choice of a successor by appointing cardinals who share his philosophy. In a similar vein, all future vicars of this new secular state could appoint functionaries committed to maintaining the hegemony of the new temporal faith and who would be inclined to choose someone of like-mind. Under the PRI, the president named and removed governors and other ranking officials as if they were bellhops, and he spent freely from a discretionary fund that was never audited—somewhat analogous to the Banco Ambrosiano's free-wheeling initiatives on behalf of the Vatican in the last quarter of the twentieth century.

In addition, the Mexican president's annual *Informe* or State of the Nation speech brings to mind *Urbi e Orbi*, literally "to the City [of Rome] and to the World," which now applies to a papal address and Apostolic Blessing that the pontiff directs not only to the City of Rome but to the entire world at Easter and Christmas.

Each September 1, Mexican chief executives use the *Informe* to make grandiose pronouncements about the country's domestic and foreign policy. This speech, which is also suggestive of a papal bull, constitutes only one of many ceremonies at which the revolutionary church's cardinals, bishops, priests, and religious brothers and sisters somberly assemble to see and be seen. Also important are the anniversary of the takeover of the oil industry (March 18), Labor Day (May 1), Independence Day (September 16), and Revolution Day (November 16).

No wonder that political scientist L. Vincent Padgett defined the nation's ruler as:

> a semidivine father-figure to the people, inherently good in caring for his children. He is never directly challenged, as for example in the press, because that would shake the very basis of secular government. He is the *jefe* of *jefes* [chief of chiefs], who makes all final decisions. Each new public work is still his gift to the people, who (especially in rural areas) petition him for the things they need in the same way that the Viceroy was petitioned centuries ago. The passage of time has changed much, but these deep-rooted practices with their supporting norms and symbols have not died—they live on the aura of the President of Mexico in the closing years of the twentieth century.[2]

In the same vein, historian Frank Brandenburg referred to the chief executive as the undisputed head of the revolutionary clan:

> He inherits Hidalgo and Morelos, leaders of Mexican independence, as godparents. He acquires Benito Juárez, nineteenth-century liberal, as his grandfather. He joins the line of successors to the first father of the Revolution, Francisco I. Madero. He usually, but not necessarily, holds the office of President of Mexico. The head of the clan exercises all power—or no power. He either delivers the definitive word on every matter, or someone else rises to take his place. Aggregation of interests can happen both inside and outside the Family, but in the last instance, all demands are judged by the head of the Family.[3]

In the words of journalist Alan Riding:

> Like the Divine Right of Kings and the infallibility of the Pope, [the myth of omnipotence] maintains the mystery of the office. The President is, after all, the heir to a pre-Hispanic tradition of theocratic authoritarianism that was enormously reinforced by the political centralism and religious dogmatism of the Spanish Colony.[4]

Pictures of the president graced the wall of all government offices much like the grandfatherly Pope Benedict XVI oversees church sanctuaries from prominently placed photographs and paintings; both the PRI, whose secular clergy manipulated elections to its advantage, and, the universal church had offices even in remote villages. In a few of the anti-clerical states, the PRI had even converted places of worship into party headquarters. Although lacking *L'Obsservatore Romano* to reiterate the reigning orthodoxy, Mexico's temporal church kept the media in line through its monopoly over the sale of newsprint and its discretion over placement of advertising for government agencies. Moreover, it firmly regulated television and radio stations, and depended on the armed forces to be the eyes and ears of an authoritarian regime that emphasized cooptation over coercion. "Mexican *presidencialismo* made the head of the federal executive the ultimate dispenser of political mobility, economic opportunities, and social justice in the country."[5]

In effect, sectoral leaders along with heads of key ministries—finance, economy, labor, defense, navy, and interior (Gobernación)—represented a revolutionary curia. The interior secretary, with responsibility for political negotiations, migration, and intelligence, shared a striking similarity to the Vatican's secretary of state, who is referred to as the Holy See's "prime minister." Especially powerful interior secretaries evoked comparisons with the role played by Cardinal Richelieu in the reign of Louis XIII. Of course, the intrepid early seventeenth-century French cleric never ascended to the throne, while the Interior Ministry once provided a springboard to Los Pinos.

The nation's governors served at the president's pleasure and represented archbishops and bishops in this secular congregation. Just as Rome sent forth nuncios as emissaries to various nations, the revolutionary church dispatched PRI delegates to manage affairs in the states, especially at the time of elections. When serving archbishops and bishops, priests dispensed the sacraments and tended to the needs of their fold. Rather than winning souls, these grassroots padres were there to round up votes and maintain the revolutionary hegemony of the new order.

In appealing to the masses, "Revolutionary Nationalism" constituted the secular church's doctrine. This nebulous ideology heralded the nationalistic tenets of the 1917 Constitution, including overt anti-clericalism, government control over petroleum and other subsoil resources, communal farms for peasants, a strong, interventionist state, and workplace rights. Enshrined in Article 123, these guarantees for workers included an eight-hour day, safety regulations, a ban on child labor, maternity leave, equal pay for equal labor by men and women, and a minimum wage for factory hands as well as farmers. With the arrival of the twenty-first century, the government had managed to implement only a portion of those laudatory provisions. In reality, Revolutionary Nationalism had turned out to be an open, protean gospel that the incumbent president, limited to a single six-year term (*sexenio*), could embellish with his own tropes.

The official creed also incorporated a profound distrust of Washington, which had seized half the homeland in the 1846-48 Mexican-American War, still known below the Rio Grande as the "War of North American Aggression." It was only 100 years later—after World War II—that some Mexican popes hesitatingly came to regard its super-power neighbor as a friendly allied monarchy. PRI pontiffs still retained misgivings about the United States' possible encroachments on sovereignty—a particular

Table 1.1
Comparison of "Revolutionary Church" and "Las Sectas"

	Revolutionary Church	PRI Figures and Practices	Las Sectas (Drug Cartels)
Pope	Strong presidents Constitutional prerogatives plus the "Dedazo," broad appointive powers, unaudited discretionary funds, selection of party candidates	Calles (1924-34), Cárdenas (1934-40), Alemán (1946-52), Ruiz Cortines (1952-58), López Mateos (1958-64), Díaz Ordaz (1964-70), Carlos Salinas (1988-94)	Jaime Herrera Nevares, Ernesto "Don Neto" Fonseca Carrillo, Pedro Áviles Pérez, Héctor "El Guëro" Palma, Miguel Ángel Félix Gallardo; Juan Nepomuceno Guerra, etc.
Prophets	Historical figures	Father Hidalgo, Benito Juárez, Flores Magón brothers, Francisco I. Madero, Lázaro Cárdenas	Jesús Malverde, the Sinaloan saint whom the narco-traffickers venerate; and Santísima Muerte.
Curia	Key Cabinet members, PRI presidents, sectoral leaders	Interior, Finance, Labor, Budget and Planning	Professional accountants who launder money and chief triggermen who carry out the orders of capos
Secretary of State/Prime Minister	Interior Secretary	Ruiz Cortines, Díaz Ordaz, Fernando Gutiérrez Barrios, Manuel Bartlett	Juan José "El Azul" Esparagoza Moreno (a negotiator among the cartels) and intermediaries between the government and the police who ensure that cartel operations proceed without official interference.
Archbishops and bishops	Governors	Agents of the president	Joaquín "El Chapo" Guzmán Loera, Ismael "El Mayo" Zambada García (Sinaloa); Beltrán Leyva brothers (a breakaway group from the Sinaloa Cartel); Ignacio "Nacho" Coronel Villarreal (Jalisco); Eduardo "El Coss"

Table 1.1 (cont.)

			Costilla Sánchez, Antonio Ezequiel "Tony Tormenta" Cárdenas Guillén (Gulf); Heriberto "The Executioner" Lazcano Lazcano and Miguel "El L-40" Treviño Morales (Los Zetas); Vicente "El Viceroy" Carrillo Fuentes (Juárez); remnants of the Arellano Félix family and their enemy Eduardo "El Tío" García Simental (Tijuana/AFO); Nazario "El Chayo" Moreno González and José de Jesús "El Chango" Méndez Vargas (La Familia); and Jorge Caro Quintero (Sonora)
Priests	Mayors	Agents of governors	Local operators such as leaders of cells that Los Zetas have created in more than a dozen states
Religious Orders	Teachers (SNTE); Oil Workers Union (STPRM); and other PRI corporatist groups	Faithful to regime at the same time pursuing their own interests	La Familia whose modus operandi and professed values leads them to urge the rehabilitation of young people. The cartel claims that its motive is to recruit youngsters into their organization to "save" them from pernicious influences
Ideology	"Revolutionary Nationalism"	Dependent on the program of the incumbent president; distrust of the United States	Amassing money and power through violence and the threat of violence
Salvation	Devotion to the PRI		Impunity that springs from enjoying princely wealth Employing violence to defeat foes without fear of being arrested
Urbi e Orbi (**Blessings at Christmas and Easter**)	*Informe* or State of the Nation address (September 1)	*Informe*	Declarations of goals by La Familia; narco-banners

Table 1.1 (cont.)

Rituals	Labor Day (May 1); Independence Day (Sept. 16); Revolution Day (Nov. 16); Day of National Dignity (March 17)	Events at which to see and be seen	→ Type of Murder **Message**
			→ Gunshots **Nothing personal; you were on the list**
			→ Torture, blows to the body, gunshot **The victim had valuable information that we had to extract**
			→ Torture, blows to the body, asphyxiation of a semi-nude victim **Revenge against someone hated by his assassins who believed his death should be slow, painful, and humiliating**
			→ Torture, blows to the body, and swathed in bandages or tape to, "mummify" the victim before shooting him or her in the head **A traitor to the cartel or someone known by his assailant**
			→ Beheading **A means to intimidate enemy who was spying on the assassins; it demonstrates that the victim was caught in flagrante; sometimes a group decapitates traitors, much like sending a finger to the family of a kidnap victim, but when a head arrives, there is no doubt about the identify of the deceased.**
			→ Strangling **Seldom used; may mean, in effect: "We have been infiltrated and we know it."**

Table 1.1 (cont.)

Symbols/ Photos of Pope Benedict XVI	Photographs of presidents in government offices	Reminder of authority figure	Jesús Malverde; Santísima Muerte; as well as devotion to the Virgin of Guadalupe (Many narcos are extremely religious and exhibit an intense fear of death)
L'Obsser-vatore Romano	Major newspapers and columnists	Stipends	YouTube; narcobanderas; websites (El Chapo's Family); notes left with cadavers; beheadings, and other acts of savagery sure to attract widespread media attention; and narco-corridos, ballads that extol the accomplishments of cartel barons
Apostolic Visitors	DFS and Federal Judicial Police	Preserve order	Cartel killers and, in terms of administration, financial operators who seek opportunities to launder money
Crusaders	Military	Combat Infidels	Los Zetas, Los Pelones, Los Güeros, La Linea, and Kaibiles (recruited by Los Zetas)
Inquisition	PRI commissions	Ouster from party of Cuauhtémoc Cárdenas, Porfirio Muñoz Ledo, other leaders of the "Democratic Current" (1987)	Specialized executioners
Martyrs	Luis Donaldo Colosio Murrieta, the PRI presidential nominee who was slain on March 23, 1994	Manuel Buendía, Enrique "Kiki" Camarena; *Zeta* editor Francisco Ortíz Franco	Fallen narco-traffickers such as Amado Carrillo Fuentes (Juárez Cartel) and Arturo "Zeta 1" Guzmán Decenas (Los Zetas)

Table 1.1 (cont.)

Calvary	Loss of Los Pinos	2000 and 2006 presidential elections	When narco-traffickers, who find themselves arrested by hooded, well-armed police officers, not only have their crimes exposed to the public but face a trial and prison sentence. Their crucifixion comes when they wind up in a high-security penitentiary from which they cannot escape. The maximum Calvary is extradition to the U.S.

Law enforcement and intelligence agencies such as the Federal Judicial Police (PJF) and the Federal Security Directorate (DFS) functioned as merciless apostolic visitors who enforced order and cracked down on dissenters. The armed forces served as loyal defenders of the faith, ready to take up arms against rebels, peasant activists, student firebrands, and, in recent years, the infidels of organized crime.

For three decades after World War II, Mexico's economy—supervised by the revolutionary church—grew 6 percent annually; its currency—the peso—maintained a stable relationship with the dollar; and investment cascaded into the country thanks to import-substitution industrialization (ISI). This strategy lavished protection and benefits on domestic and foreign entrepreneurs willing to commence and expand operations in the nation. Mexico limited ownership of energy, steel, hydrocarbon reserves, basic petrochemicals, and communications to either the state or to Mexican nationals. Otherwise, outsiders could invest in most other fields, provided, of course, they built plants in the country, complied with mutable regulations, and brought Mexican partners into their ventures—a requirement that obliging officials could waive or overlook.

As a result, U.S. equity capital and loans streamed across the border at an accelerating pace, expanding five-fold between 1950 and 1970—from $566 million to $2.8 billion. General Motors, Dow Chemical, Coca-Cola, Pepsi-Cola, Colgate-Palmolive, Goodyear, John Deere, the Ford Motor Company, Procter & Gamble, Westinghouse, Sears Roebucks, and scores of other companies headed south of the border in the postwar period. Gaudy signs flashed invitations to *"Fumé Raleigh"* ("Smoke

Raleighs") and *"Tomé Coca-Cola—La Pausa Que Refresca* ("Drink Coca-Cola—the Pause that Refreshes")—as Madison Avenue's artifices made their impact on Mexico City's Avenida Insurgentes, Paseo de la Reforma, and other broad, shop-lined boulevards. During the fifty years between 1920 and 1970, trade with the United States accounted for approximately two-thirds of Mexico's international commerce—a figure that obtained in 2009.

The "Economic Miracle" propelled by ISI inflated the power of Mexico's political pope. This initiative generated employment for the faithful in the new industries spawned by investment, gorged a rapidly growing bureaucracy with true believers, ensured attractive jobs and benefits for members of the PRI's Labor and Popular sectors, and made Mexico's revolutionary church the envy of the Third World. However, the hard-line course of President Gustavo Díaz Ordaz (1964-70) and the quixotic policies of chief executive Luis Echeverría Álvarez (1970-76) ignited social tensions.

The nation's fortunes brightened after the discovery of prolific oil and gas reservoirs in the 1970s. Commentators labeled the country "a Spanish-speaking Kuwait" and President José López Portillo (1976-82) fretted over the delightful challenge of "managing our nation's vast wealth." During his administration, the government owned PEMEX and the two firms—the Federal Electricity Commission (CFE) and Light and Power of the Center (LyFC)—that controlled the electricity sector, the major fertilizer producer (FERTIMEX), and a huge public food distribution company (CONASUPO). Smaller entities among the 1,150 state agencies included restaurants, nightclubs, movie theaters, bars, and discothèques.

In contrast to the fragmentation besetting other developing countries, Mexicans retain a strong sense of national identity buttressed by the population's commitment to Catholicism, its veneration of the Virgin of Guadalupe, and its pride in those who had spearheaded the country's independence and continuing development. Along with Fathers Hidalgo and Morelos, Juárez, and Madero, Lázaro Cárdenas assured himself a prominent place in the revolutionary church's equivalent of St. Peter's Basilica through his economic assertiveness. In 1938 he took the bold step of nationalizing the exploitative foreign oil trusts and creating Petróleos Mexicanos as a state monopoly. March 18, the anniversary of this take-over, remains a "Day of National Dignity"—a veritable holy day—when politicians and labor bigwigs chant the nationalistic credo: *"¡El Petróleo es el nuestro!"* ("The Oil is Ours!").

Notes

1. Christened as the Institutional Revolutionary Party (PRI) since 1946, in earlier incarnations, its formal name was the National Revolutionary Party (PNR) from 1929 to 1938, and the Mexican Revolutionary Party (PRM) from 1938 to 1946.
2. Quoted in L. Vincent Padgett, *The Mexican Political System* (2nd ed.; Boston: Houghton Mifflin, 1976): 187.
3. Frank Brandenburg, *The Making of Modern Mexico* (Englewood Cliffs, N.J.: Prentice-Hall, 1964): 5.
4. Alan Riding, *Distant Neighbor: A Portrait of the Mexicans* (New York: Alfred A. Knopf, 1985): 66.
5. Lorenzo Meyer, "El presidencialismo mexicano: Del Populismo al neoliberalismo." Paper presented at El Colegio de México, 1992 and cited in Francisco E. González, *Dual Transitions from Authoritarian Rule: Institutionalized Regimes in Chile and Mexico, 1970-2000* (Baltimore: Johns Hopkins, 2008): 57.

2

Wars, Prohibition, and the Antecedents of Narco Churches

Wars have spurred the production, processing, and transport of drugs in and through Mexico, as well as consumption in both countries, particularly in the United States. Raw opium was highly regarded well before the birth of Christ. However, it was not until 1805 that scientists finally refined the "miracle drug" morphine from the dried, condensed juice of poppy. Combatants in the Mexican-American War smoked marijuana, which was legal in both nations. In 1858 two American physicians first used a hypodermic needle to inject morphine directly into the blood stream. During the U.S. Civil War, Confederate and Union doctors prescribed morphine and other narcotics not only to abate suffering from wounds and crudely performed surgeries, but also to treat malaria, dysentery, and diarrhea. Elaine Shannon, author of *Desperados*, observed that morphine addiction was so pronounced that it was called "the army disease."[1] Some raised alarm about this dependence after hostilities concluded, but often the response was to substitute it with another drug.

Throughout the nineteenth century, pharmacies in both nations sold over-the-counter nostrums that contained narcotics, as well as regularly prescribed medications like laudanum and paregoric. Merck used cocaine in a surgical anesthetic. In 1884 it produced 3,179 pounds of so-called "Booger Sugar"; two years later the output spiraled to 158,352 pounds. The Sears, Roebuck and Co. catalog even touted a morphine-laced mixture that could be slipped into a wayward spouse's coffee to keep him home at night.

In "On Cocaine," a technical paper published in Vienna, Sigmund Freud popularized the use of the narcotic for treating nervous disorders, depression, and his own morphine addiction.[2]

A year after Georgia's Fulton County enacted Prohibition in 1885, Dr. John Stith Pemberton invented Coca-Cola, a carbonated, non-alcoholic beverage flavored with kola nut and containing a small portion of cocaine. Yet in 1903 the Atlanta-based company removed cocaine from its secret recipe, perhaps in reaction to hysterical claims that cocaine drove black men to rape white women. Dr. David F. Musto, a historian of America's drug policy, noted that some law enforcement agencies in the South converted from .32-caliber to .38-caliber bullets fearing that cocaine-crazed African-Americans could withstand gunshots that would fell whites.[3]

In 1898 the Bayer Company, which began marketing heroin as a non-addictive cough suppressant for children, renamed the product "heroin," derived from the word *heroisch,* German for heroic, because users felt "heroic" after a dose. As with aspirin, Bayer lost its trademark rights to heroin as part of war reparations specified in the 1919 Treaty of Versailles following Germany's defeat in World War I.

Well before the Great War, a symbiotic relationship defined the flow of narcotics between the United States and Mexico, alternating between periods of laxness and intolerance. Chinese immigrants—hundreds of whom flocked to Sinaloa—brought opium habits with them to North America. In 1880 the U.S. and Chinese governments agreed to prohibit bilateral traffic in the substance. Sinaloa, especially in the mountainous sierra, continued to serve as a center for cultivating opium poppy.

In 1906 the Chinese government spearheaded a campaign against opium use in order to spur modernization and attenuate British colonial imperialism. Anger at the mistreatment of Chinese nationals in the U.S. precipitated a voluntary boycott of American products by the regime in Peking (now Beijing). President Theodore Roosevelt sought to propitiate the Chinese by supporting their anti-opium drive. He also wanted to curb drug smuggling from the Philippines, acquired by the U.S. in the Spanish-American War. As a result, "the U.S. launched a campaign for worldwide narcotics traffic control that would extend over the years in an unbroken diplomatic sequence from the League of Nations to the present efforts of the United Nations."[4] Washington participated actively in the thirteen-nation International Opium Commission, which held conferences in Shanghai (1909) and The Hague (1911). The latter approved a convention requiring signatories to suppress opiates and limit narcotics to medical use.

Mexican Revolution

The collapse of the Díaz's dictatorship in 1911 ignited the revolution that found soldiers spreading marijuana's appeal throughout the country.

The national ban on the cultivation and marketing of marijuana (1920) and opium poppy (1926) occurred amid simmering unrest, which was finally contained by the creation of a dominant single party in 1929—the forerunner to today's PRI. President Calles, who disdained the Chinese, justified the prohibitory measures on the grounds of protecting the quality of the race, an argument embraced by some American prohibitionists.

Although it lost influence during the Civil War, the Women's Christian Temperance Union (WCTU) was so successful that, in 1879, Catherine Booth could righteously declaim that "almost every [Protestant] Christian minister has become an abstainer."[5] The WTCU and the Anti-Saloon League (ASL) formed part of a crazy-quilt coalition that encompassed pietistic Protestants in the Democratic and Republican parties, many women, African-American spokesmen, and Progressives. The ASL, which sprang to life as "an army of the Lord to wipe away the curse of drink," looked forward to "an era of clear thinking and clean living." One of its monthly publications carried the warning: "Come in and take a drop. The first drop led to other drops. He dropped his position; he dropped his respectability; he dropped his fortune; he dropped his friends; he dropped finally all prospects in this life, and his hopes for eternity; and then came the last drop on the gallows. BEWARE OF THE FIRST DROP."

The Progressive Movement emerged to improve the quality of life and invigorate the nation's moral fiber by preserving the environment, placing itself in opposition to political skullduggery, stemming the use of mood-altering substances, and proscribing the marketing of adulterated foods. One of the movement's first victories came in passage of the Pure Food and Drug Act in 1906. The measure did not prevent the sale of narcotics, but it did require the accurate labeling of patent medicines sold in inter-state commerce.

Zealots denigrated "Lucifer's liquors" and their link to wife-abuse and child beating. Tycoons like the tee-totaler Henry Ford deplored the impact of drinking on productivity in his factories. Advocates averred that outlawing the sale of alcohol would shrink corruption, quell machine politics, and uplift immigrants.

Although some states forbade the sale of alcohol, it was not until the U.S. entry into World War I that "drys" obtained enactment of national legislation. The Great War invested Prohibition with a patriotic aura since German Americans owned many breweries. The Anti-Saloon League called Milwaukee's brewers "the worst of all our German enemies" and reviled their beer as the "Kaiser's brew."[6] Once the U.S. entered the war in April 1917, Congress mandated liquor-free zones around military camps.[7]

Eight months later Congress approved the Eighteenth Amendment, and President Woodrow Wilson instituted partial prohibition to conserve grain for the war effort and, by September 1919, the president had forbidden the wartime production of beer. The constitutional change only prohibited "manufacture, sale, or transportation of intoxicating liquors … for beverage purposes." Although this was the "supreme law of the land," congressional action was needed to enforce its provisions. The patron of the enacting bill, which passed over Wilson's veto, was ultra-religious, super-dry Minnesota representative Andrew J. Volstead. "Hell will be forever for rent," trumpeted evangelist Billy Sunday, who looked forward to an America "so dry, she can't spit."

Although conceived to reduce alcoholism, promote family unity, and curb absenteeism, Prohibition had unintended consequences. The production of "bathtub gin" and proliferation of "Speakeasies"—clandestine watering holes—became a plague. Organized crime moved in, sensing an opportunity in the illegal, but popular enterprise. Chicago's Al "Scarface" Capone and his nemesis George "Bugs" Moran made fortunes through bootlegging at the same time that ax-waving G-Men smashed stills and invaded warehouses across the country. "When I sell liquor, it's bootlegging. When my patrons serve it on a silver tray on Lakeshore Drive, it's hospitality," groused the Windy City's top scofflaw.[8] As one American commentator noted: "When we erected an artificial barrier between alcohol producers and consumers in 1920, we created a bonanza more lucrative than the Gold Rush. Staggering profits from illegal booze gave mobsters the financial power to take over legitimate businesses and expand into casinos, loan sharking, labor racketeering, and extortion. Thus we created the major crime syndicates—and the U.S. murder rate jumped tenfold."[9]

The sharp increase in smuggling, violent crime, and evasion spurred repeal of what President Herbert Hoover, who opposed Prohibition, called "a noble experiment" in 1933, the year that he handed over the White House to Democrat Franklin D. Roosevelt amid the Great Depression.

In Mexico brothels and bars abounded, especially in Ciudad Juárez where, for the first three decades of the twentieth century, the "big three" underground industries were gun-running (north to south), prostitution (north to south), and liquor smuggling (south to north). Drug peddling dated from at least 1906 when the great San Francisco earthquake uprooted numerous Chinese immigrants and they relocated to Ciudad

Juárez—with opium-peddler Sam Hing becoming the first drug lord of the region. The Chinese were succeeded by a couple—Ignacia "La Nacha" Jasso and her husband Pablo "El Pablote" González—who headed the first local cartel, according to a historian of the city. In addition to selling marijuana in Ciudad Juárez, La Nacha and her organization marketed it throughout the Southwest.[10]

The next famous drug trafficker, Enrique Fernández, became known as the "Al Capone of Ciudad Juárez"—because of his ostentatious wealth and unbridled influence over officials. Governors of the Northern District of Baja California, then a Mexican territory, not only slapped tariffs on the Chinese who shipped opium from Sinaloa via Tijuana to San Francisco, they also got rich from the promotion of gambling, prostitution, and the manufacture, sale, and export of alcoholic beverages. Hollywood celebrities and even Capone himself frequented casinos and clubs in Tijuana and Mexicali, replicas of Sodom and Gomorrah and the main portals for drugs entering the U.S. from the 1930s to the 1950s. Meanwhile, María Dolores Estévez, known as "Lola la Chata," surfaced as the most important drug figure in Mexico City[11] where opium dens catered to the elite.

In the late 1930s, President Lázaro Cárdenas ordered the military to destroy marijuana and poppy crops in Sinaloa. The state's governor, Colonel Rodolfo T. Loaiza (1941-44), proposed "exterminating narcotics trafficking" and converting poppy-growing farms in the remote municipalities of Badiraguato and nearby Mocorito into bean and corn producers. In February 1944 the state executive was murdered, apparently on the orders of former War and Navy Secretary Pablo Macías Valenzuela, who ascended to the governorship and later received the prestigious Belisario Domínguez medal from the Mexican Senate.[12]

Four years after the repeal of Prohibition, Harry J. Anslinger, the zealous chief of the U.S. Bureau of Narcotic Drugs (BND), pioneered another social intervention when he convinced Congress to pass the Marijuana Tax Act of 1937.[13] The BND reformer argued that cannabis caused "murder, insanity and death." In 1969 the Supreme Court determined that the law violated the Fifth Amendment inasmuch as anyone seeking the tax stamp would incriminate himself.

Unlike opiates and cocaine, marijuana was introduced during a period of drug intolerance. The practice of smoking cannabis arrived in the U.S. with Mexican immigrants, who had come North during the 1920s to work, and it soon caught the fancy of jazz musicians.[14] Widespread use did not take place until the 1960s; forty years after marijuana cigarettes had reached America.

World War II

During World War II, the United States formally pressed Mexico to control illegal narcotics traffic. A dispatch from A.A. Berle, Jr., acting on behalf of Secretary of State Cordell Hull, to the U.S. ambassador in Mexico City, typified this stance. "Both the Treasury Department and this Department regard the illicit production of opium poppies in Mexico and the recent trend toward increased production as a menace to the health of our people. It would appear that Mexico, replacing the Far East, from which supplies are no longer available, is fast becoming the principal source of opium illicitly entering the United States."[15] Nonetheless, Japan's occupation of poppy growing regions in Asia combined with Turkey's alliance with the Axis powers forced Washington to informally seek an alternative source of opium, with which to produce morphine during World War II.

"We were concerned that our supply of opium or morphine would be cut off because the world was at war. So we needed a supply close by. But, that was one of those black box things. Who knows when it happened, who did it, and why," said Edward Heath, who later headed the Drug Enforcement Administration (DEA) in Mexico for ten years. "To supplant Middle East supplies, the United States reached a secret accord with Mexico [to] open up its uncultivated areas ... in the Western Sierra Maestra. The Sinaloan mountains were crowded with unofficial instructors from both countries who taught the local population to grow poppy. The poppy flourished [and] prosperity reached the lost people of the mountains thanks to its golden brilliance."[16]

In this period of officially-tolerated opium trade, many Sinaloans made their fortunes. "Everybody was growing it, it was institutional. Some government officials bought the harvest from the farmers to export themselves. There were even soldiers up in the hills caring for the plants," explained Dr. Ley Domínguez, a 77-year-old life-long resident of Mocorito, one of Sinaloa's most notorious poppy-producing regions.[17] Mexico became a source of morphine for the legal and illegal markets. The war also created a high demand for hemp fiber for rope, which led to large-scale cultivation of marijuana in both Mexico and the United States.

Once the Allies won, the U.S. resumed importing superior opium for medicinal purposes from Asia and the Middle East. But many Mexican farmers continued to produce opium and heroin; operations became *sub rosa*, and smuggling networks materialized to satisfy what historian Héctor Aguilar Camín termed "the insatiable North American nose." Mexico remained a source of narcotics, especially when tens of thousands of service personnel returned from overseas with a taste for, if not a full-blown addiction to, drugs.

Enrique Diarte dominated the opium trade in Tijuana and Mexicali until Max Cossman reportedly ordered his execution in 1944. Known as the "king of opium," Cossman forged links to Mickey Cohen of the old Al Capone gang. Fellow American Benjamin "Bugsy" Siegel, who launched the development of Las Vegas and was linked to the Charles "Lucky" Luciano and Meyer Lansky mobs, and his girlfriend Virginia Hill, connived with local politicians to grow poppy in Mexico's northwest.[18]

After the Axis powers surrendered, the U.S. no longer needed Sinaloa's opium. Washington once again began to twist the arm of Mexican policymakers to curb the export of illegal substances. In 1947 President Miguel Alemán Valdés (1946-52) created the Federal Security Directorate, a secretive law enforcement arm of the presidency (later transferred to the Interior Ministry), which worked with the Federal Judicial Police, the Attorney General's Office, and the Army to combat forbidden transactions. The American embassy's military attaché compared the force [DFS] to the Gestapo in light of its vast powers, use of torture, and the questionable backgrounds of its leaders.[19] We will return to the Directorate in Chapter 7.

Notes

1.   Elaine Shannon, *Desperados: Latin Drug Lords, U.S. Lawmen, and the War America Can't Win* (New York: Viking, 1988): 28.
2.   Katie Shimer, "Coke: From Where it Grows … to Your Nose," *Portland Mercury*, May 22, 2003. *www.portlandmercury.com.*
3.   David F. Musto, *The American Disease* (New Haven and London: Yale University Press, 1973).
4.   Quoted from David F. Musto, "Opium, Cocaine and Marijuana in American History," *Scientific American* (July 1991): 20-27.
5.   Catherine Booth, *Strong Drink Versus Christianity* (London: S.W. Partridge and Co., 1879): 29.
6.   "The Jazz Age: the American 1920s," *Digital History. www.digitalhistory.uh.edu/database/article_display/.*
7.   Quoted in Thomas R. Pegram, *Battling Demon Rum: The Struggle for a Dry America, 1800-1933* (Chicago: Ivan R. Dee, 1998): 144.
8.   Quoted in *Spritcaller.net www.spiritcaller.net/quotes/drugs.htm.*
9.   Quoted in Mike Gray, "We Tried a War Like This Once Before," *Washington Post*, April 12, 2009.
10.   Rafael Núñez, "A Not-So-Secret History of Vice in Juárez," *Newspaper Tree*, March 6, 2006. *www.newspapertree.com.*
11.   Luis Alejandro Astorga Almanza, *El siglo de las drogas* (Mexico City: Planeta, 1996): 62-63.

12. *Ibid.* 63-67.
13. The spelling then used for cannabis was "Marihuana."
14. Musto, "Opium, Cocaine and Marijuana in American History," p. 16.
15. The communiqué is found in William O. Walker III (ed.), "25 Mexican Opium Production and Trafficking, 1943," *Drugs in the Western Hemisphere: An Odyssey of Cultures in Conflict* (Wilmington, DE: Scholarly Resources, 1996): 123.
16. Quoted in Héctor Aguilar Camín, "Narco Historias extraordinarias," *Nexos* (May 2007). *www.nexos.mx.com.*
17. Material from this paragraph comes from Jake Bergman, "The Place Mexico's Drug Kingpins Call Home," PBS Drug Wars *www.pbs.org/wgbh/pages/frontline/shows/drugs/business/place.html.*
18. The source was Harry Anslinger, head of the U.S. Bureau of Narcotic Drugs, as reported in *Illegal Economy*, "U.S.-Mexican Cross-Border Marijuana Traffic." *www.illegaleconomy.com/drugs/us-mexico.com*; and Astorga, *El siglo de las drogas*, pp. 82-83.
19. Astorga, *El siglo de las drogas,* p. 72.

3

Two Narco Churches Emerge

After World War II, authorities on both sides of the border heralded a "special relationship" between their countries. American investment poured into Mexico to take advantage of incentives covered by the nation's import-substitution élan; bilateral trade flourished thanks to a dependable peso-dollar exchange rate; Mexico championed anti-communism; and, despite growing commerce in opiates and marijuana since the late 1940s, the question of drugs garnered scant attention when officials from the two countries met. Mexico was beginning a twenty-five-year period of robust growth, formidable industrialization, and political stability under the PRI's temporal and authoritarian church.

Operation Intercept

This era of good feelings evaporated when Richard M. Nixon (1969-74) entered the Oval Office. He faced an upswing in drug consumption, especially in marijuana, because of the permissiveness of the "anti-establishment hippie" years of the 1960s. This situation coincided with the rising heroin addiction among U.S. soldiers who had served in Vietnam. The boom in demand for controlled substances sparked a surge in production and profits south of the border.

Although he had run on a strong law and order platform, once in office the new president found that the federal government had little enforcement jurisdiction against violent felonies compared with its state and local counterparts. Unwilling to empower big-city mayors, most of them Democrats, Nixon established the Presidential Task Force Relating to Narcotics, Marijuana and Dangerous Drugs. This body set as its highest priority "an eradication of the production and refinement in Mexico of opium poppies and marijuana."

The report identified Mexico as a pivotal source of heroin and asserted that marijuana constituted a critical "stepping stone" to heroin addiction.

The White House, which claimed that abusers committed many serious crimes, vowed to stanch the influx of narcotics.[1] When Washington urged the spraying of their fields with herbicides, Mexican authorities told us—using diplomatic language—in effect, "to go piss up a rope," according to G. Gordon Liddy who had been involved in the initiative.[2]

Nixon responded with "Operation Intercept," which began in September 1969 and entailed 2,000 customs and border patrol agents meticulously examining vehicles, shoppers, and workers crossing into Mexico. Simultaneously, the U.S. Army stationed mobile radar units from El Paso to San Diego to impede northbound flights of marijuana-filled aircraft.[3] The two-week logjam of cars, trucks, and pedestrians in this "nightmarish dragnet" wreaked economic chaos in the border zone.[4]

The object was to stem the flow of Mexican brown heroin or "Mexican mud" into American neighborhoods. "Something had to be done. And we were expecting that the Mexicans would do something when asked. We requested a favor: 'Cooperate with us,'" recalled the DEA's Heath, who was close to the decision-making. When collaboration did not crystallize, the U.S. took drastic action. "Well, of course, the Mexican officials were hurt, insulted, if you can interpret that. Immediately there was some action taken through the embassy to start a dialogue of cooperation,"[5] Heath stated.

To break the impasse, Mexico City grudgingly unveiled "Operation Cooperation." In return for allowing American agents to monitor Mexican poppy and marijuana fields, Mexican soldiers began hacking away at drug plants with machetes. Aerial spraying had yet to be introduced and the joint effort proved futile. As DEA agent Jaime Kuykendall said: "The traffickers got the message for a little while that we were serious.... But it didn't last. We quit showing them we're serious, so they figured everything was hunky-dory."[6] Operation Intercept benefited big-time criminals who had access to swift boats and small planes at the expense of amateurs who could survive only with the ready cash derived from overland trafficking.[7]

The failure of interdiction aside, Nixon signed into law the Controlled Substances Act of 1970. This measure laid the foundation for the continuing "War against Drugs." Congress assigned responsibility for enforcement to the Bureau of Narcotics and Dangerous Drugs, and the chief executive renamed his strategy a "total war" on heroin and a "crusade to save our children." In 1973 the Drug Enforcement Administration was born as the entity with prime responsibility for narcotic matters.

Early on authorities thwarted the transit of high-quality morphine paste from Marseilles to New York—the "French Connection" celebrated in the eponymous film.[8] This stroke transformed the marketing and distribution patterns of heroin, giving impetus to the expanded cultivation of opium poppy in Mexico. Demand escalated for "Mexican mud," and from 1972 through 1976 Mexican *mafiosi* controlled three-fourths of the U.S. heroin market, while satisfying Americans' appetite for marijuana.[9]

Rules of the Game

The prospect of earning considerable sums by selling heroin and marijuana altered the rules of the game in Sinaloa and elsewhere. In 1957 the law enforcement agencies boasted superior firepower over the cartels, whose operatives depended on handguns.[10] But that did not matter. Relying on bribes or *mordidas*, the desperadoes pursued their illicit activities with the connivance of authorities, frequently through ad hoc pacts that might last days, weeks, or months. Loyal to the PRI, the armed forces bolstered the top-down control exercised by the state. Criminal organizations sought protection from local police, regional or zonal military commanders, and sometimes directly from governors or their representatives. Just as in other forms of corruption, authorities allocated "*plazas*"—in the case of drugs, areas and corridors where the gangs held sway to produce, store, or ship narcotics. Reportedly, they followed a "1-2-3 System": a pay-off to authorities of $1 million for an interior location; $2 million for a coastal zone; and $3 million for a U.S.-Mexico border crossing.[11]

Clashes among families or between traffickers and police happened in places such as "Mi Delirio," "Montecarlo," and other bars in Tierra Blanca, a rough-and-tumble neighborhood of the state capital, Culiacán. The inequality of power ensured that drug barons also paid danegeld to representatives of the federal government—with upfront payments of $250,000 or more. Emissaries would forward a portion of the loot upward through the chain of command. Drug dealers behaved discretely, showed deference to public figures, spurned kidnapping, appeared with governors at their children's weddings, and, although often allergic to politics, helped the hegemonic PRI discredit its opponents by linking them to narco-trafficking. Unlike Colombians, Mexico's barons did not seek elective office. In addition, they did not sell drugs within the country, target innocent people, or invade the turf or product-line (marijuana, heroin, cocaine, etc.) of competitors. As Professor Leo Zuckerman has emphasized, each syndicate had its own geographic enclave. If one lord needed to cross the territory of another, he would first ask permission and, if granted, pay the appropriate fee, known as the right of transit (*derecho de piso*). They would not attack the families of other cartel chiefs, and the Federal District, Monterrey, and Guadalajara functioned as sanctuaries, free from revenge killings or other reprisals. In 2009 only Mérida, on the Yucatán Peninsula, and Querétaro, 135 miles north of the Federal District, had attributes of sanctuary cities.

Tradition dictated that, should a conflict get out of hand in a municipality, the governor would call local officials on the carpet and, if needed, request that the military or agents of the Federal Judicial Police or the Federal Security Directorate repress the reprobates. If conditions remained the same or worsened, the state executive would receive a phone call from the secretary of interior—the revolutionary church's political consiglieri—and sometimes even directly from within Los Pinos. The message was clear: "Restore order or pack your bags."

The "no-reelection" article in the Mexican Constitution brought a new chief executive and his security entourage to power every six years. This provision sometimes changed the relative ascendancy—or even the ability to do business—of the cartels. The situation was sufficiently fluid so that should a local police or military unit refused to cooperate with a cartel, the latter would simply transfer its operations to a nearby municipality where they could cinch the desired arrangement. Analyst Luis Rubio compares drug shipments to United Parcel Service delivery; namely, the Mexicans would pick up the merchandise from the seller and deliver it to the addressee. Above it all, the PRI pope and his cardinals dictated the conduct of drug enterprises just as a church hierarchy managed corrupt dioceses and parishes throughout the nation.

The "live and let live" ethos that enveloped these activities began to change in the 1980s and 1990s when opportunities to make vast fortunes mushroomed because of changing routes for cocaine trafficking—a phenomenon that coincided with an upsurge in PAN electoral victories.

National Action Party governors and mayors reorganized law enforcement agencies in their jurisdictions, which allowed hometown cops to act with greater independence from the PJF, a longtime intermediary between the revolutionary church and organized crime. "Consequently, local power fell outside the corruption network, a situation that facilitated more autonomous actions of traffickers, federal agents, local police and corrupt officials, thereby increasing the probability of violent actions to impose new rules of the game," according to Luis Astorga.[12]

Meanwhile, Los Zetas, La Familia, and a new generation of narco-traffickers from established cartels began to manifest contempt for old ways of doing business. These sadists intimidated police and elected figures, butchered Army officers, assassinated enemies in crowded cities, subjected adversaries to unspeakable cruelty, fought hammer and tongs against rival bands, and participated in deadly intramural showdowns when a power vacuum presented itself. While PAN executives had given lip service to democracy, human rights, and clean governance, they often realized that cooperating with dubious actors was far safer and more rewarding than defying them. It's no wonder that the first two states to elect PAN governors—Baja California (1989) and Chihuahua (1992)—seethe with drug-related bedlam.

The rules of the game did not reconfigure overnight. A preview of what was to become the norm began when violence erupted near the end of Luis Echeverría's *sexenio*. To the surprise of many, in 1976 the reactive nationalist approved "Operation Condor," a follow-up to Operation Cooperation. The DEA called its side of the project "Operation Trizo," short for "tri-zone" because the eradication focused on the Sinaloa-Durango-Chihuahua "Golden Triangle."

Operation Condor involved 10,000 soldiers headed by General José Hernández Toledo. Besides hacking away with machetes, they used paraquat to defoliate illegal plantations in the mountains of Sinaloa, Durango, and Chihuahua. The Americans "flew every inch of the country and we knew what they were doing and what was there," DEA pilot Jerry Kelley told author Elaine Shannon. "It didn't matter who was corrupt. There was no way they could hide what was going on."

At the same time, reports of abuses proliferated as human rights attorneys denounced the Mexican military's shocking people with electric prods, gouging their eyes, shoving their heads into excrement-filled toilets, and forcing soft drinks and gasoline up prisoners' noses. Yet the operation garnered glittering praise on both sides of the border.

Peter Bourne, director of the White House Office of Drug Abuse Policy under President Jimmy Carter, told a Senate subcommittee: "The ongoing activities of the Mexican and American governments in the field of drug control must rank among the most exemplary forms of international cooperation existing in the world today."[13]

The intense campaign drove traffickers out of the region—with Miguel Ángel Félix Gallardo and Manuel Salcido "Crazy Pig" Uzeta impelling a move to Guadalajara, "the pearl of Western Mexico." This exodus included other high-ranking clergymen in the Narco Church: Caro Quintero, Ernesto "Don Neto" Fonseca Carrillo, Pedro Avilés Pérez, Ismael "El Mayo" Zambada García, and Arturo "*El Barbas*" Beltrán Leyva and his brothers. In addition, there were Juan José "The Blue" Esparragoza Moreno, Juan José Quintero Payán and his brother Rafael Emilio, and Joaquín "El Chapo" Gúzman Loera (commonly referred to as El Chapo or "Shorty" in the press, Gúzman Loera's friends call him "The Uncle" or "El Tío").

The newcomers displaced Ruperto Beltrán Monzón, who—after breaking out a Nayarit prison—moved to Guadalajara in 1964. He soon controlled marijuana trafficking in Jalisco, Nayarit, Sinaloa, and Sonora. Beltrán Monzón encountered no problems. Nonetheless, his wife was accused of owning a cocaine-processing laboratory and his daughter allegedly threw wild parties. Thus, the ex-convict dropped out of sight. His disappearance coincided with the arrival of the uprooted Sinaloans and their allies who established the Guadalajara Cartel and basked in impunity.

"They traveled around Guadalajara with platoons of guards armed with automatic weapons, and with suitcases full of cash [with which] they bought whatever caught their fancy. Slow to bend to civilized ways, they lived like clannish hill people, marrying cousins, entertaining one another with raucous and violent parties, settling scores with impulsive savagery."[14] At the same time, they transferred their unlawful activities to Michoacán, Nayarit, other parts of Jalisco, and nearby states in the so-called "cucaracha effect."

Such Federal Security Directorate officials as Esteban Guzmán Salgado and Daniel Acuña Figueroa helped the kingpins locate houses, introduced them to important people, provided bodyguards, and equipped them with computers. Rafael Chao López, Florentino Ventura Gutiérrez, and several other DFS commanders transferred to the Federal Judicial Police, which enjoyed broader responsibilities over narcotics' matters and enabled the dirty cops to be of greater service to their underworld contacts.

"The traffickers provided muscle and blood," one DEA informant said, "and DFS leaders contributed brains, coordination, insulation from other government agencies, and firepower in the form of thousand of smuggled automatic weapons."[15] They even assisted the lords in purchasing real estate in the Southwest United States and helped them link up with Latino communities in East Los Angeles, Texas, and Chicago—in exchange for a quarter of the syndicate's profits.[16] Meanwhile, they warned the criminals to (1) terminate their internecine conflicts, (2) refrain from opening bases in the U.S., (3) stay out of Sinaloa, and (4) establish themselves in Guadalajara.

The barons enjoyed the protection of Flavio Romero de Velasco, the PRI governor of Jalisco from 1977 to 1983. He was later found guilty of consorting with the feared and powerful Juárez cartel. Although ordered to spend two years and nine months in prison and pay a $105 fine, he avoided jail on the condition that he checked in regularly with the compliant judge in the case.

The Sinaloan Church

As mentioned previously, marijuana and poppy flourished in remote municipalities of Sinaloa and in neighboring states. Chinese involved in building railroads or those displaced by the 1906 San Francisco earthquake may have introduced poppy, which soon became a typical crop grown by local farmers. In Sinaloa the production of poppy and marijuana became a family enterprise passed down from one generation to another. The mountainous, remote municipality of Badiraguato, located fifty-five miles northeast of Culiacán, renowned as "opium central," was the home or hideout for hundreds of hoodlums.[17] Gum makers or *gomeros* converted the poppy into opium paste for sale.

As noted earlier, Prohibition had fostered the rise and consolidation of organized crime in Mexico when "rum runners" thrived during the 1920s and early 1930s. That experience had further prepared Mexican gangsters to profit from the escalating drug trade, beginning in the 1940s. The Culiacán press even urged the government to ask the United Nations for permission to legalize poppy production—as was done in Yugoslavia, India, Turkey, and Iran—to provide work and income for the state's residents.[18]

In the late 1950s, Culiacán—described as the "opium smugglers' base of operations"—became the situs for an underground economy devoted to illicit drugs destined for the U.S. Three elements—the 400-mile long coastline of the carrot-shaped state, the completion of the Pan-American Highway, and the construction of a regional airport in the 1960s—facilitated a network that enabled the Sinaloa Cartel to gain hegemony in Mexico's Pacific Northwest. Ernesto Fonseca Carrillo, known as "the Godfather," lived in Badiraguato and pioneered large-scale poppy production and trade. He also served as mentor to Rafael Caro Quintero, a shrewd and youthful entrepreneur who converted Mexican marijuana from second-rate weed to the choice of connoisseurs by perfecting a seedless variety of the plant (*sinsemillas*). In the 1960s, Jorge Favela Escobar also drew attention as a key Sinaloan smuggler. In the post-war years, Sinaloans dominated the business, beginning with opium smuggling and, depending on demand, gradually branching out into marijuana, cocaine, and methamphetamines.[19]

Another important player the 1960s and 1970s was Jaime Herrera Nevares, a former Durango state judicial policeman who managed the heroin traffic in his home state. The Herrera organization pioneered a "farm-to-arm" structure that cultivated opium poppy, processed and packed heroin, and transported it to Chicago along what came to be called the Heroin Highway. There, it was either sold locally or distributed to other U.S. cities. This network proved extremely difficult to penetrate because family members controlled the entire operation. Herrera transformed many of his profits into legitimate activities and became a pillar of the local economy.[20] The Herrera family cooperated with Sinaloans Ernesto "Don Neto" Fonseca Carrillo and Favela Escobar.

The Sinaloans eventually gained entrée to the cocaine trade. Although born in Cuba, Alfredo Sicilia Fonseca became the über-don of cocaine. A flamboyant bisexual who made a big splash in the capital's social circles, Sicilia Fonseca befriended Juan Ramón Matta Ballesteros, a shrewd Honduran chemist who introduced the Cuban to Medellín Cartel capos José Gonzalo Rodríguez Gacha, Pablo Escobar, and the Ochoa Vázquez brothers. Sicilia Fonseca lived in Guadalajara, where he acquired valuable properties. When the PJF arrested Falcón in mid-1975, Matta Ballesteros presented Rodríguez Gacha to his friend Félix Gallardo.

A semi-literate street vendor until he became a Sinaloa judicial policeman at age 17, the youthful hustler attracted the attention of Governor Leopoldo Sánchez Celis (1963-69). Félix Gallardo looked after the state executive's young boys before becoming the politician's bodyguard. He took advantage of the governor's broad network of contacts to create the largest drug syndicate in the country, moving quantities of cocaine northward comparable to shipments of the Medellín organization. Sánchez Celis acted as best man at Félix Gallardo's wedding; later Félix Gallardo became godfather to the state executive's son, Rodolfo Sánchez Duarte. While he maintained a home in Guadalajara, Félix Gallardo headed the large and growing Sinaloa Cartel, which observers call the "Blood Alliance" because of its leaders' family ties, which, until recent fractures, ensured greater cohesion than its Gulf Cartel enemies.

The Sinaloan organization was far from monolithic. Héctor Luis "El Güero" Palma Salazar, a car thief who began working as a hit man for Félix Gallardo, rose steadily through the syndicate's ranks along with

Eduardo "The Little Wolf" Retamoza. After a large cocaine shipment was lost, Retamoza was killed but El Güero survived and joined forces with El Chapo Guzmán Loera, a fellow Sinaloan.

In 1978 U.S. authorities arrested Palma in Arizona where he was sentenced to eight years in prison. Upon his release, he found that his wife, Guadalupe Leija Serrano, had run off with Venezuelan trafficker Rafael Enrique Clavel. The ruthless Clavel forced Guadalupe to withdraw $7 million from a bank account, decapitated her, and shipped her head to Palma. Clavel then took El Güero's two children, Jesús and Nataly, to Venezuela where he dropped them off the Concordia Bridge on the Colombian border. In retaliation, Palma executed the three children of Clavel, who had gone to Tijuana to work for Félix Gallardo. By bribing the Federal Judicial Police and even hiding out in the home of a PJF commander, Palma, who shared leadership of the Sinaloa Cartel with Guzmán Loera, avoided arrest until 1995.[21]

The Gulf Church

The Gulf Cartel provided the main competitor to the Sinaloans. Juan "Don Juan" Nepomuceno Guerra, who bootlegged whisky to the U.S. along the Gulf Coast during Prohibition, founded this organization in the 1970s with the complicity of DFS Commanders Chao López and Rafael Aguilar Guajardo. The criminals initially concentrated on contraband, but Nepomuceno's American-born nephew Juan García Abrego drew upon his uncle's lattice of contacts to expand into the more rewarding substance—cocaine. Collaboration with Nuevo León's PJF commander, Guillermo González Calderoni, vouchsafed the organization's success. The crooked cop had grown up in Reynosa and was a boyhood friend of García Abrego's older brother.

García Abrego, who in 1995 became the first Mexican to land on the Federal Bureau of Investigation's "Ten Most Wanted List," reached a path-breaking accord with the Colombian cartels in the early 1990s. In lieu of receiving cash, the Colombians gave half of their shipments to the Gulf Cartel, which incurred the risk of marketing the cocaine in return for pocketing the profits derived from sales. By 1994 this design became the model for all Mexican crime organizations. "This deal was a major turning point in the fortunes of the Mexican cartels. With this new business arrangement, the power and wealth of the Mexican drug cartels exploded."[22] The Mexicans established distribution outlets in Houston, Dallas, New York, Los Angeles, Chicago, and Denver. The Colombians agreed to this as long as the Mexicans left them Miami and East Coast markets. García Abrego forked over millions of dollars in bribes each month to immunize himself from arrest.

Furthermore, he may have colluded with Quintana Roo Governor Mario Villanueva Madrid, an ally of the Juárez Cartel. Together they are believed to have facilitated the flow of drugs from the Yucatán Peninsula through Campeche, Tabasco, Veracruz, Tamaulipas, and ultimately to Nuevo León.[23]

In the aftermath of the slaying of Cardinal Jesús Posada Ocampo, which is discussed in Chapter 7, public outrage and lobbying from the Vatican forced Salinas to lower the boom on the Sinaloa Cartel and the Tijuana-based Arellano Félix Organization (AFO). Still, he treated as untouchable García Abrego, who hobnobbed with the president's brother Raúl. Soon after Ernesto Zedillo Ponce de León reached Los Pinos in late 1994, he ordered the arrest of García Ábrego, who had burrowed underground. In early 1996 police nabbed the chubby culprit south of Monterrey, and the president instructed authorities to hand him over to the FBI rather than imprison him in Mexico.[24] As he was being hustled onto a jet, he scowled at the eight agents escorting him to Houston and admonished them: "You are all dead men."[25] The savage, violent, and vain honcho, who once had an operation to prune his bulbous nose, wound up in the Centennial Detention Facility, in Rate City, Colorado, to serve the first of eleven life terms.

The War on Terrorism

After 9/11 the DEA sought a role in President George W. Bush's "War on Terrorism" to justify an enlargement of its budget and activities. Administrator Karen P. Tandy told a Congress that opium production in Afghanistan "is a significant concern and a priority for the DEA because of its impact on worldwide drug supply and its potential ... to provide financial support to terrorists and other destabilizing groups."

The Administration reopened its Kabul Country Office in February 2003, and reportedly made "superb contributions under these difficult circumstances" to gathering and disseminating information to U.S. and British intelligence agencies, while supporting the Pentagon's creating a "fusion center" for multinational information sharing.

Tandy also backed "Operation Containment" to make a "concerted effort" to coordinate information among nineteen countries in Central Asia, the Caucuses, Europe, and Russia. Its aim was to "deprive drug trafficking organizations of their market access and international terrorist groups of financial support from drugs, precursor chemicals, weapons, ammunition and currency." Meanwhile, the DEA also enlarged existing offices in Europe and Southwest Asia, opened a new office in Uzbekistan, and assigned special agents to its Kabul, Ankara, Istanbul, Tashkent, Moscow, and London Offices. While concentrating on the Middle East, the DEA raised the specter that terrorists and Mexican smugglers colluded. The agency cited contacts between Mexican traffickers and guerrillas in the Revolutionary Armed Forces of Colombia (FARC).[26]

Notes

1. Ted Galen Carpenter, *Bad Neighbor Policy: Washington's Futile War on Drugs in Latin America* (New York: Palgrave Macmillan, 2003): 12.
2. G. Gordon Liddy, *Will: The Autobiography of G. Gordon Liddy* (New York: St. Martin's Press, 1980): 185.
3. Shannon, *Desperados*, pp. 47-49.
4. Carpenter, *Bad Neighbor Policy*, p. 13.
5. Interview with Edward Heath, "Drug Wars," PBS Frontline, 2000.
6. Quoted in Shannon, *Desperados*, p. 52.
7. Jerry Kamstra, *Weed: Adventures of a Dope Smuggler* (Santa Barbara, CA: Ross-Eirkson, 1983): 96.
8. Mexico's link to the French Connection was Jorge Moreno Chauvet, a major distributor of heroin, marijuana, and cocaine.
9. Drug Enforcement Administration, *1975-80 www.dea.gov/pubs/history/1975-1980.html*.
10. Authorities found cartridges from handguns at the scene of a confrontation between Ernesto Fonseca Carrillo and the police.
11. Agustín Ambriz, "Arévalo Gardoqui: la Sombra del narco," *Proceso*, May 7, 2000.
12. Quoted in Astorga, "Drug Trafficking in Mexico" www.india-seminar.com/2001/504/504%20luis%20astorga; social scientist Leo Zuckerman has also written widely on the changing "rules of the game."
13. Quoted in Shannon, *Los Desperados*, p. 65.
14. Astorga, "Drug Trafficking in Mexico," pp. 3-4.
15. Quoted in Shannon, *Los Desperados*, p. 187.
16. Shannon, *Los Desperados*, p. 187.
17. Astorga, *El siglo de las drogas*, p. 70.
18. Luis Astorga, "Drug Trafficking in Mexico: A First General Assessment," Discussion paper 36. *www.unesco.org/shs/most.*
19. Luis Astorga, "Drug Trafficking in Mexico."
20. Shannon, *Los Desperados*, p. 59.
21. Héctor Luis Palma Salzar *http://wiki.xiaoyaozi.com/en/H%C3%A9ctor_Luis_Palma_Salazar.htm.*
22. Chris Eskridge, "Mexican Cartels and Their Integration into Mexican Socio-Political Culture." An earlier version of this paper was presented at the International Conference on Organized Crime: Myth, Power, Profit, October 1999, Lausanne, Switzerland, p. 10. *www.customscorruption.com/mexican_cartels_integr.htm.*
23. Jiménez, "Identifica el Ejército tres rutas de cárteles."
24. Government Secretary Emilio Chuayffet Chemor opposed dispatching García Abrego to the U.S., while Secretary of Foreign Relations Angel Gurría Treviño and the Attorney General Antonio Lozano Gracia favored the move. Zedillo, who

had no love lost for the DEA because of Operation Casablanca, insisted that the suspect be handed over to the FBI not the DEA.

25.   Quoted in Kevin Fedarko *et al.*, "The Capture of America's Most Wanted," *Time*, January 29. 1996 *www.time.com.*

26.   Karen P. Tandy, "United States Policy towards Narco-terrorism," testimony to the Committee on International Affairs, House of Representatives, February 12, 2004 *www.usdoj.gov.dea*; and José Carreño, "DEA Confirms Nexus between Mexican Narcotics Traffickers and Colombia's FARC Guerrillas, *El Universal*, January 31, 2007.

4

The Weakening of the Revolutionary Church

The prominence of the secular pope advised by a college of cardinals, archbishops, bishops, and lower clergy masked the fissures in the foundation of the secular revolutionary church. Evidence of its low institutional capacity was seen in the inability to ensure security for its citizens, the anemic tax revenues as a percentage of Gross Domestic Product (GDP), a colonization of public education by cacique-led SNTE, the extraordinary influence of a venal union within PEMEX, and the theft of more than one-third of the electricity produced for consumers in the Mexico City metropolitan area. Other indicators were the disdain the public has for politicians and the bicameral Congress, the markedly unequal distribution of income, the conversion of the bureaucracy into a kleptocracy, the abject corruption that suffused most of the nation's more than 1,640 local, state, and federal law enforcement agencies, the dysfunctional prison system, and the brazen exploits of increasingly bloodthirsty cartels. Even though President Calderón earned plaudits for handling the spring 2009 swine flu epidemic, the PRI-fashioned health-care sector drew scorn from doctors and nurses as weak, obsolete, and fragmented. Among other gross deficiencies, the half-dozen or more public systems have different databases, which delay ascertaining the characteristics, nature, and scope of a disease.[1]

As mentioned in Chapter 1, for decades, a secular papal president bestrode the apex of an iron triangle: one side consisted of the PRI, which was embedded in the government; the other side depicted an ISI-stimulated economy. It was said that not a leaf fluttered to the ground in Los Pinos without the chief executive's knowledge.

Some analysts have traced the beginning of the PRI/government decline to the October 2, 1968 Tlatelolco Massacre when snipers and the military fired on hundreds of students and other civilians in downtown Mexico City. "From that day on Mexico was a different country. Different because channels of freedom were closed; different because an asphyxiating political system lived on; different because society was wounded, thrashed, with the assassination of its youth; different because we could not learn the truth amidst declarations about the preservation of the institutions."[2]

Others claim that the erratic policies of President Echeverría are the source of the state's debilitation. He ran up an unprecedented budget deficits, sharply increased government intervention in the economy, embarked on bald-faced populism, and alienated the "Monterrey Group" of industrialists who retaliated by reducing investment and propelling capital abroad. He crossed swords with Washington over his strident advocacy of transferring resources from the affluent "first world" to the impecunious "third world," and embroiled his administration in a costly dust-up with Jews by backing a UN General Assembly resolution declaring that "Zionism is a form of racism and racial discrimination."[3] Like his predecessor Díaz Ordaz, the obdurate Echeverría clung to the revolutionary church's deteriorating corporatist scaffolding. Neither man understood how to accommodate the new, more prosperous sectors of society spawned by the economic miracle.[4] Rather than throw open the doors of the sanctuary to potential communicants among emerging groups, these myopic autocrats repressed them on the specious grounds that they were communists and other species of subversives.

Echeverría used elements of the Federal Security Directorate, other law enforcement agencies, and the military to form anti-terrorist groups like the Falcons (*Los Halcones*) and the White Brigade (*Brigada Blanca*). Kate Doye, a researcher at the National Security Archive, has concluded that the U.S. government helped instruct the thugs. Colonel Manuel Díaz Escobar Figueroa, the alleged chief of Los Halcones, indicated that trainees in a U.S.-Mexico program were keen to learn "crowd control, dealing with student demonstrations, and riots. They would also be interested in training in physical defense tactics and hand-to-hand combat." Doyle based her assessment on secret telegrams sent by the American embassy in Mexico City.

On Corpus Christi Day, June 10, 1971, *Los Halcones*, wearing civilian attire and wielding wooden poles, chains, and billy clubs, brutally attacked peaceful student demonstrators, killing at least twenty-five protestors and maiming dozens more. Between 1973 and 1976, the *Brigada Blanca* waged a "dirty war" against dissidents during which upwards of 800 people disappeared.[5]

Echeverría's regime concluded with an economic crisis, which forced Mexico to devalue the peso and seek assistance from the International Monetary Fund (IMF), which the populist chief executive viewed as a handmaiden of avaricious capitalists.

The unveiling of massive oil deposits after López Portillo swore the oath of office in December 1976 dramatically improved the nation's economic situation for several years. At first the flamboyant chief executive—he stripped to the waist to convince *National Geographic* photographers that he hurled spears in his back yard on Sunday afternoons—spoke naively and arrogantly about learning how "to administer abundance." Several years into his term, it became obvious that he had mismanaged newly discovered oil reserves and was presiding over an orgy of corruption.

The petroleum bonanza found the profoundly arrogant president, who even placed his mistress in his cabinet, falling into the trap of "*petrolization.*" This neologism describes an economy superheated by hydrocarbon revenues; an overvalued currency; mounting dependence on external credits to import escalating amounts of food, capital, and luxuries; a moribund agricultural sector; and, above all, outsized budget deficits spawned by prodigious spending by a rapidly expanding bureaucracy. Like a heroin addict who sells his blood in the morning to buy a "fix" from an obliging, well-heeled supplier at night, Mexico reacted to hydrocarbon-induced dilemma by exchanging oil for loans.

All told, the country's private and public obligations exceeded $100 billion by the early 1980s. In the spring of 1981, though, foreign bankers stopped jetting into Mexico City when an international oil glut appeared, and a sellers' market for black gold turned in favor of buyers. Determined not to "rat on" the Organization of Petroleum Exporting Countries with which Mexico had coordinated policy, the government adhered to overvalued oil prices. Clients abandoned PEMEX either to make strategic purchases in the "spot market" or to patronize exporters offering handsome discounts.

Plummeting income deprived the revolutionary church and its secular pope of the hard currency required to fund social projects that had historically preserved the support of its followers. Mexico's economic miracle had turned out to be a mirage. The ISI protectionist cocoon meant that manufacturers in Mexico produced expensive goods of mixed quality with little regard to follow-up consumer service and replacement parts. After all, not only did these industrialists benefit from the safeguards of tariffs, quotas, import permits, subsidies, and tax breaks, but they also enjoyed monopolies or oligopolies in their segments of the economy. A lack of foreign sales networks further inhibited their ability to hold their own in the global marketplace.

At the same time, corruption reached a crescendo as López Portillo and his entourage endeavored to assure themselves a sybaritic retirement. The last year of a six-year term is called the "Year of Hidalgo"—after Father Miguel Hidalgo whose pinched face peered sternly from the ten peso coin—giving rise to the doggerel: "This is the year of Hidalgo; he's a fool who doesn't steal something" ("*Este es el año de Hidalgo: Buey el que no roba algo*").[6]

The revolutionary popes periodically convened synods in the form of PRI National Assemblies to bring consistency to recognized beliefs. López Portillo called such a conclave to announce that, amid economic woes actuated by petrolization, he would defend the peso "like a dog"—a pledge as ludicrous as it was impossible to achieve inasmuch as the peso plunged from 22 to 70 per dollar, the steepest drop in recent history.

The economic crisis that erupted in May 1982 forced López Portillo to submit to a burdensome rescue plan crafted by the United States, the IMF, and other foreign lenders. As a gesture of defiance, the aloof, whining patriarch used his last State of the Nation address, delivered on September 1, 1982, to nationalize the country's banking system, which he avowed had "betrayed us." "I can affirm" he thundered, "that in recent years a group of Mexicans, led, counseled and supported by private banks, have taken more money out of the country than all the empires that have exploited us since the beginning of our history."[7] But it was gross financial mismanagement, not a plot by financial gnomes, which unleashed the capital flight. His move was designed to conger memories of President Cárdenas' takeover of the oil industry forty-four years earlier. Some 300,000 workers, peasants, and civil servants flocked to Mexico City's central plaza to praise the intrepid action of their patriotic pope. In the opinion of one writer, "López Portillo was looking increasingly like a bullfighter awarded both ears and the tail" for his triumph.[8]

This populist gambit instantly converted the state into a shareholder in the hundreds of corporations in which the banks held stock and sharpened distrust between the business community and the government, which had enjoyed a long history of cooperative enrichment. As a scion of a powerful banking family noted: "At night, we would go to bed together; in the morning, we would get up and fight."[9]

The next protector of the faith was Miguel de la Madrid Hurtado (1982-88), who professed that he would tackle corruption and foster democracy. He ran on the reformist platform of "Moral Renovation," vowing to combat malfeasance and guarantee fair contests. When the PAN began winning local elections in the North, PRI dinosaurs crudely stole the 1986 gubernatorial contest in Chihuahua. This political sleight-of-hand detonated massive, rowdy demonstrations by admirers of the "losing" PAN nominee. Only Rome's intercession prevented the state's bishops from denying sacraments to the faithful to protest the flagrant transgression of the revolutionary church.

Prophets inveighed against the drug-motivated criminality that infused officialdom. Rather than heed the oracles, the elite silenced the truth-tellers. A case in point was that of Manuel Buendía, the nation's leading syndicated columnist who was assassination in downtown Mexico City on May 30, 1984. The 58-year-old journalist's feisty front-page commentary in the newspaper *Excelsior* had frequently exposed corruption and venality in the highest reaches of government, labor, and business. Buendía's death did not halt muckraking by other journalists. In mid-1985 the weekly magazine *Proceso* publicized the criminal exploits of José Antonio Zorrilla Pérez, the DFS chief and protector of drug barons who eventually was convicted along with four others for Buendía's murder.

Three senior journalists at the Tijuana weekly *Zeta* also paid a heavy price for prophesying about the regime's iniquities, including its contamination by drug traffickers. Assassins executed the paper's co-founder Héctor Félix Miranda (April 20, 1988) and a chief editor Francisco Ortiz Franco (June 22, 2004), while severely wounding its editor and publisher J. Jesús Blancornelas (November 27, 1997).

The country sustained a different kind of "mighty blow from hell" on September 19, 1985, when an earthquake that registered 8.1 on the Richter scale struck Mexico City; a second intense tremor assailed the capital area on the following day. De la Madrid's hesitation in response to this disaster cost the PRI dearly, particularly in the Federal District's devastated thirteen-square-mile central zone. His vacillation undermined the legitimacy of the temporal pope and the single-party church over which he presided much like the 1755 Lisbon earthquake eroded the credibility of Portugal's church hierarchy.

The paternalistic regime failed to take care of its people in their greatest moment of need, and the PRI's approval levels nosedived. In the wake of a disaster that resulted in 10,000 deaths and left tens of thousands homeless, any ward politician worth his patronage allotment would have clamped on a hard hat, rolled up his sleeves, and waded into the smoking debris. While average Mexicans organized to rescue stricken family members, neighbors, and fellow workers, one diplomat noted that de la Madrid appeared to behave more like an "accountant scrutinizing a balance-sheet" than a concerned patriarch of a tormented national family. The "vaunted organizational talents of the PRI were nowhere in evidence" and "the party's labor and agrarian wings, which on numerous occasions had bused in hundreds of thousands of trade unionists and peasants for political rallies, failed to mobilize anybody to aid the earthquake victims."[10]

Colorless technocrats on de la Madrid's team lacked either popularity or well-cultivated rapport with the people, and many of the old guard proved incompetent and corrupt. Police demanded bribes from men and women who begged to cross security lines to search for loved-ones. The capital's residents coped with the crisis with minimal official help. Taxis metamorphosed into ambulances, ham-radio operators devised a communications network, and agile young people—known as "moles"—dug with their hands to locate victims in the rubble of collapsed buildings. "We realized for the first time that we could help each other without relying on the government," recalled a community activist.[11]

A crisis linked to drug trafficking erupted six months before the natural disaster; namely, the brutal torture and execution of DEA agent Enrique "Kiki" Camarena Salazar—a martyr to the cause of fighting the cartels. The case, which also highlighted self-serving official malfeasance, will be analyzed in Chapter 9.

The post-earthquake reconstruction gave rise to a new generation of technocratic leaders. Epitomized by Planning and Budget Secretary Carlos Salinas, these young policymakers constituted a virtual religious order. Many of its members had served their novitiate at prestigious universities in the United States and Europe, spoke English fluently, had served as acolytes in the Finance Ministry, Central Bank, or other sanctums of the financial bureaucracy, were cosmopolitan, and regarded the continuance of muscular import-substitution as an economic sin that had exacerbated Latin America's purgatory-like "lost decade" of the 1980s. These men and women realized that the country's patriarchs had clung too long to the ISI model, making their nation dependent on the vagaries of the international market, particularly with respect to petroleum. They were also cognizant of the free-enterprise homilies delivered by U.S. President Ronald Reagan, U.K. Prime Minister Margaret Thatcher, and Spain's Prime Minister Felipe González.

The technocrats moved to open the economy gradually by raising the prices of state-sold goods like gasoline, natural gas, fertilizer, and electricity, while reducing the barriers to competition. They spearheaded Mexico's affiliation with the General Agreement on Tariffs and Trade (now the World Trade Organization or WTO) and signed a Bilateral Framework Agreement on trade and investment with the U.S. en route to negotiating the North American Free Trade Agreement (NAFTA), which took effect on January 1, 1994.[12]

Meanwhile, the new generation of technocrats who had negotiated those trade agreements questioned PRI's dogmas, structures, and goals. The increasingly secularized brothers and sisters supervised the return of the banking system to private hands, and sold off Teléfonos de México (TELMEX) and hundreds of other state-owned enterprises. This historical shift has parallels with the Second Vatican Council (1962-65), which Pope John XXIII had convened in reaction to the tremendous challenges actuated by political, social, economic, and technological developments. That Roman Church conclave advocated ecumenism, reevaluated time-worn beliefs, expanded lay participation in Church affairs, and replaced Latin with the vernacular in sacramental worship.

Just as European-educated priests had taken the lead in moderniz-ing the Roman Catholic Church, the implementation of the Council's directives on liturgy was carried out under authority of a special papal commission and later incorporated in the Congregation for Divine Wor-ship and the Discipline of the Sacraments, acting under the scrutiny of national bishops' conferences.

Whenever core values of an institution are challenged and targeted for change, a counter-revolutionary reaction will arise. The appearance of the Thermidorian response to the excesses of Robespierre's Jacobin revolu-tion in eighteenth-century France was one of many similar backlashes. The shifts associated with Vatican II outraged conservative Archbishop Marcel Lefebvre, who was excommunicated for ordaining four bishops in 1988 without the Pope's permission.

Likewise, the Mexican revolutionary church had fervent believers who resisted the reproach to true orthodoxy. Cuauhtémoc Cárdenas, former governor of Michoacán and son of canonized President Lázaro Cárdenas, Porfirio Muñoz Ledo, former PRI president, and other dissenters objected to the new credo and its dismissal of revolutionary doctrine. Neo-liberal-ism represented heresy against the tenets of Revolutionary Nationalism. Salinas *et al.* were simply acting like latter-day Luthers. The traditional-ists, who formed the Democratic Current (CD) within the PRI/government church in October 1986, championed *intra*party "democracy" and decried the use of the *dedazo* to select the next presidential nominee. For them, the concept of "neoliberalism" reeked of blasphemy. Such altruistic positions concealed the CD's real goal; namely, to fend off the technocrats' assault on a statist, corporatist regime. The CD openly campaigned for Cárdenas' selection as the PRI standard-bearer in the 1988 presidential campaign—an action that offended the previously unchallenged dictate that an incumbent president had the right to anoint his successor.

Following de la Madrid's consecration of Salinas as the candidate, Cárdenas accepted the nomination of the small Authentic Party of the Mexican Revolution, which eventually cast its lot with the CD and a farrago of leftist groups to form the Democratic National Front (FDN). In reaction to this "violation" of party statutes, the Church excommunicated Cárdenas, Muñoz Ledo, and other key schismatics in the Democratic Current.

After Salinas won the highly controversial presidential showdown with the aid of mysterious computer failure, Cárdenas and many of his FDN brethren created the leftist-nationalist Democratic Revolutionary Party (PRD).

The Harvard-educated secular pope repressed the PRD even as he propitiated the PAN to advance his neoliberal initiatives, which eventually crystallized in NAFTA. The U.S.-Canadian-Mexican pact required rewriting laws that covered twenty-two of Mexico's economic sectors. Amid such an upheaval, only 25 or 30 percent of the population might be expected to benefit in the short- to medium-term. How could Salinas maintain the support of—or, at least, appease—the majority of shantytown dwellers and poor campesinos for whom the accord bore no proximate relevance?

The president astutely employed three tools to convey to the downtrodden that, profound changes aside, he had not forgotten them even as he weakened labor unions, peasant organizations, and other corporatist structures. Specifically, he cultivated the armed forces, the Roman Catholic Church, and participants in the National Solidarity Program called PRONASOL or "Solidarity."

He lost no opportunity to ingratiate himself with the military, many of whose members reportedly voted against him. He attended their ceremonies, praised their unflinching "loyalty" to the state, and increased their budget.

While in office, Salinas improved relations with the Roman Catholic Church, which the church of revolutionary nationalism previously had treated as an archdemon. He steered passage of legislation to amend the most objectionable anticlerical provisions inherent in the 1917 Constitution. In addition, he renewed diplomatic relations with the Vatican that had been severed in 1857. And he warmly greeted Pope John Paul II when the pontiff arrived in Mexico in 1990. As a progressive, Salinas considered anticlericalism as outmoded as a droopy Pancho Villa mustache. If an atheistic nation like the Soviet Union could send an ambassador to the Holy See, as President Mikhail S. Gorbachev had done in late 1989, why could not an overwhelmingly Catholic country like Mexico make peace with the Vatican?

Rather than offering beatitude-like assurances for the next life, Salinas's endeavored to uplift the poor in the here and now through PRONASOL. A community or neighborhood desiring to take part in the program could contact Solidarity directly. The Mexico City-based agency then would dispatch a representative to an assembly open to all local residents. After extensive and frequently boisterous deliberations, average people elected a board of directors, set their priorities, and decided whether they would match the government's contribution to, say, a clinic either with pesos or their own "sweat capital." The disbursement of funds from the capital directly to beneficiaries by-passed sticky-fingered governors, mayors, and other PRI minions. This program poured disproportionate resources into PRD bailiwicks to undermine the newly created party and attract coverts to the temporal church. The initiative also burnished the image of Luis Donaldo Colosio Murrieta, the party president who would go on to head PRONASOL before receiving Salinas' imprimatur as his successor in 1994. Salinas toyed with the idea that the 100,000 Solidarity committees could provide a base for his returning to Los Pinos in 2000 if Colosio could eliminate the constitutional ban on reelection.

In May 1990 Pope John Paul II invested legitimacy in the Solidarity plan. He celebrated Mass in Chalco, a slum near the D.F. that teemed with scruffy dogs, postage stamp-sized yards, unpaved streets that exuded either mud or dust, and cinder block shacks that housed some 300,000 residents. Thanks to PRONASOL, Chalco acquired new schools, access to potable water, and electric power lines. The Vicar of Rome stressed that "the Church has always raised its voice and acted in the defense of each and every man, most of all the weakest and most defenseless." He pledged that it would continue to do so. In a transparent reference to the revolutionary church, he said that too often people have been led by "false pastors" ... [who served] "not truth and well-being but special interests, ideologies and systems that turned themselves against man."[13]

President Salinas was eager to cooperate with Washington as well as Rome. He knew that narco-violence and ubiquitous venality could thwart the North American Free Trade Agreement that he had so enthusiastically championed. During a mid-1990 trip to the U.S., the Mexican leader agreed to the presence of armed DEA agents in Mexico, as well as the deployment of spotter aircraft and surveillance satellites to detect drug operations.

To demonstrate his commitment, he established a Center for Drug Control Planning (CENDRO), which carried out intelligence functions; the National Drug Control Program (PNCD) to set goals; and the National Institute to Combat Drugs (INCD), a Mexican version of the DEA under the jurisdiction of the Attorney General's Office.

One of the most bizarre events during Salinas's term involved the murder of Cardinal Posadas Ocampo in broad daylight in Guadalajara on May 24, 1993. The official version of the incident holds that the prelate, garbed in full clerical dress, wearing a conspicuous pectoral cross, and ensconced in the rear of a large black limousine, was mistaken for "El Chapo" Guzmán Loera. Assassins yanked open the car door and riddled the cardinal's throat and chest with fourteen bullets. Also killed were the clergyman's driver and five others. It was presumed that the assailants acted on behalf of Tijuana's Arellano Félix Organization, which had vowed to eliminate Guzmán Loera because of its territorial conflict with the Sinaloa Cartel.

Doubts about the "mistaken identity" theory surfaced when *30Giorni*, an Italian journal, reported that Posadas Ocampo's housekeeper claimed that the prelate's phone had been tapped a week before his death, that someone had broken into his home, and that a mysterious stranger shadowed his residence for a week before the assassination and was not seen again after the killing. A delay, just long enough for the triggermen to board a Tijuana-bound Aeromexico flight after the shooting, also suggested premeditation.

Domestic and international outrage forced federal authorities to hunt down the drug barons who were responsible. For his part, Guzmán Loera unobtrusively escaped by taxi from the airport, drove to Mexico City, and then took refuge in the mountains of neighboring Guatemala. Two weeks later, he was apprehended and sentenced to a twenty-year prison term.

Ten months later Donaldo Colosio, the PRI's first presidential candidate for the 1994 election, also died from a killer's bullet, becoming another martyr for the Institutional Revolutionary Party and its dogma. Mexican laws restricting the pool of candidates who could run for president several months before an election left Salinas with few options. He selected Ernesto Zedillo, a political neophyte, a Yale Ph.D., and a votary of the magic of the marketplace, to replace the murdered contender on the ticket. The "December crisis"—a state of near-bankruptcy—exploded three weeks after the new revolutionary pope's investiture and produced Mexico's worst economic downturn since the Great Depression. A first-rate economist but an inexperienced politician, Zedillo devoted himself to righting the storm-tossed economy. The debilitation of the Mexican state soon became even more obvious.

Again, Mexico had to seek an economic lifeline. When the U.S. Congress balked at funding a rescue scheme, President Bill Clinton took matters into his own hands. He teamed up with Speaker of the House Newt Gingrich, the U.S. Treasury, the IMF, and leery European governments to craft a $52 billion international aid plan. In exchange for access to these funds, the Mexicans agreed to furnish timely, accurate data to lenders and to guarantee repayment of the loans with PEMEX revenues that would be deposited in New York's Federal Reserve Bank.

President Zedillo, who lacked a political base among his party's senior clergy, infuriated PRI cardinals and bishops by holding conversations with the PAN, the PRD, and smaller parties as he sought to resolve the emergency that had been dumped in his lap. To his credit, he ordered the incarceration of the ex-president's older brother, Raúl Salinas, in connection with the 1994 murder of José Francisco Ruiz Massieu, the PRI's second-in-command and a former Salinas brother-in-law whose divorce had precipitated a family uproar. Zedillo's action against Raúl broke a salient precept of his party: a sitting chief executive would not ventilate the dirty linen of his predecessor, who—in turn—would not meddle in the affairs of the secular church. In January 1999 a judge declared Raúl Salinas guilty of ordering the murder and sentenced him to fifty years in prison. In June 2005 an appellate court overturned his homicide conviction. Still, party graybeards have never forgiven Zedillo's unprecedented sanction against the Salinas family.

In the past, the revolutionary pope named and removed governors like they were choir boys. Zedillo's weakness manifested itself in his inability to extract PRI stalwart, Roberto Madrazo Pintado, from Tabasco's governorship in the aftermath of a 1994 fraud-drenched election. The chief executive offered Madrazo a major cabinet post, which the Tabascan initially accepted. A wilier pontiff would have publicized the appointment. Zedillo neither made such an announcement nor asked for a written pledge. He was playing under new rules and believed that two gentlemen had reached a good faith accord. Madrazo was more akin to a Machiavellian cardinal raised under the patronage of the revolutionary church. The Tabasco governor succeeded in defying the PRI's temporal pope, whose decisions until then had represented the will of God for party faithful. PRI militants lauded Madrazo's resistance to executive pressure and later elected him party president in a move to restore the secular version of pre-Vatican II practices. Madrazo went on to became the PRI's hugely unsuccessful standard-bearer in the presidential election that the PAN's Felipe Calderón won in 2006.

Like the political system, Mexico's judiciary has been infused with PRI-fashioned mores. Zedillo's lack of confidence in Mexico's courts shaped his decision to dispatch Juan García Abrego, the chief honcho of the infamous Gulf Cartel, to the United States rather than having him tried in Mexico. Not only was Los Pinos concerned about that drug lord's ability to bribe Mexican judges, police officers, and prison guards, but it was feared that he would continue to run his business from behind bars while awaiting trial. "There is a better chance that the truth will emerge in the U.S., said a senior Mexican official. "We aren't afraid of that happening."[14]

Worst of all was the revelation that General Jesús Gutiérrez Rebollo, whom Zedillo had appointed director of the National Institute to Combat Drugs (INCD) in December 1996, was actually in the pocket of the Juárez Cartel. The bulldog-faced Gutiérrez Rebollo commanded the Fifth Military Region, embracing several west-central states, including the drug trafficking center of Guadalajara. The general—initially reputed to be a tough officer brimming with personal integrity—had had extensive experience in running Army operations against drug traffickers in western Mexico.

Praised by U.S. officials, the forty-two year Army veteran was called upon to clean up anti-drug police agencies. Washington's own drug czar, General Barry McCaffrey, lauded Gutiérrez Rebollo as "a guy of absolute unquestioned integrity." Despite initial efforts at a cover-up, military authorities arrested the general on February 18, 1997. Confronted by Defense Secretary Enrique Cervantes Aguirre, Gutierrez Rebollo angrily denied any wrongdoing. His daughter claimed that he was then forcibly sedated and bundled off to the Central Military Hospital. Twelve days later, General Cervantes assembled his commanders for an extraordinary televised address. He denounced the former drug-enforcement chief as a Judas and claimed that Gutiérrez Rebollo had a heart attack when confronted with evidence of his treason. In a separate statement, President Zedillo said the arrest confirmed his regime's ''unshakable determination to pursue and punish drug trafficking and combat corruption."[15]

A little more than a month after his arrest, Gutiérrez was replaced as INCD chief by Mariano Federico Herrán Salvatti, a former prosecutor and law professor who reportedly underwent a most rigorous background investigation.[16] In light of endemic corruption and inefficiencies in the INCD, the attorney general dismantled the agency in late April 1997. The Institute was succeeded by the Special Prosecutor's Office for Crimes against Health (FEADS) and staffed by personnel who were supposedly better paid, trained, and vetted.[17] Six years later, Attorney General Rafael Macedo de la Concha dissolved FEADS, describing the agency as a corrupt "dung heap."[18]

The PRI's losses—its majority in Congress (1997), the Mexico City mayoralty (1997), several governorships (late 1990s), and the presidency (2000)—further weakened the once-hegemonic party. The incompetence of Fox, who took office on December 1, 2000, debilitated the state even more. A superb vote-winner but a hapless politician, Fox failed to unite his National Action Party behind his ever-changing program, much less reach out to his coalition partner, the Mexico Green Ecological Party (PVEM). He hoped to curry favor with the Zapatista National Liberation Army, but the Chiapas-based rebels scorned his overtures. He quickly abandoned a plan to construct a new Mexico City airport, the "center-piece" of his public works agenda, when machete-waving dissidents decried the project. Fox's weakness became obvious in April 2002 when he sought permission to briefly visit Canada and the United States. For the first time in history, Congress denied a president's request to leave the country, reminiscent of popes held captive hundreds of years earlier. In essence, Fox had become a lame duck with four years left in his term. As leader of the PAN's deputies from 2000 to 2003, Calderón had a front row seat from which to observe his predecessor's fall from grace.

An astute observer of Fox's anti-narcotics strategy noted: "While effective at raising the number of individuals arrested and drug shipments confiscated, this policy fell far short from the government's objective of defeating the cartels. Moreover, the capture of some cartel leaders was tantamount to kicking around hornets' nests without having the means to spray the rattled insects."[19] The apprehension of Benjamín Arellano Félix, capo of Tijuana's AFO (2002) and Osiel Cárdenas Guillén, head of the Gulf Cartel (2003), kindled a virulent war within and among the criminal organizations, as ambitious lieutenants battled to assert or reassert domain over territory, resources, and manpower.

Much to President Fox's chagrin, the Sinaloa Cartel may have secreted a spy deep within his government. The alleged insider was Nahum Acosta

Lugo, who coordinated travel for the chief executive's private secretary
from 2001 to 2005. Authorities accused Acosta of passing confidential
details of Fox's whereabouts and schedule to Arturo Beltrán Leyva of
the Sinaloa syndicate. The president said security would be increased
because "organized crime has challenged the Mexican state and we are
not going to tolerate that at all."[20] After several months in prison, Acosta
was released for lack of evidence.

Calderón's interior secretary, Fernando Gómez Mont, has castigated
previous administrations, including that of Vicente Fox, for shortcomings in reining in the cartels. Fox's first interior secretary, Santiago Creel
Miranda, bristled at this charge and retorted that it was "inopportune
and irresponsible" to criticize his boss.[21] On the prestigious "Meet the
Press" television news program, U.S. Defense Secretary Robert M. Gates
also praised Calderón's anti-drug efforts and reaffirmed Gómez Mont's
indictment of previous Mexican leaders.[22]

Although the revolutionary church lost to the PAN again in 2006, Fox
had proved inept in confronting drug trafficking and other nightmares
that bedeviled his flock. In addition to the cartel menace and a flagging
economy, Calderón had to manage the spring 2009 influenza outbreak
and a number of other serious problems cited near the end of the text. As
a result, powerful PRI cardinals of the true faith—über-Senator Manlio
Fabio Beltrones, Mexico State governor Enrique Peña Nieto, and party
president Beatriz Paredes Rangel—delighted in the prospect of recovering the power lost in 2000.

The once-hegemonic party proposed neither new liturgy nor new rituals; however, Paredes spoke of a "twenty-first century PRI" as capable
of uplifting the faithful. She planned to demonstrate her congregation's
strength in the July 5, 2009 Chamber of Deputies' election, as well as
in eleven states whose citizens cast ballots for state or local officials on
the same date. In pursuit of this goal, she recruited congressional candidates from all theological tendencies to overcome past schisms. These
nominees included such traditionalists as Federico Madrazo (son of 2006
presidential candidate), Manuel Cavazos Lerma (former Tamaulipas
governor), Manuel Ángel Núñez Soto (former Hidalgo governor), Emilio
Chuayffet Chemor (former Mexico State governor), and Enrique Burgos
García (former Querétaro governor). Paredes vied for a deputy seat with
an eye to becoming the PRI's leader in the lower house—a position that
would advance her presidential aspirations. We will return to the election
in the Conclusions.

Notes

1. Ruth Rodríguez and Thelma Gómez Durán, "Sistema de salud, por los suelos," *El Universal*, May 14, 2009.
2. Julio Scherer and Carlos Monsiváis, *Parte de guerra: Tlatelolco 1968* (Mexico City: Aguilar, 1999): 13.
3. George W. Grayson, *The United States and Mexico: Patterns of Influence* (New York: Praeger, 1984): 48.
4. González, *Dual Transitions from Authoritarian Rule*, 55.
5. González, *Dual Transitions from Authoritarian Rule*, 56.
6. Susan Kaufman Purcell and John F.H. Purcell, "State and Society in Mexico: Must a Stable Polity be Institutionalized?" *World Politics* 32 (January 1980): 200.
7. Quoted in *Excelsior*, September 2, 1982, p. 1-A.
8. *Latin America Weekly Report*, November 19, 1982, p. 6.
9. Agustín F. Legorreta, interview by author, August 19, 2002, Mexico City.
10. Jonathan Kandel, *La Capital: The Biography of Mexico City* (New York: Random House, 1988): 571.
11. Kandel, *La Capital*, 570.
12. George W. Grayson, *The Mexico-U.S. Business Committee: Catalyst for the North American Free Trade Agreement* (Rockville, MD: Montross Press, 2007).
13. Clyde Haberman, "Pope, Amid Mexico's Poor, Laments," *New York Times*, May 8, 1990.
14. Kevin Fedarka *et al.*, "The Capture of Mexico's Most Wanted," *Time Magazine*, January 29, 1996.
15. Tim Golden, "U.S. Officials Say Mexican Military Aids Drug Traffic," *New York Times*, March 26, 1998.
16. In January 2009, authorities incarcerated Herrán Salvatti, who had served as an official in the Chiapas government, for "corruption, criminal conspiracy, illegal use of public resources and abuse of power charges against the government of Chiapas and society"; see, "Mexican Drug Czar Arrested on Corruption Charges," *Latin American Herald Tribune*, February 15, 2009. www.laht.com/article.asp?CategoryId=14091&ArticleId=326449.
17. This section draws on an excellent paper by Graham H. Turbiville, Jr., "Law Enforcement and the Mexican Armed Forces: New Security Mission Challenges the Military" *http://fmso.leavenworth.army.mil/documents/mxcoparm.htm.*
18. "La corrupción en corporaciones antinarco," *El Universal*, November 23, 2008.
19. González, "To Die in Mexico: Rumblings of a Drug War."
20. "Fox: Drug Trafficking Reached Presidency," *UPI*, February 8, 2005 <www.upi.com/Top_News/2005/02/08/Fox_Drug_trafficking_reached_presidency/UPI-25821107894052/>.
21. Arladna García, "Acusa Segob omisiones de Fox," *Reforma*, February 25, 2009; and Jorge Ramos and Ricardo Gómez, "Narco confronta a panistas; Creel refuta Gómez Mont," *El Universal*, February 26, 2009.
22. "En México no se enfrentó a narco.—Gates," *Reforma*, March 1, 2009.

5

Diaspora of the Narco Churches

The narco churches share several characteristics with evangelical Protestant denominations, known as *"sectas"* in Mexico. The sects require less formal studies for ordination of their leaders, are often in conflict with Catholics, and are prone to fragmentation. It is scriptural differences that generate ruptures in fundamentalist churches, but it is more likely to be power struggles, leadership conflicts, and control of *plazas* that produce cleavages within drug organizations. And while competing sects rely on Biblical interpretations to consolidate their positions and win converts, drug traffickers depend on force, weapons, and savagery to gain followers and ensure submission. The religious sects engage in good works to help the poor and dispense alms and charity; the narco churches are loyal to their friends, their nurturing communities, and those who will protect their privacy—and they reward the faithful with money, jobs, paved roads, lighting, parks, and schools. The religious sects believe in the baptism of water and ceremonies and sacraments of bread and wine; narco churches depend on ceremonies and rituals of blood and bullets. Religious sects operate in the market of faith; cartels in the market of drugs.

Sinaloa Cartel and the Beltrán Leyva Brothers

On April 8, 1989, Sinaloan Miguel Ángel Félix Gallardo awoke to find a twelve-man police taskforce at his door. He offered them $5 million in exchange for his freedom, but PJF Commander González Calderoni, acting under strict orders from President Salinas who sought to fortify relations with Washington, arrested the kingpin. A judge convicted the crafty Sinaloan of drug trafficking, bribery, and illegal possession of weapons. When first incarcerated, he directed his lucrative empire via mobile phone, lawyers, and through intermediaries visiting his well-appointed apartment above the warden's office. One of the striking aspects of his accommodations was a large framed photograph of the drug lord with Pope John Paul II. An avid reader, with a bulging collection of books, he had been patron to José Luis Cuevas, Martha Chapa, and other artists. Unfortunately for him, most of those indulgences ended in 1992 with his transfer to the top-security La Palma prison west of capital.

Authorities believe that Félix Gallardo, the "capo of all capos," distributed *plazas* to his lieutenants from behind bars in order to minimize intramural conflicts. According to the Attorney General's Office, he granted the territories as follows:

1. Joaquín "El Chapo" Guzmán Loera (Mexicali and San Luis Río Colorado, Sonora, which lies along the U.S. border at the intersection of Sonora, Baja California, Arizona, and California);
2. Rafael Aguilar Guajardo (Ciudad Juárez);
3. Héctor Luis "El Güero" Palma Salazar (Nogales and Hermosillo);
4. Jesús "El Chuy" Labra Avilés, mentor to the Arellano Félix brothers who were Félix Gallardo's nephews (Tijuana);
5. Ismael "El Mayo" Zambada García (Sinaloa).
6. Pedro Avilés Pérez (Jalisco).

With the growing popularity of methamphetamines and other synthetic drugs, the Milenio Cartel sprang to prominence in Michoacán under the dominance of Luis and Armando Valencia Cornelio; the Colima Cartel emerged in Colima state headed by the brothers José, Adán, and Luis Amezcua; and the Oaxaca Cartel, led by Pedro Díaz Parada, began operations in the Isthmus of Tehuantepec.

This modus vivendi, designed by Félix Gallardo, depended on the various factions respect for the territories of other crime syndicates. It quickly evaporated when the Arellano Félix Organization broke with El Chapo in an effort to control all of Baja California and even began making incursions into Sinaloa and Durango.[1]

These actions notwithstanding, Guzmán Loera rose to the top of one of the country's most remunerative enterprises. During the mid- and late 1980s, the U.S. government's "Operation Hat Tricks" had successfully disrupted Colombian supply routes through south Florida, forcing the Medellín and Cali gangsters to find another avenue to the United States. They increasingly turned to El Chapo and other Mexican entrepreneurs to move the product to American consumers. As Samuel Logan noted, the U.S.-Mexican border became the "soft-underbelly" of drug commerce.[2] Later NAFTA facilitated the free bilateral flow of goods and services, which provided more opportunities to export illegal substances. Between 1999 and 2008, the number of containers moving through west coast ports in Michoacán and Guerrero exploded from 4,475 to 197,149 per year.[3]

Guzmán Loera developed alternative routes through Central America to avoid the increasing use of radar scans. He also shifted his role from simply transporting Colombian cocaine to ownership of it. To shuttle cocaine from Mexico to the United States, he dug sophisticated, structurally sound tunnels under the border. He excavated a 1,500-foot, concrete-reinforced, air-conditioned tunnel between Tijuana and Otay Mesa near San Diego; and another subterranean passage afforded access to Douglas, Arizona.

El Chapo and his counterparts have shown enormous ingenuity in smuggling drugs into the biggest market on Earth. They have stuffed beer cases, shoes, dolls, and surfboards with their merchandise. A woman captured in Tijuana had a protruding belly, caused not by pregnancy but by a packet holding several pounds of tightly wrapped cocaine. Another female carried cocaine that had been surgically implanted in her buttocks. She died of blood poisoning when a container burst upon her arrival at the Mexico City airport.[4] In 1993 authorities in Tecate, Baja California, seized a U.S.-bound 7.3-ton cocaine shipment that had been concealed in cans of chili peppers. In May 2008, U.S. Customs agents found in a car trunk a 6.6-pound statue of Jesus fabricated from plaster blended with cocaine. The driver, who managed to escape back into Mexico, explained that she was guaranteed $80 to transport the figure to the Laredo bus station.[5]

El Chapo directed his operations much like a multinational corporation—with a deadly difference. A federal drug agent who has long tracked his behavior noted that "when Donald Trump calls you into the boardroom, you might lose your job. But when Chapo Guzmán calls you in, you might lose your life." In other words, "his business is crime."[6]

When captured in 1991, El Chapo retrieved $50,000 from a suitcase and dumped it on the desk of a Mexico City law enforcement chief, who allowed him to go free. In the same way, he reportedly gave a police commander $1 million and five Dodge Ram Chargers to permit two drug-laden cargo planes to land in Jalisco.[7]

Guzmán Loera was eventually arrested in Guatemala and charged for his role in the assassination of Cardinal Posadas Ocampo. Behind bars he conducted transactions from a luxurious cell, where he imbibed fine wines, chit-chatted with Dan Rather and other media mavens, and started an affair with inmate and ex-police officer Zulema Julieta Hernández.

He maintained continual contact with the extremely powerful Arturo Beltrán Leyva and his brothers (Héctor Alfredo "El H," Mario Alberto "El General," and Carlos), other lethal offspring of the municipality of

Badiraguato. On January 19, 2001, a few days before a scheduled extradition to the U.S., El Chapo fled from the Puente Grande maximum-security prison in Jalisco state, where he had been serving his twenty-year sentence for criminal association and bribery.

The Beltrán Leyvas, Zambada, "El Azul" Esparragoza, and dozens of other conspirators helped orchestrate this blatant escape, which made inventive use of a prison laundry cart after El Chapo's electronically controlled cell door inexplicably flew open during a period when video cameras temporarily went dark. The feat became known as the "golden kilogram"—an allusion to the weight of the gold used to bribe those who helped the inmate gain his freedom.[8] A federal investigation led to the arrest of seventy-one prison officials, and comedians began calling Puente Grande (the "Big Bridge") Puerta Grande—(the "Big Door"). El Chapo once boasted that he spent $5 million each month on bribes to police and other officials. "He remains fairly safe in Mexico because of his influence and ability to corrupt," affirmed DEA Special Agent in Charge Jack Riely.[9]

After his escape, Guzmán Loera met with "El Mayo" Zambada, "El Azul" Esparragoza, and Arturo Beltrán Leyva in Monterrey. He contrived with them to undercut the Tijuana Cartel's growing influence, break the hegemony of the Carrillo Fuentes family over Ciudad Juárez, and exterminate Los Zetas, which Osiel Cárdenas Guillén had formed to protect the Gulf Cartel. He pursued his goals by leading authorities to the AFO's top dog, Benjamín Arellano Félix, and orchestrating the murder of Rodolfo "Golden Baby" Carrillo Fuentes, the youngest brother of Amado and Vicente.[10]

Although it is unclear whether he ran the show alone or with the help of "El Barbas" Beltrán Leyva—since they had never enjoyed a close relationship—El Chapo hatched sinister projects from a remote ranch near La Tuna, a five-hour drive from Badiraguato. Like any good soap opera, the plot thickened when a hit man, allegedly acting on orders from Gulf Cartel leader Cárdenas Guillén, murdered El Chapo's younger brother, Arturo "El Pollo"/"The Chicken," inside La Palma in late 2004.[11]

The Beltrán Leyvas suffered a body blow on January 20, 2008, with the arrest of Alfredo, who allegedly oversaw large-scale smuggling and money-laundering projects. Commonly called "El Mochomo" after a big, red stinging ant, Alfredo was believed to be in charge of two assassin groups, Los Pelones in Guerrero and Los Güeros in Sonora. Agents arrested him and three bodyguards at a house in Culiacán where they found an AK-47 and other firearms, eleven expensive watches, a luxury SUV, and two suitcases stuffed with approximately $900,000.[12] El Mochomo's own Colt pistol bore the oft-recited revolutionary mantra: "I'd rather die on my feet than live on my knees."

Nearly a year later, the Mexican Army apprehended Adrián "El Primo Rivera" Rivera García, another key Beltrán Leyva operative who cooked methamphetamines and had responsibility for La Montaña area of Guerrero state, which they control in concert with Los Zetas. In addition to drug trafficking, Rivera and his accomplices, "Los Primos," stole automobiles, engaged in kidnappings, and extorted money from businessmen.[13]

El Universal reported that Arturo Beltrán Leyva, who holds Guzmán Loera responsible for his brother's capture, signed a pact with Los Zetas, thus fracturing the so-called "La Federación" composed of the Sinaloan capos and their allies in Michoacán, Colima, Jalisco, Nayarit, and Sonora.[14]

In early May 2009 the Federal Preventative Police (PFP) seized Alberto "El Borrado" Pineda Villa, who headed the Beltrán Leyvas' logistics and operations in Morelos and Guerrero. The Pineda Villa crime family once acted independently but after La Familia kidnapped El Borrado's brother and failed to release him following receipt of a 7-million-peso ransom, they cast their lot with the Beltrán Leyvas.[15]

Later in the month, an anonymous tip enabled the Army to apprehend Rodolfo "El Nito" López Ibarra, who had just taken over the *plaza* in San Pedro Garza García, Nuevo León, one of Mexico's wealthiest municipalities. A spokesman for the Seventh Military Zone said that the 33-year-old Ibarra had flown in from Acapulco where he attended a baptism organized by Arturo Beltrán Leyva.[16] On June 26, 2009, the Army made another successful strike in San Pedro Garza García when they took into custody César "La Borrega" or "El 34" Niño García, who admitted extorting up to 100,000 pesos monthly from local nightclubs and restaurants. Linked to three executions, the former state SWAT team member also had in his briefcase the names of thirty-three police officers who may have received payment from the Beltrán Leyvas.[17]

In mid-April 2009, the Army clashed with the forty members of the Beltrán Leyva group in the municipalities of San Miguel, Totolapan, and Arcelia in southern Guerrero's Sierra Maestras. When the smoke cleared, fifteen gangsters, almost all from Sinaloa, and one soldier lay dead.[18] The armed forces also took into custody Rubén "The Small One"/"Nene" Granados Vargas, the Beltrán Leyvas' assassin, trafficker, and kidnapper in Guerrero's Costa Grande, which lies just below the Tierra Caliente where Guerrero, Michoacán, and Mexico State converge.[19] Still, the Beltrán Leyvas and their Zeta allies hold the whip in Guerrero where the small guerrilla band, the Insurgent People's Revolutionary Army briefly reappeared in May 2009.

The group's leader Omar Guerrero Solís, who had escaped from an Acapulco prison in 2002, began to issue statements that took on the tone of vigilante justice. "El ERPI will continue promoting self-defense; we will not countenance what is happening in Ciudad Juárez ... where a mother must pay off criminals so they will not hurt her children when they return from school.[20]

On January 29, 2009, the Federal Police apprehended Arturo Beltrán Leyva's cousin, Jerónimo Gámez García, another of the gang's financial adepts. Upon arresting him just outside Mexico City, they found in his home $1 million, an assortment of firearms, armored vehicles, and a computer crammed with information about the organization's business ventures.[21]

A bloody battle for control of the Mexico City's Benito Juárez International Airport, the focus and cornucopia of drug activities, contributes to the El Chapo-Beltrán Leyva split. The Beltrán Leyvas, who purportedly control Monterrey's airport, sought to oust Jesús "The King" Zambada García, brother of Ismael Zambada and ally of El Chapo, from the lucrative D.F. airport *plaza*. That skirmish took the lives of hit men for both contenders and may have triggered the deaths of two PFP commanders and their escorts, Edgar Millán Gómez (May 8, 2008) and Igor Labastida Calderón (June 26, 2008), who allegedly had ties to organized crime.

The airport remains a sewer of criminality despite the jumble of 1,700 PFP, city, and private police assigned to the facility.[22] Because everyone has responsibility, no one is actually in control and miscreants can freely dab Vicks VapoRub on the noses of drug-sniffing dogs to impair their efficiency.[23] This situation prompted Calderón to relieve retired General Víctor Gutiérrez Rosas from his post as chief of federal police at the airport, replacing him with the Army's 46-year-old inspector general, Hugo Ignacio Tinoco Gutiérrez, effective May 1, 2009.[24]

The violence and bloodbath escalated and continued to touch family members of the capos when gunmen assassinated Guzmán Loera's son, Édgar Guzmán Beltrán, in the parking lot of the City Club shopping mall in Culiacán on May 8, 2008. Also killed was Arturo Meza Cázares, son of Blanca Margarita "La Emperatriz" Cázares Salazar, presumed chief financial operator and money launderer of El Mayo Zambada. Witnesses say that at least twenty men armed with AK-47s, R-15s, .9 mm weapons, and even a bazooka launched the attack.[25]

Another close friend on the hit list was El Chapo's prison girlfriend, Zulema Hernández Ramírez. On December 23, 2008, police in Ecatepec discovered her body crammed into the trunk of an automobile. She and a male companion had been dispatched with gunshot wounds to the head, and were rolled in a green quilt that was bound with fine tape. Her abductors, most likely Los Zetas, had carved blackened "Zs" on her back, breasts, abdomen, and buttocks.

The PGR and SIEDO have linked the Beltrán Leyvas to the execution of twenty-five men found near Mexico State's La Marquesa Park in September 2008. Former police commander Raúl "El R" Villa Ortega, arrested for participation in the mass murder, is an operator of Édgar "La Barbie" Valdez Villarreal, the brothers' chief enforcer and head of Los Negros, another narco-military gang.

Born in the United States in 1973, "La Barbie" acquired his nickname because his light complexion and corn-flour blue eyes that resemble those of Mattel's Ken doll. In February 2009 authorities captured Valdez Villarreal's cousin, Gerardo "Tony the Liar" González Benavides, who sold drugs in bars and discothèques in the Federal District and Mexico State for the Beltrán Leyvas. Also seized were nine other operatives, including two federal police officers who provided protection for the organization in Tultitlán, Mexico State.[26]

Earlier the Beltrán Leyvas made headlines when they placed informants high up in Mexico's Attorney General's Office, and they infiltrated the U.S. embassy in Mexico City. Despite this security breach, a U.S. government spokesman averred "we have not lost confidence [in Mexican officials]... We have full confidence that the Mexican government is pursuing the traffickers."[27]

On May 20, 2009, the respected Mexican newspaper *Reforma* revealed that in recent years the Beltrán Leyva brothers had been using the Mariano Matamoros Airport in Temixco, Morelos, to expedite cocaine shipments from South America. The syndicate then sold the drugs in Mexico or the United States.

In mid-2009 the Federal Police rounded up nine suspected Beltrán Leyva underlings in Sonora. The prisoners included César Alberto "El César" Escárreaga, responsible for surveillance along the border between Nogales and the U.S., and José "El Chito" Damasio Gutiérrez, recruiter of couriers to transport drugs to Tucson.[28]

This internecine war aside, the thriving Sinaloa Cartel continues to do business throughout Mexico, along the Southwest border, in the Western and Midwestern regions of the U.S., and in Central America. Its traditional route runs from Chiapas to Ciudad Juárez, passing through nine or more states.[29] The syndicate also imports cocaine via Lázaro Cárdenas and other Pacific ports from the remnants of the Medellín and Cali cartels—the so-called *cartelitos* scattered throughout Colombia. Nicaragua's military and police chiefs have reported that 90 percent of Colombian cocaine reaches Mexico through a Pacific corridor in international waters off the Nicaraguan coastline.[30] Besides smuggling cocaine, the Sinaloans distribute heroin, from Mexico and Southeast Asia, and Mexican marijuana in the United States and other countries.

Access to abundant marijuana supplies has provided the Sinaloa Cartel with an advantage over the Gulf Cartel because the U.S. Justice Department rarely prosecutes carriers apprehended with fewer than 500 milligrams of cannabis. Guzmán Loera has continually claimed that, in contrast with the Gulf and Tijuana cartels, his organization does not kill innocent people. It does employ, however, fifty tough-as-nails "Sinaloan cowboys," another group of thugs known as La Gente Nueva, and law enforcement officers to protect its *plazas* and personnel.[31] In reaction to Los Zetas, the Sinaloans assembled their own force called *Los Pelones*, literally "the baldies" but typically understood to mean "new soldiers" because of the shaved heads of military inductees. Deserters from the armed forces and turncoat policemen form this group. After breaking with Guzmán Loera, the Beltran Leyvas established the paramilitary Special Forces of Arthur (*Las Fuerzas Especials de Arturo*—FEDA) made up of former security officials and gangsters from Mexico and the United States.[32]

Rather than denounce El Chapo as a lawbreaker, his neighbors venerate him for his largesse and the thousands of jobs created by poppy cultivation. He has financed the construction of sidewalks, lighted the cemetery, repaired churches, and paved roads in the Badiraguato area. He also hands out money to the poor. After all he grew up with an abusive father in humble surroundings before attaching himself to cartel leaders.

Pundits joke that local peasants wear no clothing except for hats, which they can doff when encountering Guzmán Loera. "They see him as a hero. They cover for him. When any stranger comes into the communities, they warn him," observed Deputy Attorney General José Santiago Vasconcelos. A resident told the *Los Angeles Times:* "When the cops pass El Chapo on the road, they call him boss." He has become a folk hero, extolled in songs known as *corridos*. The group *Los Buitres* (*The Vultures*) recorded a ballad, only one of many within narco-culture that glorifies Guzmán Loera's life on the run and the exploits of other disreputable grandees.

He sleeps at times in homes,
at times in tents
Radio and rifle at the foot
of the bed
Sometimes his roof is a cave.[33]

Guzmán Loera revels in this mythic role as someone who vanishes just before the military or police zero in for an arrest. He "chalks up more sightings than Elvis. He is everywhere, and nowhere—a long sought criminal always a step ahead of the law, yet always in sight or mind." "It's similar to trying to find Osama bin Laden," a U.S. law enforcement official said.[34] Despite the $5 million bounty on El Chapo's head, he remains at large, probably because of complicity by Army and law enforcement personnel.

In early 2009 *Forbes* magazine added another dimension to Guzmán Loera's persona by listing him as one of the wealthiest people in the world. The publication ranked El Chapo number 701 with an estimated fortune of $1 billion. Already on edge because of "failed state" allegations, President Calderón blasted the article, saying that "magazines are not only attacking and lying about the situation in Mexico but are also praising criminals." Attorney General Medina Mora asserted that *Forbes* was defending lawlessness by "comparing the deplorable activity of a criminal wanted in Mexico and abroad with that of honest businessmen."[35]

Not to be outdone, *Time* magazine named El Chapo one of the "most influential people" of 2009, calling him "the new Pablo Escobar, a kingpin testing the ability of a nascent democracy to control organized crime." He appeared in the category of "leaders and revolutionaries" along with President Barack Obama, Secretary of State Hillary Rodham Clinton, French President Nicholas Sarkozy, and German Chancellor Angela Merkel.[36]

El Chapo's brazenness knows no bounds. In late 2007 he became enamored of Emma Coronel Aispuro, an 18-year-old contestant for "Queen of the Great Guayaba and Coffee Festival" held in La Angostura, Sinaloa, situated cheek-by-jowl with Durango. He reportedly had a ghostwriter pen love letters that he sent to his new flame. To gain support for her candidacy, Senorita Coronel Aispuro sponsored a dance on January 6, 2008, the Day of the Three Kings. At 11 a.m. 200 motorcycles roared into town, carrying black-hooded men hefting high-powered weapons. They immediately secured the ten entrances to the town, including one that only accommodated horses. Then, a five-seat plane landed, carrying the popular musical group, "Los Canelos de Durango."

In late afternoon, El Chapo stepped out of one of six aircraft that had just touched down. With him was Ignacio "Nacho" Coronel Villarreal, a native of Canelas, chief of the Jalisco Cartel, and Emma Coronel's uncle. Guzmán Loera was decked out in light tweed slacks, a jacket, a natty hat, and black leather tennis shoes. He had an AK-47 strapped across his chest, and a pistol that matched his clothing thrust into his belt.

Los Canelos struck up *Cruzando Cerros y Arroyos* (Crossing Hills and Arroyos), the favorite tune of Joaquín and Emma. On hand were her mother and father, who beamed with happiness because of the rich, influential man who had swept their daughter off her feet. Their delight brought to mind *Sin tetas no hay Paraíso [No Paradise without Breasts]*, a novel by Colombian author Gustavo Bolívar Moreno, who describes how mothers enhance the breasts of teenage daughters so they can catch the eye of narco-traffickers and their sons. This book was turned into a wildly popular television soap opera.

Also joining in the festivities were Alfredo Higuera Bernal, Sinaloa's former attorney general, and the local PAN mayor, Francisco Cárdenas Gamboa. The fiesta continued until late in the night and, at 11 a.m. the next day, the visitors departed as quickly as they arrived. Only on January 8 did 150 soldiers from Infantry Battalion 72 appear on the scene. Emma finished number-one in the pageant and went on to become El Chapo's third wife. The couple exchanged vows on July 2, 2008, her eighteenth birthday, and immediately departed for their honeymoon—a day before a military squad reached Angostura.[37]

Ismael Bojórquez Perea, the intrepid editor of the Sinaloa weekly *Ríodoce*, published an account of a rare public appearance by Guzmán Loera at the upscale La Palmas restaurant on a busy Culiacán street in late 2007. The don's henchmen instructed the other diners to remain seated and hand over their cell phones before their boss entered. He promptly went from table to table shaking hands with the forty customers like a Chicago assemblyman schmoozing for votes. He then retired to a private dining area, feasted on a juicy steak with all the trimmings, and quietly left by a back door. To their delight, the diners discovered that he had paid for their meals with a fistful of cash.[38]

In November 2004 the armed forces came closest to capturing El Chapo when 200 paramilitaries swooped down on his Sierra Madre stronghold in Blackhawk helicopters. His voice had been heard on a tapped phone line half an hour earlier, but the drug king got away. All the troops could do was blow up his Hummer and Dodge Ram pick-up truck. In June 2005 they grabbed his brother, son, two nephews and a niece. They also seized nine houses and six vehicles. But once again they missed the main man. Also in November 2005 El Chapo was seen eating out with his retinue at one of his favorite restaurants.

The account mirrors that of Bojórquez. Someone told the clients: "Gentlemen, please. Give me a moment of your time. A man is going to come in, the boss. We ask that you remain in your seats; the doors will close and nobody is allowed to leave. You will also not be allowed to use your cellulars. Do not worry; if you do everything that is asked of you, nothing will happen. Continue eating and don't ask for your check. The boss will pay. Thank you. The diners stayed where they were, surprised, expectant. It was one of the first days of November. Eight at night. The restaurant, Las Palmas, on Xicoténcatl Boulevard, in Colonia Las Quintas, was filled with people."

Fifteen men entered the restaurant; including the boss, El Chapo and his henchmen, carrying the ubiquitous AK-47. The diners sat still, stupefied, embarrassed, and frightened amid wooden chairs and tables and wooden chairs piled high with goat's meat, bottles of cold beer, plates of octopus and shrimp. El Chapo reportedly came in through the front door. "He walked among the tables, squarely between the patrons; his entry more stalking than walking; tranquil and proud. He greeted each person there. 'Hello, nice to meet you. How are you? I'm Joaquín Guzmán Loera. A pleasure. At your service.' He circled the room full of tables occupied by families, couples, and businessmen, who had gathered to eat and to drink. Nobody was spared the greeting, the squeezing of the hand, the benediction."[39]

El Chapo retired to the private salon inside the restaurant where the house specialties are expensive cuts of beef and fist-sized shrimp. A group of his associates and gunmen trailed him into the reserved room. The other half sat with the diners, watching and speaking in low voices. Guzmán Loera spent two hours behind a locked door, feasting on seafood, and blood-red steaks. The meal finally ended. El Chapo departed without fanfare; a moment later his triggermen left as well.[40]

In view of the deference that local authorities show him, the narco-cardinal Guzman Loera has a higher prospect of being killed, as occurred with his son, by rivals in other cartels than by law enforcement agencies.

The left-leaning weekly *Proceso* has alleged that the Calderón administration has either ignored or cast its lot with the Sinaloans, who claim a presence in thirty-eight countries. This publication and other critics asserted that Washington encouraged *Forbes* magazine to spotlight El Chapo to pressure the Mexicans' pursuit of him and his entourage.

On March 19, 2009, the Mexican Army cast doubt on any claims of "untouchability" when it apprehended Vicente "El Vicentillo" Zambada Niebla, son of Sinaloa Cartel stalwart El Mayo Zambada.[41] At the same time, federal and state authorities have attempted to curb flights by the 300 small aircraft in the zone, requiring them to use only authorized landing strips. The goals is to prevent the numerous air taxis in the region from contributing to the drug commerce—with a focus on makeshift, clandestine airfields in Sinaloa (Badiraguato, Sinaloa de Leyva, and Cosalá), Chihuahua (Guadalupe and Calvo), and Durango (Topia, Canelas, San Dimas, and Tamazula). The representative of Pitty air service, whose company makes six to eight flights daily into the mountains of Durango and Sinaloa, scorned the initiative on the grounds that it would leave residents of isolated areas stranded, especially if they required medical care.[42]

In June 2009 Army and Federal Police engaged in a shootout with criminals in Durango. The confrontation took the life of Israel "El Paisa"/"The Confidant" Sánchez Coral, chief of the *plaza* and an El Chapo chief lieutenant. Captured in this face-off were El Paisa's girlfriend, marijuana distributor Miguel Ángel Piedra Gallardo, and José Alfonso Sánchez Gutiérrez, who reportedly sold 300 kilograms of marijuana daily for his Sinaloan boss.

The Sinaloa Cartel collaborated with the Juárez, Milenio, Jalisco, and Colima criminal organizations in "The Federation" before the execution by El Chapo's hit men of Rodolfo Carrillo Fuentes, a Juárez Cartel stalwart.

Milenio Cartel

The Milenio Cartel began operations in 1997 under the leadership of the Valencia brothers—Armando, Luis, Juan, and Ventura—who cooperated with Guillermo Moreno Ríos and other Colombians. Armando "Juanito" Valencia Cornelio had previously lived in Anaheim and Sacramento, where he earned enough money to invest in avocado growing in the Uruapan area of Michoacán. In California he became acquainted with Nemesio "El Mencho" Oseguera Cervantes, who became chief of this cartel's liquidators (*sicarios*). In the United States, he also may have gotten to know Wenceslao "El Wencho" Álvarez Álvarez who worked in concert with La Familia, as described in Chapter 8.

In addition to avocado production, the Valencias entered the drug business, concentrating their activities within their home state, which was the entry point for enormous quantities of Colombian cocaine. They also cooperated with the Sinaloans in Jalisco, Colima, and Nayarit.

The newly formed Milenio Cartel endured a setback in October 1999, when the Federal Judicial Police arrested Guillermo Moreno Ríos, the organization's chief operator in Zapopan, along with three other Colombians and an American.[43]

Still, early in first decade of this century, the DEA claimed that the Milenio Cartel was supplying one-third of the cocaine consumed in the United States—with a focus on California, Texas, Chicago, and New York. In mid-2003 Mexican authorities captured "Juanito," the organization's head honcho. His arrest left the leadership in the hands of his brothers, Luis, Juan, and Ventura. In mid-April 2007 their enemies gunned down Ventura in Tepalcatepec, Michoacán, bastion of La Familia. The killers hammered a nail in his chest with the message: "Greetings, Luis Valencia Valencia, Óscar Nava Valencia, Armando Valencia González," which was signed "MENCHO," believed by the PGR to be a reference to Nemesio Oseguera Cervantes, once the Milenio Cartel's chief gunman ("Mencho" is the nickname for Nemesio).[44] The killer or killers also destroyed part of Ventura's skull and deposited a dead dog at his feet.[45]

Inter-cartel violence escalated in Michoacán during the Fox administration, which did relatively little to combat the threat. The Sinaloa Cartel invaded the territory of the Tamaulipas-based Gulf Cartel, headed by Osiel Cárdenas Guillén. Cárdenas Guillén counter-attacked by sending Los Zetas to seize transit routes through Michoacán, whose Pacific Ocean ports serve as open conduits for narcotics. When the Arellano Félix brothers and the Juárez Cartel cast their lot with the Gulf Cartel, they encountered ferocious opposition from the Sinaloa Cartel and their allies in the Milenio, Jalisco, and Colima organizations. The number of drug-related murders in Michoacán soared from a few dozen in 2000 to 543 in 2006 before falling in 2007 (238) and 2008 (233)—with more than 255 fatalities reported through the first week of August 2009.

On December 15, 2006, as part of "Joint Operation Michoacán," federal authorities arrested four of the Milenio band's lieutenants: Jesús Arellano García, Elías Valencia Valencia, José Valencia Lara, and Eleodoro López Torres.

The Milenio Cartel apparently worked with Zhenli Ye Gon, who imported chemicals for methamphetamine production in super-laboratories concealed amid the verdant hills of Apatzingán and other municipalities. The shadowy Chinese-Mexican multi-millionaire reportedly provided precursor drugs to Luis Valencia Valencia and Óscar "El Lobo" Nava Valencia. Other figures in the Milenio Cartel include Arturo and Sergio Ureña Partida (Apatzingán), Ramón and Ramiro Castañeda (Turicato), and Alejandro and Ángle Béjar Chávez (Marcos Castellanos), and Fernando "El Fernandón"/"The Big Fernando" Santana.[46]

Jalisco/Guadalajara Cartel

As mentioned earlier, Beltrán Monzón moved to Guadalajara. He soon controlled marijuana trafficking in Jalisco and neighboring states, only to drop out of sight when the powerful Sinaloans roared into town in the aftermath of Operation Condor. The death of Pedro Avilés and the arrest of Félix Gallando opened the way for an ally of El Chapo to take control.

Born in Veracruz in 1954,[47] Ignacio "Nacho" Coronel Villarreal now heads the Jalisco Cartel and is closely associated with Guzmán Loera who, as mentioned earlier, married his niece. He learned the drug business as an apprentice to Amado Carrillo Fuentes—first in Zacatecas and later as logistics chief in the Juárez Cartel. By 2002 he had become the leading handler of amphetamines and methamphetamines, earning the nickname "Crystal King." His organization operates state-of-the-art clandestine super-labs in Michoacán and Jalisco, while his supply network extends from Nogales, Sonora, to Arizona, New Mexico, Texas, Oklahoma, Kansas, and the entire eastern seaboard.

This cartel's domestic structure stretches from Morelia, Michoacán, along Mexico's Pacific coast through the Yucatán Peninsula and the states of Nayarit, Sinaloa, and Sonora. In December 2006 the federal government severely weakened its links when it incarcerated a half-dozen of Coronel's allies in Guadalajara. In press releases related to a posted $5 million reward for Nacho, the FBI noted that "the scope of its influence and operations [of Coronel's cartel] penetrate throughout the United States, Mexico, and several other European, Central American, and South American countries [and] ... now considered one of the most powerful drug-trafficking organizations in Mexico ... [working] directly with Colombian sources of supply by purchasing multi-ton quantities of cocaine."[48] In early March 2009, El Nacho Coronel suffered another blow when assailants gunned down one of his lieutenants, Miguel Ángel Bátiz López, in a bar in Zapopan, Jalisco. A search of the deceased's residence turned up drugs and a .22-caliber submachine gun.[49] Nacho, also known as "El Cachas" or "The Hunk," decorates his weapons with precious stones, has secure residences in Jalisco and Yucatán, and frequently hides out in El Molino, a small community between Guatimapé and Canatián in southern Durango state. He reportedly underwent plastic surgery to alter his appearance.[50]

Sonora Cartel

The Sonora Cartel, allied with the Sinaloans through Caro Quintero's past relationship with Félix Gallardo and Fonseca Carrillo, functions mainly within its own state and nearby border areas, relying heavily on small planes to convey marijuana, cocaine, and methamphetamines to the United States and to bring back dollars and guns. In their cat-and-mouse game with authorities, smugglers recently developed an ultra-light aircraft to minimize detection by radar, according to *USA Today*. It resembles a scooter with a hang glider attached, and authorities have identified several of these contraptions in mid-flight over the border with more than 100 pounds of marijuana attached. They have also discovered wreckage of these makeshift machines.[51]

Caro Quintero, a native of Badiraguato, cultivated enormous marijuana plantations, complemented by huge drying sheds, in Sonora and neighboring Chihuahua. He bribed police commanders in both states so they would steer clear of his sophisticated industry. In November 1984 the federal police raided Caro Quintero's property at El Búfalo, Chihuahua, and destroyed between 5,000 and 10,000 tons of high-quality seedless marijuana, which had a street value estimated at $2.5 billion. They had been alerted to the site by DEA agent Camarena, who was subsequently tortured and murdered as described in Chapter 9.

After the imprisonment of his brother Rafael, Miguel Ángel Caro Quintero took charge the operation with his six siblings (Genaro, Jorge, María del Carmen, Blanca Lili, Melida Caro de Arce, and María Manuela Caro de Sesteaga). They continue to specialize in marijuana cultivation on ranches in the north, using small planes to transport the drug into Arizona. Although the organization relies on cannabis, it also ships cocaine and methamphetamines.

On December 20, 2001, authorities apprehended Miguel Ángel Caro Quintero with the aim of extraditing him to the U.S. In all likelihood, leadership passed to Genaro, who has sight and hearing disabilities.

A major drug-related event in Sonora occurred after midnight on May 16, 2007, when fifteen trucks carrying men armed with AR-15 assault rifles rumbled into Cananea, a copper-mining town twenty miles south of the Mexico-Arizona border. The menacing convoy snaked through the sleepy Sonoran municipality for an hour before its gunmen opened fire on five policemen and two civilians. The attackers then fled into the Sierra Madre Mountains where they were tracked down by the PFP and local police. The incident concluded with the death of twenty-three individuals and left several wounded.

Public Safety Secretary García Luna attributed this bloodshed to a turf battle between the Gulf Cartel and its Sinaloa rival, with whom the Caro Quintero clan had been traditional allies. Francisco "Dos Mil" Hernández García, the driving force of a gang known as "Los Números" or "Los Güeros" and a former ally of the Sinaloans, had switched allegiance to the Gulf Cartel and was trying to recoup a *plaza* in the state. According to U.S. agencies, Los Zetas have furnished weapons to support their new allies, Los Números.

The Cananea episode enraged Sonora's influential, wealthy PRI governor, Eduardo Bours Castelo. He initiated a shake-up of federal police in the state and ushered in a period of relative tranquility. A quasi-peace following the dust-up during which the sound of gunfire was replaced by the noisy takeoffs of drug-ferrying Cessnas bound for clandestine airstrips the United States.

In the spring of 2008, the Sinaloa Cartel—once preeminent in the zone—renewed its battle with the Gulf Cartel for dominance of the Sonoran-Arizona corridor, the most desired piece of real estate along the U.S.-Mexico border, according to Anthony Coulson, DEA assistant special agent in charge of the Tucson District Office.

The route remains one of the best ways to move drugs northward, with a combination of cities and roads on both sides of the frontier and a vast expanse of harsh desert that impedes the apprehension of traffickers. Even with a slight decrease in 2008, Arizona accounted for 43 percent of all seized marijuana along the southwestern U.S. border despite covering only 13 percent of the 2,000-mile frontier. Although the cities of Hermosillo and Caborca remain important, Nogales has become the epicenter of smuggling, accounting for 60 percent of all drugs entering Arizona, Coulson averred.[52] "Never in my life have I seen anything as terrible as what's going on over there," said Nogales-born Tony Estrada, sheriff of Santa Cruz County, Arizona.[53]

In mid-October 2008, the U.S. State Department warned travelers about the spiraling violence in Nogales, a city of 200,000 people that lies just sixty-five miles south of Tucson. A week later a running gun battle took the lives of ten gangsters. No law enforcement agents died in the fracas, but shrapnel injured several policemen as the fleeing suspects lobbed grenades at their pursuers.

In early November 2008, heavily armed gunmen killed Juan Manuel Pavón Félix, director of Sonora's State Preventive Police. The previous week, the U.S. Marshals Service had honored Pavón Félix and other Mexican law enforcement officers for their assistance in apprehending American fugitives in Mexico. Earlier in the day, Pavón Félix had made security sweeps in Nogales.

A PRD legislator has asserted that the federal government subsidizes agricultural enterprises owned by members of the Caro Quintero clan in the state. In a news conference, Deputy Nora Ruvalcaba Gámez presented documents that allegedly demonstrated that such aid-to-the-poor programs as Assistance and Services for Rural Marketing (ASCA) and Direct Assistance to the Countryside (PROCAMPO) had provided funds to relatives of several narco-traffickers. The purported recipients included Jorge Luis Caro Payán, uncle of Rafael Caro Quintero, and Jaime Pérez Quintero, brother of deceased gunman Lamberto Quintero Payán.[54] "The narcos don't need the money," noted Deputy Antonio Ortega, "but this is a good way to launder funds by purchasing tractors, all types of machinery, and products that they can use to justify their income and expenses."[55]

Colima Cartel

The Guadalajara-centered Colima Cartel was once chief supplier of methamphetamines to the United States. The brothers Jesús, Luis Ignacio, and Adán Amezcua Contreras, who began their careers smuggling illegal immigrants in 1988, earned fame as the "Kings of Meth." They used superior expertise and a finely textured organization to supplant motorcycle gangs and independent traffickers who once held sway over meth commerce. They manufactured the psychotropic in laboratories situated both in Mexico and the U.S., using the precursor chemical ephedrine that the cartel illegally imported from Germany, India, Thailand, and Pakistan through the ports of Veracruz, Lázaro Cárdenas, and Manzanillo. The capture and imprisonment of the three brothers in the late-1990s devastated the organization even though their sisters are struggling in a futile effort to conduct business as usual. Their wives are said to have to borrow the bus fare to visit their spouses in prison. In contrast, families of affluent dons incarcerated in La Palma have purchased luxurious homes in well-to-do neighborhoods in nearby Mextepec, which has driven up real estate prices in the area.

Gulf Cartel

As alluded to in Chapter 3, the Gulf Cartel suffered a reversal when the Zedillo administration delivered García Abrego to the FBI in 1996. Why did Mexico dispatch him to the U.S. so quickly? No doubt to prevent him from continuing to operate his empire while awaiting trial. Before his own arrest in 1997, Oscar Malherbe de León, one of García Abrego's top lieutenants and moneymen, seemed poised to become the cartel's next top honcho thanks to his connections with the Juárez Cartel. His major competitor was Salvador "El Chava" Gómez. However, in 1996 El Chava died at the hands of his friend Cárdenas Guillén, and in so-doing Cárdenas Guillén earned the sobriquet "Friend Killer" or "El Mata Amigos" for his treachery. In the late 1990s, three groups cast their lot with Cárdenas Guillén—Los Flores Soto, Los Ortiz Medina, and La Mexican Mafia—who had severed ties with González Calderoni and other brothers-in-arms of García Abrego.

In 1999 El Mata Amigos overplayed his hand by trying to snatch an informant whom FBI and DEA agents were transporting through Matamoros. A tense standoff occurred when the U.S. law enforcement personnel refused to release the man. After this incident, Washington stepped up pressure on Mexico City to apprehend Cárdenas Guillén.

Although the police captured Cárdenas Guillén in a shootout in Matamoros in March 2003, he continued to administer his empire from La Palma. Capos enjoyed comfortable prison accommodations, including TV sets, air conditioners, telephones, liquor, and conjugal visits from wives and girlfriends. Later in the month, agents of the state public security agency arrested the drug lord's possible successor, Víctor Manuel "El Memeloco"/"Crazy Guillermo" Vázquez Mireles while he was drinking publicly with pals in Veracruz.

From his cell, Cárdenas Guillén organized public relations stunts to present himself as the genuine benefactor of average people, while depicting the military and the police as their enemies. On April 30, 2005, the drug kingpin sponsored a "Children's Day" celebration in a bullring in Ciudad Acuña, Coahuila, complete with cherry-nosed clowns, breast-beating wrestlers, mouth-watering desserts, and a vast array of toys for the youngsters. On the *mafioso*'s congratulatory note to the boys and girls appeared the inscription: "Zindicato Anónimo Altruizta"—a variation on "Anonymous Altruistic Syndicate."

A year later, he embellished that act by treating 18,000 people to a Children's Day party at the Adolfo López Mateos baseball stadium in Reynosa, near McAllen, Texas. The event featured masked wrestlers and cavorting clowns. As the festivities wound down, two large vehicles lumbered in weighed down with toys for distribution with notes from Osiel Cárdenas Guillén. The message read: "Constancy, Discipline and Effort are the bases of success. Continue studying in order that you become a great example. Happy Children's Day 2006. With all my affection for tomorrow's winner, your friend, Osiel Cárdenas Guillén." An advertisement in *El Mañana* ran under a headline proclaiming: "Osiel makes thousands of children happy."[56]

The January 2007 extradition of Cárdenas Guillén to the United States ignited a battle among contenders to succeed him: Osiel's brother Antonio Ezequiel "Tony Tormenta"/"Tony the Tormentor" Cárdenas Guillén, who is deemed the weakest of three; Eduardo "El Coss" or "The Shadow" Costilla Sánchez; and Heriberto "The Executioner" or "El Lazca" Lazcano Lazcano, leader of Los Zetas, which are examined in Chapter 8.

Second-tier players enmeshed in the power struggle included the incredibly vicious Miguel Ángel "El 40" or "El Comandante" Treviño Morales (Nuevo León), Arturo "El Grande" Basurto Peña (Quintana Roo), Iván "El Talibán" Velásquez Cabala, who investigators believe is the Zetas' local enforcer in Nuevo Laredo, and Gregorio "El Goyo" Sauceda Gamboa and his brother Arturo (Nuevo Laredo). Cárdenas Guillén had no love lost for El Goyo, whom he suspected of colluding with the rival Sinaloa cartel. On April 29, 2009, the police arrested El Goyo in Matamoros. Antonio Arcos Medina (Michoacán) and Edgar Alonso Villarreal (Acapulco) also are important figures.[57] In early May 2009, the Army nabbed Ángel Vélez Morales, also known as José Manuel Figueroa Martínez."[58] A spokesman for the Defense Ministry named him as the syndicate's principal operator in Cancún, although it is unclear to whom he owed allegiance. The increasing separation and friction between Los Zetas and the Gulf Cartel has reconfigured elements of this organization.

Before Los Zetas charted their own agenda, Matamoros constituted the Gulf Cartel's hub of operations, with spokes thrusting westward along the U.S.-Mexican border through Reynosa, Miguel Alemán, Nuevo Laredo, and surrounding communities.[59]

Such internecine battles aside, the Gulf Cartel not only continues to ship drugs abroad, but is allegedly engaged in arms-exporting. In late November 2008, Mexico's Federal Investigative Agency (AFI) detained two South Africans carrying large sums of money possibly earmarked to purchase firearms and explosives from the syndicate.[60]

Juárez Cartel[61]

After Operation Condor, five small organizations fought for supremacy over the shipment of drugs between Ciudad Juárez and El Paso. Guadalajara Cartel leader "Don Neto" Fonseca Carrillo, an ally of Félix Gallardo, ordered former DFS Commander Rafael Aguilar Guajardo to

Ojinaga in the early 1980s to learn about border operations. His mentor was Pablo Acosta, the scar-faced *padrino* who controlled a lucrative 250-mile stretch of the U.S.-Mexico border and shipped a staggering sixty tons of cocaine per year into the United States.

A cocaine addict who gulped El Presidente brandy, inhaled crack-laced Marlboro cigarettes, wore Texas Stetsons, and drove sparkling new Ford Broncos, Acosta bragged about murders, smuggling, and payoffs, as well as his charitable works. His struggle to defend his expanding domain against predators mounted. "Pablo Acosta was the first 'modern' drug capo to emerge in Northern Chihuahua state—ruthless, single-minded, cruel, and completely dedicated to consolidating his power and eliminating his enemies and competitors at all costs."[62] Acosta died on April 24, 1987, in an ambush arranged by FBI agents. Amado Carrillo Fuentes, Don Neto's nephew, eventually took control of the Ojinaga operation upon Acosta's demise. The scheming Comandante González Calderoni, who killed Acosta, later defected to the U.S., and was granted asylum after informing the FBI about Mexico's presidential family and their involvement in drug trafficking.[63]

In the same year, Carrillo Fuentes helped broker a deal that enhanced the Medellín and Cali cartels' international heroin trafficking. The Colombians had sought him out to help arrange meetings with leaders of Durango's Herrera clan, which had been in the heroin trade for generations and had expertise the Colombians coveted. Carrillo Fuentes set up sessions in Torreón. Details of the deal are not known. But for years, most of the heroin seized on the U.S. eastern seaboard had been produced in Colombia. In return, the Colombians apparently agreed to stay out of the traditional Herrera heroin markets in the Midwest. As the competing Arellano-Félix brothers and the Gulf Cartel started to climb in the ranks of top-tier drug networks, Amado Carrillo decided to take the initiative and usurp the Ojinaga *plaza*.

In 1987 Carrillo Fuentes had his first and last brush with the Mexican legal system when he was arrested in Guadalajara. He told authorities that he was a cattleman with ranches in northern Mexico. He admitted smuggling marijuana with the late Acosta, but did not implicate his uncle, Ernesto Fonseca Carrillo, or any other Federation cartel. Officials confiscated several of his airplanes, and he spent a few weeks in jail. Although charged with crimes against the public health and possession of illegal weapons, he was never brought to trial.

After his release, Carrillo Fuentes continued to fulfill the role as coordinator for Acosta's successor, Aguilar Guajardo. Following Félix

Gallardo's arrest in 1989, the devious don ascended to *número uno* in the Juárez Cartel. In 1991 Carrillo Fuentes fashioned a partnership with Gilberto and Miguel Rodriguez Orejuela of the Cali Cartel. At one point, Carrillo Fuentes was exporting four times more cocaine to the U.S. than any other trafficker. He garnered the nickname *"El Señor de los Cielos"* (The Lord of the Skies) for his intrepid use of a fleet of 727 aircraft to transport Colombian cocaine to municipal airports and dirt airstrips around Mexico and in other countries. El Mayo Zambada worked closely with this airborne capo.

Carrillo Fuentes took advantage of his links to Colombian kingpins. His organization specialized in moving cocaine, heroin, and marijuana to storage bases in Guadalajara, Hermosillo, and Torreón until the drugs could be shipped to American destinations. In the mid-1990s, the cartel reportedly generated billions of dollars a year in illegal profits and had forwarded $20 to $30 million to Colombia for each major transaction.

The Juárez organization even expanded into traditional Colombian enclaves on the U.S. East Coast. Mexican police launched a concerted manhunt for the multi-millionaire, who flew on private jets to Russia, Turkey, Brazil, Costa Rica, Ecuador, Argentina, and Chile in search of a safe haven. According to a report in *Proceso*, General Gutierrez Rebollo indicated that "A.C.," presumably Amado Carrillo, "does not intend to surrender." Rather, he wanted to negotiate a pact with his captors. He would "act like a businessman, not a criminal," help the government eliminate "unorganized narcotics trafficking," and sell drugs only in the United States and Europe, not in Mexico.[64]

Possessed of a low-keyed and diplomatic mien, Carrillo Fuentes arranged accords with rival cartels. He even managed to co-opt Zedillo's drug czar, General Rebollo Gutiérrez. While the three-star general had battled criminal organizations, he had concentrated his efforts against the Arellano Félix Organization and other antagonists of the Lord of the Skies.

At the same time, concerns arose that sensitive intelligence—including information about U.S. drug agents—had been compromised by the general, while other reports linked him and two aides to a wave of kidnappings and disappearances of suspected drug traffickers in the months preceding their arrests.[65]

His love of horses contributed to Gutiérrez Rebollo's downfall. When he commanded the Guadalajara area, the cavalry officer began buying alfalfa from a farm owned by the father of one of Carrillo Fuentes' top associates. After AFO gunmen wounded the farmer's son, the young man offered to supply information about the Arellano Félix enterprise. This intelligence propelled a sweep by hundreds of soldiers through several Tijuana neighborhoods. The March 2006 strike won accolades as an extremely effective anti-drug venture, and it brightened Gutiérrez Rebollo's image. In July Arellano Félix's desperadoes killed a close aide to the general and, later, assassinated the police commanders in Tijuana and Mexico City. This violence strengthened ties between Carrillo Fuentes and sectors of the police and Army. The general's superiors either did not notice or overlooked his sybaritic lifestyle. He had purchased two thoroughbreds, acquired a fleet of automobiles and armed Jeeps, and assigned soldiers as cooks, drivers, and gardeners to his wife's household and to the homes of two mistresses.[66]

Gutiérrez Rebollo carved an enduring mark on Mexico's criminal landscape. During his brief tenure at the INCD, he dispatched loyalists to the institute's local offices, especially in the north. Even if they had been clean before arriving, the local officials were soon corrupted. Some entered the initial ranks of Los Zetas along with ex-GAFES commandos. Another spawning ground for Los Zetas was local PGR delegations where in 1995, under Pilot Plan Chihuahua, Zedillo and his Attorney General Jorge Madrazo Cuéllar substituted military men for Federal Judicial Police cadres.

Gutiérrez Rebollo was not Carrillo Fuentes' only military contact. In 1996 an Air Force flight specialist admitted that he had guided the drug baron's planes into Guadalajara's airport. Others in league with the Juárez Cartel were Brigadier General Alfredo Navarro Lara, who was charged with drug corruption, bribery, and criminal association; and Brigadier General Arturo Cardona Pérez, accused of being the principal intermediary between Gutiérrez Rebollo and Carrillo Fuentes.[67]

On the eve of President Zedillo's September 1, 2000 *Informe*, his administration arrested two more senior officers linked to Amado Carrillo: recently retired General Francisco Quiroz Hermosillo, who had held high posts in the intelligence and military transport directorates of the Army; and General Mario Arturo Acosta Chaparro, a counter-insurgency specialist whom human rights organizations had long accused of repressing and torturing leftists in Guerrero state.[68]

Carrillo Fuentes died in mid-1997 while undergoing facial plastic surgery and stomach liposuction to change his appearance. The operation took place on July 3 at the Santa Mónica Hospital in the Polanco district of Mexico City. During the eight-hour procedure, the patient apparently succumbed to complications arising from either an overdose of the sedative Dormicum or a malfunctioning respirator. Bizarre theories have circulated that Carrillo Fuentes' bodyguards, who were in the operating room, smothered him with a pillow or that the PGR tortured him first and then faked the medical procedure. *El Financiero* even reported that the corpse was the drug lord's cousin, presuming of course that Carrillo Fuentes bribed someone to substitute his relative's identification, dental records, fingerprints, and blood samples. Respected TV journalist Pedro Ferriz de Con claimed that the narco-baron was suicidal, allegedly saying: "If I die, nobody killed me. The only person who can kill Amado Carrillo is Amado Carrillo."[69]

Residents of Guamuchilito, Sinaloa, paid homage to the Lord of the Skies with a large and costly funeral at his mother's property in his hometown, where citizens revered him as a local "Robin Hood," according to the *Diario de Juárez*. He was known for giving hundreds of people money, cattle, and presents that encompassed Ram Chargers, Grand Cherokees, Chevrolet Suburbans, and Lincoln Continentals. He even built the village church. Although condemned as a drug lord by federal agents, friends and family glorified Carrillo Fuentes as "a noble soul, loving with his family," a simple man who "loved baseball and enchiladas stuffed with hot red chile." "He was a master at maintaining alliances," said Phil Jordan, a former DEA agent. This skill extended to relationships with law enforcement agents. "There is no arrest or search warrant for Amado Carrillo Fuentes in Juárez now or before his death," Chihuahua State Police spokesman Ernesto Garcia said on July 21. "As far as we know, he has neither committed nor been a part of any illegal activities here."[70]

Shortly after he died, Mexican newspapers published a photograph of Carrillo Fuentes in Jerusalem with a Mexican priest in mid-1995. Other clerics said that Carrillo Fuentes gave generously to the Catholic Church—in what are known in Mexico as nacro-alms or *narcolimosnas*.[71]

In 2001 authorities captured one of his key lieutenants, Alcides "El Metro" Ramón Magaña, who had responsibility for flying Colombian cocaine in lightweight aircraft to covert runways in Central America; from there, small launches or *pangas* ferried the drug into Chetumal, Quintana Roo, where tanker-trucks picked up the cargo bound for the United States via Reynosa. It is presumed that El Metro enjoyed the cooperation of Mario Villanueva Madrid, who served as governor of Quintana Roo until disappearing from sight after failing to appear at his successor's inauguration in March 1999.[72] The PGR believes that Ramón Magaña paid the "Crooked One," as Villanueva was known, $400,000 to $500,000 in cash for each 500- to 1,000-kilogram shipment of cocaine.[73] Police apprehended the gaunt, pony-tailed, ex-state executive in May 2001.

Amado's brother, Vicente "The Viceroy" Carrillo Fuentes, who took command of the debilitated cartel, represented a new breed of kingpin. At first he played second fiddle to Ricardo "El Doctor" Garcia Urquiza, a surgeon with an entrepreneurial vision who was imprisoned in November 2005. Before his capture, García Urquiza generated as much as $1 billion per month in profits and was responsible for 20 percent of the drugs that reached the U.S. He performed as a modern professional who employed encrypted e-mails, satellite communications, and other state-of-the-art technology.[74] Gilberto Lugo, the lieutenant in charge of the cartel's North Texas operations, pled guilty to federal drug charges in September 2005. This ended a two-year investigation that chronicled the flow of cocaine from the violence-torn U.S.-Mexico border from which Interstate 35 passes through the Dallas area and extends to the shores of Lake Superior.[75]

Witnesses in the so-called "*Maxiproceso*" super-trial of Juárez Cartel members claimed that Amado had little confidence in Vicente, that the latter chafed living in the shadow of his successful brother who thought that he was not intelligent.[76] Rather than remain inconspicuous as Amado and García Urquiza had done, The Viceroy enjoyed executing foes, drinking heavily, consuming drugs, patronizing strip clubs, and carousing with women. To show his might, he offered a $200,000 reward for anyone who killed a DEA agent on Mexican territory.[77]

The flamboyant Viceroy, wanted for multiple crimes in southeast Texas, perfected his swagger even as he continued to indulge his taste for strong rum, luxurious automobiles, gaudy mansions, platoons of bodyguards, and sexy women. He foreshadowed the *cachorros or* "pups" of the drug sector who, in contrast to their fathers and grandfathers, relish an ostentatious life. Other puppies include El Mayo Zambada's son, Vicente "El Vincentillo" Zambada Niebla, and Archibaldo "El Chapito" Guzmán.[78]

The mercurial Vicente Carrillo Fuentes changed what had been a pyramidal structure by knitting horizontal alliances with other capos. These included: Ismael Zambada, who cast his lot with the Sinaloa Cartel after the Lord of the Skies' death; Juan José "El Azul" Esparragoza, a crafty veteran who enjoyed good relations with Félix Gallardo and Amado Carrillo Fuentes and had convinced the Morelos state police to ignore drugs arriving at the Cuernavaca airport; Amado's son by his first wife, Vicente "The Engineer" Carrillo Leyva, who reportedly laundered money through the Versace boutiques that he owns; and the Beltrán Leyva brothers. Centrifugal forces beset the Juárez organization when scores of its members defected to the Sinaloa cartel after Guzmán Loera escaped from prison in 2001.

Tensions mounted when El Chapo had Vicente's brother, Rodolfo, gunned down in the heart of Culiacán on September 11, 2004—an act that strained Vicente's relations with El Mayo Zambada. El Viceroy rejoiced at the assassination of Guzmán Loera's brother, Arturo, in La Palma three and a half months later. A federal judge convicted Daniel "El Mochaorejas"/"The Ear Chopper," who was thought to have been paid by Cárdenas Guillén, for the crime. The executions ignited a turf war, which was suspended during 2005 and 2006 when the Sinaloans became engaged in a no-holds-barred battle with the Gulf Cartel. *The El Paso Times* reported 1,603 murders in 2008, and it appeared that the conflict between the Sinaloan and the remnants of the Juárez cartel had recommenced to the point that President Calderón sent thousands of troops to Juárez in the spring of 2009.

The death of Rodolfo Carrillo Fuentes led to a restructuring of the cartel with García Urquiza introducing a new business plan before his incarceration. In addition to engendering up-to-date technology, he added two major drug thoroughfares: the Pacific route involved dispatching Colombia drugs to the Galapagos Islands (Ecuador) and from there along the Central American coast, winding up in Oaxaca, Michoacán, and Guerrero; the Caribbean corridor began at the ports of Cartagena, Barranquilla, and Santa Martha, Colombia, passed through Panama, Costa Rica, Puerto Rico, Dominican Republic, Guatemala, Nicaragua, Honduras, Jamaica, Cayman Islands, and Belize, and entered Mexico through Quintana Roo.

As the man in charge of the receipt and traffic of northbound Colombian cocaine, the Doctor could have emerged as Amado's heir. Instead, his arrest ensured that Vicente Carrillo Fuentes retained the top spot.

The Viceroy has disappeared from sight in recent years. In 2003 the FBI traced him to a house in El Paso but failed to capture him. The agents did find his picture on a credential, the *charola*, bearing the name of a PGR commander. He is also known to hide in Lerdo, Durango, where he has three residences. In that city, he also hid out with Arturo "El Chaky" González Hernández, the Juárez cartel's top gunman who was arrested in April 2005.

The House of Death

The House of Death episode placed pressure on the government to apprehend Vicente Carrillo Fuentes and Vicente Carrillo Leyva. In this venture, U.S. Immigration and Customs Enforcement (ICE), a division of the Department of Homeland Security, penetrated the cartel with an informant, Guillermo "Lalo" Ramirez Peyro, a former policeman whom they paid more than $220,000. The goal of the sting was to arrest Heriberto "The Engineer" Santillán Tabares, a notoriously savage lieutenant of the Carrillo Fuentes mob, and to crack a parallel cigarette-smuggling ring.

In August 2003 Lalo bought the quicklime used to dissolve the flesh of the criminal's first victim, Mexican lawyer Fernando Reyes, and then helped administer the coup de grâce; he recorded the murder secretly with a bug supplied by his handlers. That the spy had helped commit first-degree murder threw ICE's staff in El Paso into a panic. They feared they would have to close down the operation. Yet high-level officials of the U.S. Department of Justice flashed the green light to proceed.

Lalo's cartel bosses told him whenever they were planning another killing, using a grisly codeword—*carne asada* or barbeque, and involved him in several murders. His U.S. Immigration handlers neither instructed him to avoid the dirty work nor removed him from the case. Finally, U.S. authorities arrested Santillán in El Paso where he was convicted of trafficking and homicides. When senior DEA agent Sandy Gonzalez protested the complicity of the U.S. government in the murders, he was forced to resign from the agency.[79]

The whereabouts of Juárez Cartel chieftains remained unknown for years. Rumors circulated that they might be in El Paso, Chile, Argentina, or Central America. On April 1, 2009, elements of the Army and PGR apprehended the bespectacled, nerdy looking Vicente Carrillo Leyva. They captured him while he was jogging in an Abercrombie and Fitch warm-up suit in Mexico City's upscale Bosques de las Lomas area. Neighbors described him as a "discreet and friendly" businessman who lived under the name, "Alejandro Peralta Álvarez."[80] Lic. Peralta Álvarez epitomizes another breed of "narco-puppies," who wear Armani suits, reside in exclusive neighborhoods, mingle with the elite, and are conversant with the latest in technology.[81]

His arrest gave impulse to the search for his uncle, Vicente Carrillo Fuentes who remains among Mexico's most powerful drug lords.

The latter's mother, who laments of suffering persecution because of the Carrillo name, says that she has not seen Vicente [Carrillo Fuentes] in more than ten years.[82] Nevertheless, he and Vicente Carrillo Leyva reportedly control 521 gangs in Ciudad Juárez, ninety of which are regarded as extremely dangerous. Other bands—Los Aztecas and Los Mexicles—concentrate on recruiting hit men, collecting payoffs, and distributing drugs. Local business, religious, and university leader have condemned the mounting violence to no avail.[83] Just as Mexico risks becoming a failed state, Ciudad Juárez—a miniature Chicago of the 1920s—exhibits aspects of a failure as a city.

Stratfor Global Intelligence reports that the cartel's major enforcement arm is "La Linea," headed by José Luis "JL" Ledesma and composed of current and former Chihuahua police. Chihuahua's attorney general stated that these cops-turned-killers tortured and executed Benjamín LeBarón and his brother-in-law in early July 2009. LeBarón, leader of the polygamous Mormon community in Galeana, had publicly and aggressively inveighed against the impunity enjoyed by drug organizations in the state. A spokesman for La Linea denied the group's involvement, and the PGR indicated that the Sinaloa Cartel, which operates in Casas Grandes, Ascensión, Palomas, Zaragoza, Madera, and other municipalities in the northwest region of the state, may have authored the heinous crime.

Tijuana Cartel/Arellano Félix Organization (AFO)

The middle-class couple, Francisco Arellano Sánchez and Alicia Isabel Félix Azueta, raised eleven children in Sinaloa, five of whom (Francisco Rafael, Carlos, Benjamín, Ramón Eduardo, and Francisco Javier) dedicated themselves to smuggling clothing and electronics before entering the drug trade. All the children were nephews of Félix Gallardo. Benjamín attracted the attention of their uncle's lieutenant, Javier Caro Payán. After the arrest of Félix Gallardo, Caro Payán, to whom Félix Gallardo had awarded the Tijuana *plaza*, fled the country only to be arrested in Canada. Jesús Labra Avilés and Benjamín Arellano Félix filled the vacuum left by Caro Payán's absence. This coup against Payán, a cousin of Caro Quintero, gave rise to the lingering and intense enmity between the AFO and its Sinaloan and Sonoran rivals.

Until his arrest on March 11, 2000, "El Chuy" (a diminutive for "Jesús") Labra Avilés headed the organization, which specialized in selling protection to business and political figures. Benjamín functioned as chief strategist, and Ramón directed violence against their foes in a manner reminiscent of Sonny Corleone in the *Godfather* films. Other key AFO figures were Ismael "El Mayel" Higuera Guerrero, chief operations officer, money-launderer, and boss in Ensenada, and Arturo Everado "El

Kitty" Páez, who recruited violent youths from good families in Tijuana. He dispatched these insolent toughs to torture, dismember, and assassinate targeted individuals. They also sent brutal messages to those who attempted to utilize the Mexicali/Tijuana corridor without paying the transit tax demanded by the Arellano-Félix syndicate.

Extending its tentacles from Tijuana to the streets of San Diego, the AFO once was considered the most violent and unpredictable of the Mexican crime families. This organization maintained well-armed and well-trained security forces, was described by Mexican enforcement officials as paramilitary in character, and relied on foreign mercenaries as advisors, trainers, and members.

In May 2001 authorities nabbed Arturo "Kitty" Páez, a young lieutenant in the cartel, who was flown to San Diego and sentenced to thirty years in prison for smuggling cocaine; next authorities apprehended Higuera Guerrero and "Chuy" Labra Avilés; in 2002 the police killed Ramón in Mazatlan Sinaloa; and they arrested Benjamín—the real power in the cartel—later in the year. In 2006 the U.S. Coast Guard captured the cruel, flamboyant, and reclusive Francisco Javier, who—like a playboy—favored fast women and faster boats. He was arrested aboard a 43-foot recreational craft "Doc Holliday" named after a nineteenth-century Old West gunslinger. Acute fear of Benjamín and, to a lesser extent, of the degenerate Francisco Javier, meant that captured AFO thugs would not say a word to authorities about the cartel's operations until the barbarous brothers were out of the picture.

These setbacks left in charge university-educated family member Eduardo, known as "El Médico"/"The Doctor" because of his training as a physician. His sister Enedina Arellano Félix, an accountant, who is often described as the titular head of the AFO, neither plays a role in the drug business nor is sought by the police (Appendix 3 describes the activities of women in narco-trafficking). Benjamín's loyalists have staked out their own territories, as described in Table 5.1 in Chapter 5. The cartel now faces difficulties acquiring cocaine from Colombia through its shattered network, which had once extended from the Guatemalan-Chiapas border through the western states to Tijuana.[84] At the same time, it has expanded output from local cannabis fields and increased it production of methamphetamines. The DEA believes that the Arellano Felix brothers excavated the massive and sophisticated drug tunnels discovered at the California-Mexico border in January 2006. The AFO also may have constructed the so-called "Taj Mahal" of tunnels that linked Tijuana to San Diego and featured concrete floor and lighting.[85]

The late Jesús Blancornelas, a prize-winning journalist and editor at *Zeta*, the Tijuana weekly newspaper that has no relationship to the paramilitaries by the same name, argued that setbacks aside, the AFO remained a potent force thanks to a solid corporate structure. He claimed that Gustavo "El EP1" Gustavo Rivera Martínez—subsequently arrested—took charge of day-to-day affairs, and that the cartel's business-like orientation enabled it to contact any of its regional representatives within an hour.[86]

The Arellano Félix family has challenged the Mexican state more than any other syndicate. Involved in the death of Cardinal Posadas Ocampo in 1993, it precipitated a wave of killings when Zedillo flew to Baja California in 2000 to reaffirm his fight against organized crime. The following year, cells of the Arellano Félix Organization were uncovered in Mexico City. It also cultivated contacts with Colombia's FARC guerrillas[87] and criminal organizations in Peru, Venezuela, and the United States. In light of the number of arrests of prominent members, it is now a fragmented, disorganized, and virtually leaderless group composed of *mafiosi* whose defensiveness has enhanced their viciousness.

Recent arrests and fewer opportunities to dispatch cocaine northward have prompted the AFO to diversify its range of criminal involvement: it has embarked upon kidnappings, auto thefts, extortion, murders-for-hire, human smuggling, and other locally-focused felonies. Furthermore, it has taken advantage of supplying the expanding local market: Tijuana has some 200,000 addicts, the largest per-capita number in the country.[88]

Since El Médico's arrest in October 2008, Enedina's nephew, Luis Fernando "The Aligner" Sánchez Arellano, has assumed leadership of the cartel whose strength lies in western Tijuana and Rosarito. His cousin, right-hand man, and chief operator is Fernando "The Engineer" Zamora Arellano. One of their comrades is Melvin "El Camacho" Gutiérrez Quiroz, several of whose henchmen were arrested in February 2009.[89] Two months later, the Army apprehended Isaac Manuel "Dany"/"Martín" Godoy Castro, another AFO stalwart, along with six members of his cell.[90]

The Arellano Felix Organization is trapped in bloody battle for dominance in Tijuana with Teodoro "El Teo" García Simental, also known as Eduardo García Simental. Once a cartel *pistolero*, the chubby-cheeked El Teo broke with the Arellano Félix family over the capture of his brother "El Cris" in early 2005 and now claims backing from El Chapo Guzmán and El Mayo Zambada. The remnants of the AFO have reinforced their ranks with the support of Los Zetas, the Beltrán Leyva brothers, and Vicente Carrillo Fuentes.[91]

The Aligner and The Engineer believe that the abduction of professionals, business leaders, and political elites is counterproductive. In contrast, the thirty-something García Simental stands out for his self-indulgence, unscrupulousness, and brutality. He allegedly bets heavily on horse races on isolated ranches, chases women, hires hoodlums at $400 per week to guard caged abductees, prepares barrels of caustic chemicals to dispose of victims, and even murders individuals at parties, delighting at their stunned reactions. "Criminals earn respect and credibility with creative killing methods," an official told the *Los Angeles Times*. "Your status is based on your capacity to commit the most sadistic acts. Burning corpses, using acid, beheading victims… This generation is setting a new standard in savagery."[92] One of El Teo's key allies, Raydel Rosalio López Uriarte, prides himself on the moniker "The Crutches," because he has disabled so many adversaries. Equally dangerous is El Teo's brother, Manuel García Simental.

In late November 2008, the murder of El Teo's 25-year-old girlfriend, the gorgeous and voluptuous Karla Priscila "la del Telcel"/"the cell phone enthusiast" Carrasco Agüero, may have detonated a killing spree. García Simental and his allies in the Sinaloa Cartel struck at the presumed assassins, Los Zetas and the Arellano Félix brothers. When bullets stopped flying, thirty-seven people lay dead, including three children and five policemen.[93] Informed official sources reject this account in favor of the theory that the death of the young woman, which took place inside a business that she had just purchased for $180,000, resulted from a botched kidnapping. The AFO was attempting to send El Teo a message that it kept tabs on the whereabouts of him and his lover.

In 2009 authorities apprehended four of El Teo's henchmen: Jesús Alfonso "El Profe"/"The Professor" Trapero Ibarra (March); "Benjamín "El Benji" Guzmán Quintanilla, who received $300 for every state policeman he killed (April); José Filiberto "The Bitch" Parra Ramos (June);[94] and Luis Ibarra (July).

Officers assigned to eastern Tijuana, El Teo's stronghold, cover their license tags with tape and patrol in groups of two or three cruisers. If they see a procession of Ford F-250s and Cadillac Escalades—the vehicles of choice for García Simental and his brigands—they keep away. "We're scared," said one policeman. "There's no way U.S. cops would work under these conditions."[95] It was reported that El Teo's fearless hit men even executed the top bodyguard of Jorge Hank Rhon, an immensely wealthy ex-mayor and business tycoon in Tijuana.[96]

A *narcocorrido* that praises García Simental includes the verse: "Pay attention, President … In Tijuana, I rule." Another ballad boasts: "We'll show you what a real war is like."[97]

The splintering of several cartels appears to have emboldened Attorney General Medina Mora to make a promise to replace the military with civilian police in the fight against organized crime by the time Calderón leaves office in December 2012. That claim appears unrealistic in light of the continuing climate of violence in Tijuana that has continued even after the decimation of the AFO. Narco-trafficking evolved from a discreet, managed enterprise into a vicious free-for-all between and among heartless criminals. With respect to the government's strategy, David Shirk, director of the University of San Diego's Trans-Border Institute, concludes: "At least in the first two years, it hasn't led to smaller and more manageable [cartels], it's just led to smaller and more violent [ones]."[98]

Oaxaca Cartel

Pedro Diaz Parada, "The Oaxaca Boss," began sowing marijuana in San Pedro Totolapa, Oaxaca, in the 1970s. He quickly became the number-one producer in the Isthmus of Tehuantepec. He established headquarters in Santa María Zoquitlán, Oaxaca, and Arriaga, Chiapas, and used speed boats and light aircraft to extend trafficking—in marijuana and cocaine—across the south, as well as to Chihuahua, Durango, Tamaulipas, Durango, and Veracruz. He also cultivated buyers in Brownsville and Houston.

In addition, he purchased cocaine from Colombia, smuggling it across the Guatemala border. The Oaxaca Boss first allied with El Chapo and, after the Sinaloan's arrest, with the Tijuana Cartel.[99] He accumulated an immense fortune through narcotics, transportation, restaurants, nightclubs, and loan sharking.

Authorities first apprehended Díaz Parada in 1985, and he was condemned to thirty-three years behind bars. Upon hearing the verdict, he rasped at Judge Villafuerte Gallegos: "I will go and you will die." Six days later the drug lord escaped from Oaxaca's Santa María Ixcotel prison and, in September 1987, murdered the judge near his Cuernavaca home, pumping thirty-three bullets into his body—one for every year of the announced sentence.

Federal police recaptured the Oaxaca native in January 2007, and most of his syndicate's 400 members have been apprehended. Surrounded by masked, machine-gun toting AFI and military officers, Díaz Parada no longer appeared as a strutting, untouchable cartel leader, but as a haggard-looking man dressed simply in jeans and a short-sleeve shirt. Los Zetas are attempting to fill the vacuum left by this arrest.

Table 5.1
Mexico's Major Drug Cartels

Cartel (and Founding)	Founders	Current Leaders	Area and Type of Operations
Sinaloa Sinaloa 1970s The need for Colombians to ship cocaine through Mexico greatly increased its power and wealth in the mid-1980s.	Jaime Herrera Nevares; Ernesto "Don Neto" Fonseca Carrillo (captured April 8, 1985); Pedro Avilés Pérez (killed Sept. 9, 1978); Miguel Ángel Félix Gallardo (captured April 8, 1989); and Héctor Luis "El Güero" Palma (captured June 24, 1995), who was extradited to the U.S. to face drug trafficking charges on January 19, 2007; on February 25, 2009, the DEA and other U.S. agencies participating in "Operation Xcellerator" spurred the arrest of more than 755 men and women linked to Sinaloa Cartel.	Joaquín "El Chapo" Gúzman Loera; and Ismael "El Mayo" Zambada García. Arturo Beltrán Leyva and his brothers have broken with El Chapo to align with Los Zetas in Guerrero and other areas. Juan José Esparagoza Moreno—nicknamed "El Azul" or "The Blue" because of the bluish tint of his skin—is a murky figure who enjoys productive linkages with the Sinaloa Cartel and other criminal bands thanks to his role as a "consiglieri," along with the respect he commands for his negotiating skill.	Northwest Mexico, Sinaloa, Durango, Chihuahua, Baja California (Mexicali), Sonora (Nogales, Agua Prieta, and San Luis Río Colorado), Nuevo León (Monterrey), Michoacán, Acapulco, and Guerrero; moves cocaine, heroin, and marijuana into U.S. Gúzman Loera claims to shun unnecessary violence, yet he employs his "Sinaloan Cowboys," Los Pelones, and police against foes.
Milenio (Allied with Sinaloa Cartel) Michoacan, December 1997; worked with	Armando "Juanito" Valencia Cornelio was the top dog until his arrest in mid-2003; Calderón's "Joint Opera-	Luis and Juan Valencia operate a crippled organization; destabilization in Michoacán has further weakened	Early in the decade, the DEA claimed that it supplied one-third of cocaine to U.S.—with distribution focused on California, Texas, Chicago, and New

Table 5.1 (cont.)

Colombian Guillermo Moreno Ríos in the meth trade.	tion Michoacán" (December 2006) succeeded in jailing four Valencia lieutenants. Juanito's arrest bestowed leadership on his brother Juan and cousin Luis, who is closer to the Beltrán Leyva brothers than to Guzmán Leyva.	their power, as La Familia, a multifaceted organization, and Los Zetas, have expanded their activities in Michoacán and neighboring states.	York. Its home state of Michoacán, along with Jalisco, Colima, and Nayarit, provide major entry points for cocaine and pre-cursor drugs.
Sonora (Allied with Sinaloa Cartel) Sonora 1970s Cultivated enormous and sophisticated marijuana farms in Sonora and Chihuahua, including El Búfalo, which was discovered by DEA agent Enrique "Kiki" Camarena.	Badiraguato natives Rafael Ángel Caro Quintero (arrested April 5, 1985) and Miguel Caro Quintero (arrested December 20, 2001); the cartel allied with the Sinaloa Cartel because of the Caro Quintero's ties to Félix Gallardo and Ernesto Fonseca.	Miguel Caro Quintero's siblings (Genaro, Jorge, María del Carmen, Blanca Lili, Melinda, and María) are struggling to hold the cartel together; Genaro, who is missing from sight, is the presumed leader; Francisco "Dos Mil" Hernández García, a former ally of the Sinaloans, has cast his lot with the Gulf Cartel and is trying to recoup a plaza in the state.	In its heyday, it exported marijuana, cocaine, and heroin to the U.S., using small, low-flying aircraft; scene of confrontations between the Sinaloa and Gulf cartels; Governor Eduardo Bours cracked down on police following the May 16, 2007, shoot-out in and near Cananea, which took the lives of 23 criminals; the assassination of State Police Commander Juan Manuel Pavón Félix in November 2008 indicates continued bloodshed.
Colima (Allied with Sinaloa Cartel)	Amezcua Contreras brothers (José de Jesús, Ignacio, Adán, and Ven-	Imprisonment of brothers has left the organization in shambles—	Imported precursor drugs from Thailand and India via Veracruz and Manzanillo to

Table 5.1 (cont.)

Colima 1980s Began as an alien smuggling ring.	tura); all are dead or behind bars.	with day-to-day management having passed to two sisters of the Amezcua Contreras clan—one of whom, Patricia, is married to Tijuana Cartel member Jaime Ladino Ávila.	produce methamphetamine and "ecstasy," which were exported to the U.S.; supplied meth to AFO and trafficked in cocaine in association with Cali Cartel.
Oaxaca Oaxaca 1970s Launched to grow and sell marijuana	Pedro Díaz Parada and his family.	Arrest of Díaz Parada in 2007 emasculated the organization; los Zetas seek to gain control of areas the cartel once dominated.	In its salad days, the syndicate moved marijuana and cocaine throughout the Isthmus of Tehuantepec, a half-dozen other states, and Texas cities; it cooperated with the Sinaloa Cartel and, later, with the Tijuana Cartel.
The Beltrán Leyva Brothers	Sinaloans who for years worked with El Chapo and El Mayo	Arturo "El Barbas," Héctor Alfredo "El H," Mario Alberto "El General," and Carlos Beltrán Leyva.	Sinaloa, Mexico State, Jalisco, Durango, D.F., Morelos, certain municipalities in the Tierra Caliente; Mexico City and Monterrey airports; cooperate with Los Zetas in Guerrero and, possibly, in the D.F.; Stratfor reported that, since the arrest of their Colombian drug supplier Villafane Martínez, the Beltrán Leyvas have courted Víctor and Dario Espinosa, leaders of Colombia's Norte del Valle Cartel.

Table 5.1 (cont.)

Gulf	Juan Nepomucen-	Power struggle	Tamaulipas, Nuevo
Tamaulipas 1930s	to Guerra (died 2001); Juan García Abrego (close to Raúl Salinas) was jailed and extradited to U.S in 1996 by Zedillo; Salvador "El Chava" Gómez (killed 1999) lost battle with Osiel Cárdenas Guillén (extradited to U.S. in Jan. 2007).	among: Eduardo "El Coss" Costilla Sánchez; Zeta leader Heriberto "El Verdugo" Lazcano Lazcano; and Antonio Ezequiel "Tony Tormenta" Cárdenas Guillén.	Laredo, Nuevo León, Gulf Coast to Quintana Roo, Oaxaca, Guerrero, and Michoacán; moves Colombian cocaine into U.S.; practices extreme violence via Zetas, which have branched into other criminal activities.
Juan Nepomucento was a bootlegger in the 1930s. His nephew persuaded him to move into drugs in the 1960s; the need for Colombians to ship cocaine through Mexico greatly increased its power and wealth in the mid-1980s.			
Los Zetas	GAFES recruited	Heriberto "El	Cellular organiza-
Tamaulipas; early in first decade of twenty-first century; ex-GAFES.	by Osiel Cárdenas Guillén as protectors and enforcers; while occasionally cooperating with Gulf Cartel, Los Zetas now act on their own; in addition to drug smuggling, they have taken up murder-for-hire, kidnapping, the sale of protection, extortion, human smuggling, loan-sharking, and wholesale contraband commerce.	Verdugo" Lazcano Lazcano; and Miguel "40" Treviño Morales; and, in November 2008, authorities arrested Jaime "El Hummer" González Durán, the third ranking member of the paramilitaries.	tion in Tamaulipas, Veracruz, Villahermosa (Tabasco), Quintana Roo, Guerrero, Oaxaca, Michoacán, Aguascalientes, Durango, San Luis Potosí, Jalisco, Hidalgo, Mexico State, and D.F., the U.S. (Atlanta, Dallas, and Los Angeles), and Guatemala.

Table 5.1 (cont.)

Juárez (Territorial Accords with Gulf Cartel) Chihuahua mid-1970s.	DHS Commander Guajardo facilitated its activities; Pablo Acosta Villarreal, an operator in Ojinaga, was killed in 1987; Amado Carrillo Fuentes (died in 1997); in late 2004, Ricardo Garcia Urquiza took control until his arrest in DF in Nov. 2005.	Vicente Carrillo Fuentes; on April 1, 2009, masked police officers arrested Carrillo Fuentes' nephew, Vicente Carrillo Leyva, son of Amado.	Although still in business, this cartel has been weakened; alliance with Beltrán Leyva brothers; Chihuahua's attorney general believes that "La Linea," the syndicate's main enforcement arm, may have tortured and executed Mormon leader and anti-crime activist Benjamín LeBarón and his brother-in-law in early July 2009.
Tijuana/Arellano Félix Organization or AFO (Allied with Gulf Cartel) Baja California 1980s Launched after 1989 arrest of Félix Gallardo, who distributed plazas to maintain order; the need for Colombians to ship cocaine through Mexico greatly increased its power and wealth in the mid-1980s.	After the arrest of Félix Gallardo, power devolved to (1) Javier Caro Payán, who (2) was displaced by Jesús "El Chuy" Labra, (3) whose capture placed control in the hands of the Arellano Félix brothers; authorities apprehended the group's CEO Ismael "El Mayel" Higuera Guerrero (2000); killed Ramón A/F (2002), arrested Benjamín A/F (2002); Javier A/F (2006); and Eduardo A/F (2008).	Weak leadership at the top has found the loyalists of Benjamín, the only family member who could enforce discipline, staking out their own plazas: Jorge "el Cholo" Briseño López (Rosarito); and Eduardo "El Teo" García Simental (Tecate area). In March 2008, authorities arrested Eduardo Gustavo Rivera Martínez, who had held sway in Ensenada; Enedina's nephew, Luis Fernando "The Aligner" Sánchez Arellano, and her son, Fernando "The Engineer"	Tijuana, BC, parts of Sinaloa, Sonora, Jalisco, and Tamaulipas; difficulty obtaining Colombian cocaine, although it has increased marijuana production and handles meth; severely weakened by deaths and arrests of several brothers; recruits youngsters from well-to-do area families and uses these pampered hoodlums to practice torture and dismember foes; once nurtured ties with Colombia's FARC.

Table 5.1 (cont.)

		Zamora Arellano, together are competing for control of Tijuana against El Teo.	
La Familia Michoacán early part of first decade of twenty-first century	Sprang to life as La Empresa, which worked with the Gulf Cartel to expel Los Valencias from Michoacan; evolved into La Familia, which sought both to curb Los Zetas' activities in the state and to fight the sale of methamphetamines to youngsters; now involved in murder-for-hire, extortion, human smuggling, kidnapping, and the wholesale distribution of contraband; some elements of La Familia exhibit a strong messianic religious orientation; extraordinarily violent, including the beheading of foes; hurt in the May 26, 2009 arrest of 27 public officials.	José de Jesús "El Chango" Méndez, Nazario "El Chayo"/"El Más Loco" Moreno González, Antonio "El Toñón" Arcos, Servando "El Profe" Gómez Martínez, and Dionisio "The Uncle" Loya Plancarte; on July 11, 2009, Federal Police captured Arnold "La Minsa" Rueda Medina, the syndicate's number-three operative; major sectors of the organization show intense messianic zeal.	Aguascalientes, Colima, D.F., Guanajuato, Jalisco, Mexico State, Michoacán San Luis Potosí, part of Guerrero, and the United States.

Table 5.1 (cont.)

Oaxaca	Pedro Díaz Parada founded the cartel that focused on marijuana trafficking; it was alleged that he also had ties to Colombia cocaine dealers; arrested and sentenced to 33 years in prison in 1985, Díaz Parada escaped twice—in 1987 and 1992; he reportedly pumped 33 bullets into the body of the sentencing judge to match the length of his prison term.	The January 2007 arrest of Díaz Parada decapitated the cartel; los Zetas are among the groups filling the vacuum left by his incarceration.	The Isthmus of Tehuantepec and the south—with ties to the Tijuana Cartel to ship supplies into several northern states.
1970s as a marijuana-growing venture.			

Notes

1. This account by journalist Ricardo Ravelo appears in Patricia Dávila, "La boda del Capo Mayor," *Proceso*, September 1, 2007.
2. Samuel Logan, "Mexico's Internal War," *Power and Interest News Report*, August 14, 2006 <http://www.pinr.com>.
3. Mónica Serrano, "The Parallel Economy," *BBC World News Service www.bbc. co.uk/worldservice/news/2008/11/081029_marcoec*.
4. Marc Lacey, "Mexico's Unsuccessful Drug War, Painfully Preserved and Hidden," *New York Times*, November 27, 2008.
5. "Mexico Drug Smugglers Make Jesus Statue of Cocaine," *Reuters*, June 1, 2008.
6. Tracey Eaton and Alfredo Corchado, "Mexico Intensifies Hunt for Drug Lord, *Dallas Morning News*, April 13, 2005.
7. Richard Bourdeaux, "Mexico's Master of Elusion," *Los Angeles Times*, July 5, 2005.
8. Guy Lawson, "The Making of a Narco State," *Rolling Stone Magazine*, March 4, 2009. *www.rollingstone.com/politics*.
9. Riely, Interview by National Public Radio, July 15, 2008.
10. Ricardo Ravelo, "El capo del panismo," *Proceso*, March 16, 2009.
11. Council on Hemispheric Affairs, "COHA's Report on Mexico's Prison System: Yet Another Blemished Aspect of Fox's Failed Presidency," May 1, 2006. *www. coha.org*.
12. "Mexican Military Special Forces Arrest Alfredo Beltrán Leyva, One of the Main Leaders of the Sinaloa Cartel. Cash, Firearms, and 3 Others Arrested," *Narcotic*

News, January 21, 2008. *www.narcoticnews.com/Cocaine/2008/Jan/Cocaine_2008_Jan_21_Culiacan_Sinaloa.*

13. "Capturan a operador de Beltrán," *Reforma*, January 8, 2009.
14. "'Zetas' y Beltrán crean megacártel," *El Universal*, May 19, 2008.
15. "Rolando Herrera and Héctor Raúl González, "Atrapan en Morelos a sicarios de Beltrán," *Reforma*, May 7, 2009; and "Caen en Morelos 14 integrantes de los Beltrán Leyva, *Noroeste.com*, May 7, 2009.
16. "Captura la PGR a 23 en Acapulco," *Reforma*, May 25, 2009.
17. "Detienen a operador de los Beltrán en NL," *Reforma*, June 28, 2009.
18. Juan Cervantes and Adriana Covarrubias, "Ejército busca a pistoleros de Arcelia en la Sierra Maestra," *El Universal.com*, April 18, 2009.
19. Jorge Alejandro Medellín, "Detienen a presunto líder de sicarios," *El Universal*, April 15, 2009.
20. "Reaparece en Guerrero el comandante 'Ramiro,'" *Reforma*, May 12, 2009.
21. "Don formal prisión a "El Primo,'" Reforma, April 28, 2009.
22. "Templo Mayor," *Reforma*, January 29, 2009.
23. Marc Lacey, "In Drug War, Mexico Fights the Cartels and Itself," *New York Times*, March 30, 2009.
24. Luis Brito, "Relevan a General de cargo en AICM," *Reforma.com*, May 6, 2009.
25. Fred Burton and Scott Stewart, "Mexico: Examining Cartel War Violence through a Protective Intelligence Lens," *Stratfor*, May 14, 2008 *www.stratfor.com*; and Francisco Gómez, "Sus 'cachorros,' talon de Aquiles de los carteles," *El Universal. com.mx*, April 3, 2009.
26. "Internan en Jalisco a 'Tony La Mentira,'" *Reforma.com*, May 6, 2009.
27. Anthony Placido, director of intelligence for the DEA, quoted in "Descarta DEA cambiar agentes por infiltración del *narco* en Embajada," *El Universal*, October 27, 2008.
28. "Caen 9 sicarios de los Beltrán en Sonora," *Reforma*, June 26, 2009.
29. Benito Jiménez, "Identifica el Ejército tres rutas de cartels," *Reforma*, June 14, 2007.
30. In 2006 and 2007, Nicaraguan authorities arrested six Mexican traffickers, closed down a clandestine airfield, and broke up a cocaine network; see, José Meléndez, "El cártel Sinaloa busca constituirese en Nicaragua," *El Universal*, February 1, 2009.
31. Congressional Research Service, "Mexico's Drug Cartels," October 16, 2007. *www.fas.org/sgp/crs/row/rl34215.*
32. Hal Brands, "Mexico's Narco-Insurgency and U.S. Counterdrug Policy," Department of the Army, Strategic Studies Institute, United States Army War College, May 2009.
33. Richard Boudreaux, "Since his Escape, Drug Cartel Chief Joaquín 'Shorty' Guzmán has Expanded his Empire, Waged War on Rivals, and Become a Legend," *Los Angeles Times*, July 5, 2005.
34. Tracy Wilkinson, "Mexican Drug Lord Seems Everywhere—and Nowhere," *Richmond Times-Dispatch*, November 5, 2008; and Richard Boudreaux, "Mexico's Master of Elusion."
35. Adriana Gómez Licón, "Mexico Angry that Drug Lord Joaquín "El Chapo" Guzmán on Forbes Billionaires List," *El Paso Times*, March 14, 2009.
36. "The 2009 Time 100," *Time Magazine*, May 1, 2009.
37. His first wife, Alejandrina María Salazar Hernández, whom he married in 1977, bore four children; his second wife was Laura Álvarez Beltrán; see, Dávila, "La boda del Capo Mayor."

38. Wilkinson, "Mexican Drug Lord Seems Everywhere—and Nowhere."
39. This vivid account draws heavily on *MySpace.com*, "The Cartel Report." *http:// profile.myspace.com/index.cfm?fuseaction=user.viewprofile&friendID=3677770 93.*
40. *Ibid.*
41. Ravelo, "El capo del panismo"; and María de la Luz González, "Detienen al hijo de El Mayo Zambada," *El Universal*, March 19, 2009.
42. Javier Cabrera, "Control aéreo en Triángulo Dorado," *El Universal*, April 24, 2009.
43. PGR *Boletín No. 333/99*, October 15, 1999.
44. "Se suma nueve ejecuciones a la ola de violencia en todo el país," *El Universal*, April 18, 2007.
45. ¿Quiere saber dónde se producen las células rojas? April 17, 2007. *www.milenio. com.*
46. Operators for the Gulf Cartel in Michoacán are Sergio Orozco Barajas, Ramón Moreno Madrigal and Uriel Pacheco Arzate (Apatzingán) and Baldomero Alvarado Rodríguez, David Carrillo and Ismael Ambriz Vargas (Churumuco, La Huacana, and Tumbuscatío), as well as Alberto "El Tico" Espinoza Loya and José Luis "Pepillo" Méndez Vargas; see, "Pelean Michoacán Zetas y Familia," *Reforma*, September 18, 2008.
47. Authorities report that he also has documents indicating that he was born in Culiacán or Canelas, Durango.
48. Federal Bureau of Investigation, "Wanted: Ignacio Coronel Villareal" www.fbi. gov/wanted/fugitives/cei/villareal_ic.htm; *and* Sam Logan and Kate Kairies, "*U.S. Drug Habit Migrates to Mexico," February 7, 2007,* Americas Program, Center for International Policy.
49. Mae López Aranda, "Ejecutan a operador de 'Nacho' Coronel," *El Universal*, March 4, 2009.
50. "'Nacho' se expande mientras cárteles riñen," *El Universal*, October 9, 2008.
51. Emily Bazar, "New Tool in Pot Trade Ups the Ante," *USAToday*, March 6, 2009.
52. Brady McCombs, "Es Nogales el premio de guerra entre cárteles," *Arizona Daily Star*, September 19, 2008.
53. Quoted in Mccombs, "Es Nogales el premio de guerra entre cárteles."
54. "Denuncian ayuda de Procampo a narcos," *El Siglo de Torreón*, October 28, 2008.
55. Gardenia Mendoza Aguilar, "Indagan mal uso de programas oficiales," *La Opinión*, October 31, 2008.
56. Quoted in Olga R. Rodriguez, "Mexico Denies Drug Suspect Paid for Party," *Boston Globe*, April 30, 2006; and Francisco Gómez, El cártel del Golfo y su disfraz de altruismo," *El Universal*, January 7, 2008.
57. Gustavo Castillo García, "Guerras internas del narco; la más cruenta, en el cártel del Golfo, *La Jornada*, February 18, 2007; and "Drug Cartels: the Growing Violence in Mexico, *Stratfor*, October 2006.
58. "Cae operador del Cártel del Golfo in QR," *Reforma*, May 9, 2009.
59. "Drug Cartels: the Growing Violence in Mexico, *Stratfor.*
60. "Exporta Cártel del Golfo armamentos y explosivos," *Reforma*, November 26, 2008.
61. The section relies heavily on *MySpace.com*, "The Cartel Report"; and Terrence E. Poppa, "Pablo Acosta" *www.laits.utexas.edu/jaime/jnicolopulos/cwp3/ncg/ pablo_acosta.htm.*
62. Núñez, "A Not-So-Secret History of Vice in Juárez."

63. Calderoni was killed in Matamoros in February 2003.
64. Quoted in Tim Golden, "U.S. Officials Say Mexican Military Aids Drug Traffic," *New York Times*, March 26, 1998.
65. Julia Preston, "Drug Corruption Links Mexican Military to Spate of Abductions," *New York Times*, March 9, 1997.
66. Sam Dillon with Craig Pyres, "Court Files Say Drug Baron Used Mexican Military," *New York Times*, May 24, 1997.
67. *Ibid.*
68. Tim Weiner, "Mexico Imprisons Two Generals, Longtime Suspects in Drug Cases," *New York Times*, September 2, 2000.
69. Quoted in Jeff Barnett and Ana María Ruiz-Brown, "Top Drug Lord Reported Dead; Juárez Cartel Changes Hands" *www.nmsu.edu/~frontera/old_1997/aug97/897amado.htm.*
70. *Ibid.*
71. Quoted in *Ibid.*; and Anderson, "After Death Kingpin's Life Is an Open Book."
72. "Da juez 47 años de cárcel a 'El Metro,'" *El Diario*, June 21, 2007.
73. PGR, "Mario Villanueva Madrid Case," August 18, 2007, Press release 400/07; Villanueva acquired the nickname "El Chueco" because of his partially paralyzed face, although it could have applied also to his behavior.
74. "Report Ties Ex-official to Juárez Cartel," *The Herald* (*El Universal*), January 21, 2006. *www.eluniversal.com.mx/miami/16675.html*; and Carmen Jaimes, "Cae successor de Amado Carrillo," *Noticieros Televisa*, November 21, 2005.
75. Jason Traham *et al.*, "Drug Wars' Long Shadow," *Dallas Morning News*, December 13, 2005.
76. Ricardo Ravelo, "El cártel de Juárez: poder creciente," *Proceso*, July 10, 2005.
77. *Washington Post*, October 26, 2000.
78. Gómez, "Sus 'cachorros,' talón de Aquiles de los cartels."
79. David Rose, "The House of Death," *The Observer*, December 3, 2006. guardian. co.uk/world/2006/dec/03/.
80. Eduardo Castillo, "Mexico Reports Arrest of Major Drug Suspect," *Associated Press*, April 2, 2009; and María de la Luz González and Juan Veledíaz, "Vivía como un discreto empresario en las Lomas," *El Universal*, April 3, 2009.
81. "Los narcocachorros," *El Universal*, June 28, 2009.
82. "Nos persiguen por 'estigma': Carrillo Fuentes," *Noroeste*, December 12, 2008.
83. Rubén Villalpando, "La violencia en Ciudad Juárez provoca éxodo de 3 mil familias," *La Jornada*, November 17, 2008.
84. Jiménez, "Identifica el Ejército tres rutas de cárteles."
85. Authorities discovered this passage in 1994; see, "Smuggling Tunnels Get Plugged with Concrete," *The Herald* (*El Universal*), May 17, 2007.
86. Blancornelas was interviewed for the article, "Arellano Corp.," *Proceso*, September 3, 2006. *www.proceso.com.*
87. Jorge Fernández Menéndez, "La verdadera historia de los Arellano Félix," *Arcana*, March 1, 2002. *www.drogasmexico.org.*
88. Emilio San Pedro, "In the Shadow of the Cartels," *BBC World Service. www.bbc. co.uk/worldservice/news/2008.*
89. "Caen sicarios de los Arellano en Tijuana," *Reforma*, March 1, 2009.
90. "Cae operador de los Arellano Félix en BC," *Reforma*, April 25, 2009.
91. Richard Marosi, "Mystery Man Blamed for Gruesome Tijuana Deaths," *Los Angeles Times*, December 18, 2008.
92. Quoted in Marosi, "Mystery Man Blamed for Gruesome Tijuana Deaths."
93. Julieta Martínez, Asesino de novia de 'capo' avivó la violencia," *El Universal*, December 2, 2008.

94.   "Cae operador de 'El Tio' en Tijuana, *Reforma*, March 2, 2009. Guzmán Quintanilla reported that his paymaster was García Simental's operative, Francisco "El Pancho" Javier Copetillo Angulo, a former member of the state preventative police; see "Caen 21 sicarios de los Arellano en BC," *Reforma*, April 8, 2009.
95.   Quoted in Marosi, "Mystery Man Blamed for Gruesome Tijuana Deaths."
96.   "Cobra el hampa 38 vidas en 7 estados; 19, solo en Tijuana," *La Jornada*, December 1, 2008.
97.   Richard Marosi, "A Tijuana Blood Bath," *Los Angeles Times*, October 6, 2008.
98.   Quoted in Elliot Spagat, "An Infamous Mexican Cartel Totters, Violence Grows," *Associated Press*, March 26, 2004.
99.   Colleen W. Cook, "Mexican Drug Cartels," Congressional Research Service Report to Congress, February 25, 2008 *http://assets.opencrs.com/rpts/RL34215_20080225.pdf.*

6

Calderón's Anti-Drug Strategy

In seeking the presidency, Calderón, a moderate who hoisted the banner of the center-right National Action Party, emphasized three major goals: creating jobs, combating poverty, and fighting crime. By the time he took office, he lasered in on the cartels in a fashion that seems to modeled on President George W. Bush's steely eyed focus on al-Qaeda in the aftermath of the 9/11 attacks on the World Trade Center and the Pentagon. The difference was that U.S. officials mislead the public about weapons of mass destruction to inflate the danger of terrorism and gain support for the Iraq invasion. In contrast Mexico was under siege by well organized bands of deadly killers who posed a threat to the nation's institutions, as well as its very sovereignty.

These brigands even threatened his life during the campaign, and one American official estimated that 5 million to 10 million in narco-dollars flowed into 2006 mayoral and contests.[1] "It was a factor that was considered, especially the municipal elections, because from there they [the cartels] could gain control of the local police forces," stated Attorney General Medina Mora.[2] During the five months between his July 2, 2006 victory and his swearing-in, narco-violence extinguished the lives of more than 1,000 people, raising the yearly total to 2,231; an increase from 1,537 in 2005 and 1,304 in 2004. In 2007 the drug-related death toll spiraled to 2,794, according to Reforma, with the number nearly doubling to 5,207 in 2008, and climbing to 3,628 through the first week of August 2009.[3]

Figures in Table 6.1 below speak for themselves. Yet the numbers fail to reveal the mounting bestiality of the killings and their locations, with the murders often bearing the mark of *Mafia*-style executions.

In the past, TV, radio, and newspaper stories about the brazenness of cartels and their chieftains pressured law enforcement agencies to pursue the culprits. In recent years, fear of the assassination of journalists and bombings of printing plants has prompted *El Mañana* chain, which pub-

Table 6.1
Murders in Mexico, 2001 to mid-2009

Year	Number of Murders
2009	3,628 (Through August 7)
2008	5,207
2007	2,275
2006	2,120
2005	1,537
2004	1,304
2003	1,365
2002	No consistent figures found
2001	1,080

Source: Office of the Attorney General; James C. McKinley, Jr. "With Beheadings and Attacks, Drug Gangs Terrorize Mexico," *New York Times*, October 26, 2006, and the newspaper *Reforma*, which publishes a weekly tally of murders in its "National" section.

lishes editions in the border cities of Reynosa, Matamoros, and Nuevo Laredo, and other newspapers, to tone down and in most cases eliminate coverage of narco-crimes. A drug gang reportedly added at least one American journalist to its hit list.[4]

The Paris-based Reporters without Frontiers cited ninety-five attacks on journalists during the first half of 2008, while a World Journalists' Report on Press Freedom castigated Mexico as "one of the most dangerous countries for journalists in the world"—with twenty-eight reporters killed, eight missing, and dozens threatened, intimidated or harassed for practicing their profession during the last eight years.[5]

The Writers in Prison Committee of International PEN expressed particular outrage at the murder of Michoacán-based newspaper editor Miguel Angel Villagómez Valle in early October 2008. Abducted on his way home from work, the editor and publisher of the daily tabloid *Noticias de Michoacán* suffered multiple gunshot wounds before his body was thrown on a garbage pile in Guerrero State, about thirty miles from Lázaro Cárdenas. He was one of twelve journalists killed in Mexico during the year.

The motive for the murder of Villagómez is not yet known; however, it was probably linked to his profession. He had received a threatening phone call from a member of Los Zetas about a month before his death and had warned his family to be alert. *Noticias de Michoacán* often reports on organized crime, corruption, and drug trafficking. Neither the state police nor the PGR's Special Prosecutor for Crimes of Violence against Journalists, created in February 2006, turned up suspects.

Eight Ciudad Juárez journalists received intimidating calls from self-described cartel members in January 2008. The messages all said, "Don't get mixed up with the wrong people" or face the consequences. José Armando Rodríguez Carreón of *El Diario* was one of those contacted. When he reported the threat to the Chihuahua state prosecutor's office, he was told he should get out of the city for there was no way to guarantee his safety. After two months El Choco, as he was called, returned to work, while other journalists preferred self-exile. Triggermen gunned him down on November 13 when he was driving his three children to school. There were menacing calls to reporters during his funeral the next day. As a result, the number of journalists leaving the region or the country increased.[6]

Michoacán State has one of the highest levels of violence in Mexico, with regular confrontations between and among the Milenio Cartel, Los Zetas, and La Familia. Abductions, disappearances, and murders of journalists are common. For example, Mauricio Estrada Zamora of *La Opinión de Apatzingán* and *La Opinión de Michoacán* has been missing since February 14, 2008, and José Antonio García Apac of *Ecos de la Cuenca* since November 20, 2006. Gerardo Israel García Pimentel of *La Opinión de Michoacán* was shot dead on December 8, 2007.[7] Rodríguez Carreón was the eleventh writer killed in Mexico in 2008.

Gangsters are not the only ones who direct violence toward reporters. For example, in mid-March 2009 cops in Puebla stopped a vehicle carrying reporters for *Intolerancia*, *El Columnista*, and *Cambio*. When the police learned their profession, they said that the press humiliated law enforcement officers. They threw the three men to the ground, handcuffed them, and continuously beat and threatened them during a twenty-five-hour detainment. Each year newspapers, TV networks, radio stations, and press associations report scores of incidents of similar brutal treatment.[8]

Alejandro Junco de la Vega, owner and publisher of major dailies (*Reforma*, *El Norte*, *Mural*, and *Palabra*), has moved to Texas in response to threats. In a letter to Nuevo León's governor, the newspaper tycoon said he considers himself a "refugee" and faced the dilemma of either "compromising the editorial line of the paper[s] or protecting my family," adding that: "We lost faith."[9] In late May 2009 banners dotted the landscape in Torreón warning soldiers and journalists to "watch out." The names of El Chapo and the unknown Cartel of the West (Cártel del Poniente) graced the placards, which appeared one day after the discovery in an irrigation canal of the bullet-ridden body of Elisio Barrón Hernández, a 36-year-old crime reporter for *Milenio-Torreón*.[10] In mid-June 2009 five suspects were arrested for Barrón's execution. One

Table 6.2
Mexican Journalists Murdered in 2008 and during the First Half of 2009

2008

* Claudia Rodríguez Llera, founder of the publication *CineMagazine* and host of the news program *En Pantalla Grande* on Radio Mix of Ecatepec, Mexico State; shot in the temple (January 7).

* Francisco Ortiz Monroy, correspondent for the daily newspaper *El Diario de México*; shot dead in Camargo, Tamaulipas (February 5).

* Bonifacio Cruz Santiago and his son Alfonso Cruz Pacheco, director and editor respectively of the weekly *El Real de Ciudad Nezahualcóyotl*; killed in Chimalhuacán, Mexico State (February 7).

* Felicitas Martínez Sánchez and Teresa Bautista, radio journalists for an indigenous station "La Voz que Rompe el Silencio," in San Juan Copala, Oaxaca; shot to death (April 7).

* Candelario Pérez Pérez, independent journalist and editor for crime magazine *Sucesos*; shot dead in Ciudad Juárez (June 24).

* Miguel Ángel Gutiérrez Ávila, anthropologist, linguist, author, and indigenous rights activist; beaten to death in Guerrero state (July 25 or 26).

* Alejandro Zenón Fonseca Estrada, host of the news program "El Padrino" on radio station "Exa FM" in Villahermosa; assassinated by commandos (September 23).

* David García Monroy, columnist for *El Diario* and contributor to various publications in Chihuahua; killed along with ten other people in a shoot-out in a bar (October 9). The incident was apparently unrelated to the murder of Villagómez.

* Miguel Angel Villagómez Valle, publisher and editor of *Noticias de Michoacán*; executed near Lázaro Cárdenas (October 8 or 9).

* Francisco Javier Salas, spokesman for *El Mexicano* of Tijuana: killed for having reported threats to authorities (October 17).

* José Armando Rodríguez Carreón, reporter for *El Diario* (Juárez); killed while taking his children to school (November 13).

2009

* Jean Paul Ibarra Ramírez, photographer for *El Correo de Iguala*, Iguala, Guerrero; shot on his motorcycle after covering a story (February 13).

* Luís Daniel Méndez Hernández, reporter for *La Poderosa* of the Radiorama chain; shot four times in the back in la Huasteca region of Veracruz (February 22).

* Juan Carlos Hernández Mundo, director of the local newspaper *El Quijote*; assassinated in Taxco de Alarcón, Guerrero (February 27).

* Carlos Ortega Samper, reporter for *El Tiempo de Durango*; shot dead in Santa María del Oro, Durango (May 3).

* Elisio Barrón Hernandez, crime reporter for *Milenio-Torreón*; kidnapped from his home on May 25; shot eleven times; and found dead in an irrigation canal in Torreón (May 26).

* Martín Javier Miranda Avilés, reporter for *Panorama* and correspondent for *Quadratín* news service; found dead with two knife wounds, Zitácuaro, Michoacán (July 12).

* Ernesto Montañez Valdivia, editor for *Enfoque del Sol de Chihuahua*; shot dead in Ciudad Juárez (July 14).

* Juan Daniel Martínez Gil, host of news program *Radiorama* (Mexico City); tortured and found dead in Acapulco (July 27).

Source: "Mexico: Incontenible el ritmo de asesinatos de periodistas; caen tres en un més," Federación Latinoamericana de Periodistas, Mexico City, April 5, 2009; "Amenaza narco a periodistas y soldados," *Reforma*, May 28, 2009; and La Fundación para la Libertad de Expresión, "Siete Periodistas Asesinados Este Año; Ayer Uno en Acapulco," July 29, 2009.

of the men, Israel Sánchez Jaime, confessed membership in Los Zetas and admitted to killing the kidnapped reporter.[11]

Kidnappings

Almost as alarming as these killings are the kidnappings, which have ascended to epidemic proportions. The rate jumped by 9.1 percent during the first five months of 2008 compared with the year before, raising the average number of monthly number of abductions to 64.6 from 62.5, according to Mexico's Attorney General's Office.[12] Figure 6.3 shows the burgeoning number of abductions in recent years. This data only reflect reported kidnappings. An academic study confirms the conventional wisdom that families do not inform police in up to nine out of ten abductions because they believe that law enforcement agents and other government officials may be accomplices in the crime.[13]

Especially unsettling is the participation of the police in the capture, ransom, and all too frequent liquidation of the victims. A cause célèbre occurred on the streets of Mexico City on June 4, 2008, when malefactors snatched Fernando Martí, the 14-year-old son of the wealthy owner of the largest chain of sporting goods stores in the country. Even though the family bought ads in major newspapers pleading for their son's freedom and they had delivered hundreds of thousands of dollars in ransom, on August 1 authorities found the decomposed bodies of the youngster and his chauffeur jammed into the trunk of an automobile.

One of the suspects in this highly publicized case is Lorena González Hernández, a former deputy inspector of the anti-kidnapping squad of the Federal Preventative Police, who had worked in one or more federal law enforcement agencies since 1999. Mexico City authorities linked her to a group known as La Flor, a seven-cell organization and one of many dangerous gangs dedicated to kidnapping in the capital.[14]

Three days before the discovery of young Fernando's corpse, a family of six was found dead in their home in western Jalisco state, allegedly targeted by abductors who were aided by corrupt cops. The killers shot four victims in the head, including two children, slashed the throat of a teenage boy, and asphyxiated his mother with a plastic sack.

To show hostility towards the government and evince solidarity with the grief-stricken Martí family, more than 150,000 people, dressed in white and carrying symbolic candles, marched through the center of Mexico City on August 29, 2008. But there seems no way to convert grassroots' seething into major changes in public policy. "We are prisoners in our own homes," said Maricarmen Alcocer, a housewife. "They are more bloodthirsty, they make their victims disappear, they mutilate them [and], they cut their ears off just [as] in the case of my daughter [seized in 2004]. We do not know where she is," she added.[15]

The outrage is palpable! "They should put their eyes out, so they can't commit any more crimes," bemoaned Ignacio Noriega, who says he no longer feels safe anywhere. "Prison isn't a solution anymore. They just form their own gangs inside prison and come out stronger," the 26-year-old university student told a reporter.[16]

Mexico City's PRD Mayor Marcelo Ebrard Casaubon, a presidential aspirant, created a police investigative agency to replace its old corruption-ridden detectives' unit. In addition, he announced plans to enlist 300,000 neighborhood anti-crime representatives in the metropolis of 8.7 million people and set up an anti-kidnapping hotline with rewards of up to 500,000 pesos (approximately $49,400 in 2008) to people who furnished information leading to the capture of kidnappers. Meanwhile, the federal government pledged to establish five national anti-kidnapping centers and push for the cleanup of its law enforcement agencies.[17]

These steps were too late to prevent the kidnapping and murder of Silvia Vargas Escalera, the beautiful 18-year-old daughter of the prominent ex-director of the National Athletic Commission, Nelson Vargas Basáñez. Amid a tsunami of public outrage at one of the world's highest and incrementally growing kidnapping rates, Vargas expressed bitterness and frustration at the slow, ineffective work of the Attorney General's Office and the PFP in pursuing leads that he had given them after the September 2007 abduction. For instance, he pointed out that their former driver, Oscar Ortiz González, might have been involved. In fact, two of the chauffeur's brothers belonged to Los Rojos, a kidnapping gang, according to police. During the news conference, Vargas asked how the police could have missed that fact. "So I ask myself, where is the intelligence? They don't see the obvious. What can we expect from their investigations?" he said.

"I have cried. I have begged. I am now demanding that Attorney General Eduardo Medina Mora and Public Safety Secretary Genaro Garcia Luna resolve this case," Vargas said during a news conference where he constantly struggled to steady his voice and hold back tears. "Find my daughter. Find my Silvia," he pleaded.

The PGR confirmed to reporters that the Ortiz brothers were wanted on suspicion of kidnapping but said investigators did not know that Oscar Ortiz had worked for the family until Vargas informed them in October 2008. The Vargas family reiterated that they had told police about the chauffeur shortly after the kidnapping.

The newspaper *Excelsior* outlined the reported errors made by police, including failure to identify the cell phone number used by the kidnappers when they first contacted the family; failure to examine images from at least forty video cameras along the route the young lady took to school; and failure to take fingerprints from the bag the abductors sent as proof that she was still alive. Vargas said he told police his suspicions. Only later, Vargas said, did a tipster who had seen news coverage of the case tell him that Ortiz's brother was one of Mexico's top kidnapping suspects. The Vargas family driver was apprehended in southern Mexico in November 2008 month and is being investigated, but he has denied involvement, police said. His brother Raúl was sentenced to sixteen years in prison for kidnapping in 1996 but escaped in 2000 by hiding in a clothes container that was being removed from the prison.[18] In late July 2009, Federal Police apprehended other suspects, including Raúl "El Azul" Ortiz González, leader of Los Rojos gang.

"Express kidnappings" have also gained notoriety in Mexico's murky underworld. Although the victims generally survive, these acts often begin when a passenger climbs into one of the tens of thousands of unauthorized or "pirate taxis" whose owners bribe officials in Mexico City and elsewhere in order to operate illegally. The driver, or his accomplice, whips out a knife or gun and demands credit cards, cash, jewelry, cellular phones, or immediate withdrawals from ATM accounts. Once the loot is obtained, they often release the traumatized victim. In addition, "[o]ne increasingly disturbing spin is that the criminals may contact your family and not release you until a hefty ransom is paid."[19]

In a cruel irony, American anti-kidnapping specialist Felix Batista traveled to Torreón and Saltillo in Coahuila state on December 6, 2008, to make presentations to the local business community about kidnapping risks and prevention. The 55-year-old Cuban-American also met with law enforcement officials in connection with his efforts to negotiate the freedom of kidnap victim José Pilar Valdés, the former head of security for Grupo Industrial Saltillo and a contact of Batista's in Coahuila. While answering a cell phone call outside the acclaimed El Mesón Principal restaurant in Saltillo, six armed men heaved him into a white sport-utility vehicle and sped away. Batista consults for the Houston-based ASI Global security firm, which "provides a portfolio of crisis management, prevention and pre-incident services to private clients and families, financial institutions and major corporations worldwide." It identifies its "K&R"—kidnapping and ransom—consultants as having "the very best minds in the business."[20]

In April 2009 the PFP apprehended Germán "El Zeta 25" Torres Jiménez in Veracruz for the disappearance of Batista. It was reported that the Cuban-American had gleaned inside information about the organization's cell in Saltillo that Torres Jiménez had headed before a dispute broke out between him and his comrades. Although authorities tracked down Zeta-25, who had fled the state, they had not determined the whereabouts of Batista by mid-2009.[21]

In a late 2008 survey about the "worst" occurrences in 2008, respondents placed kidnappings (24 percent) one point behind narco-trafficking (25 percent) and ahead of unemployment (20 percent) and price increases (14 percent).[22]

This rising influx of illegal substances, accompanied by mounting deaths and kidnappings, prompted the U.S. ambassador to Mexico, Antonio O. Garza, to warn Americans "to exercise extreme caution," adding that: "Drug cartel members have been known to follow and harass U.S. citizens traveling in their vehicles particularly in border areas including Nuevo Laredo (Nuevo León) and Matamoros (Tamaulipas)."

Calderón Emphasizes Extraditions

To set the tone for his regime, Calderón wasted no time before extraditing drug kingpins to the United States. Although Fox was also prepared to use this measure, the National Supreme Court of Justice (SCJN) tied his hands on the grounds that Mexican citizens could not be tried in countries that imposed sanctions not authorized at home—namely, sentences longer than sixty years and capital punishment. Moreover, Fox had been challenged by abstruse injunctions known as "*amparos*," multi-layered lower courts, and Kafkaesque procedural technicalities.

Nonetheless, he managed to send scores of criminals to the United States, many of whom were citizens of America or third countries. During Fox's term, the number of those extradited shot up from seventeen in 2001 to sixty-three in 2006. However, with the exception of the May 2001 dispatch of the right-hand man of the Arellano Félix Organization, few high-level chiefs appeared in this number. In November 2005 the Supreme Court partially reversed its earlier decision and determined that life imprisonment without parole was not cruel and unusual punishment. Two months later it ruled that U.S. extradition requests only had to satisfy the 1978 bilateral extradition treaty, not Mexican domestic statute on international extraditions. These findings permitted the extradition of Francisco Rafael Arellano Félix, who was the highest-level trafficker sent to the U.S. under Fox.

Calderón's appointment of Santiago Vasconcelos, an expert in extradition, to the post of assistant attorney general for judicial and international affairs, foreshadowed his readiness to hand over criminals to the

Table 6.3
Kidnappings in Mexico, 2000-2008

Year	Number of Kidnappings
2009	Not Available
2008	1,028
2007	751 (PGR)
	438*
2006	595*
	601**
2005	325* **
2004	334* **
2003	436* **
	362 (PGR)
2002	433* **
2001	521* **
2000	601* **

Sources: Unless otherwise noted a single asterisk (*) indicates Instituto por la Seguridad y la Democracia, AC http://www.insyde.org.mx/: a double asterisk (**) denotes the Instituto Ciudadano de Estudios sobre la Inseguridad, AC www.icesi.org.mx/icesi/index.asp/; and the 2008 figure comes from "Iguala 2008 a 1997 en plagios," *Reforma*, December 30, 2008.

Americans. Seven weeks after taking office, the new regime turned over fifteen suspects to U.S. authorities. The most infamous was Osiel Cárdenas Guillén, who since his 2003 arrest had been running the Gulf Cartel from his well-appointed cell at La Palma maximum-security prison. Three other extradited potentates appeared on the Bush administration's "kingpin list," including Héctor Luis Palma Salazar, a top lieutenant of Guzmán Loera. Had he not escaped from prison in 2001, El Chapo too might have traveled abroad at government expense.

"El Güero" Palma fully epitomized the image of the strutting drug lord. He paid princely sums in protection fees to the Guadalajara police, carried a handgun bejeweled with diamonds and emeralds, and dressed in a flamboyant style embellished by gold chains and snakeskin boots. He was arrested in 1995 flying to a wedding when engine troubles forced his Lear jet to crash land in Nayarit. He was accompanied by seven gunmen and thirty-three heavily armed members of the Federal Judicial Police, who served as his bodyguards.[23] The composition of his team "confirmed what most Mexicans had long known—in Mexico, the police are for sale, and the criminals are buying...."[24] In addition, authorities extradited two other arch criminals in the Arellano Félix Organization.

In response to these initiatives, U.S. Attorney General Alberto R. Gonzales effused: "Never before has the United States received from Mexico such a large number of major drug defendants and other criminals for prosecution in this country."[25] As mentioned earlier, extraditions are not unalloyed blessings; they often ignite vicious power struggles within the wounded cartel, as well as encroachments from rival criminal organizations.

In July 2007 Santiago Vasconcelos asked Washington to extradite to Mexico Zhenli Ye Gon, who was mentioned in Chapter 5. The affluent Shanghai-born businessman had managed to gain Mexican citizenship several years before he was eligible. Earlier in 2007, U.S. law enforcement agencies discovered that Ye Gon sat on a trove of cash in an opulent Mexico City mansion west of Chapultepec Park. The Americans passed along the information to the PGR, which searched the premises and discovered $227 million in cash and travelers' checks, much of the loot stashed in closets and behind false walls. The U.S. government called it "the largest single drug cash seizure the world has ever seen."[26]

The PGR also found a cache of luxury automobiles, high-powered rifles, and equipment to manufacture amphetamine pills. This wealth undoubtedly came from the importation of pseudoephedrine from China, a decongestant used to manufacture methamphetamines. Ye Gon's import volume exceeded two to three times the country's legitimate needs. Despite a pending arrest warrant, Ye Gon took possession of at least four more large shipments of chemicals through the Pacific port of Lázaro Cárdenas, marketed them to cartels and independent laboratories, obtained government-issued identification papers, and traveled back and forth to the United States at will. He had particularly close relations the Michoacán-based Milenio Cartel. Ye Gon had even found time to lose $126 million playing baccarat at swanky Las Vegas hotels.

His lawyers asserted without proof that "a substantial part" of his cash consisted of funds from Felipe Calderón's National Action Party delivered to Ye Gon's home by campaign officials. In an interview in New York, the chemical importer testified that a Mexican cabinet member, who made a throat-slashing gesture, gave him the option to "cooperate or have his neck slashed" (*"coopelas o cuello"*).[27] On July 23, 2007, DEA agents captured Ye Gon in an Asian restaurant in Wheaton, Maryland, before the suspect could tuck into his meal of codfish and baby carrots. Mexican officials have requested his extradition, and it appears that U.S. prosecutors may comply in view of "evidentiary concerns" that would make Mexico a better place to try him.[28]

During its first two years, the Calderón administration extradited 178 criminals to the United States and other countries—eighty-three in 2007 and ninety-five in 2008. During the same period, Washington surrendered forty-three suspects to Mexico, according to the PGR. On January 1, 2009, Mexicans authorities announced the dispatch of ten leading drug traffickers. These included "El Chuy" Labra Avilés, the erstwhile financial brains of the Arellano Félix Organization; Efraín Pérez Archiniega, arrested in mid-2004 for trafficking and enforcement activities in Tijuana and Ensenada; Jorge "El Macumba" Aureliano Félix, who worked under Pérez Archiniega's supervision; and Armando "The Crazy Duarte" Martínez Duarte, an ex-federal police commander who provided muscle and protection for the AFO in Mexicali.[29]

Hot Spots

Violence is endemic in all Mexican border states—Chihuahua, Baja California, Sonora, Coahuila, Nuevo León, and Tamaulipas—and the murder rate has more than tripled from 732 (2006) to 2,648 in 2008 to upwards of 1,500 during the first seven months of 2009. Chihuahua leads the pack, with a jump from 130 (2006) to 1,652 (2008)—with more than 1,093 deaths through early August 2009. Chihuahua's largest city, Ciudad Juárez, which lies cheek-by-jowl with El Paso, Texas, stands out as a horror spot. Once a watering point for the numerous cattle drives from Chihuahua City to Santa Fe, New Mexico, drovers and their herds would often spend weeks or even months waiting there to cross what was often a raging river. This was truly a town of the Wild West with cattle drives, gunfights, saloons, and bawdy houses. Over the years it has known such notables as Wyatt Earp, Billy the Kid, Sheriff Pat Garrett, and later on Pancho Villa.[30]

Now it is has infamously become Mexico's grisly killing field, especially for young women. "Residents even point out that on a map, it looks like a vulture with its beak stuck under New Mexico, its craggy back pushed up against El Paso and its claws sunk deep into the Mexican state of Chihuahua, [with] soldiers with machine guns stand[ing] guard on the Mexican side of the border bridge, giving Juárez a tense, we-are-not-in-Kansas-anymore feel."[31]

Tijuana competes with Ciudad Juárez as Mexico's most dangerous city. In the 1920s and 1930s, the economy boomed by catering to Americans' insatiable tastes for vice, silver jewelry, and handicrafts. The number of visitors, which spiked at 4.5 million in 2005, often reflected the state of the U.S. economy. The fabled Agua Caliente casino and racetrack thrived during Prohibition and attracted such Hollywood stars as Charlie Chaplin and Gary Cooper. Sailors from San Diego flocked to the city in the post-World War II period. Now Tijuana is a ghost town at night as tourists opt for San Diego's attractions: the Gas Lamp District, Sea World, the San Diego Zoo, or the Hotel del Coronado, where the Marilyn Monroe classic, *Some Like It Hot*, was filmed. Customers are few and far between in the Tijuana's strip clubs—to the point that whores are willing to engage in risky sex. "I'll do that now—let the customer go without a condom—if they pay me an extra $10," Katia, a longtime Tijuana prostitute, said in an interview. "I know I shouldn't, but I need the money."[32]

Even the famous tourist resort of Acapulco—once lauded as the "Pearl of the Pacific"—has been informally renamed *Narcopulco* after numerous murders have befouled the erstwhile Eden where Elizabeth Taylor celebrated one of her many marriages and John Wayne and Tarzan star Johnny Weissmuller threw extravagant soirees at Los Flamingo Hotel. The Sinaloa Cartel traditionally controlled narcotics in Acapulco where rows of 1950s mansions bleed into modest, working-class houses. Drug honchos owned posh, waterfront homes, dined at luxurious bistros, frolicked in the ocean with their wives and children, and assiduously avoided drawing attention to themselves. But open warfare erupted in 2005 when the rival Gulf Cartel sought retaliation for the Sinaloan incursions into Nuevo Laredo and other venues along the Texas border it had claimed for itself. As discussed in Chapter 5, the Gulf Cartel dispatched its paramilitaries, Los Zetas, to gain revenge against their malevolent competitors.[33]

In the words of one reporter: "Assaults on police stations killing seven, a chopped-up body discarded in rubbish bags, three execution-style murders and foreign tourists grazed by bullets: it's been a nasty week in the resort city of Acapulco, defying a much-flaunted crackdown on drug-related violence and delivering a serious blow to Mexico's tourism industry."[34] The two-lane coastal highway between Acapulco and the resort city of Ixtapa-Zihuatenejo pierces verdant mangroves and offers views of spectacular beaches. "It is also one of the country's busiest drug-trafficking corridors."[35]

According to *Latina* magazine's Mariela Rosario, the Beltrán Leyvas, allied with Los Zetas in Guerrero state where Acapulco is located, provoked a June 6, 2009 showdown when Mexican armed forces, acting on a tip, invaded Avenida Rancho Grande—a suspected hideout of Sinaloan cut throats. The soldiers ran headlong into an intensive barrage that lasted two hours. At its conclusion, they had killed sixteen suspected gangsters and had lost two of their own. The Army also seized thirty-six assault rifles, two grenade launchers, thirteen pistols and 3,500 rounds of ammunition from the scene, the Defense Ministry reported.

In retaliation, unidentified trigger-men opened fire on two police stations just days later, killing three more Mexican law enforcement officers. Armed with AK-47s, the gunmen stepped out of two luxury vehicles and began shooting at a police station in the Ciudad Renacimiento neighborhood of Acapulco. A half-hour later, they assaulted another precinct. Since then, soldiers in tanks and helicopters swarmed over the popular tourist destination. After the horrendous effects of the swine flu, the local chamber of commerce worries that the late spring blood bath will hobble the economy of Acapulco and other popular resort areas.

Security Cabinet

To confront the violence, Calderón assembled a more cohesive team than Fox's "Montessori Cabinet," a puckish allusion to its members' preference for self-expression rather than pulling together. Interior Secretary Fernando Gómez Mont, who replaced Juan Camilo Mouriño Terrazo, a member of the Calderón's inner-circle who perished in a November 4, 2008 plane crash, shares responsibility for the anti-drug effort with several colleagues: Attorney General-designate Arturo Chávez Chávez, Public Security Secretary Genaro García Luna, Defense Secretary Galván Galván, and Navy Secretary Mariano Francisco Saynez.

Guillermo Valdés Castellanos, another Calderón confidante, heads the Center for Investigation and National Security (CISEN), a Mexican version of the CIA that falls under the legal rubric of the Interior Ministry but is a de facto dependency of Los Pinos. In early April 2009, Monte Alejandro Rubido García replaced Sigrid Arzt Colunga, an expert in security matters, as technical secretary to the National Security Council. This body is composed of the president, the CISEN director, and nine secretaries, whose ministries are involved in the war against organized crime. For the previous seven months, Rubido García Monte had functioned as executive secretary of the larger National Public Security System, which acts as a liaison between the federal government and state and local officials. He took over that post from political activist Roberto Campa Cifrián in September 2008, only to relinquish it to Jorge E. Tello Peón, who is discussed below. Customs officers, who report to the Finance Ministry, are deployed at borders and at international airports to interdict contraband. The Bank of Mexico also operates its own security division, which is charged with enforcing banking and monetary laws, including counterfeiting, fraud, and money laundering.

While at first exhibiting more harmony than Fox's entourage, intramural skirmishes have occurred. The sensational revelation of Ye Gon's fortune incited jurisdictional tensions between the Attorney General's Office and the Public Security Ministry. Rumors abound that the officer who developed a thick archive on Ye Gon took advantage of this information to blackmail his contacts. Reportedly, José Nemesio Lugo Félix, head of an intelligence unit that focused on cartels, threatened to blow the whistle on his unscrupulous underling. Before he was able to do so, an unidentified gunman killed Lugo Félix on May 15, 2007.

SSP chief García Luna had also crossed swords with Santiago Vasconcelos, who resigned his post in the Attorney General's Office two months before perishing in the same crash that extinguished Mouriño's life and meteoric rise to power. As deputy attorney general in 2005, Vasconcelos claimed that corruption suffused the ranks of Federal Investigative Agency or AFI, then-headed by García Luna. Moreover, Campa Cifrián clashed repeatedly with the secretary of public security before stepping down.

The military has also shown its animus towards García Luna because of his identification with the Fox regime. On April 4, 2008, a spokesman for the secretary reported that two days earlier his agency had spearheaded the capture of ex-GAFES José Alberto Martínez Medrano and four accomplices of Los Zetas, who had had $6 million in their possession. The SSP indicated that it had asked the Army to take custody of the money and weapons seized.

The Defense Ministry immediately disseminated its own communiqué "to clarify" that, in fact, the Army's 5th Motorized Cavalry Regiment had accomplished the April 2 arrest and that the amount seized was $6,110,950. Similar disputes have arisen over anti-drug strikes in Tampico and Colima.[36]

Finance Secretary Agustín Carstens reportedly has warded off García Luna's efforts to take control of his ministry's contingent that investigates money laundering and other financial crimes.

Calderón's naming Gómez Mont as interior minister helped bring discipline to this fractious entourage. A month earlier, the president selected Jorge Tello Peón, a veteran law enforcement expert, as a virtual national security czar. A protégé of intelligence and police guru Jorge Carrillo Olea, Tello Peón was seen as a wunderkind of Mexican security. He participated in the dismantling of the DFS (discussed below), the creation of CISEN, the Planning Center for the Drug Control (CENDRO), an intelligence organ of the PGR, the National Institute to Combat Drugs (INCD), and the Federal Preventative Police (PFP). Except for three years in the Attorney General's Office, he spent seventeen years during his previous two decades in public service in the Interior Ministry. President Fox did not trust security/intelligence mavens, believing they were agents of the PRI. Thus, he had discharged Jorge Tello Peón as undersecretary of public security after El Chapo's dramatic escape from prison in January 2001.

In early December 2008, the Calderón administration appointed General Javier del Real Magallanes, commander of the Army's Fourth Region that embraces Nuevo León, to serve as the SSP's undersecretary for strategy and police intelligence. An ally of Tello Peón, the 63-year-old Real Magallanes gained notoriety as a public security official in Mexico City in 1996 and 1997, when gang members from the dangerous Buenos Aires slum died mysteriously after a crackdown by elite forces.[37]

A month later another general, Alfredo Fregoso Cortéz, was named as coordinator for Regional Security of the PFP, replacing Eduardo Pequeño García, who apparently had been unsuccessful in restructuring the PFP's Anti-drug Division. In this post, Fregoso has responsibility for 8,000 police distributed among thirty-four commands overseeing highways and thirty-two airports.[38] In a move to further strengthen military control over the police, General Rodolfo Cruz López became coordinator of Federal Support Forces of the Federal Police (*Fuerzas de Apoyo de la Policia Federal*), which are responsible for safeguarding strategic installations and spearheading public security operations throughout the country.[39] Cruz López and his squad have been on the scene—or have announced—many recent arrests of cartel gangsters.

The move to shine more sunlight on government operations has taken its toll on security matters. In late 2008, a now-former employee of the Interior Minister apparently placed on the organization's web site information about acquisitions sought by the Center for Investigation and National Security, which Calderón has provided with vastly more resources and personnel. The material included the location of 124 CISEN installations and their configurations. In addition, details appeared about Director Valdés Castellanos' armored vehicle, including its license number, and the spy agency's bids for motorcycles, automobiles, explosive detectors, uniforms, semi-automatic weapons, and a host of other items. Such disclosure was unnecessary inasmuch as the Federal Transparency Law exempts from public bidding goods and services needed for national security.[40] This setback aside, CISEN is creating a new, state-of-the-art training center for its operatives.

Table 6.4
Mexico's Security Cabinet

Position	Incumbent	Date and Place of Birth	Education	Professional Background
Attorney General (PGR)	Arturo Chávez Chávez	Sept. 4, 1960, Chihuahua	Law degree (ITESM, Chihuahua)	PGR delegate in Chihuahua's state atty gen; undersecretary of Interior; good rapport with Mont.
Deputy Attorney General for Judicial and International Affairs	Juan Miguel Alcántara Soria	March 18, 1955, Irapuato, Gto.	Law degree (Escuela Libre de Derecho); post-graduate studies in Madrid (U. of Complutense and Instituto Universitario Ortega y Gasset; diploma in philosophy (U. Panamericana).	Practiced law; attorney general of Guanajuato; Federal deputy (1988-1991; 1997-2000); state legislator (1994-97).
Deputy Attorney General for the Specialized Investigation of Organized Crime (SIEDO)	Marisela Ibánez Morales	March 1, 1970; D.F.	Law degree (UNAM); M.A. (Criminology).	Mexico City Attorney-General's Office, worked closely with Rafael Macedo de la Concha; 1993-97; PGR, 1997-2005.
Secretary of Public Security (SSP)	Genaro García Luna	July 10, 1968, D.F.	Degree in mechanical engineering (Universidad Autónoma Metropolitana).	Director de AFI (2005-06); general coordinator of intelligence for prevention in PFP (1998-2000); CISEN (1989-98).
Subsecretary of SSP for Police Intelligence and Strategy	Gen. Javier del Real Magallanes	Dec. 22, 1944, Zacatecas.	Heroico Colegio Militar; Superior War College (ESG).	Previously commanded the Fourth Military Region (Nuevo León) and Second

Table 6.4 (cont.)

				Military Region (Mexicali); served as head of S-2, the Army's intelligence service, as well as in CISEN.
Coordinator for Regional Security (PFP)	Gen. Alfredo Fregoso Cortéz	Sept. 6, 1945; Jalisco.	Heroico Colegio Militar; Superior War College (ESG).	Various Army posts, including commander of the Fourth Military Zone.
Coordinator of the Federal Support Forces of the Federal Police	Gen. Rodolfo Cruz López	Sept. 11, 1943, Orizaba, Veracruz.	Heroico Colegio Military; Superior War College (ESG).	Various Army posts, including group commander of the Seventh Military Region.
Secretary of National Defense (SEDENA)	Gen. Guillermo Galván Galván	Jan. 19, 1943, D.F.	Heroico Colegio Militar; Superior War College (ESG).	Various Army commands.
Secretary of the Navy (SEMAR)	Adm. Mariano Francisco Saynez Mendoza	Sept. 20, 1942, Veracruz, Veracruz.	Heroica Escuela Naval Militar.	Various naval commands.
Secretary of Interior (SEGOB)	Fernando Francisco Gómez Mont	Jan. 11, 1963, D.F.	Law degree (Escuela Libre de Derecho).	Son of PAN founder; federal deputy (1991-94); Zedillo wanted to name him attorney general, but Gómez Mont had not reached the minimum age, 35; resigned position on PAN executive committee to devote himself to his prestigious law firm, Zínser Esponda y Gómez Mont; defended such controversial clients as Carlos and Raúl

Table 6.4 (cont.)

				Salinas, former PEMEX Director Rogelio Montemayor, and Channel 40 against TV Azteca.
Director of Center for Research on National Security (CISEN)	Guillermo Valdés Castellanos	May 24, 1955, Guadalajara, Jalisco.	Degree social sciences (ITAM) Positions in the ministries of social development, planning and budget, and education; director of GEA-ISA; and confidant of the president.	Adviser to his friend Calderón in the presidential campaign; director of polling and consulting company, GEA-ISA; held positions in the ministries of Social Development, Planning and Budget, and Public Education.
Executive Secretary of Mexico's National Public Security System (SNSP) Composed of the president, the attorney general, the 32 governors, and the secretaries of interior (who presides), public security, national defense, and Navy (As part of the Crime Prevention Strategy,	Jorge Enrique Tello Peón	May 22, 1956; Yucatán	Degree in civil engineering (UAM); M.A. in hydrology (UNAM); and M.A. in public administration (CIDE).	In the course of 17 years in the Interior Ministry and the PGR, he participated in the design and creation of CISEN, CENDRO, INCD, FEADS, and the PFP; from 2001 to 2008 served as a vice president for security at CEMEX.

Table 6.4 (cont.)

the secretaries of education, health, social development, and communi- cations and transport may meet with the CNSP.				
Technical Secretary of National Public Security Council (CNSP) Composed of the president, the attorney general, CISEN, and the secretaries of interior, public security, national defense, navy, foreign relations, finance, public function, and communication and transport.	Monte Alejandro Rubido García	Jan. 27, 1954; D.F.	Law degree (UNAM); and graduate study at the Sorbonne.	Executive secretary of the National System of Public Security/SNSP (September 2008- April 2009); Subsecretary of SSP; secretary for Prevención, Vinculación and Human Rights; and technical secretary of CISEN's council; and CISEN's director of strategic studies.

Notes

1.   Lacey, "In Drug War, Mexico Fights the Cartels and Itself." The Gulf Cartel had reportedly taken out a contract on Calderón's life; see, Steve Fainaru and William Booth, "As Mexico Battles Cartels, the Army Becomes the Law," *Washington Post*, April 2, 2009.
2.   Quoted in Fainaru and Booth, "As Mexico Battles Cartels, the Army Becomes the Law."
3.   *Reforma* presents weekly updates on the number of narco-casualties in each states, as well as nationwide.
4.   In the wake of the threat, the *San Antonio Express-News* temporarily reassigned its Laredo correspondent; see, Jose Simon and Carlos Lauría, "Mexican President Must Protect Freedom of Expression," *San Francisco Chronicle*, July 23, 2007.
5.   "Shocking Culture of Impunity and Violence" *www.freemedia.at/cms/ipi/statements_detail.html?ctxid=CH0055&...&year=2008*.
6.   "The Dilemma Mexican Journalists Face: Self-censorship, Exile or Certain Death," *Mexidata.info*, January 26, 2009.
7.   International Pen, "Mexico: Editor Abducted and Shot Dead," October 15, 2008. *www.internationalpen.org.uk.*
8.   "Mexico-Media Safety: Police Assault and Threaten Three Journalists, IFEX, March 19, 2009. *www.newssafety.org.*
9.   "Por qué se fue Alejandro Junco," *Reporte Indigo*, September 12, 2008. *www.reporteindigo.com.*
10.   "Amenaza narco a periodistas y soldados," *Reforma.com*, May 28, 2009.
11.   Elisabeth Malkin, "Mexico: Arrests in Reporter's Death," *New York Times*, June 13, 2009.
12.   "Secuestran a dos personas al día en promedio: PGR," *El Imparcial* (Hermosillo), September 15, 2008.
13.   Researchers at Mexico's National Autonomous University (UNAM) reported a 90 percent non-reporting rate; see Barnard R. Thompson, "Kidnappings are out of Control in Mexico," *Mexidata.Info*, June 14, 2004 www.mexidata.info.
14.   Zemi Communications, "Mexico, Politics and Policy," September 9-15, 2008; and Icela Lagunas, "Los siete pétalos de 'La Flor,'" *El Universal*, December 2, 2008.
15.   The quotations appeared in "Over 150,000 March in Mexico against Crime," *Reuters*, August 31, 2008.
16.   Quoted in Mark Stevenson, "Mexico Outraged over Corrupt Police, Kidnappings," *Associated Press*, August 21, 2008.
17.   Reed Johnson, "Mexico Unveils Anti-kidnapping Measures," *Los Angeles Times* ("La Plaza" Blog), August 12, 2008.
18.   The material in this section, including quotations, benefits from William Booth, "Mexico Kidnapping Death Stokes Outrage," *Washington Post*, December 14, 2008.
19.   Quoted in Solutions Abroad, "Kidnappings in Mexico" *www.solutionsabroad.com/en./security.*
20.   William Booth, "Kidnap Consultant Taken in Mexico," *Washington Post*, December 16, 2008, A15.
21.   "Detienen a presunto plagiario de Batista," *Reforma*, April 25, 2009.
22.   Rodrigo León and Alejandro Moreno, "Encuesta/Destacan el crimen," *Reforma*, January 1, 2009.
23.   The Federal Investigations Agency (AFI) replaced the extremely corrupt Federal Judicial Police (PJF) in 2002.

24.   Quoted in Andrés Oppenheimer, *Bordering on Chaos: Guerrillas, Stockbrokers, Politicians, and Mexico's Road to Prosperity* (Boston: Little Brown and Co., 1996): 298.
25.   James C. McKinley Jr., "Mexico Sends 4 Kingpins to Face Trial in the U.S., *New York Times*, January 21, 2007, p. 15; Héctor Tobar, "Drug Kingpin Extraditions Will Likely Help Calderón," *Los Angeles Times*, January 22, 2007.
26.   Paul Duggan and Ernesto Londoño, "Not Your Average Drug Bust; Suspect Wanted in Mexico Found in Wheaton Restaurant," *Washington Post*, July 25, 2007.
27.   Ricardo Ravelo, "Cómplices, encubridores, beneficiarios...," *Proceso*, July 8, 2007.
28.   Del Quentin Wilber, "Justice Dept. Wants Charges against Mexican Man Dropped," *Washington Post*, June 23, 2009.
29.   Greg Moran and Sandra Dibble, "U.S. Given Four Ranking Drug Cartel Members," *San Diego Union Tribune*, January 1, 2009.
30.   *History of Ciudad Juárez. http://www.blines.com/page2.html.*
31.   Jason Beaubien, "Economy, Drug Wars Hurt Cross-Border Business," *Morning Edition*, National Public Radio, December 4, 2008. *www.npr.com.*
32.   Quoted in Manuel Roig-Franzia, "Tijuana Strip Turns Ghostly in Wake of Drug Violence," *Washington Post*, June 16, 2008; and "A Real Tijuana Hangover," *Los Angeles Times*, February 17, 2008.
33.   Indira A.R. Lakshmanan, "Drug-related Violence Moves into Acapulco," *Boston Globe*, July 30, 2006. *www.bostonglobe.com.*
34.   Jo Tuckman, "Drug Wars Cast a Long Shadow over Acapulco's Future," *The Guardian*, February 10, 2007.
35.   Fainaru and Booth, "As Mexico Battles Cartels, the Army Becomes the Law."
36.   Fred Álvarez P., "Fue sedena, no SSP," April 5, 2008. *www.fredalvarez.blogspot.com/2008/04/fue-sedena-no-ssp.html.*
37.   The Buenos Aires episode took place on September 8, 1997; see, "Tuvo General paso polémico por la SSP-DF," *Reforma*, December 6, 2008.
38.   Luis Brito, "Refuerzan PFP con otro General," *Reforma*, December 19, 2008.
39.   Agencia Reforma, "México: Refuerzan Policía Federal con otro general," *La Estrella Digital*, December 19, 2008 *www.disariolaestrella.com;* and "Fusiona la SSP a PFP y la AFI," *El Mañana*, April 4, 2008.
40.   "Balconea Segob autos, casas y armas del Cisen," *Milenio.com*, May 12, 2009.

7

Crusade against Evil Antagonists

In contrast with the ineffectual policies of Zedillo and Fox, Felipe Calderón has sent more than 40,000 federal police and troops to combat the insidious lawbreakers. The early deployments or "operations" averaged 2,000 federal police and military personnel. He has also dispatched units to many more areas of the country and did so without notifying the mayor (Tijuana) or governors (Michoacán, Guerrero, etc.) in advance of the strikes. This was an about-face and a more focused strategy than the one used by his predecessor. Vicente Fox continuously altered priorities in what had more in common with a "flavor of the month" style of making decisions. In the face of the mounting body count, in 2005 he unveiled his *"Plan México Seguro"* ("Safe Mexico Plan") with the dispatch of forces to Nuevo León, Tijuana, and Acapulco. But Fox's defense secretary did not want to involve the Army in interrogations, nor assign it to guarding checkpoints and conducting searches. He argued that "drug work would inevitably discredit the armed forces, and feared that the soldiers would become abusive after months of being stationed in impoverished areas and subject to elevated stress and boredom."[1] Instead, the military was assigned to tasks of interdiction, crop eradication, and intelligence gathering. Vicente Fox shied from a scorched-earth policy in the run-up to the bitterly contested 2006 presidential contest. In contrast, Calderón zeroed in immediately on the crime issue, accentuating his determination to "take back the country from criminals."

Failure of Government Officials

In reaction to a palpable, deep-seated outrage against rising violence, Calderón used his September 1, 2008 state of the national address to reaffirm his commitment to the battle. "I wish to tell you that my Government will continue working every day to find and apply solutions for the issues that most worry you and your family. The goals of transforming

Mexico require the effort and commitment of all. We have problems, yes; we are confronting them, and we are going to overcome them and move ahead."[2]

While nodding approval, moguls in the audience continued to fork over millions of pesos for armored cars, skilled drivers, bodyguards, weapons, alarm systems, sophisticated locks, security consultants, microchip implantations in family members and executives, and other protective devices.

The chief executive's optimistic words aside, lawmakers seemed to pursue "*Populismo Penal*" ("Punishment Populism"); namely, posturing in a get-tough stance rather than developing proposals that transcend rhetoric and actually get tough on crime. To its credit, Congress did approve a bill, which became effective in late August 2009, that allows authorities to seize and dispose of the assets of "everyone connected to the commission of a crime." The legislators also extended jurisdiction over drug-related offenses—once the sole responsibility of federal authorities—to state and local law enforcement agencies. In addition, it approved a constitutional amendment to revamp the judicial system, which is examined later in this chapter.

Interior Secretary Gómez Mont presides over the National Public Security Council (CNSP), which also encompasses the secretary of national defense, the secretary of the navy, the secretary of communications and transport, the attorney general, the mayor of Mexico City, and the thirty-one governors. Its purpose is to coordinate the police activities in the various jurisdictions among which there is, at best, a modest exchange of information and intelligence.

The CNSP has considered imposing life-in-prison sentences for malefic acts, compensating kidnap victims' families, outlawing payments to kidnappers, combating corruption, encouraging neighborhood-watch groups, cleaning up the judiciary, offering anonymity (and even stipends) to informants, tracking the numbers of cell phones used in the commission of felonies, and, in accord with recent legislation, confiscating the property of criminals and their enablers.

These and other proposals were embedded in the "A National Accord for Legality, Justice and Security." This anti-crime pact, was subscribed to on August 21, 2008, by all the governors, Mexico City's mayor, and representatives of the Church, trade unions, the private sector, the mass media, and non-governmental organizations (NGOs). This document stated, in part, that: "the Mexican society is profoundly disturbed by the impunity, corruption, lack of coordination among authorities, as well as the [prevailing] climate of violence and insecurity." The signers also affirmed that: "the State and society face a critical situation arising as much from common criminal activities, which threatens families every day, as from the attacks of organized crime, which is a complex phenomenon … that transcends borders."[3]

One hundred days after signing the accord, Calderón evaluated how it had functioned. He noted a slight decline in kidnappings—to 237, of which Mexico State (100), the D.F. (24), and Michoacán (17) led the country. He also emphasized the break-up of fifty-three dangerous kidnapping gangs, the smashing of a La Familia cell in Ecatepec, the liberation of 184 kidnap victims, the seizure of La Flor leader along with Fernando Martí's presumed abductor Lorena González, and the arrest of Zeta big shot Jaime "El Hummer" González Durán. During this period, authorities also took into custody Jesús "The King" Zambada and fifteen Sinaloa Cartel gangsters, the Gulf Cartel's purported Reynosa chief Antonio "The Yellow One" Galarza Coronado, and cartel spies who had infiltrated the security bureaucracy. In addition, the Army had commandeered $26.2 million from the home of El Mayo Zambada in Culiacán; and, in Reynosa, it seized the largest arms' stockpile in Mexico's history—288 assault rifles, 126 pistols, a rocket grenade launcher, 287 grenades, and 428,000 rounds of ammunition.

On the negative side of the ledger were the following entries:

* The September 15 grenade attack in Morelia;
* 1,561 executions (seventy-four of which involved multiple victims);
* Six group kidnappings;
* Assaults on consulates, newspaper offices, businesses, and police headquarters;
* Uprisings in a dozen prisons and jails;
* The proliferation of "narco-messages" mainly through hundreds of banners;
* The execution of the mayor of Ixtapan de la Sal, México State; and
* The slaying of 114 police officers (twenty federal, fifty-three state, and forty-one municipal cops), fifteen members of the armed forces, and two journalists.[4]

Although the national government provided no comparable data, Mexico City officials reported a surge in criminality—with the number of street crimes increasing from 13,921 in July to 15,626 in October 2008. In this period, robberies rose from 7,680 to 8,469[5]—a figure likely to grow because of the economic recession.

Roman Catholic Church

The Roman Catholic Church has also weighed in on the surge in narcotics-related bloodshed. Bishop Gian-Franco Girotti, director of the Vatican's Apostolic Penitentiary (the papal board that has responsibility for questions of repentance), has reviled the consumption and sale of drugs as "capital sins."

Nonetheless, various figures in Mexico's clergy have shown ambivalence toward the narco churches, thus posing a dilemma for President Calderón. The government spends billions of dollars on anti-poverty and community development programs such as OPORTUNIDADES, SEDESOL, and PROCAMPO. Meanwhile, the drug-traffickers provide gifts to children, assist victims of natural disasters, generate employment in poor areas, and make generous donations to the Church.

In 1997 Raúl Soto Vázquez, the canon of the Basilica of Guadalupe, raised eyebrows in a homily when he suggested that more Mexicans should follow the example of kingpins Rafael Caro Quintero and Amado Carrillo Fuentes, who had made offerings of millions of pesos.[6] When politicians alleged that the cleric was stamping his approval on drug activities, the Church's first response was that it was the duty of authorities, not religious organizations, to investigate the origin of funds placed in its coffers. Father Alberto Athié, executive secretary of the Social Pastoral Committee of the Episcopate, affirmed that the hierarchy does not accept donations from the "culture of death" and that the government was free to audit its accounts.[7]

Church-narco ties had previously elicited attention in the 1990s when photographs were published of Amado Carrillo Fuentes visiting the Holy Land in the company of Father Ernesto Álvarez Valenzuela of Culiacán and Father Benjamín Olivas. Álvarez Valenzuela justified his action as a token of appreciation for the drug baron's generosity to the Ciudad de los Niños (City of Children), an orphanage in the Sinaloa state capital.[8]

The bishop of Aguascalientes, Ramón Godínez Flores, has developed a latter-day theory of medieval alchemy; namely, that ill-gotten funds contributed for the Church's social mission can magically be transmuted into legitimate resources.[9]

Carlos Aguiar Retes, bishop of Texcoco and president of the Mexican Episcopal Conference, raised the possibility that the government recruit as "counterspies" narco-traffickers who confess their sins and abandon wayward lives in order to gather intelligence about cartels. "They are very generous with the people in their communities, and in general they install electricity, telecommunications, highways, roads, paid for by them," Aguiar Retes affirmed. The narcos should be afforded a way of starting a new life through a witness protection program similar to the one in Colombia, he suggested.[10] He also cited the example of Colombia, where guerrillas who had deserted the FARC assisted in the rescue of former presidential candidate Ingrid Betancourt.

In early March 2009, the six Chihuahua bishops exhorted criminals to stop "staining our Patria and our state with blood," adding:

> We invite those implicated in violence to consider that no one's life should be taken. We cry with the hearts of pastors: repent and change your life. God is disposed to pardon you, but this pardon carries with it the obligation to step back, repair the damage you have done and cease committing murders.[11]

The murder of Cardinal Posadas Ocampo provoked vexing questions about the Church's relationship with the underworld. One of the investigators in the case, sociologist Fernando M. González, described a subterranean "narco-catholic culture" among the Tijuana clergy. "This culture was sustained by close relationships between the drug lords and the priests in which the clergy administered the sacraments to the bosses and their families, and in turn received large donations without ever asking where they came from."[12]

In July 1994 Archbishop Girolamo Prigione, the Machiavellian papal nuncio to Mexico, admitted private conversations with both Ramón and Benjamín Arellano Félix. He used his entrée to Los Pinos to pass along to President Salinas a message from the pious delinquents. At first, Prigione agreed to cooperate with law enforcement agents, but later reversed his decision, inferring that he could not violate the privacy of their confessions. Father Gerardo Montaño Rubio, who facilitated the meeting between nuncio and the Arellano Félix brothers, received large sums from the clan to finance an ostentatious Seminario del Río in Tijuana.[13] *El Financiero* quoted Tijuana priest Isidro Puente as saying that Montaño Rubio had "organized trips for seminarians to homes of the rich drug lords with swimming pools and tennis courts."[14]

In mid-April 2009 Héctor González Martínez, the archbishop of Durango, stirred media frenzy by indicating that "everyone knows," except the authorities, that fugitive El Chapo Guzmán lives in Guanaceví, a mining village in northwest Durango. Wedged between Sinaloa and Chihuahua and lying atop Zacatecas, this state is prized by cartels for its smuggling trails through the forbidding Eastern Sierra Madres en route to the U.S. The archbishop asserted that the criminals had incited a "chaotic psychosis" in San Bernardo, El Oro, Santiago Papasquiaro, Pueblo Nuevo, Tepehuanes, and other municipalities near Giamacevî.[15]

A few days after González Martínez' pronouncement, hit men seized two undercover Army intelligence agents in Durango, tied their arms, taped their eyes shut, and riddled their bodies with AK-47 shells. They left behind a taunting note, saying: "You'll never get El Chapo—not the priests, not the government."[16] Even in the wake of these executions Durango's archbishop refused to accept protection from the government, expressing a readiness to confront the gangsters even if they killed him.

In reaction to the archbishop's statement, Durango's PAN president maintained that a form of "parallel state" existed in which criminals carried out traditional government functions such as collecting taxes (in the form of extortion) and providing security (in return for payments).[17]

Faustino Armendáriz Jiménez, bishop of Matamoros, indirectly criticized his fellow cleric by averring that all priests should exercise "prudence when voicing opinions, especially if they can't back them up."[18]

Mons. Raul Vera López, the progressive bishop of Saltillo, disagreed. He castigated Calderón's "famous" war on drugs and insisted that the people live in a "state of pure terrorism." He bemoaned the "impunity" enjoyed by the cartels and urged the ouster of public officials linked to "narco-trafficking."[19] He may have been referring obliquely to the PRI's 2009 gubernatorial nominee in Colima state, outgoing Colima city mayor Mario Anguiano Moreno, who became a brunt of criticism: his brother Humberto, known as "The Frog," is serving a ten-year sentence in Mexico for selling methamphetamines; his first cousin Rafael Anguiano Chávez was sentenced to twenty-seven years behind bars in the United States for the same offense. Both men reportedly worked with the Amecua brothers, leaders of the Colima Cartel, to which the family of the outgoing Colima governor is allegedly connected.

José Guadalupe Martín Rábago, the archbishop of León, lamented that cartels had also invaded Guanajuato, producing "the same dynamic of violence that has engulfed the majority of states of the Republic …."

He rendered this *cri de coeur* following a late June 2009 confrontation between Los Zetas (and their allies) and elements of the Army, Federal Police, and state police. This battle took place in Apaseo El Alto, and ended with the death of twelve narco-criminals, and the capture of a dozen more culprits. At least six of the delinquents were Zetas.[20]

Non-Christian Religious Icons

For all of these men, and for other narco-traffickers, religious figures loom large in their lives. Whether involved in licit or illicit activities, an overwhelming majority of the population resonates to the message of the Virgin of Guadalupe whose basilica attracts 20 million visitors each year. Mobsters are pathologically afraid of dying, and like many other Mexicans are deeply afraid of the consequences for their worldly actions throughout eternity. While many are *guadalupanos* and contribute to the Catholic Church, they cover all of their bets and rely on other religious figures to protect them.

Jesús Malverde has become most famously identified as "The Narco Saint."[21] During the dictatorship of Porfirio Díaz (1877-1911), bandits flourished in Mexico's mountains and back roads. The light-skinned, mustachioed Jesús Malverde became a folk hero because, like Robin Hood, he allegedly stole from the rich and gave to the poor. His admirers insist that the agents of the caudillo hung the bandit and left him to rot on May 3, 1909, the anniversary of which is celebrated every year at the Malverde shrine and chapel in Culiacán. Historians have found no concrete evidence that Malverde existed, and he is likely the amalgam of two outlaws—Heraclio Bernal from western Sinaloa and Felipe Bachomo from the north. "If he lived, faith in him is a remarkable thing," said dramatist Sergio López, who has written and researched the life of Malverde. "If he never lived, it's even more remarkable because people have created this thing to achieve the justice that is denied them." Journalist and author Sam Quiñones reports that: "Smugglers come to ask Malverde for protection before sending a load [of drugs] north. If the trip goes well, they return to pay the shine's house band to serenade the bandit, or place a plaque thanking Malverde for 'lighting the way'...."[22]

In addition to Malverde, narco-traffickers seek the good offices of *Santísima Muerte* (Saint Death), especially in Tepito in the heart of Mexico City's thieves market and along the border with the United States. She takes the form of a clothed skeleton squeezing a scythe with her bony hand, who—from a distance—may resemble the Virgin of Guadalupe. "The narco-traffickers have always been very religious; they are no atheists." To the contrary, they are extremely superstitious said University of Nuevo León psychologist José María Infante. "She [*Santísima Muerte*] is a figure who accords with their activities where life and death are closely intertwined," he added.[23] As journalist Reed Johnson reported: "In the tough Tepito neighborhood [of Mexico City], where poverty, corruption and violence are daily realities, there is a beloved 'saint' who understands and forgives the frailties of all human flesh. Her domain is a labyrinth of grimy streets lined with auto body shops and humble mom-and-pop stores. From her perch behind a glass-encased altar adorned with candles, decayed flowers and shot glasses of tequila, she watches scruffy curs pick through garbage while a constant stream of pilgrims lays offerings at her feet."[24]

In March 2009 chapels built to venerate Malverde and Santísima Muerte were bulldozed in Tijuana. Devotees pledged to rebuild the shrines. While Mayor Jorge Ramos Hernández denied any role in leveling the crude structures, he expressed opposition to anything that promoted "narcoviolence" in the city. A similar sentiment lay behind the government's decision to deploy backhoes to crush more than thirty shrines of the robe-covered skeleton spread throughout the border city of Nuevo Laredo. David Romo, founder and high priest of the Santísima Muerte church urged his 5 million followers to take to the streets to protest "religious intolerance."[25]

It's not just religious figures who give rise to myths. Pancho Villa, born Doroteo Arango, earned fame because he continuously eluded the punitive expedition of General John J. "Blackjack" Pershing after the hard-riding freedom fighter attacked Columbus, New Mexico, in March 1916. Some nine decades later, El Chapo Guzmán shares elements of a mythic image similar to the revolutionary hero. El Chapo is every-where—but nowhere. One of his *corridos* or ballads alludes to hiding in caves, something that Pancho Villa was forced to do in the declining years of his influence. The authorities seem unable to capture El Chapo. Some observers have suggested that his birth on Christmas Day invested him with supernatural powers.

El Chapo and fellow thugs have increasingly found their way into an emerging genre of "narco-literature," which includes such books as Élmer Mendoza's *El Amante de Janis Joplin* or *Un asesino solitario*, Leonardo Alfaro's *Tierra Blanca*, Eduardo Antonio Parra's *Nostalgia de la sobra*, Juan José Rodríguez's *Mi nombre es Casablanca*, and Martín Solares' *Los minutos negros*.[26]

A Colombia-produced soap opera—*El Cartel de los Sapos* [translated as The Cartel of Traitors]—garnered a large audience in Mexico and served to whet interest in criminal activity. It remains to be seen if Mexican production companies will venture into the field of "narco-novels."

Vocalists, bandas, and tambora bands have created best-selling *narco-corridos*, which not only venerate drug lords but provide a form of popular "musical newspaper."[27] Artists who cater to one criminal group risk revenge by its enemies. Los Zetas gunned down Valentín "El Gallo de Oro" Elizalde after a November 2006 concert in Reynosa. Assassins of the "The Golden Rooster" struck because the star performer had sung *A Mis Amigos*, which supposedly represented an anti-Zeta threat from El Chapo Guzmán Loera. The *Arizona Daily Star* reported the death of Sergio Gómez, 34, founder of the popular group K-Paz de la Sierra, which features fast-paced drums and brass horns. A Chicago resident, Gómez disregarded warnings not to perform in his native state of Michoacán before being abducted and murdered. The same week gangsters shot and killed Zayda Peña of Zayda y Los Culpables in a hospital in Matamoros. Samuel González Ruiz, former chief of a federal organized crime unit, said: "The cartels don't care about how they are seen by the public, they are worried about showing their absolute control of their territory, and they will impose their control at all costs ... [killing a singer] is like planting the flag of their cartel in the ground."

Operation House-Cleaning (Operación Limpieza)

Some government officials may depend on divine intervention, but others take no chances and safeguard themselves through bribes. In mid-2008 a protected witness in the U.S. fingered the head of the PGR's unit for the Specialized Investigation of Organized Crime (SIEDO), Noë Ramírez Mandujano as someone on the Beltran Leyvas' payroll. In pursuing his mandate, Ramírez Mandujano had concentrated his investigations on the Gulf Cartel and Los Zetas, to the exclusion of any Sinaloans.[28] On July 31, 2008, Medina Mora named Marisela Morales Ibáñez to replace the low-profile official, who was dispatched as the PGR representative to the United Nations Office on Drugs and Crime in Vienna, Austria. Morales Ibáñez had worked extremely closely with Vicente Fox's first attorney general, General Rafael Macedo de la Concha, and has been praised from domestic and foreign observers for her no-nonsense, take-charge approach. Two of her top assistants are Nicandra Castro Escarpulli, who remains head of the PGR's Special Kidnapping Investigation Unit, and Irving Barrios Mojica, one of several general coordinators of SIEDO.

In late summer 2008, his adversaries attempted to oust Medina Mora. The attorney general told President Calderón that he could accept his resignation at any time. During that same meeting, Medina Mora presented the chief executive with evidence from a protected witness with the code name "Felipe" that Ramírez Mandujano had collected some $450,000 in bribes from the Beltrán Leyva brothers to provide information and advance notice about government probes. Santiago Vasconcelos, who previously directed SIEDO, and Public Security Secretary García Luna had recommended Ramírez Mandujano for the PGR post.

Calderón reaffirmed his confidence in Medina Mora, who then sought a subtle means to lure Ramírez Mandujano back into the country without arousing the suspicion of the iguana-eyed former SIEDO chief. Under this pretext, the attorney general instructed all PGR attachés to attend a two-day session in Mexico City beginning on November 18, 2008.[29] The purported reason for the meeting was to improve coordination between the Attorney General's Office and law enforcement organizations in the countries where attachés were currently assigned. While present for the first day of the program and the next morning session, Ramírez Mandujano failed to return after lunch on the second day. Speaking off the record, another attaché remembered thinking: "This guy is really smart; he's dining in an upscale restaurant rather than eating government-provided food." The PGR announced his arrest two days later.

Morales Ibáñez played a key role in "Operation House-Cleaning," designed to uproot other insiders who were supplying cartels with information about the administration's anti-drug strategy. This initiative, which focused on high-level government corruption, yielded impressive results. Not only was Ramírez Mandujano charged with accepting jumbo-sized payoffs, but other law enforcement personnel stood accused of collaborating with the Sinaloan gangsters.

Debauchery that would make Roman emperor Claudius blush characterizes Mexico's drug environment. In October 2008 100 ski-masked federal police stormed the opulent mansion of a Colombian cocaine drug merchant known as "El Cornejo" or "the Rabbit." The raid interrupted a lavish party complete with bountiful supplies of cocaine, high-end prostitutes, free-flowing alcohol, a movie theater, an arsenal of assault rifles embellished with diamonds and gold, and crocodiles and a hippopotamus sculpted from glass and cement. These creatures may have been statues, but real animals also roamed a faux-jungle complex of caves, pools, and pagodas. An in-house zoo held two African lions, two white tigers, and two black jaguars. "Very Noah-like. Each pair was a male and female. There was also a monkey, sans partner."[30] Law enforcement agents invited in the media to document the "narco fantasia," as one publication called it.

That was the bowdlerized account of the episode. A few days later another version emerged:

The *federales*, it turns out, had turned the takedown into a violent shakedown. According to witnesses, the police burst into the mansion screaming, 'Fucking bitches! Daughters of whores! Now the real party has begun!' For the next 24 hours, the cops went on a crime spree of their own. They pocketed Cartier and Rolex watches, diamond rings, [and] mounds of pesos. They stole a honey–colored English bulldog, which was carried to the back seat of an armored police car. They dragged the prostitutes into the screening room and administered electric shocks to the men. Then they filled the swimming pool with ice and forced the men into the freezing water, as a way of extracting names and addresses from them—not to arrest other traffickers, but simply so police could be dispatched to their residences to steal from them as well. All told, seven houses were robbed of nearly $600,000. One narco was instructed to come up with half a million dollars in cash, which was stuffed into two Winnie the Pooh bags for delivery to the officer in charge of the raid.[31]

It turned out that PFP Commissioner Víctor Gerardo Garay Cadena threw himself into the sybaritic environment with reckless abandon. While awaiting the arrival of the hush money, he selected four of the thirty prostitutes and retired to a room in the basement designed to look like a cave. As he cavorted with the women in a heated Jacuzzi, he ordered one of his bodyguards to bring a portion of the seized cocaine. It was "for the whores," the police commissioner explained. In the morning, discarded condoms covered the floor of the cave. By then, the police were focused more on looting than making arrests. They did capture fifteen alleged traffickers and released nine Mexicans working as waiters and disc jockeys, but the Rabbit scampered away. A gardener detained with the others swore that the police threatened to feed him to lions and tigers during the bust.[32]

DFS and PGR: Source of Original Sin for Law Enforcement Agencies

In most cases there is little evidence of a successful housecleaning, but Operation House-Cleaning yielded large dividends. The U.S. hailed Calderón's commitment to stamping out organized crime. Some 15 percent of $400 million in the initial antinarcotics aid to Mexico—called the Mérida Initiative (addressed in Chapter 9)—was earmarked to cleanse and professionalize Mexico's police forces. But Edgardo Buscaglia, a visiting professor of law and economics at Mexico's Autonomous Institute of Technology, has misgivings about initiatives such as the House-Cleaning venture. He believe they are only a response to pressure from wealthy Mexicans—many of whom have had children kidnapped in recent months—and do not represent an overall and comprehensive strategy that will strike police corruption at its roots.

Mexico is encouraging state and municipal authorities to use various methods—background checks, polygraph examinations, scrutiny of as-

Table 7.1
Major Apprehensions Arising from Operation House-Cleaning

Suspect	Position	Date of Capture	Alleged Crime(s)	Status
Noë Ramírez Mandujano	PGR delegate in Vienna; former head of SIEDO	November 20, 2008	Received more than $450,000 from Beltrán Leyva brothers over a two-year period	Western Federal Penitentiary "El Rincón" (Nayarit)
Miguel Colorado González	General Technical Coordinator (SIEDO)	July 2008	Spied since 1997 for the Beltrán Leyva brothers	In custody; U.S. is seeking his extradition
Víctor Gerardo Garay Cadena	Ex-PFP chief, who had been in charge of the Group of Special Operations	December 4, 2008	Organized crime, robbery, abuse of authority, and to furnish protection to the Beltrán Leyvas	Western Federal Penitentiary "El Rincón" (Nayarit)
Jorge Cruz Méndez	PFP	November 2008	Organized crime and crimes against health; protection of Jesús " El Rey" Zambada's criminal organization	Western Federal Penitentiary "El Rincón" (Nayarit)
Fernando Rivera Hernández	Adjunct Director of Intelligence in Technical Coordination (SIEDO)	July 31, 2008	Organized crime and crimes against health	Western Federal Penitentiary "Puente Grande" (Jalisco)
Édgar Enrique Bayardo del Villar	Former deputy attorney general in Tlaxcala; ex-head of PFP in Guerrero; and PFP anti-drug agent	October 20, 2008	Organized crime and presumably supplying information about police movements to "El Rey" Zambada	Protected Witness

Table 7.1 (cont.)

Ricardo Gutiérrez Vargas	PFP and ex-director of Interpol in Mexico	November 16, 2008	Organized crime and crimes against health; spied for the Beltrán Leyva brothers	Western Federal Penitentiary "El Rincón" (Nayarit)
Rodolfo de la Guardia García Deployment (AFI)	Director of Regional	October 29, 2008	Between 2003 and 2005 maintained contacts with organized criminal groups that gave him monthly payments in dollars for information about anti-drug activities	Western Federal Penitentiary "El Rincón" (Nayarit)
Arturo González Rodríguez	Major (EMP)	December 26, 2008	Received $100,000 monthly from Beltrán Leyva brothers	Western Federal Penitentiary "El Rincon" (Nayarit)— until freed by a judge on March 12, 2009
Francisco Navarro Espinosa	General director of special operations for Coordination of Federal Support Forces	November 2008	Organized crime, robbery, abuse of authority, and furnished protection to the Beltrán Leyvas	Western Federal Penitentiary "El Rincón" (Nayarit)
Javier Herrera Valles	Ex-coordinator of regional security (PFP)	November 17, 2008	Receipt of $35,000 every 15 days to protect a cartel plaza in Tabasco; also involved in criminal activity in Guerrero where he had been previously assigned (groups not specified)	Western Federal Penitentiary "El Rincón" (Nayarit)

Table 7.1 (cont.)

Marco Antonio Valadez Rico	Deputy inspector (PFP/SSP)	October 20, 2008	Organized crime, crimes against health, and possession of unauthorized firearms; captured with "El Rey" Zambada García	Central Federal Penitentiary Almoloya de Juárez (Mexico State) Formerly La Palma
Carlos Gerardo Castillo Ramírez	Agent (AFI/SSP)	October 20, 2008	Organized crime, crimes against health, and possession of unauthorized firearms; captured with "El Rey" Zambada García	Central Federal Penitentiary Almoloya de Juárez (Mexico State) Formerly La Palma
José Guillermo Báez Figueroa	Agent (PFP/SSP)	October 20, 2008	Organized crime, crimes against health, and possession of unauthorized firearms; captured with "El Rey" Zambada García	Central Federal Penitentiary Almoloya de Juárez (Mexico State) Formerly La Palma

Sources: "Detenido el jefe de Interpol México en el marco de la 'Operación Limpieza,'" *El Periódico.com/Internacional*, November 18, 2008; Silber Meza, "'Imita' Sinaloa Operación Limpieza," *Noroeste.com*, November 23, 2008; and PGR, "Se Libran y Cumplén Órdenes de Aprehensión," *Boletín 980/08*, December 5, 2008.

sets, and competency tests—in return for increased federal funding. Of more the more than 56,065 officers in state and municipalities tested since January 1, 2008, approximately one half failed the competency assessment.[33] Even though U.S. law enforcement agencies vet high-level Mexican officials with whom they are willing to share information, leaks continue. Nevertheless, Calderón trumpeted the imposition of fines on 11,500 public servants, totaling nearly $300 million during his two years in office at the UN-sponsored International Anti-Corruption Day celebrated on December 9, 2008.[34] Cynics said that "everyday should be international corruption day in Mexico," because in 2007 an estimated $2.6 billion—more than $24 per person—went to pay bribes in the country, according to the non-governmental agency Transparency Mexico.[35]

A *tour d'horizon* of all of Mexico's law enforcement establishment lies beyond the scope of this book. Nevertheless, the skullduggery within the Federal Security Directorate (DSF)—and its most conspicuous figure, Fernando Gutiérrez Barrios—and the Federal Judicial Police (PJF) have so corrupted the federal law enforcement that its salvation represents a will-o'-the-wisp. The DSF and PJF provided blunt but effective mechanisms that the revolutionary secular church and the PRI mafia relied on to control its adversaries—with a nefarious side effect of establishing egregiously venal baselines of morality that continue to bedevil Mexican law enforcement. The scope of corruption uncovered in Operation House-Cleaning reveals the depth to which this has reached. In addition to Fernando Gutiérrez Barrios, the rogue's gallery of DFS strongmen also displays Miguel Nazar Haro, José Antonio Zorrilla Pérez, Luis de la Barreda Moreno, Javier García Paniagua, and General Jorge Carrillo Olea.

In 1946 Miguel Alemán Valdés became the first civilian to attain the presidency since the formation of the PRI. He was eager to ingratiate himself with the United States in order to attract investment for an import substitution industrialization plan (ISI) that he hoped would drive economic diversification. To that end, he enthusiastically cooperated with Washington in a Cold War anti-communism struggle that became evident in the Truman Doctrine (1947), the Marshall Plan (1948) and the formation of the North Atlantic Treaty Organization (1949), along with the creation of other intelligence-gathering and collective-security bodies. During World War II, Americans had complained about the quality of Mexico's intelligence service, particularly its difficulty in tracking the movement of Axis spies. Determined to woo U.S. capital, the chief executive created the DFS in late 1946 or early 1947 as a key instrument of control responsive to his beck-and-call.[36]

Although adept at gathering a hodge-podge of information and suppressing dissidents, the DFS epitomized the worst in police forces. It recruited poorly educated individuals, mostly men aged 30 to 45; its roster included both civilians and military personnel; it demanded that operatives show loyalty to their individual sponsors, thus privileging personal commitments over institutional loyalties; it paid relatively low salaries and turned a blind eye when members supplemented their incomes by trafficking in drugs, extorting money, or selling protection to hapless businessmen and prostitutes. It also suffered high turnover as its agents, once having learned the ropes of criminality, gravitated to more lucrative endeavors—most often in the underworld. Moreover, the agency was a loose cannon whose activities often overlapped or conflicted with those of the Federal Judicial Police, state and local forces, and the military—that is, it engaged in reckless intelligence gathering, crime promotion, the illegal investigation of lawful behavior, and political espionage.

As a stalwart U.S. ally during the Cold War, the DFS tapped telephones; photographed individuals entering the Soviet embassy, and later, snapped pictures of passengers flying from Mexico to Cuba; and it readily exchanged information with the newly established Central Intelligence Agency (CIA). In return, American authorities sometimes assisted their DFS peers by bending the rules to spirit Mexican dissidents in the United States back to their homeland.[37]

Above all, the DFS nourished the image of a tough "elite" organization that could ignore the law because it was fighting communists, PRI malcontents inside and outside of the party, and other conspirators. "We were not run-of-the-mill police. We were smartly dressed and well turned out. We were extremely well received and well known. We were special. We were pure tigers," explained a member of the force.[38] The FBI even assisted in haphazard training of these men who adopted a ferocious tiger face as their emblem.

The organization's identification card—known as the *charola* or collection plate—provided a license to abuse civil liberties, intimidate suspects, make false arrests, procure prostitutes, protect cronies, and extort money. In addition to paid employees, the director invited several hundred members of the armed forces, civilians, and agents of other police units to serve as honorary DFS affiliates. They, too, could use their badges for legitimate or illegitimate purposes. They also functioned as informants for paranoid leaders, who had an unquenchable thirst for information about plots and schemes that communists, radicals, and other subversives supposedly had hatched. Presidents Gustavo Díaz Ordaz (1964-70), Luis Echeverría Álvarez (1970-76), and José López Portillo (1976-82) gave free rein to the political police.

By far the most prominent "enforcer" of the *priísta* regime was Fernando Gutiérrez Barrios (1927-2000). Son of a military officer, a graduate of the Heroic Military College, and an Olympian horseman, Gutiérrez Barrios rose to the rank of captain before joining the DFS soon after its inception. One of his first assignments as a 28-year-old plainclothes policeman was to keep tabs on the PRI's opponents.

In that context, he first met Fidel Castro and Ernesto "Ché" Guevara, who were in his home state of Veracruz training to overthrow Cuban dictator Fulgencio Batista. The tyrant's intelligence service, the Mexicans, and the FBI had the would-be revolutionaries under surveillance. At the request of the Cuban government, the group was rounded up in preparation for what might have been their extradition to Havana. After interrogating the young rebels, Gutiérrez Barrios developed a strong and long-lasting friendship with Castro. "He was a kind and gentlemanly policeman who conversed agreeably and even had some leftist ideas," the Cuban revolutionary later said. For his part, Fernando Gutiérrez Barrios never regarded Fidel as a criminal, but as a young idealist who yearned to overthrow a despot. He released the Cubans, and they went on to win an insurgency.[39]

Gutiérrez Barrios rose steadily through the ranks, ascending to DFS deputy director in 1958 before serving as director from 1964 to 1970. He directed the agency in 1968 when security forces gunned down hundreds of unarmed demonstrators before the Mexico City Olympics and the dirty war against "subversives" took place. Later as subsecretary of the interior, he continued to run the directorate by proxy through subordinates. Even though the DFS had been disbanded two years earlier, Gutiérrez Barrios remained a fixture to be reckoned with when Salinas named him secretary of interior in 1988. Between stints with the secret police, he headed the Directorate of Federal Highways and Bridges (1982-86), a lucrative honey pot, and subsequently captured the governorship of his home state, Veracruz, known for its many political aficionados.

As the official or de facto chief of the DFS, Gutiérrez Barrios, was distinguishable by his 1950s-style gray pompadour, dapper dress, a meticulously-trimmed mustache, manicured fingernails, and quiet, sonorous voice. He earned both fear and respect as evidenced in the "Don Fernando" appellation that he received ("Don Fer" to close friends). In a biographical essay, journalist Mary Beth Sheridan indicated that the security guru "was a pragmatist who would use violence only after all else failed."[40] Stories about his negotiating skills are legendary. It is said that if university radicals hoisted the hammer-and-sickle, Gutiérrez Barrios would send DFS goons to arrest them: He would then offer the rabble-rousers one of two options: scholarships to study in Europe or execution. He also jailed foreign leftists and, in return for their release, forced them to spy for him on their internal counterparts. A longtime associate insisted that Don Fernando never employed or implied threats and that he never resorted to profanity.[41]

Activist Primitivo Rodríguez recalled how left-wing parties planned to demonstrate in Mexico City on behalf of Puerto Rican independence in 1977. Gutiérrez Barrios offered them a deal. If they cancelled the gathering, he would publicly support the island's emancipation from the United States. But it is too late to call off the widely publicized march, Rodríguez insisted. "He [the DFS chief] told us: 'Don't worry. The announcements canceling it are already on the radio,'" Rodríguez recalled. Next Gutiérrez Barrios dolled out envelopes of cash.[42] He may have preferred conciliation to coercion; still, Don Fernando did not hesitate to use violence in defending the system that he cherished. It was said that, if you cut his wrists, he would bleed red, white, green blood—the colors of the nation and the PRI.

A *New York Times* correspondent offered a less sanguine view: "Like all good spies, Mr. Gutierrez was by reputation an essentially amoral man. With one arm, he embraced Fidel Castro, avatar of Latin American leftists... With the other, he aimed to squeeze the life out of the left in Mexico. In more than three decades as a top official, Mr. Gutierrez Barrios, a suave and sophisticated man ... oversaw the arrests, tortures and murders of dozens, perhaps hundreds, of opponents of the governing party...."[43]

Thanks to informants and electronic eavesdropping Gutiérrez Barrios filled dossiers with titillating information about members of the political, business, intellectual, and social establishment. His archives earned him the reputation as "the best informed man in Mexico"—the country's version of J. Edgar Hoover, the autocratic founder and longtime director of the Federal Bureau of Investigation.

In 1977 President Echeverría named Javier García Paniagua to head the DFS, and Don Fernando moved to the Interior Ministry, where he oversaw the quashing of dissidents. The savage García Paniagua, who employed crude, abusive techniques in interrogating suspects, also helped conduct the violent counterinsurgency campaign that virtually wiped out several leftist guerrilla groups. He and his colleagues deployed fearsome units to suppress rural and urban insurgents.

An even greater villain was Miguel Nazar Haro, who succeeded Paniagua at the helm of the Directorate. He once bragged to strangers at a wedding dinner about having just cold-bloodedly shot three alleged kidnappers. Before Nazar Haro left the DFS in 1982, the FBI, the California State Police, and U.S Attorney William H. Kennedy had received evidence that the Mexican gendarme was involved in a car theft ring in San Diego. Hoodlums stole luxury models from dealerships, handed them over to middlemen, who—in turn—passed them along to Mexican officials. These recipients wanted the flashy vehicles not for personal use but as gifts for bosses with whom they hoped to curry favor. When

Kennedy confirmed elements of a newspaper article about the investigation, the U.S. Department of Justice fired the prosecutor. He was replaced with Peter K. Núñez, who immediately contacted Washington about the curious sensitivity of the case. He received, at best, a lukewarm reception to pursuing it.

What was the roadblock? It emerged that Nazar Haro was the—if not one of the—top agents for the CIA's and FBI's counterintelligence operations in Latin America. "It was a very complicated circumstance. We [in San Diego] had spent considerable time trying to charge him, and the Justice Department in Washington and some of the U.S. intelligence agencies did not want us to go ahead," Nuñez said.

The Justice Department waffled on indicting Miguel Nazar Haro, but he eventually received a grand jury summons and was later imprisoned. His lawyer quickly posted the $250,000 bail, obtained proper U.S. Customs authorization for travel, and returned his client to Mexico. He never again appeared publicly in the United States.[44]

In 1994 Nazar Haro was charged with having apprehended, tortured, and disappeared 21-year-old Jesús Piedra Ibarra twenty-four years earlier. The accused claimed the young man belonged to the 23rd of September League, a small guerrilla band. The court found Nazar Haro guilty and imprisoned him at the Topo Chico penitentiary in Monterrey. Because he was 80-years-old and debilitated by pneumonia and other recurring ailments, a judge soon allowed him to complete his sentence at his comfortable Mexico City home—much to the dismay of human rights advocates.[45]

The next DFS director, José Antonio Zorrilla Pérez, emerged from the same mold. Not only was he joined at the hip with drug traffickers, but he had masterminded the assassination of journalist Manuel Buendía in 1984. Convicted of the crime in 1989 and sentenced to thirty-five year behind bars, he was granted an early release from the Reclusorio Preventivo Oriente after nineteen years as a result of "good behavior."[46] The report of his early release was greeted with great dismay and concern by many of Mexico's veteran journalists and columnists—particularly by the respected Miguel Angel Granados Chapa.[47]

The most notorious paramilitary group was the previously described White Brigade, whose existence was always officially denied, although it was active in the 1970s and the early 1980s, when the government dismantled it. This unit consisted of soldiers and policemen who harshly repressed guerrilla movements and civilian dissenters. Published reports held that the White Brigade was responsible for the "disappearance" of several hundred leftists, most of whom the government claimed were killed in fights between rival radical bands. Politically motivated disappearances tapered off sharply during the 1980s, but were once again reported in the mid-1990s in connection with the uprising by the Zapatistas in Chiapas.

Conflation of the dirty war, the murder of Manuel Buendía by a DFS director, l'affaire Camarena, and other scandals forced former President Miguel de la Madrid to dismantle the Directorate. The ineffectual Direction of Investigation and National Security (DISEN), headed by Pedro Vázquez Colmenares, replaced the DFS. Yet following several years of bureaucratic churning CISEN emerged as the number-one intelligence agency in 1988. During the 1980s, ambitious politicians like Secretary of Interior Manuel Bartlett Díaz, the devious García Paniagua, and Tamaulipas Governor Emilio Martínez Manautou began forging their personal mini-spy operations in hopes of achieving the presidency. Mexico State, which established the State Security Agency (ASE) in 2006, is one of a handful of jurisdictions that have formed their own intelligence arms.

Don Fernando's influence had seriously waned under Salinas. The image of a tough-minded policeman and anti-clerical mason, clashed with the progressive face that Salinas endeavored to project after his controversial electoral victory in 1988. Moreover, members of the chief executive's inner circle—especially, chief of staff and presidential alter ego José "Pepe" Córdoba Montoya and the appointed Mexico City mayor Manuel Camacho Solís—regarded Gutiérrez Barrio with a jaundiced eye. He threatened their power bases, and unfounded rumors circulated that he would make a bid for the PRI nomination for Los Pinos in 1994. Salinas signaled his intentions by removing CISEN from the jurisdiction of the Interior Ministry, which Don Fernando headed. In January 1993 the president unceremoniously ousted him as secretary in a "manotazo" (a strong blow), awarding him a Senate seat as a consolation prize.

President Ernesto Zedillo prevailed upon Don Fernando to organize the first PRI presidential primary in November 1999. "From the point of view of democratic idealism, it seems crazy. But from the practical point of view, it was a perfect strategy," stated prominent historian and PRI critic Enrique Krauze. "Yeltsin was a Communist. Gorbachev too.... You need a strong man to reform from inside," he added. Astute observer José Antonio Crespo agreed: "Who else can force people to accept the [electoral] laws, stop the [PRI] governors from playing dirty games, stop the caciques [local power bosses]?"[48] The warhorse died on October 30, 2000—the year in which his beloved PRI lost the presidency.

Leftist activist Rosario Ibarra de Piedra, who is convinced that her son Jesús had been murdered in the dirty war, said of the suave spymaster: "What Fidel Castro saw as a friendly hand was the hand of repression in this country. And death does not change a person's deeds."[49] The whereabouts of Don Fernando's vaunted archives, bulging with information about many current politicians, is as mysterious as the meaning of Olmec hieroglyphics.

Even with the dissolution of the DFS, other agencies—the Federal Judicial Police (PJF) and the Federal Highway Police (PFC), in particular—attracted denunciations for torture, wrongful arrests, drug trafficking, corruption, and other abuses. Although it remained one of the smaller law enforcement agencies, the PJF tripled in size between 1982 and 1984, from 500 personnel to an estimated 1,500. In 1988 an assistant attorney general's office for investigating and combating drug trafficking was formed with 1,500 additional Federal Judicial policemen. In 1990 the PGR section was expanded and given interagency coordinating functions in the battle against narcotics.

Some former DFS agents remained in the spy business. Few if any Directorate alumni serve in the previously mentioned Center for Investigation and National Security or CISEN. Since its creation by President Salinas, this agency has had eight directors and suffered a severe loss of funding and key personnel. The picture changed when Calderón named the highly respected Guillermo Valdés Castellanos as director and substantially expanded its budget and human resources. In an effort to make law enforcement more professional, President Zedillo formed the Federal Preventive Police from elements of the Federal Highway Police, the Third Military Police Brigade, some Navy personnel, the small migration police, and the fiscal police. This organization sought to prevent crimes, while the Federal Investigations Agency (AFI), which supplanted the ignominious Federal Judicial Police in 2001, concentrated on solving them. President Fox hoped that AFI would become Mexico's version of the FBI—an analogy that the latter abhors. The dissolution of the PFP and AFI will be addressed later in this chapter.

In 1991 Attorney General Enrique Álvarez del Castillo, who reportedly impeded several human rights investigations of the police, was abruptly removed and replaced by Ignacio Morales Lechuga. Morales Lechuga promptly announced a crackdown on corruption, including a reorganization of the Federal Judicial Police, the creation of special anticorruption and internal affairs units, as well as a contingent to protect citizens against crimes committed by the police. In addition, he placed all federal police under a civilian deputy attorney general. New high-level officials supervised police activities in sensitive border areas. These measures were taken after a jailed drug baron took control of a prison in Matamoros, claiming that PJF agents aligned with another drug lord had threatened his life.

Despite Morales Lechuga's reputation for effectiveness, Salinas replaced him early in 1993 with Jorge Carpizo MacGregor, a respected human rights advocate. The new attorney general acknowledged the symbiotic relationship between criminals and law enforcement agencies and produced his own program to eliminate deficiencies and corruption among the police. His changes brought limited progress; members of the security forces were charged and sentenced; and human rights violations declined. But the so-called "culture of impunity" still prevailed. In early 1994, Carpizo left the PGR and was replaced by respected jurist Diego Valadéz.

The 1994 assassination of PRI presidential candidate Donaldo Colosio shook the highest levels of federal law enforcement. After failing to make significant progress on the Colosio murder, Attorney General Valadéz stepped down in favor of Humberto Benítez Treviño. Initially declaring that a lone gunman performed the killing, the Attorney General's Office revised its theory after videotapes derailed their interpretation. Evidence suggested that as many as six individuals may have helped the gunman approach the nominee during a crowded rally in Tijuana. The post of attorney general underwent yet another change in early 1996 when President Zedillo replaced Benítez Treviño with an opposition congressman, PAN deputy Fernando Antonio Lozano Gracia—the first time that a non-*priísta* had headed the PGR.

Late in 1994 the assassination of José Francisco Ruiz Massieu prompted a special investigation headed by Deputy Attorney General Mario Ruiz Massieu, brother of the slain politician and brother-in-law of former president Salinas. After calling dozens of PRI officials to testify, the erratic Ruiz Massieu resigned abruptly in November. He then accused ranking party functionaries of complicity in the murder of his brother and of impeding further progress in the investigation. He then took his own life rather than face money-laundering charges in the United States. His suicide note blamed President Zedillo for both his own death and the assassination of José Francisco. He offered no evidence to support these denunciations. What's more, he had conducted a protracted legal struggle to frustrate four attempts by Washington to extradite him to Mexico to face charges of graft, money laundering and abuse of power.

Appendix 4 highlights the evolution of Mexico's federal police, anti-drug, and intelligence services from the late nineteenth century to 2009.

A number of smaller law enforcement bodies exist at the state and local level. Each of the country's thirty-one states and the Federal District has its own judicial police—the State Judicial Police and the Federal District Judicial Police. State police report to the governor; the Federal District Judicial Police fall under the control of the Federal District's Attorney General. Most offenses fall under the jurisdiction of state authorities. Offenses against the government and those involving several jurisdictions lie within the domain of the federal police. The distinction among crimes under the rubric of state and federal authorities is sufficiently vague that negotiations often take place to determine who will accept the responsibility for investigating and prosecuting them. Before Congress changed the law under Calderón, narcotics-related violations fell under the purview of federal authorities, which often permitted state executives to shrug their shoulders and say, in effect, "That's not our responsibility." And to complicate things even more, the agents involved in deciding the agency that should pursue specific cases may be overwhelmed by staggering levels of police incompetence and public mistrust of them.

President Calderón revealed that 61.6 percent of municipal police failed psychological, toxicological, medical, academic, and background checks—with the figure especially high in Baja California (88.9 percent), Zacatecas (70.7 percent), Coahuila (69 percent), and San Luis Potosí (64.7 percent). The results led to the dismissal of 220 law enforcement officers in Tijuana.[50]

The lack of confidence in the police has spurred the president to enlist citizens in his "Clean up Mexico" scheme (*"Limpiemos México"*). This program involves (1) "Taking Back Public Spaces" with emphasis on 750 zones, (2) drug-testing in schools, (3) a national program to treat and prevent drug and alcohol addiction, and (4) inviting citizens to use e-mail and cell phones to report illegal activities. The wave of narco-violence will limit the denunciation of criminal activities even further. Although devoted to family and close friends, most Mexicans have become disillusioned by the corruption and inaction of authorities, and consequently have little reason to feel any obligation to their community. Even worse, they fear that the police may be in league with the criminals. This cynicism gave impulse to a movement whereby citizens went to the polls on July 5, 2009, and spoiled their ballots to protest the corruption, ineffectiveness, and insensitivity of parties and politicians.

When a former PFP official was linked to the kidnapping of Fernando Martí, *Reforma*'s "Templo Mayor" column reported that the head of the Public Security Ministry (SSP) "looks more fragile than Humpty Dumpty." As indicated earlier, the number of critics of García Luna expands each day, and more and more people are actively challenging him. Not only is he engaged in a turf battle with Medina Mora, but the Attorney General had misgivings about creating a "Policía Federal"—to the point that journalist Raymundo Jiménez García referred to "an underground war" between the two men. In September 2009 Medina Mora was replaced by Arturo Chávez Chávez, ally of PAN VIP Diego Fernández de Cevallos.

Although not activated by Medina Mora, in late September 2008, 180 members of the 5,400-member Federal Investigative Agency—a dependency of the Attorney General's Office—marched from their office to the PGR headquarters to protest any fusion with the Federal Preventative Police, considered an inferior force by many AFI agents.

García Luna's detractors notwithstanding, there are several reasons why President Calderón appears determined to keep his secretary of public security on the job. First, the chief executive is extremely reluctant to dismiss officials with whom he has a good rapport, especially with a plethora of local and state elections in 2009, 2010, and 2011.

Second, many members of the president's entourage believe that ousting the cabinet member, who continuously receives death threats, would show weakness in the anti-crime battle.

Third, in contrast to many naysayers in the media and academic communities, García Luna exudes a cautious optimism. He argues that Mexico is in the midst of a transformation and there must be no retreat in the crusade against the syndicates. In a lengthy interview, he used the example of the *Mafia* in the U.S. to argue that criminal violence is unrelated to alleged Mexican corruption or incompetence. "That is how it has been all over the world," he said. "Look at Chicago, New York, Italy."[51]

Fourth, García Luna is a tough, no-nonsense professional who did not hesitate to purge police commanders whom he considered corrupt or incompetent. This move displaced 284 AFI and PFP commanders throughout the country. He pledged that each would be subjected to psychological analysis, drugs tests, polygraph examinations, background probes, and physical check-ups conducted by the SSP's National Center of Confidence Control.[52] Meanwhile, he replaced them with officials, many of whom had undertaken training programs in the new police academy and had been carefully vetted to screen out mob infiltrators, according to the *New York Times*.

Fifth, he has established a working rapport with the U.S. embassy in Mexico and law enforcement agencies in the United States.

Sixth, the SSP boss is a disciple of the controversial admiral, Wilfrido Robledo Madrid, who—after holding various high-profile law enforcement posts—serves as a security adviser to business guru Carlos Slim Helú, one of the world's five wealthiest men and the major shareholder in TELMEX and scores of other corporations. Indeed, García Luna selected former TELMEX executive Francisco Niembro González as chief of evaluation and institutional development at SSP. In this position, Niembro will construct the "Mexican Platform" in cooperation with INTERPOL protocols. The link means that Mexico will automatically have access to INTERPOL's databases on wanted persons, pilfered and lost travel documents, and stolen motor vehicles while it updates its own crime databases. When a Mexican police officer finally gains access to a national database, he can simultaneously receive INTERPOL information.

Finally, García Luna is close to Jorge Tello Peón, whom Calderón named in October 2008 as the de facto security czar, and who—as mentioned earlier, has helped to diminish intramural battles within the Security Cabinet. Five months later, the president appointed the tough-minded law enforcement expert executive secretary of the National Public Security System.

Based on these factors, García Luna appears to be secure in his assignment unless the charges of corruption leveled at his associates turn out to be true, and there is hard evidence that he has ties to the underworld.

Although President Calderón wound up relying on the military to spearhead the anti-cartel war, he is laboring to achieve a root-and-branch overhaul of the nation's civilian police. On December 13, 2006, he announced plans to incorporate 7,500 soldiers and 2,500 marines into the PFP for three months, but the proposal came a cropper due to opposition from military personnel, who claimed that such a move would harm their salaries, benefits, opportunities for promotion, and reputations. As a result, only 600 soldiers and fifty marines have been assigned to the federal police agency.

Criminal organizations have terrorized and suborned substantial numbers of the two federal police forces, the Federal Investigations Agency and the Federal Preventative Police. In reaction, Calderón has lobbied Congress to replace them with a single, highly professional organization modeled on Spanish or French national agencies.

In 2007 the president placed the two forces—the PFP and the AFI—under a single command headed by a Ministry of Public Security official. Meanwhile, he relied heavily on the militarized Support Forces of the

Federal Police run by General Cruz López.[53] Specifically, the 3,500-member elite force proves "assistance to civil authorities to combat organized crime of threats to security of the nation...." It acts on orders of the chief executive, but depends on the Defense Ministry for technical, operational, and administrative matters. It is distinguishable by cappuccino-colored uniforms and black berets. The establishment of this unit reinforces dependence on the military for the fight against criminals.[54] Cruz López can activate several dozen or several hundred of its members to carry out specific assignments. After completing these missions, they return to their regular duties.

In light of the problems with current officers, the Ministry of Public Security took steps to improve the training of new, carefully selected cadets. On October 15, 2007, President Calderón inaugurated the police academy in San Luis Potosí, which features a rigorous curriculum, instruction in "vanguard" crime-fighting technology, leadership training, and emphasis on human rights and civic responsibility. Although its graduates will receive attractive compensation, the sordid reputation of law enforcement personnel poses a major obstacle to attracting applications from middle class young men and women. "They look upon policemen not as professionals but as strange creatures, as Martians," lamented García Luna.[55] The legacy of the DFS and PJF for poor standards, criminality, corruption, and impunity mean that Calderón and García Luna confront the Herculean task of convincing upright young people that police work is an honorable career. The issue is not simply to reform corrupt organizations, but to create a new law enforcement capability from scratch.

Professional training cannot overcome bureaucratic obstacles. Some 350 cadets who completed six-months of instruction in Mexico City to join the PFP found themselves with neither an assignment nor a salary on January 31, 2009. Of the program, a cadet said: "It was a waste of time. We never had the basic law enforcement training necessary.... We showed up and listened to speeches from people who supposedly were qualified, but who were not accredited."[56]

Opposition to merging the AFI and PFP was strong, persistent, and widespread. Congress was wary that a professional force might investigate its wayward members. And of course, the SSP honcho has never bowed and scraped before legislators, many of whom have an inflated opinions of themselves. When a member of the lower house asked what García Luna thought to be an uninformed question, he responded: "How is this possible ... that you as a deputy don't know...."

Defense Secretary Galván Galván also harbored profound reservations about a combined federal force. The armed forces feared that launching such a body would siphon money from an underfunded and understaffed military, require Army and Navy personnel to train the new recruits, and do little to diminish the flagrant corruption that envelopes the nation's gendarmes. Senior officers also decry the physical condition of the police, seven out of ten of whom cannot run 100 meters without becoming winded. An official report showed that 70 percent of the officers suffered from obesity, high cholesterol levels, diabetes, hypertension, eye problems, and other deficiencies.[57] As in the United States, post-traumatic stress plagues Mexican cops who confront family, economic, and life-threatening challenges.

Roberto Campa Cifrián criticized the proposed AFI-PFP merger until, in early September 2008, loud, continuous clashes with García Luna spurred his forced resignation as executive secretary of the National Public Security System, which, as mentioned earlier, functions as an intermediary between the federal government and state and local officials.

Of course, the governors, who behave like archbishops and religious potentates in their dioceses, overwhelming opposed a single Federal Police, which if successful, could expose the wrongdoing that many state executives either prosper from or to which they appear deaf, dumb, and blind.

It was an open secret during the first half of 2009 that the PRI would have liked to replace the tart-tongued García Luna with Jesús Murillo Karam, its 61-year old party secretary-general who has served as governor of Hidalgo and undersecretary of public security.

Enemies of the SSP chief have leaked like colanders to any media mavens who have shown an inclination to undermine the nation's top cop. They have alleged linkages of Luis Cárdenas Palomino, whom García Luna named as the PFP's general coordinator for Intelligence to Prevent Crimes, to both the killing of a taxi driver in the 1980s and the 1994 extortion of Enrique Salinas, youngest brother of Carlos, who was killed ten years later.

These impediments have deterred neither Calderón nor his security advisers from revamping both the AFI and PFP. In late May 2009, the former became the Federal Ministerial Police (PFM) with responsibility for helping prosecutors investigate and prepare cases; on June 1, the latter morphed into the Federal Police (PF) with investigative powers such as the right to seek telephone taps of conversations related to organized crime. The PF will also secure crime scenes, execute arrest warrants, and collect and process reports submitted by various authorities. Based on past experience, changes in names and duties of police agencies are not likely to improve law enforcement. It is unclear whether the data in Table 7.2 on the decline in the deaths of police officers indicates more professionalism in discharging their duties or the preponderant role of the armed forces in fighting the cartels.

Unprofessional Judiciary

The judiciary, which remains pivotal to any legal reform, still shows laxness toward narco-traffickers. In late 2008 federal judge Jesús Salvador Fausto Macareno released four of thirteen suspects in Monterrey, even though the detainees had been arrested in possession of arms, drugs, AFI uniforms, money-counting machines, and stolen automobiles. On similar occasions in the past, the freed men have hunted down and executed both the commander who had spearheaded their capture and the local judge who placed them behind bars.[58]

Attempting to contribute to modernizing Mexico's judiciary, representatives of the U.S. Agency for International Development have spoken positively about the changes in the laws of Mexico State, Chihuahua, and several other states and classified them as genuine "judicial reform"; in reality, the changes undertaken represent little more than window dressing. The over-all issue is "one-half law and one-half existing structures and culture. The elimination of corruption and bureaucracy is not easy, even with legal tools."[59]

In March 2008 Mexico's Congress approved a constitutional amendment to replace secretive proceedings and inquisitorial techniques with a U.S.-style adversarial approach. The change included open trials, allowed recorded phone calls admitted into evidence if one of the participants

Table 7.2
Deaths of Police Officers: December 1, 2006 to June 9, 2009

Year*	AFI	PFP	TOTAL
2007	20	19	39
2008	28	73	101
2009	10	17	27
TOTAL	58	109	167

* No police officers died during December 2006
Source: Ministry of Public Security.

agreed, and permitted prosecutors to hold organized-crime suspects without charges for up to 80 days.[60] The reform also introduced a presumption of innocence, the right of the defendant to face his accuser, and evidence-based procedures—with a greater emphasis on forensics and meticulous fact-gathering. "In what experts say is nothing short of a revolution, Mexico is gradually abandoning its centuries-old Napoleonic structure of closed-door, written inquisitions—largely a legacy of Spanish colonial rule—that had long been criticized as rife with corruption, opaque decisions, abuse of defendants and red tape that bogged down cases for years."[61]

In early 2009 legal specialists, with the help of U.S. attorneys, were attempting to iron out the protocols of this legislation, which will not be implemented in all of the thirty-one states and Federal District before 2016. Meanwhile, "we work with the same system that was used during the Spanish Inquisition," avers Alberto Barbaz, Mexico State's attorney general. For example, information derived from electric shocks and other coercive interrogation techniques constitutes credible evidence. "In America, prosecutors investigate, but the judge and jury decide the facts," said human rights lawyer Santiago Aguirre Espinoza. "Here, statements made to prosecutors are facts. There is no cross-examination or right to confront accusers. If a person in Mexico confesses to a prosecutor, it is considered sufficient evidence for a detention—so there is an inherent incentive to obtain confessions."[62] One survey found that 71 percent of convicted defendants said they never saw a judge before they were sentenced. About 47 percent of inmates in Mexico City's prisons are serving sentences for robbery involving sums of fewer than $20, law professor Ana Laura Magaloni said. Those who fall into the system are often subject to "arbitrary treatment," she added.[63]

The judiciary received a black eye with the March 2009 disclosure that retired Supreme Court justices not only benefited from a generous pension (150,000 to 255,000 pesos per month), a chauffeur, and complete medical care, but they had charged sumptuous meals to taxpayers. All but one on the thirty-five retirees had spent collectively almost a half-million pesos wining and dining themselves and friends on the public tab in the best restaurants in the Federal District, Cancún, Cozumel, other Mexican cities, as well as in foreign cities like Vancouver, British Colombia. Members of Congress immediately introduced legislation to ensure that no public servant earned more than the president whose monthly gross salary is 208,648 pesos.[64] "This is what people miss when they analyze Mexico. Drug trafficking feeds on a country that has a very precarious, if not nonexistent, rule of law," stated Mexican political scientist Denise Dresser.[65]

Prisons

Authorities nominally control Mexico's penitentiaries, especially the nine high-security federal facilities. In reality, pay-offs to prison officials and guards, combined with the proliferation of organized gangs behind bars, give well-heeled convicts unparalleled influence. Inmates sometimes settle scores with adversaries behind bars—most notoriously exemplified in the 2004 murders of El Chapo's brother Arturo Guzmán and his associate Miguel Ángel Beltrán Lugo inside La Palma prison. At the same time, drug lords carry on negotiations behind bars. Former Assistant Attorney General Santiago Vasconcelos acknowledged that the Gulf Cartel's Osiel Guillén cut a deal to cooperate with Tijuana's Benjamín Arellano Felix while both were locked up in the same prison.[66]

In January 2005 gangsters seized six employees of the Matamoros penitentiary and handcuffed, blindfolded, and shot them, leaving their cadavers in a white sport utility vehicle parked opposite the facility. This savagery may have been a response to the seizure six days earlier of La Palma prison by 750 federal police and military. Clearly, drug dealers had corrupted the guards and were overseeing violent networks from inside. In early December 2008 enemies are believed to have executed two Zetas in the Mazatlán detention center.[67]

Thanks to widespread access to cell phones, prisoners find it easy to engage in extortion. A committee of the Chamber of Deputies estimated that convicts had extorted 186,620 million pesos in the 2001-2007 period. The equipment installed in 2007 to block telephone signals in eleven prisons fell into disrepair and no longer functions.[68] This situation prompted Mexico State to invest 10 million pesos to block telephone signals in its four largest penitentiaries, Neza-Bordo (Nezahualcóyotl), Barrientos (Tlalnepantla), Chiconaultla (Ecatepec), and Almoloya de Juárez (Santiaguito).[69]

Just as in the United States, drugs flow freely inside Mexico's prison walls. Of the 37,000 inmates in Mexico City's penal institutions, an estimated 25,900 are addicts. Authorities admit that the availability of the substances, which may generate 15.5 million pesos a month, represents a convenient way to minimize melees and curb other violent outbursts. As a prison official told a city councilman: "Sir, if I cut off the flow of drugs, there will be a mutiny the next day."[70] In late 2008, authorities discovered fifty-one packets containing 119 kilograms of marijuana covered with sacks of toilet paper and boxes of soft drinks aboard a truck seeking to enter the capital's Reclusorio Sur.[71]

In February 2003 guards apprehended Natividad Hernández Hernández, head of a group of women who smuggled marijuana into Mexico City's Reclusorio Norte in their vaginas.[72] So serious is the problem that messianic populist and former presidential candidate Andrés Manuel López Obrador urged that the Army take over the prison system,[73] something that it was forced to do in so-called "centers of social readaptation" in Ciudad Juárez (CERESO), Puebla, Guanajuato, Durango, San Luis Potosí, Tamaulipas, Aguascalientes, and elsewhere in 2009.

Between January 1 and December 19, 2008, guards in Mexico City's ten prisons discovered 1,397 cell phones and 167.7 kilograms of marijuana–up from 18.9 kilograms in 2007. The number of psychotropic pills found increased from 5,801 tablets to 8,449 tablets during the same period, while the quantity of cocaine fell from 6.4 to 4.7 kilograms. Penal authorities also decommissioned 17,063 knives, shanks, blades, and other dangerous objects.[74]

On New Year's Eve 2008, Mexico City penal officials sought to calm nearly 40,000 inmates with a special dinner featuring Jalisco style pozole, pork, tostadas with cream, buñuelos of wheat tortillas, and fruit tea. They were also provided a Mass and alcoholic beverages; the latter was not so much a treat as recognition that prisoners can easily obtain beer, wine, and liquor on their own.[75]

Overcrowding accentuates turmoil. Of Mexico's 439 federal, state, and local penal institutions, 228 are stuffed with an excessive number of inmates. In Mexico City's Reclusorio Oriente, seventy prisoners occupy one six-by-five square meter cell. This means that they must sleep standing up, lie in hallways, seek out green spaces to stretch out, or pay for access to a bunk.[76] Wealthy "deluxe prisoners" grease the palms of guards, who—for the right price—will permit them to exit the facility for a few hours to conduct business, love-making, or criminal ventures.

The SSP has sent twenty-four guards, administrators, and staff members for penology training in Santa Fe, New Mexico. These graduates will become instructors at the First Academy of the National Penal System, situated in Jalapa, Veracruz. More and better-trained personnel are required, not only for existing institutions, but also for a recently completed "super-maximum" penitentiary that will be used exclusively for kidnappers, in Guasave, Sinaloa.[77]

It is hoped that this facility will contain prisoners, who took part in twenty-two escapes and forty-three uprisings in other institutions during the first three months of 2009. An especially brazen escape happened in Zacatecas on May 16, and all of it is available for public viewing on *YouTube*. Before dawn, thirty or more heavily armed thugs believed to be Zetas, riding in trucks with AFI logos, stormed into the Cieneguillas penitentiary as one of their helicopters whirred overhead. In the blitzkrieg assault, they extricated fifty-three prisoners, including Zetas, members of the Beltrán Leyva family, and other narco-felons. State and federal authorities immediately began apprehending escapees even as they investigated the director and his fifty subordinates to determine who fostered the escape.[78] One of several inmates recaptured was Osvaldo "The Vampire" García Delgado, a kidnapping specialist whose Los Cotorros gang coordinates activities with Los Zetas in the state of Hidalgo.

The sheer volume of these escapes and riots has required the government to talk about penal reform and consider policy alternatives. A classic attempt involved "El Pueblo de La Mesa" facility in Tijuana. This prison-turned-village allowed family members to live with inmates, shop at stores in the compound, and support their spouses as they learned new skills. The pragmatic concept gave rise to "a class structure mirroring that of the larger Mexican society." The rich amassed computers, televisions, phones, DVD players, and tequila bars. They also bribed guards and surrounded themselves with servants and bodyguards hired from among their poor, who scrambled to survive. A humane setting did not humanize hard-core criminals in "El Pueblito." Drug sales, extortion, and murders increased, and some convicts even built a sophisticated meth laboratory. In 2000 the National Human Rights Commission (CNDH) called the penal institution the worst in the country because of overcrowding and privileges for prosperous prisoners. Two years later, the Army relocated the inmates, evicted their families, and shuttered the facility. As one observer noted: "The Big House is no longer a home."[79]

Ever the optimist, in June 2009 García Luna pledged to curb overcrowding by the end of Calderón's term. He made public a plan to construct twelve new penitentiaries and enlarge ten existing ones. When completed, the new and expanded facilities will accommodate an additional 41,412 convicts—a figure that approximates the 44,982 men and women behind bars in mid-2009.

Effect on Children

While outraged by the illicit drug trade and its associated bloodshed, Calderón, the father of three young children, has expressed alarm at the escalating domestic consumption of substances once earmarked for export. "I know the anguish and pain of mothers who realize, sometimes too late, that their children have fallen into the claws of drugs," he said.[80] Mexico City authorities have identified 4,000 locations in the capital where drugs are sold, often to pre-teens and teenagers.[81] In early August 2007 Attorney General Medina Mora reported that drug addiction within the country had increased from 15 to 30 percent annually since 2000.[82]

A study by the Ministry of Public Education (SEP) found that many preparatory-school students know where to purchase drugs: Mexico City (55 percent), Baja California (50 percent), and Sonora (40 percent). Nationwide, 20 percent of youngsters could identify fellow classmates who brought weapons to school.[83]

Equally upsetting is the allure of the gangster lifestyle for children in Michoacán's Tierra Caliente. Brenda, a twelve-year-old carrying a .9 mm toy pistol, told a researcher: "Here the narcos enjoy respect because they help the people and have a great deal of power. Not even mayors help as much when someone dies or doesn't have a job."[84]

According to the Defense Ministry, 610 children died in the drug war between December 2006 and March 2009. One-hundred-and-ten were caught in crossfires; seventy three were executed along with their families; and 427 died during fighting among the several crime families. Officials reported the largest number of casualties in Chihuahua (43), Baja California (26), Zacatecas (23), Guerrero (19), Michoacán (17), Sinaloa (15), Nuevo León (13), Tabasco (11); Tamaulipas (9), and Durango (7).[85]

Violence targeting parents has orphaned at least 3,700 children. Most young people witnessing such savagery become traumatized; others become inured to the bloodshed as an expected, even acceptable, part of life. In Tijuana, a child held up ten little fingers to depict the number of dead bodies he had recently seen outside his primary school. Then, he stuck up two more, for there had been a dozen bodies in all. "'They chopped out the tongues,' the boy said, seemingly fascinated by what he saw at the mass-killing outside Valentín Gómez Farías Primary School three weeks before. 'I saw the blood,' offered a classmate, enthusiastically. 'They were tied,'" piped up another.[86]

Concerned that the violence increases truancy among students and drives instructors from dangerous areas, the SEP has sent 1,200 teachers to Chihuahua, Durango, and Sinaloa. They will concentrate on providing instruction to poor, indigenous, and migrant youngsters. The teachers have pledged that they will focus on their objective and "neither see nor hear" anything about criminal organizations.[87]

Primary Role of the Armed Forces

The obstacles to creating reliable civilian agencies have spurred the chief executive to rely on Mexico's armed forces, which—while not free from corruption—are less contaminated than the 1,666 federal, state, local, and quasi-private police forces. "One of the most critical elements in the decision to use the military was the amount of violence between the election and when we took over," a senior presidential adviser said. "The executions, the decapitations, the confrontations between the drug gangs [gave rise to] ... a perception in society of lawlessness, that there was no state."[88]

Calderón began by mending relations between the presidency and the Army after his predecessor Vicente Fox raised hackles among the brass. He had named a mediocre "desk general," Clemente Vega García, as defense secretary; appointed a lower-ranking general as attorney general, a position superior to defense secretary; and created a National Security Council led by a left-wing politician, who failed to garner respect from more experienced officials supposedly under his purview.

To make matters worse, President Fox slighted the military in a post-9/11 interview on *The Larry King Show*. When the TV host asked if his nation would join the war against terrorism, the inept Mexican leader stated that: "Militarily speaking, we don't count. I mean, we are not a military country. We don't have a strong Army. That is not the way we contribute."[89] This comment ricocheted through the Defense Ministry like a photon in a laser cavity.

In contrast Felipe Calderón has wasted no time in courting the armed forces.[90] Initially, he had feared a disturbance of his inaugural ceremonies by loyalists of López Obrador, the PRD's 2006 presidential nominee who subsequently proclaimed himself the nation's "Legitimate President" and continues to barnstorm the country. To guard against this threat, the chief executive-elect accepted the presidential sash from Vicente Fox cradled by a cadet from the Heroic Military College, Mexico's version of West Point, just after midnight on December 1, 2006.

The military ensured that the public investiture in Congress took place with minimal disruptions. Later in the morning, Felipe Calderón went to the Campo Marte near Los Pinos presidential residence. Accompanied by Defense Secretary Galván Galván and Navy Secretary Saynez, he reviewed troops, received a 21-gun salute, and raised an enormous flag before praising the loyal men in women in uniform whose "commitment to the security and well-being of Mexicans must be justly recognized and compensated."

During his first *Informe*, he stressed the necessity of austerity but promised to grow the budget of the armed forces and other security institutions. In 2009 Mexico earmarked $9.3 billion for national security, nearly a 100 percent increase since Felipe Calderón affirmed the presidential oath.[91] In February 2007 he awarded up to a 46 percent pay raise to the military, while he voluntarily took a personal 10 percent salary cut. One of the goals of increasing compensation was to reduce the contagion of desertions (discussed below), which approximated 100,000 soldiers between 2000 and 2006, and consequently provided recruits for the cartels.[92] Calderón even visited the 43rd Military Zone in Apatzingán, a no-man's land of narco-activities in Michoacán. There, he donned a floppy military tunic and sported an olive-green field hat bearing five stars and the national shield—all symbols of the commander-in-chief—to underscore his solidarity with the federal forces assigned to confront drug-traffickers. On another occasion, the president's two young sons wore military uniforms as they observed the 2007 Independence Day parade alongside their parents and the secretaries of defense and navy. On "Army Day" in February 2008, the chief executive announced a 500-peso pay increase for soldiers, bringing average monthly salaries to 5,717 pesos or $531.32.[93]

The chief executive's wife also played her role by inviting the children of members of the Presidential Military Staff to a party at los Pinos to express thanks for the contribution that their fathers and mothers made to the First Family's security.

Meanwhile, the government commended the armed forces in television commercials and appointed to attaché posts in distant countries generals threatened by cartels. Felipe Calderón's deference towards the military and his increased use of troops to combat rampant drug violence helped bump up his approval rating. The armed forces have committed themselves to confronting the cartels because of their respect for the president, their nationalistic ethos, and their concern over the loss of sovereignty over broad areas to which the narco-barons have laid siege. In addition, military personnel enjoy greater protection than civilians who, even if they have several domiciles, find themselves vulnerable.

As described in Chapter 3, Mexican officials have turned to the military to help drive marijuana and heroin-poppy producers from their sanctuaries in the rugged folds of the western Sierra Madres in the late 1970s. Operation Condor temporarily dislodged the drug lords, and it gave rise to committing some 20,000 men of the Army's then 150,000 soldiers to eradication forays.

The campaign proved a source of pride for a military that does not have to worry about securing the country's borders, except for random encroachments by Guatemalan soldiers. Still, proximity to drugs has ignited allegations that senior officials—including a former defense minister, a secretary of the navy and several senior Army commanders—have also colluded with the traffickers. The low educational level of many soldiers has prompted the Defense Ministry to use comic books to warn against the ills of narcotics use and as instruction tools for conducting anti-drug operations.[94]

The assignment of the armed forces to undertake law enforcement duties also has sparked charges of human rights abuses. On June 1, 2007, soldiers at a checkpoint in the Sierra Mountains of Sinaloa fired more than a dozen rounds into an automobile, killing three children and two unarmed women. In the aftermath of the bloodbath, the Defense Ministry, which has established a human rights' office, arrested three officers and sixteen soldiers. Nevertheless, on March 26, 2008, soldiers killed five more civilians whose car failed to stop at a guardhouse in Badiraguato.[95] Spokesmen for NGOs fear that trying the accused in military courts will yield either exoneration or slaps on the wrist. Representatives of the National Human Rights Commission and sister organizations have asked that allegations of human rights abuses be heard by civilian, not military, courts. They argued that of the 500 suspected human rights violations presented to the Army between January 1, 2006, and December 31, 2008, only 174 investigations were initiated, just eleven suspects were apprehended and no sentences were handed down.[96]

Military tribunals hear most criminal cases against soldiers and they often treat them as disciplinary matters rather than crimes. The defense secretary, an advocate of the current system, appoints all military judges whom he can remove at his discretion. Verdicts are not made public, and the accused have no recourse to civilian appellate courts. When the New York-based Human Rights Watch asked for examples of any cases in which soldiers had been convicted of crimes, the Defense Ministry failed to provide information.[97]

Such issues led Mexico's Supreme Court (SCJN) to review the jurisdiction of military tribunals. Proponents of curbing their authority cite Article 13 of the Mexican Constitution, which refers to "crimes and violations against military discipline" but does not apply to crimes in general. If the SCJN removes the case involving the deaths in Badiraguato from military judges, it will be heard by a civilian district court.[98]

Calderón's anti-drug war has aroused criticism from other quarters. For instance, the president of the Sinaloan Civic Front excoriated Operation Culiacán-Navolato that was centered in her state. She observed that 1,200 violent deaths occurred in 2008 and that hit men have made three attempts on the life of Navolato's mayor during this intervention. "Despite the arrival of federal forces, she asserted, "we live [in] the most cruel wave of insecurity, including repeated attacks on state and local officials...."[99] Since Calderón's inauguration, the internationally respected Centro de Derechos Humanos Miguel Agustín Pro Juárez, A.C., has recorded 120 complaints, while Mexico's National Human Rights Commission has received 1,230 accusations of abuses by the military.[100] The CNDH received 588 complaints in 2008 alone—up from 395 in 2007.[101]

In the same vein, a non-governmental organization, The National Front against Repression, demanded the removal of armed forces from the streets because of their harsh treatment of citizens. "The grave violations of human rights and the attacks on lives by the military spurs an increase in crime that multiplies in an alarming manner," said a spokesman for the group.[102] Nevertheless, 62 percent of respondents to a survey applauded the use of military force, while support for Calderón's approach to combating organized crime rose from 58 percent in March 2007 to 74 percent in February 2009. Respondents showed their animus toward hit men and cartel chiefs by endorsing their torture (60 percent) and execution (65 percent).[103] However, pollster Dan Lund found that the approval rating of the Army falls when it is deployed in a state. "Strong support for the Army is where they are not," he said.[104] This assertion flies in the face of growing public backing for the armed forces, even in theaters of operations where citizens increasingly provide the military with information about cartel activities.

Proceso scorned the drug war as "Calderón's Iraq," and Jorge Castáñeda has castigated the president for failing to clarify his objectives. "Do we want to defeat and banish the cartels, or just force them back to their lairs? Do we want to spare Mexico (but not the United States) by sealing off Mexico's southern border, thereby rerouting drug shipments from South America to the United States via detours in the Caribbean and the gulf?," queried the former foreign secretary.[105] The police's venality left the president with two alternatives at the beginning of his administration: either sit on his hands or put boots on the ground.

In Nuevo León, Los Zetas, with the collaboration of local police, have tried to take advantage of human rights violations by giving poor people—often children—cell phones, school supplies, and toys. In return for these and other gifts, the recipients hoist banners, shout slogans, and mobilize opposition to the presence of the military and federal police in their state. "Soldiers Go Home!" "We Want Peace; Out with the Army," "The Soldiers Scare Us!"—were among the various chants intoned by these so-called "Hidden Ones" or "*Tapados,*" who may number 30,000 individuals in the metropolitan Monterrey area.[106]

In early May 2009 municipal police in San Nicolás de los Garza, Nuevo León, aided the escape of local Zeta leader "El Comandante Colosio," probably the pseudonym for Sergio Peña Solís (who also goes by René Solís Carlos) during a firefight between the Army and the criminal gang. Police from the nearby municipality of Apodaca also fired on the armed forces. Authorities apprehended two police officers and several of the cartel chief's bodyguards.[107]

Like his predecessor, Secretary Galván Galván has appeared before congressional committees to discuss the behavior of troops and to apprise legislators' of their needs. In these appearances and in public statements, he has emphasized that the Army's supplies will last only twelve days, fewer in the case of howitzers (5.5 days), grenades (nine days), 7.62 mm shells for PC-7, PC-9, Bell 212 helicopters, and MD-530 helicopters (five days).

In addition to a shortage of munitions, the cabinet official pointed out that the 594 units of 13-year-old night-vision equipment and the GPS devices employed by Special Forces had "seen their best days." Also, out-of-date were 150,392 anti-fragment helmets, and 41,160 bulletproof vests would last only through 2009.

The Army and Air Force have approximately 200,000 members, only about 80,000 to 100,000 perform combatant roles.[108] At any given time, tens of thousands of troops are on leave, injured, ill, in training, in detention, away without leave (AWOL), or otherwise unable to serve. Professor Roderic Ai Camp, America's leading expert on the Mexican military, expresses grave misgivings about the interdiction strategy and argues that major troop deployments mean that the "armed forces are stretched to the limit."[109] General Galván will have to expand his forces significantly to continue to confront the drug syndicates unless Calderón introduced a new policy—something he seemed prepared to do in mid-2009.

The defense secretary said that the materials of the 11,700-member Air Force, a branch of the Army, were in even worst shape—in terms of bombs, air-to-air missiles, and .20 mm ammunition.[110] To enhance this service's role in the anti-narcotics war, Galván Galván named as the new commander of the Air Force General Leonardo González García, 61, who has directed reconnaissance flights over drug plantations and other cartel facilities.[111] Priorities for new weapons include twelve F-16 aircraft (to replace the old F-5s), four anti-aircraft batteries for the southeast of the country, and radar that would provide the nationwide coverage that is now lacking. In addition, the Defense Ministry would like to add 10,000 members to the Cuerpo de Fuerzas de Apoyo Federal, the force that has made gains under General Rodolfo Cruz López.[112]

In early March 2009 Admiral Michael Mullen, chairman of the U.S. Joint Chiefs of Staff, met with Galván Galván and Saynez in Mexico City. The American visitor voiced "concern for the challenge of organized crime and narco-trafficking" and expressed appreciation for the vigorous efforts to improve security. In addition, he stated a willingness to provide unmanned spy planes to collect intelligence, carry out reconnaissance missions, and help locate criminals. The Pentagon subsequently announced that it would earmark $12,945,000 for Mexico's armed forces "to reduce [the area] of ungovernable territory that can be exploited by violent terrorist organizations." These resources are in addition to those provided under the Mérida Initiative. Such aid aside, Mexico's secretary of defense adamantly rejects the introduction of U.S. troops on his nation's soil. Mexican leaders also expressed alarm over the demand by U.S. border governors, including Texas' Rick Perry's, to deploy National Guard units along the Texas-Mexico frontier.[113]

The military brass believes that shortages of aging equipment contribute to the Army's extremely high desertion rate, which has been estimated to be 150,000 officers and soldiers during the period from 2001 to 2008—including 18,128 in 2008. Jorge Justiano González Betancourt, a retired general who presides over the Chamber of Deputies' National Defense Committee, claims that 80 percent of the deserters are young men who find they lack a military vocation. The drug lords seek to accentuate this disenchantment through inhumane acts. For example, in late December 2008, authorities discovered the tortured and decapitated bodies of eight officers and enlisted men in Chilpancingo, Guerrero. The soldiers, assigned to the 41st Infantry Battalion of the Military Zone 35, apparently were ambushed when returning to barracks after a leave. General Galván Galván said that such treachery would only "reinforce the commitment to combat effectively this scourge in order to recover spaces occupied by narco-traffickers and ensure the security and social peace that Mexicans demand."[114] This butchery may have been designed to provoke an over-reaction by the Army and thus amplify claims of human rights abuses. If this was the objective, the Defense Ministry said it would fail, according to a document released in late December 2008: "The members of this institution will always carry out their duties within the framework of the law and with complete respect for the individual guarantees of cities...."[115]

Elites have also gone AWOL. Between 1994 and 2004, 1,383 members of the Airborne Special Forces Groups or GAFES and other elite personnel deserted; this figure fell to 177 between 2005 and 2008. The military budget has grown in recent years—from 22 billion pesos (2001) to 35.3 billion pesos (2008) to 43.6 billion pesos (2009).[116]

Issues of promotion complicate matters! A graduate of the Heroic Military College, Mexico's version of West Point, will attain the rank of captain in approximately eight years. At that point, he or she may seek to enter the Superior War College (CSG), analogous to the U.S. Army's Command and General Staff College at Ft. Leavenworth, Kansas. Only about 25 percent of the applicants gain admission to the three-year CSG course, whose graduates receive the General Staff Diploma (Diploma del Estado Mayor—or DEM). This distinction places the holder on the fast-track to advancement and prestigious assignments. The remaining 75 percent may remain in the Army in hopes of reaching the rank of colonel; others may resign their commissions to take security jobs in the private or public sectors; some will try to enter the United States illegally; and a handful will cast their lot with drug cartels, as did the original Zetas.

The Navy, which Defense Ministry officers consider a little brother, has played an increasingly effective role in the anti-drug conflict without the personnel problems besetting the Army. In contrast to past personality clashes, Saynez seems to get along well with Galván Galván, and the leaders often attend each other's ceremonial functions. Saynez has shrewdly maintained a low-profile as the 50,000-member Navy has spearheaded major seizures of narcotics and cash in accord with the secretary's pledge to give "unconditional support" to Calderón's objectives.[117] This assistance crystallized in the seizure of twenty-three tons and 562 kilograms of cocaine aboard a ship that had arrived in Manzanillo from Colombia in October 2007. Six months later, the Navy intercepted $12 million in U.S. currency along with illegal goods on board a vessel bound for Panama.

Marginalized during the Fox administration, the Marines, who number 19,328 men and form part of the Navy, have been given more responsibilities since December 2006. As a result, they have won recognition for ferreting out and destroying drug crops. In April 2009 Marines burned

700,000 marijuana plants on twenty-five farms with a combined size of 130,747 square meters. This eradication took place in the Michoacán towns of Las Tinajas, Zapotillos, La Coralilla, and La Manguera. In nearby Las Peñitas, they destroyed 100 kilograms of dry marijuana. Marines also undertook successful operations against growers near Topolobampo and Mazatlán, Sinaloa.[118]

Several factors explain why the Navy suffers relatively few desertions. It attracts many more middle-class applicants for the Heroic Naval Academy, carefully vets these men and women, conducts follow-up tests once they are on active duty, enjoys more prestige as a service, and produces cosmopolitan officers who may have visited many countries. In addition, there are fewer obstacles to reaching the upper echelons of the service.[119]

The Navy has shown greater readiness to innovate and to work with private contractors. In 2004 it began to deploy Spot ERMEXS satellites not only to track the movement of criminal organizations but also to detect marijuana and poppy fields in Nayarit, Jalisco, Campeche, Quintana Roo, and Veracruz. Naval officials are now negotiating with three technology firms—Geo Eye, Digital Globe and Imágenes Satelitales, SA—to enhance its ability to combat narco-trafficking.[120]

In April 2009 the Mexican Navy joined its counterparts from ten other countries in "Unitas 50-09," a maritime exercise sponsored by the United States and held off the coast of Mayport, Florida. This marked the first time in the fifty-year history of the event that the Mexicans had taken part as full contributors to this multilateral venture.[121]

Governors and mayors are actively pursuing individuals with military backgrounds to serve in public safety positions, often in large jurisdictions. As seen in Table 7.3, retired ranking officers are discharging security functions in more than a dozen states and large municipalities.

While by no means new to Mexico, this approach offers several advantages. First, many of the officers selected have served as regional or zone commanders and have years of experience combating the drug mafias.

Second, they are likely to have ties to—and the confidence of—current regional and zonal military chiefs with whom they often coordinate assaults on cartels.

Third, whether retired or on leave, military officers may be familiar with the tactics of Los Zetas, the original contingent of which served in the Army's elite Special Forces Airmobile Group. General Rolando Eugenio Hidalgo Heddy, Public Security Secretary in Aguascalientes, headed these commandoes.

Table 7.3
States and Municipalities with Military Men in Senior Public-Safety Posts

State/ Municipality	Position	Incumbent	Date Appointed
Acapulco (Guerrero)	Director of Municipal Traffic and Protection	Brig. General (ret.) Serafín Valdez Martínez	Jan. 2, 2009
Aguascalientes	Secretary of Public Security	Div. General Rolando Eugenio Hidalgo Heddy; former commander of IX Military Zone headquartered in Culiacán; and ex-head of GAFES	Oct. 6, 2008
Baja California	Director of State Police	Brig. General Florencio Raúl Cuevas Salgado; former commander of II Military Zone headquartered in Tijuana	March 27, 2008
Ciudad Juárez	Director of Public Security

Director of Security Operations | Div. General (ret.) Julián David Rivera Bretón
Col. (ret.) Alfonso Cristóbal García Melgar | March 16, 2009

March 16, 2009 |
| **Coahuila** | Director of State Police

Undersecretary of Prevention and Social Readaptation | Brig. General (ret.) Jesús Ernesto Estrada Bustamante
General José Luis García Dorantes | Aug. 12, 2008

Feb. 24, 2009 |
Gómez Palacio (Durango)	Director of Municipal Public Security	Lt. Col. Antonio Horacio Ramírez Morales (Ret.)	Feb. 14, 2008
Guerrero	Secretary of Public Security	Div. General (ret.) Juan Heriberto Salinas Altés, former Army chief of staff	April 1, 2005
Morelos	Secretary of Public Security	General (ret.) Gastón Menchaca Arias	May 15, 2009

Table 7.3 (cont.)

	General Coordinator of the State College of Public Security	Brig. General (ret.) Héctor Andrés Alvizu Hernández	April 22, 2008
Oaxaca	Secretary of Citizen Protection	Lt. Col. (ret.) Javier Rueda Velásquez	March 31, 2008
Puebla	Secretary of Public Security	Div. General (ret.) Mario Ayón Rodríguez; former director-general of personnel for Defense Ministry	March 1, 2005
Saltillo (Coahuila)	Director General of the Municipal Preventative Police	Brig. General (ret.) Marco Antonio Delgado Talavera	Jan. 29, 2009
Tabasco	Acting Secretary of Public Security	Mayor (ret.) Sergio López Uribe	Feb. 1, 2009
Tijuana (Baja California)	Municipal Secretary of Public Security	Lt. Col. (ret.) Julián Leyzaola Pérez	Dec. 2, 2008
	Operational head of the city's police force	Captain Francisco Ortega Zamora	March 19, 2009
	Commander of the forces strategic central area	Air Force Captain Víctor Manuel de la Cruz	March 19, 2009
	Assistant Commander of this the central area	Lt. Adrián Hernandez	March 19, 2009
Tlaxcala	Secretary of Public Security	Div. General-(ret) José Leopoldo Martínez González	Jan. 1, 2009
Veracruz	Secretary of Public Security	Div. General Sergio López Esquer; former zone commander for states of Coahuila, Baja California, Baja California Sur, and Veracruz	July 1, 2008

Source: Jésica Zermeño, "Toman Generales Mandos Policiacos," *Reforma*, February 15, 2009; Zermeño *et al.*, Optan estados por mando militar," *Reforma* ("Enfoque"), February 15, 2009; "Encabezan los hermanos Ayón Rodríguez mandos policiacos en el país," February 15, 2009, *E-consulta* www.e-consulta.com/index; and "Border Militarization Spreads and Deepens," *Frontiera NorteSur*, March 19, 2009.

Fourth, generals, admirals, and colonels have the background to bring a culture of discipline to civilian police forces that have often acted in a venal, free-wheeling manner—to the point that thousands of serious kidnappings and other felonies go unreported because many citizens believe that the cops are in league with the miscreants.

Even if military leaders cannot change behavioral patterns, they can oust incompetents and malefactors. For instance, General Salinas Altés removed 200 elements of Acapulco's Municipal Preventive Police when he took over as Guerrero's security boss.

Fifth, officers are in a good position to recruit active-duty or retired members of the armed forces as policemen in the jurisdictions that they serve.

Finally, every public-opinion survey shows that the military enjoys a much better reputation than do the police. Praise centers on their efforts in disaster relief, as well as their anti-crime missions.

The Other Side of the Coin

These factors must be weighed against the different professional preparation of Army and Navy personnel vis-à-vis officeholders. The former are taught to employ force to subdue an enemy. While encouraged to acquire diplomatic skills, repression is emphasized. In contrast, good politicians need to negotiate with average citizens who are angry or agitated, attempting to resolve disputes through conciliation rather than resorting to a physical or armed response.

As Carlos Luken, a Mexico-based businessman and consultant, astutely observed:

> A soldier is trained to fight, kill and be victorious. When a good soldier does his job, he uses tactics and strategies, not rights and negotiation. People get hurt. A politician is trained to buy time for argument, concession and to seek accommodation. Their methods are totally different. It is a colossal error to have one and ask him to behave like the other. Doing so is not only fruitless and confusing, but dangerous as it eventually pits them against each other. In the short outcome the rules of engagement eventually overrun the rules of order, while in the long run both lose.[122]

Respected author Charles Bowden agrees. In an article enlivened with grisly anecdotes, he implies that the Mexican Army is the "biggest cartel of all" and focuses not on Calderón's successes but on "a second Mexico where the war is *for* drugs, where the police and the military fight for their share of drug profits, where the press is restrained by the murder of reporters and feasts on a steady diet of bribes, and where the line between the government and the drug world has never existed."[123]

Then, there is the danger that these men face. Los Zetas, in particular, have homed in on military personnel. They are believed to have decapitated the eight Army officers and enlisted men in Guerrero in December 2008. After this tragedy, the mayor in charge of Chilpancingo, Héctor Astudillo Bello, sought closer collaboration with the local zonal commander concerning security issues.[124]

These paramilitaries stand accused of having methodically broken his arms and legs when torturing retired Brigadier General Mauro Enrique Tello Quiñones, and then driving him into the jungle and executing him with a shot to the head. His mangled corpse and those of two aides were discovered on February 3, 2009, two days after the mayor of Cancún had hired Tello Quiñones to form a SWAT team to fight criminals in the resort city.[125] One week later, the Army arrested Octavio "El Gori 4" Almanza Morales and six other Zetas for the crime.[126] El Gori 4's brothers, Raymundo and Eduardo, have evaded capture. In late May 2009 the military grabbed the Cancún *plaza*'s new head honcho, who had been using two names: Félix Camacho Pérez or José "El Boti" Hernández González. They also took into custody his lieutenant, Julio César "El Gastón" Guerra Alvarado.[127]

Tabasco's Governor Andrés Granier Melo has had trouble keeping military safety chiefs because of threats from the underworld. Retired Major Sergio López Uribe is the fourth ex-military man to function as the state's secretary of public security.[128]

Ciudad Juárez's police chief, retired Major Roberto Orduña Cruz, stepped down on February 20, 2009, after several officers were slain during the week and the killers posted handwritten signs saying a policeman would be executed every forty-eight hours until he resigned. More than 1,350 people died in Ciudad Juárez last year in a wave of unspeakable violence that included the beheadings and murder of more than sixty police officers.

Even bodyguards of the governor of Chihuahua, the state where Ciudad Juárez is located, fell under attack on February 22, 2009, during which one escort died and two were seriously wounded. The state's death toll had already reached 878 during the first half of 2009. In mid-March, at the suggestion of Defense Secretary Galván Galván, Ciudad Juárez's mayor named retired General Julián David Rivera Bretón as the city's new security chief.[129]

In late April 2009, 150 preventative police agents went on strike to protest the alleged harsh treatment by Public Security director Col. Arturo Navarro López. Three days later, he was assassinated.[130]

Interjecting military personnel into sensitive posts can also breed corruption. On January 17, 2009, Chiapas Governor Juan Sabines ousted retired General Marco Esteban Juárez Escalera as director of state police because of his alleged involvement in illegal activities. As mentioned above, the removal of retired General Gutiérrez Rosas as head of the federal police at the Mexico City airport furnishes another example.

Such actions have not prevented mayors from working with the Defense Ministry to recruit military policemen as law enforcement officers in their cities. Ciudad Juárez alone is seeking to attract 500 to 1,000 soldiers, offering a salary of 9,800 pesos per month ($726) compared with their current pay of 3,600 pesos ($267).[131]

Private companies are also making recruiting offers to members of the armed forces to safeguard businesses, individuals, their families, and foreign visitors. Ricardo de León, president of the National Council of Private Security, estimates that 40 percent of bodyguards in the private sector are ex-military—generally between the ages of twenty-eight and forty. Not only do their display rigorous discipline and dress neatly, but they retain the lifetime right to carry a firearm, something not permissible for private security guards. De León calculates that they earn from 12,000 to 20,000 pesos per month. This pay, which supplements any military pension and other benefits received, may account for the record number of middle-grade officers who retired in 2007: 171 second lieutenants, 313 lieutenants, and 182 captains.[132]

Younger officers—like their senior counterparts—no longer mask frustration at putting their lives and those of their troops in harm's way amid ever more piercing attacks from NGOs, while politicians amass fortunes conniving with and protecting narco-criminals. When asked privately if Mexico is winning the drug war, many captains and majors will say off the record: "No, the civilians are losing it."

In a flight of speculative fancy, *Reforma*'s René Delgado has even expressed fear that a protracted, open-ended conflict could eventually persuade military and police commanders that they have a vested interest in its continuation in terms of increased budgets, higher salaries, faster promotions, and improved equipment. Although Delgado admits that such a development is unlikely, a symbiotic relationship between armed institutions and the cartels—a latter-day version of the converging goals of Baptists and bootleggers during Prohibition—would ensure Mexico's failure as a state.

Table 7.4
Calderón's Anti-Drug Operations

Operation	Date	Personnel	Goal
Michoacán I	Dec. 10, 2006	Initial deployment of 6,784--4,260 Soldiers, 1,054 marines, 1,420 federal police, and 50 detectives.	To eradicate drug cultivation and to combat by land, sea, and air Los Valencias, Los Zetas, and La Familia; marijuana and poppy fields destroyed, weapons seized, boats and vehicles confiscated and 1,301 suspects arrested, including Alfonso "Ugly Poncho" Barajas, a low-level leader of a Zeta unit.
Tijuana	Jan. 1, 2007	1,242 federal police and soldiers.	To restore order in a city beset by murders and kidnappings by the AFO, which engages in various criminal acts, including drug smuggling; 2,443 suspects arrested among whom were three foreigners.
Guerrero	Jan. 13, 2007	7,600 federal police, Army, and marines.	To end horrendous murders, especially in Acapulco; arrested 494 suspects and seized weapons, vehicles, communications equipment, and police uniforms.
Golden Triangle/Sierra Madre (Chihuahua, Durango, and Sinaloa)	Feb. 13, 2007	9,054 soldiers, 40 airplanes, 20 helicopters, and 25 trained dogs.	To destroy marijuana crops, and collect weapons and vehicles used by narco-traffickers; 442 surveillance flights facilitated the destruction of 3,151 hectares of marijuana and poppy, as well two laboratories; 2,188 suspects arrested; weapons, aircraft, and $34,000 seized.
Nuevo León-Tamaulipas	Feb. 17, 2007	3,499 soldiers with three airplanes and six helicopters.	To capture members of the Gulf Cartel and Los Zetas; 1,396 suspects arrested, including 7 foreigners.

Table 7.4 (cont.)

Tabasco	March 17, 2007	200 PFP and 20 Army personnel.	To rein in drug activities believed to be spearheaded by local law-enforcement officials who belonged to the shadowy "La Hermandad" or "The Brotherhood"; three police chiefs and a state official arrested.
Operation Dragon	Early and mid-2007	DEA authorities in cooperation with the PGR.	To captured Chinese-Mexican chemical importer Zhenli Ye Gon whom the DEA apprehended in Maryland on July 23, 2007; previously, authorities had found in his luxurious D.F. homes $227 million in cash and travelers' checks; in addition, the PGR discovered a cache of expensive automobiles, high-powered rifles, and equipment to make amphetamine pills.
Michoacán II	Spring-Summer 2007	4,579 federal police and soldiers.	To curb murders and kidnappings as gangs warred over drug routes.
Veracruz	May 11, 2007	1,200 PFP and soldiers.	To affirm the rule of law in the aftermath of the murder of four bodyguards protecting the three sons of Enrique Peña Nieto, the governor of Mexico state.
Sonora	May 16, 2007	PFP and soldiers.	To quell the raging turf battle between Gulf and Sinaloa cartels; 3,833 suspects arrested since Dec. 1, 2006.
Michoacán III	Oct. 20, 2007	100 members of the military, the AFI, and the PFP.	To stymie narco-activities in the state, with a focus on the port of Lázaro Cárdenas through which cocaine and precursor drugs pour into Mexico.

Table 7.4 (cont.)

Manzanillo (Colima)	Oct. 30, 2007	Navy, PFP, Army, Customs, and AFI.	To thwart illegal drug shipments; found 23 tons and 562 kilograms of cocaine in a vessel that had arrived at Manzanillo from Colombia—the largest such seizure recorded in Mexico.
Tamaulipas "Northeast Operation"	Jan. 22, 2008	Hundreds of GAFES.	To relieve local police of duty and disarmed their officers in Nuevo Laredo, Matamoros, and Reynosa as Army troops searched for evidence that might link them to ever-more violent traffickers in the state.
Tamaulipas-Nuevo León Operation	Feb. 28, 2008	110 soldiers of the Special Forces 10th battalion.	To combat intra-cartel violence as several lieutenants sought to take charge of the Gulf Cartel after Osiel Cárdenas' 2007 extradition to the U.S.
Manzanillo (Colima)	March 6, 2008	Navy, Customs, and federal police.	To intercept illegal goods and cash; seized nearly $12 million in U.S. currency, which originated in Toluca and was found on a ship bound for Panama, a major trans-shipment point for Colombian traffickers.
Southern Area "Clean-up Operation"	March 2008	Army and civilian authorities.	To scrutinize small aircraft from Colombia, Venezuela, and Panama to prevent entry of drugs into Mexico.
Joint Chihuahua Operation I	March 23, 2008	485 soldiers from D.F., including 200 members of the Corps of Special Forces who belonged to the Parachute Brigade. At least three Guatemalan commandoes known as Kaibiles assisted in the strike.	To seize cocaine, marijuana, heroin, and meth; captured 42 individuals, 37 weapons, and 51 vehicles.

Table 7.4 (cont.)

		Hercules C-130, Boeing 727, and Barreta .50 mm machine gun employed.	
Joint Chihuahua Operation I (Expanded)	March 27, 2008 (Reinforcements in April)	400 federal police; military provided 2,526 troops, 180 tactical vehicles, 3 aircraft; 46 mobile control posts sent to violence-afflicted Ciudad Juárez.	To curb mounting and Unprecedented bloodshed sparked by turf disputes between the Sinaloa and Juárez cartels; captured several big shots in the Juárez Cartel, as well as armored vehicles and high-powered weapons.
Operation in Tijuana, Ciudad Juárez, and Culiacán	May 10, 2008	Armed forces and federal, state, and local police.	To combat the proliferation of drug-related violence— exacerbated by inter-cartel strife—in these three cities.
Culiacán-Navolato	May 13, 2008	3,000 members of the armed forces and federal police.	To counter, in three stages, the severe resistance from Beltrán Leyva loyalists, as well as from local police; Gen. Rodolfo Cruz López, who commanded the action, complained that the criminals had more lethal weapons than his troops; captured 6 tons and 280 kilos of marijuana, 425 kilos of cocaine, troves of weapons and vehicles, and $5.3 million in cash.
Crossed Swords (Armas Cruzadas)	June 9, 2008	Joint effort by U.S. government (ICE and AFT) and Mexican authorities.	To curb cross-border arms shipments; gave rise to the seizure of 1,628 weapons, 189,446 bullets, approximately $21 million, and 391 criminals.
Michoacán IV	July 28, 2008	Federal police and soldiers from the 21st Military Zone.	To stem the contagion of kidnappings that had reached 30 by late July 2008, compared with 33 during all of 2007; Army confiscated high-powered weapons, ammuni-

Table 7.4 (cont.)

			tion, and fragmentation grenades, while dismantling a house that served as operations' center of the extortionists.
Tabasco	Sept. 5, 2008	Army's 17th Infantry Battalion and federal police took control of the municipality of Cárdenas.	To reduce the firepower of criminal organizations linked to police in 11 of the state's 17 municipalities; captured scores of rifles and pistols, as well as military equipment and 13 vehicles; soldiers confined state police to their headquarters to inspect their weapons; authorities took the state police director to Mexico City for questioning.
Michoacán V	Sept. 15-16, 2008	Soldiers from the 21st Military Zone, federal, state, and local police.	To restore order and apprehend the culprits who threw two fragmentation grenades into a large crowd in Morelia amid the Sept. 15 Independence Day celebration.
Project Reckoning	Sept. 16, 2008	Italian authorities; U.S. agencies including the Justice Department, DEA, FBI, Internal Revenue Service, U.S. Marshals Service (During his 2007 visit to Italy, President Calderón discussed cooperation on drug issues with local law enforcement officials).	To crack an international drug and money-laundering scheme; seized $60 million, 40 tons of narcotics, and 175 suspects, including second-tier Gulf Cartel members.
Operation House-Cleaning (Operación Limpieza)	Late Summer/ Fall 2008	Attorney General's Office in cooperation with the DEA.	To apprehend bribe-taking officials working for the cartels; authorities arrested former SIEDO chief Noê Ramírez Mandujano and

Table 7.4 (cont.)

			other high-level officials for leaking information to drug barons.
Mapache	Oct. 8, 2008	PGR (SIEDO).	To shut down a complex network, involving the shipment of drugs from Mexico to Atlanta, Philadelphia, and Indiana; captured Wenceslao "El Wencho" Álvarez Álvarez, an operator for both the Gulf Cartel and La Familia.
Joint Chihuahua Operation II	November 2008	1,200 troops of the Army's airborne and motorized brigades.	To diminish the wave of violence pounding the state and especially Ciudad Juárez.
Operation Xcellerator	21 months culminating in the Feb. 24, 2009 announcement	The DEA and various U.S. law enforcement agencies.	To apprehended more than 755 Individuals believed to be linked to the Sinaloa Cartel in the U.S.
Joint Chihuahua Operation III	Feb. 28 and March 1, 2009	3,000 members of the Army's 20th Motorized Cavalry Regiment; 1,200 of these troops were brought in by air.	To fortify the effort against the tsunami of violence in Chihuahua in general and in Ciudad Juárez in particular; deemed unsuccessful, giving rise to a new strategy in mid-July 2009.
Michoacán VI	May 26, 2009	Federal forces swept into Michoacán, concentrating on Lázaro Cárdenas and trafficking corridors from the port. They arrested twenty-seven officials, including ten mayors.	To disrupt narco-trafficking in this violent state and to demonstrate that public servants involved with cartels did not enjoy impunity.
Operation Summer 2009	July 11 to August 24, 2009	SSP, in conjunction with relevant agencies, deployed 7,000 Federal Police, 1,700 patrol units, and 9,150 elements of	To provide additional security to protect tourists, focusing on highways, airports, and bus terminals. Four other initiatives formed part of this venture: (1) "30 Delta"

Table 7.4 (cont.)

		the Federal Support Forces.	concentrated on the mental and physical condition of drivers; (2) "Carousel and Radar Observing" to enforce speed limits on highways; (3) "Buckle-up" to ensure that automobile drivers and passengers used seat belts; and (4) "Detection and Anti-assaults" to zero-in on high crime zones, as well as employ metal detectors and other devices to prevent the presence of guns in airports and bus depots.
Michoacán VII (Operative Conjunto)	July 11, 2009	Armed forces and Federal Police sent 5,500 elements to Michoacán and Guanajuato.	To stanch La Familia's attacks on Federal Police and Army installations in retaliation for the arrest of the syndicate's leader Arnoldo "La Minsa" Rueda Medina.

Sources: Sam Logan, "Mexican President Calderón Overhauls Security," *Mexidata. info*, January 22, 2007 www.mexidata.info; Laurence Pantin, "Combate al narcotráfico," *Enfoque* ("*Reforma*"), June 17, 2007; Secretaría de Defensa, *Comparencia ante la comisión de defensa nacional de la Cámara de Diputados, April 26, 2007*, "Mexico: Semana sombria para las ofensivas anti-delito," *Informe Latinoamericana*, May 17, 2007; "México—Conducirán la Operaciones Juárez con tácticas Kaibiles," *Offnews.info*, March 29, 2008 *www.offnews.info/verArticulo.php?contenidoID=10743*; "'Blindarán' Juárez, Culiacán y Tijuana contra guerra de carteles," *El Diario*, May 10, 2008; "Arraigan a cinco mandos policiacas por Operación Limpieza," *Excelsior*, November 21, 2008; Benito Jiménez, "Alistan militares para Chihuahua," *Reforma*, November 25, 2008; "Van mil 200 militares más a Cd. Juárez," *Reforma*, March 1, 2009; and "Alista la SSP operativo de verano," *Reforma*, July 11, 2009.

Notes

1. Castañeda, "Mexico Goes to War: Calderon's drug crusade is winning fans, but can he win the fight? *Newsweek* (International Edition), May 28, 2007.
2. Gobierno de México, *Segundo Informe*, September 1, 2008 *www.presidencia.gob. mx/*.
3. "Responde hampa con violencia," *Reforma* (Enfoque), November 30, 2008.
4. "Responde hampa con violencia," *Reforma* (Enfoque); and "Seguridad, tarea pendiente," El *Informador*, January 3, 2008.
5. "Responde hampa con violencia," *Reforma* (Enfoque).
6. Alonso Garza Treviño, bishop of Piedras Negras, stated that drug baron Osiel Cárdenas Guillén contributed tons of food for the victims of floods that afflicted Coahuila in 2006; see, Leopoldo Ramos, "Rechazan que el narco financie a la iglesia," *El Siglo de Torreón*, October 21, 2006; in 1997 Raúl Soto, the canon of the Basilica of Guadalupe, suggested in a homily that more Mexicans should follow the example of kingpin Rafael Caro Quintero and Amado Carrillo Fuentes who had given millions of pesos to the church; see, Carlos Fazio, "Polémica con la Iglesia en México por narcolimosnas," *Clarin.com*, September 25, 1997.
7. Carlos Fazio, "Polémica con la Iglesia en México por narcolimosnas," *Clarin.com* (Buenos Aires), September 25, 1997.
8. "Monseñor de oro," *Milenio.com*, December 19, 2008.
9. Miguel Angel Granados Chapa, "Plaza Pública: Bendito lavado de dinero," *El Diario*, April 7, 2008.
10. Lawrence Iliff, "Mexico's Drug Traffickers are Financing Churches, Bishop Says," *Dallas Morning News*, April 5, 2008.
11. Quoted in Efraín Klérigan and Roland Herrera, "Piden paz Obispos a narcos," *Reforma*, March 3, 2009.
12. Quoted in *El Financiero*, March 20, 2005; see, Bill and Patty Coleman, "Church Queried in Mexican Murder Probe," *National Catholic Reporter*, March 31, 2005.
13. Granados Chapa, "Plaza Pública: Bendito lavado de dinero."
14. Bill and Patty Coleman, "Church Queried in Mexican Murder Probe."
15. Mónica Perla Hernández, "'El Chapo' vive en Durango: arzobispo," *El Universal*, April 18, 2009.
16. William Booth, "Mexican Archbishop: 'Everyone Knows' Where Drug Lord Lives," *Washington Post*, April 23, 2009.
17. "Provoca crimen organizado un Estado paralelo en Durango," *Terra*, May 12, 2009.
18. Quoted in Booth, "Mexican Archbishop: 'Everyone Knows' Where Drug Lord Lives."
19. Noemí Gutiérrez, "Políticos dan soporte al narco desde el gobierno, acusa obispo," *El Universal*, April 23, 2009.
20. "Advierte Arzobispo invasión de sicarios," *Reforma*, June 29, 2009.
21. For an extended analysis, see James H. Creechan and Jorge de la Herrán García, "Without God or Law: Narcoculture and Belief in Jesús Malverde," *Religious Studies and Theology* 24, no. 2 (2005): 53.
22. Sam Quiñones, "Jesus Malverde," *Front Line: Drug Wars*, PBS *www.pbs.org/ wgbh*.
23. "El culto a la Santísima Muerte, un boom en México," *Terra. www.terra.com/arte/ articulo/html/art9442.htm*.
24. Quoted in Reed Johnson, "A 'Saint' of Last Resort," *Los Angeles Times*, March 19, 2004.

25.   "Destruyen 'narcocapillas' in BC," *Reforma*, March 25, 2009; and Olga R. Rodriguez, "Mexico Targets Death Saint Popular with Criminals," *Associated Press*, April 18, 2009.

26.   Sergio González Rodríguez, "Narcoliteratura mexicana," *Reforma*, March 25, 2009.

27.   See Elijah Wald. *Narcocorrido : A Journey into the Music of Drugs, Guns, and Guerrillas* (New York, NY: Rayo, 2001).

28.   At the time, the Beltrán Leyvas were still allied with Guzmán Loera and El Mayo Zambada.

29.   The PGR has attachés or liaison offices in Madrid, Vienna, Guatemala City, Bogotá, Washington, D.C., Chicago, Los Angeles, San Diego, San Antonio, and El Paso.

30.   Tracy Wilkinson, "Lions and Tigers and Drugs," *Los Angeles Times*, October 31, 2008.

31.   Quoted in Lawson, "The Making of a Narco State."

32.   *Ibid.*

33.   Sara Miller Llana, "Setbacks in Mexico's War on Corruption," *Christian Science Monitor*, December 30, 2008.

34.   *Ibid.*

35.   Ken Ellingwood, "Corruption Hurting Mexico's Fight against Crime, Calderón Says," *Los Angeles Times*, December 10, 2008.

36.   Sergio Aguayo Quezada, *La charola* (Mexico City: Grijalbo, 2001): 62.

37.   The National Security Archive at Washington University has increasingly added material and archives from this period *www.gwu.edu/~nsarchiv/*.

38.   Aguayo Quezada, *La charola*, p. 66.

39.   Philip Gunson, "Fernando Gutiérrez Barrios," *The Guardian*, November 2, 2000.

40.   Mary Beth Sheridan, "Fernando Gutiérrez Barrios; Mexico's Spy Chief," *Los Angeles Times* October 31, 2000.

41.   Jaime Castejón Díaz, Interview with author, March 10, 2009, Mexico City.

42.   Mary Beth Shcridan, "Conducting an Overt Operation," *Los Angeles Times*, June 30, 1999.

43.   Tim Weiner, "Fernando Gutiérrez, Head of Secret Police in Mexico, *New York Times*, November 1, 2000.

44.   Peter K. Núñez, Telephone interview with author, May 28, 2009.

45.   Víctor Hugo Michel and Dora Irene Rivera, "Mexican Miguel Nazar Haro Was Protected by the CIA," *Mexidata.info*, February 24. 2004; and "Convicted Ex-Chief Flown Home," *El Universal*, November 29, 2004.

46.   Filiberto Cruz Monroy, "Asesinos de Buendía cumplieron sentencia," *Excelsior*, February 20, 2009.

47.   Miguel Angel Granados Chapa, "Gran golpe o gran puesta en escena." *Reforma*, May 31, 2009.

48.   Quoted in Sheridan, "Conducting an Overt Operation."

49.   Quoted in Gunson, "Fernando Gutiérrez Barrios."

50.   Claudia Guerrero and Ariande García, "Desconfía Gobierno de 60% de la policía," *Reforma*, November 28, 2008.

51.   Quoted in Daniel Kurtz-Phelan, "The Long War of Genaro García Luna," *New York Times Magazine*, July 13, 2008.

52.   David Osborne, "Mexico Purges Top Police in Battle against Corruption, *The Independent* (London), June 28, 2007; a handful of these commanders were reinstated, but the SSP was reluctant to fire any of them lest they pursue careers in the underworld.

53.   By assuming direct control of the unit, the president would be liable before the International Court of Justice should the special corps commit crimes.

54.   "Crea Sedena el Cuerpo de Fuerzas de Apoyo Federal," *El Universal.com*, May 9, 2007; and Jorge Ramos Pérez, "Publican reform que crea Cuerpo de Especial del Ejército, *El Universal.com.mx*, September 17, 2007.

55.   Presentation to the Center for Strategic & International Studies, Washington, D.C., January 31, 2008.

56.   Quoted in "'Arrumba' PFP a 350 cadetes," *Reforma*, March 2, 2009.

57.   Study by the Federation's Superior Auditor of Public Accounts and reported in Antonio Baranda, "Abundan policías de carrera … corta," *Reforma*, March 21, 2009.

58.   "Templo Mayor," *Reforma*, December 28, 2008.

59.   Security expert Raúl Benítez Manaut quoted in Inter-American Dialogue, *Latin American Advisor*, March 13, 2008.

60.   Olga R. Rodriguez, "Mexican Senate Approves Judicial Reform," *Associated Press*, March 7, 2008.

61.   Quoted in Randal C. Archibold, "Mexican Prosecutors Train in U.S. for Changes in their Legal System," *New York Times*, April 24, 2009.

62.   Lawson, "The Making of a Narco State."

63.   Héctor Tobar, "Mexico Gives Final OK to Judicial System Reform," *Tampa Bay Online*, March 7, 2008 www2.tbo.com/content/2008/mar/07/.

64.   Carlos Avilés, "Los lujosos manjares de ex ministros," *El Universal*, March 9, 2009.

65.   Quoted in Spencer S. Hsu and Mary Beth Sheridan, "Anti-Drug Effort at Border Is Readied," *Washington Post*, March 22, 2009.

66.   "Mexican Army Urged to Take Over Prisons," *USA Today*, August 1, 2005.

67.   "Executan a 'zetas' en cárcel in Mazatlán," *Reforma*, December 14, 2008.

68.   Daniel Venegas, "Diputados exigen alto a la extorsión desde cárceles," *Milenio*, October 19, 2008.

69.   "Inhiben señal de celular en 4 cárceles," *Reforma*, December 31, 2008.

70.   Quoted in Henia Prado, "Toleran autoridades drogas en penales," *Reforma*, November 16, 2008.

71.   Icela Lagunas, "Detectan 119 kilos de mariguana en aduana del Reclusorio Sur," *El Universal*, December 15, 2008.

72.   "Robo y homicidio, los principales delitos que cometen mujeres," *El Mexicano*, March 24, 2008 *www.oem.com.mx/elmexicano*.

73.   "Mexican Army Urged to Take Over Prisons."

74.   Antonio Baranda, "Rompe récord droga decomisada en penales," *Reforma*, December 25, 2008.

75.   Yáscara López, "Festejan reos con cena, misa y alcohol," *Reforma*, December 31, 2008.

76.   "Llevan cárteles a penales guerra por territorios," *El Universal*, October 18, 2008; and Claudia Bolaños, "Cárceles, infierno de pobres," *El Universal*, May 16, 2009.

77.   "Activarán en junio la Primera Academia del Sistema Penitenciario," *Milenio. com*, May 12, 2009.

78.   Luis Brito, "Amotina el narco penales," *Reforma*, May 24, 2009.

79.   Sabastian Rotella, "Doing Time in Tijuana," *Los Angeles Times Magazine*, March 27, 1994; and David, PTO Administrator, "La Mesa Prison in Tijuana Mexico," *World Prison News*, August 23, 2002.

80.   Quoted in Dudley Althaus and Marion Lloyd, "Calderón Unveils Anti-Drug Initiative," *Houston Chronicle*, July 3, 2007.

81. Fernando Martínez, "Ubican 4 mil puntos donde venden droga," *El Universal*, July 7, 2007.
82. Carlos Camacho, "Las adicciones han crecido entre 15 y 20 por ciento annual, dice Medina Mora," *La Jornada*, August 3, 2007; the text of the article indicated 15 to 30 percent; the headline indicated 15 to 20 percent.
83. Sonia del Valle, "Ingresan a escuelas armas y narcóticos," *Reforma*, April 6, 2009; and David, PTO Administrator, "La Mesa Prison in Tijuana Mexico," *World Prison News*, October 22, 2002.
84. A study carried out by the State Population Council entitled "La niñez y juventud en Michoacán"; reported in "Aspiran niños a ser sicarios," *Reforma*, July 29, 2007.
85. "Han muerto 610 niños en las guerras por la droga: Sedena," *La Jornada*, April 12, 2009.
86. Quoted in Marc Lacey, "Drug Killings Haunt Mexican School Children," *New York Times*, October 19, 2008.
87. Nurit Martínez, "Prometen dar clase y 'no oír o ver nada,' en área de narcos," *El Universal*, March 25, 2009.
88. Quoted in Fainaru and Booth, "As Mexico Battles Cartels, the Army Becomes the Law."
89. Quoted in "Mexico Pledges to Help U.S. Fight Terror," CNN.com./US. http://archives.cnn.com/2001/US/09/29/gen.terror.mexico/.
90. His proclivities to support the military have been caricatured by many editorial cartoonists who frequently depict him wearing an oversized military fatigue outfit.
91. Fainaru and Booth, "As Mexico Battles Cartels, the Army Becomes the Law."
92. Stephanie Hanson, "*Backgrounder: Mexico's Drug War*," Council on Foreign Relations, June 28, 2007.
93. Claudia Herrera and Jesús Aranda, "Lealtad contra la delincuencia, pide Calderón a la tropa; les aumenta $500," *La Jornada*, February 20, 2008.
94. Jorge Alejandro Medellín, "Táctica militar antinarco en comics," *El Universal*, January 30, 2009.
95. "Mexico to Try 19 Soldiers in Civilian Shootings," *Reuters*, June 11, 2007 *www.reuters.com*; and Víctor Fuentes, "Acepta Corte revisar fuero militar," *Reforma*, April 1, 2009.
96. Liliana Alcántara and Jaime Hernández, "Demandan suprimer el fuero militar en lucha antinarco," *El Universal*, March 21, 2009.
97. "Barracks Law," *The Economist*, April 30, 2009.
98. Fuentes, "Acepta Corte revisar fuero militar."
99. Javier Cabrera, "Urgen reviser operativo policiaco," *El Universal*, November 30, 2008.
100. Centro de Derechos Humanos Prodh, "La Justicia militar propicia impunidad," *Boletín de Prensa*, March 9, 2009.
101. Silvia Garduño, "Persisten en México abusos militares—EU," *Reforma*, February 26, 2009.
102. Luis Carlos Cano, "ONG protestan contra las acciones militares," *El Universal*, November 30, 2008.
103. "Crece aprobación," *Reforma*, June 1, 2007; and Ulises Beltrán, "Apoya 60% la tortura a narcos," *EXonline*, March 2, 2009.
104. Quoted in Sara Miller Llana, "As Mexico's Drug War Rages, Military Takes over for Police," *Christian Science Monitor*, December 5, 2008.
105. Quoted in "Can Calderón Win Mexico's Drug War?" *Newsweek International*, May 28, 2007.
106. Juan Alberto Cedillo, "Pandillas al servicios del narco," *El Universal*, March 3, 2009.

107. "Facilitan policías huida de jefe 'Zeta'," *Reforma.com*, May 5, 2009.
108. The figures used, which may be dated, come from *Military Balance*, 107 (London: Institute for Strategic Studies, 2007).
109. Roderic Camp, electronic mail to author, May 26, 2009.
110. Jorge Alejandro Medellín, "En combate, las armas del Ejército alcanzan sólo para 12 días: Sedena," *El Universal*, January 2, 2009.
111. Benito Jiménez, "Va experto antidrogas a la FAM," *Reforma*, January 14, 2009, p. 10.
112. "¿Degradación del poder military?" *El Blog de Fred Álvarez*, December 3, 2008.
113. "Propone EU lucha militar conjunta," *Reforma*, March 7, 2009; Juan Arivizu and Andrea Merlos, "México no acepta ayuda de tropas de EU: Sedena," *Reforma*, March 20, 2009; and Doris Gómora, "EU dio partida para 'liberar territorios'," *El Universal*, March 25, 2009.
114. Quoted in Europa Press, "Encuentran nueve cadávares decapitados, entre ellos los de ocho soldados, en el suroeste de México," *Hispavista Noticias*, December 22, 2008.
115. "Reitera Sedena combate al narco con respeto a derechos humanos," *El Periódico de México*," December 30, 2008.
116. Juan Arvizu and Andrea Merlos, "Este año van 18 mil: diputados," *El Universal*, December 4, 2008; and "Desertan en 8 años 150 mil soldados," *El Siglo de Durango*, December 4, 2008.
117. Benito Jiménez, "Apoya Marina estrategia contra narco," *Reforma*, December 18, 2008.
118. "Destruye Semar 55 plantíos de droga en Michoacán y Sinaloa, *Milenio.com*, April 14, 2009.
119. "Reliability Tests Keep Officers away from Corruption—Mexican Navy," *BBC Monitoring Latin America*, November 16, 2008.
120. Jorge Alejandro Medellín, "Negocian servicios de satelite militar privado," *El Universal*, January 27, 2009.
121. "Mexican Navy Will Join US Navy in Multinational Maritime Exercise, MXC The Mexico Times Co., April 7, 2009.
122. Luken, "Politics versus the Mexican Military's War against Crime," *Mexidata. info*, August 11, 2008.
123. Quoted in Charles Bowden, "We Bring Fear," *Mother Jones*, July/August 2009: 31.
124. Jesús Guerrero, "Prevén pedir colaboración a Ejército," *Reforma*, January 3, 2009.
125. William Booth, "Warrior in Drug Fight Soon Becomes a Victim," *Washington Post*, February 9, 2009.
126. "Arraigan a 'El Gori 4' y a otros seis 'zetas' por muete del general Tello," *Noticaribe*, February 13, 2009.
127. María de la Luz González, "Cae 'El Boti' en Cancún," *El Universal*, May 28, 2009.
128. His predecessors were retired generals Francisco Fernández Solís (Jan. 1,2007-June 30, 2007); Alberto Espinoza Ramírez (June 30, 2007-Feb. 6, 2008); and Héctor Sánchez Gutiérrez (Feb. 6, 2008-Dec. 22, 2008). A sinister gang known as Hermandad (The Brotherhood), possibly headed by Roberto Vidal Méndez, may have attempted to assassinate General Fernández Solís, a former secretary of public security in Tabasco under Governor Roberto Madrazo (1994-2000) and ally of super-cop Admiral (ret.) Wilfredo Robledo Madrid; see, Rodulfo Reyes, "Atribuyen a Vidal Méndez de La Hermandad, autora de atentado al general Francisco Fernández Solís," *La Crónica*, April 8, 2009.

129.   "General en retiro assume el control de la seguridad pública en Ciudad Juárez," *La Jornada*, March 17, 2009.
130.   "Reconocen corrupción policiaca en Guerrero," *El Porvenir.com*, March 17, 2009; and "Ejecutan a director de Seguridad Pública de Piedras Negras, *El Porvenir*, April 26, 2009.
131.   Pedro Torres, "Reclutará el Municipio soldados como policías," *El Diario*, August 20, 2008.
132.   César Díaz, "Contrata la IP a ex militares," *Reforma*, November 9, 2008.

8

Emerging and New Narco Sects— Los Zetas and La Familia

Introduction

Drug-related violence in the border town of Nuevo Laredo, the major portal for U.S.-Mexican commerce, left the city of 350,000 without a police chief until printing-shop owner Alejandro Domínguez Coello valiantly stepped forward to accept the post on the morning of June 8, 2005. "I'm not beholden to anyone. My commitment is to the citizenry," stated the fifty-six-year old father of three. Within six hours, he lay in a curdling pool of blood after hit men, believed to belong to Los Zetas paramilitary force, pumped more than thirty bullets into his body. Their message was clear: narco-traffickers control the streets of Nuevo Laredo. "They are openly defying the Mexican state," said Mexico City political scientist Jorge Chabat. "They are showing that they can kill anybody at any time. It's chilling."[1]

The brutal, daylight murder of Domínguez provides an aperçu into why Mexican scholar Raúl Benítez insists that "Los Zetas have clearly become the biggest, most serious threat to the nation's security."[2] Meanwhile, the U.S. Drug Enforcement Administration advises that these brigands "may be the most technologically advanced, sophisticated and violent of these paramilitary enforcement groups."[3]

Origins

In early 1997 the Gulf syndicate began to recruit military personnel whom General Gutiérrez Rebollo had assigned as representatives of the Attorney General's Office in northern states. In the aftermath of the officer's imprisonment, Attorney General Jorge Madrazo Cuéllar created the National Public Security System (SNSP), which incorporated military personnel into the short-lived Special Prosecutor's Office for Crimes against Health (FEADS) to reinforce the fight against drug cartels, especially along the border.[4]

In the late 1990s, Osiel Cárdenas Guillén, who was in a no-holds-barred fight for leadership of the notorious organization, began courting local military personnel. One of his first contacts was with Lt. Antonio Javier Quevedo Guerrero, a former member of the 21st Cavalry Regiment of Nuevo León. After Quevedo's capture, Cárdenas reportedly told Lt. Arturo Guzmán Decenas that he "wanted the best men possible." The deserter replied: "They are only in the Army." As a result, the Gulf Cartel sought out veritable heretics, members of the Army's elite Airborne Special Forces Groups[5] or GAFES to provide protection and perform other vital functions. Arturo Guzmán Decenas, his top recruit, brought with him thirty other deserters enticed by salaries substantially higher than those paid by the Mexican government.[6] The original defectors, whose nicknames include "El Winnie Pooh," "The Little Mother," and "El Guerra," had belonged to the 15th and 70th Infantry Battalions and the 15th Motorized Cavalry Regiment.[7] Appendix 2 lists their names and the status of the GAFES turncoats.

One of Los Zetas' first tasks was to eradicate Los Chachos, a group led by Dionicio "El Chacho" Román García Sánchez, when he switched his allegiance from the Gulf Cartel and gave it to the Arellano Félix Organization. Originally fifty or sixty cross-border auto thieves, the Chachos competed for control of drug smuggling in Nuevo Laredo with the Flores Soto gang, headed by Mario Flores Soto. The Gulf Cartel sought unfettered access to Laredo's transportation network and wanted the right to charge other groups for traversing their turf. When Los Chachos kidnapped and killed Mario Flores Soto's youngest brother and ten of his associates, Los Zetas responded by virtually decimating the gangsters. El Chacho was found dead in women's underwear in Tamaulipas on May 13, 2002, after being abducted by a heavily armed, commando-style group. Also killed was his right-hand man, Juvenal "El Juve" Torres Sánchez.[8] Once Osiel Cárdenas Guillén had consolidated his position, he expanded the responsibilities of Los Zetas to collect debts, secure his *plazas* for cocaine supply and trafficking routes, discourage defections from the cartel, and execute—often with grotesque savagery—his foes.

Two years after the military killed Guzmán Decenas (November 2002), it captured the new Zeta chief, Rogelio "El Kelín" González Pizaña along with fourteen of his comrades. They were incarcerated on Mexico's version of a racketeering statute. At this point ex-GAFE Heriberto "The

Executioner" Lazcano Lazcano, also known as "El Lazca," ascended to the apex of the paramilitary wing of the Gulf Cartel. The arrest (March 2003) and deportation to the United States (January 2007) of Cárdenas Guillén changed the panorama for Los Zetas. Their strategic reaction at the loss of their patron was to "accelerate their rhythm of collecting taxes" from small-time drug vendors, illegal gambling establishments, houses of prostitution, and contraband sellers.[9]

This success emboldened Lazcano and his top henchman—military deserter Jaime "The Hummer" González Durán and former PJF commander Miguel "40" Treviño Morales—to act independently of other savage contenders to head the cartel: Osiel's brother Ezekiel and former municipal policeman Jorge Eduardo "El Coss" Costilla Sánchez. "The Gulf Cartel created the lion, but now the lion has wised up and controls the handler," stated a U.S. law enforcement official. "The Zetas don't ask the Gulf Cartel permission for anything anymore. They simply inform them of their activities whenever they feel like it."[10] Mexican police believe that the Gulf Cartel and Los Zetas at one time may have shared "gatekeepers"—those men and women responsible for bribing customs agents, military personnel, policemen, and lookouts, while lining up truckers or other mules to carry drugs across the border sector for which they are responsible. These facilitators reportedly earn $200 for every kilogram of drug handled—with shipments averaging 500 to 3,000 kilograms. Now there is a widening chasm between the paramilitaries and their erstwhile partners in crime.

Although the Gulf Cartel is hunkered down in Matamoros, Los Zetas run the show in at least 70 percent of Tamaulipas, a state in which they have hand-in-glove ties with local politicians. This dominance means that in 2008 Tamaulipas and neighboring Nuevo León, where Los Zetas also hold the upper hand, endured the fewest executions of the six states bordering the United States—with the exception of Sonora where the governor has assumed a tough law-and-order approach.

Goals

In addition to conducting activities along the border, they are striving to encircle the country. Los Zetas are active throughout the Gulf Coast with centers of operations in Veracruz, in the southern states of Tabasco, Yucatán, Quintano Roo, and Chiapas, and in the Pacific Coast states of Guerrero and Oaxaca, as well as Aguascalientes and Zacatecas. The also hold sway in Mexico State and Hidalgo, which they use as an entrée to Mexico City.[11]

Table 8.1
Executions in Border States, 2006 to mid-2009

State	Executions (through Aug. 7, 2009)	Executions 2008	Executions 2007	Executions 2006	Total
Tamaulipas	28	110	88	181	407
Nuevo León	37	79	107	50	273
Coahuila	115	53	29	17	214
Chihuahua	1,093	1,652	147	130	3,022
Sonora	47	137	125	61	370
Baja California	172	617	154	163	1,106
Nationwide	3,628	5,207	2,275	2,120	13,230

Source: "Ejecuciones 2009," *Reforma*, August 10, 2009.

The capital and adjoining states (México, Morelos, Hidalgo, and Puebla) embrace nearly 30 percent of the nation's population. As a result, Los Zetas vie with the Sinaloa Cartel, the Beltrán Leyvas, and La Familia in this megalopolis (Los Zetas cooperate with the Gulf Cartel in the D.F.). The fierce competition triggered many of the 260 executions in 2008. An official of the Mexico State Security Agency labels as the "black zone" where Ecatepec, Naucalpan, Chalco, and other cities of the state adjoin the Federal District.[12]

In Michoacán, El Lazca's operatives encountered fierce resistance from the locally-based Jalisco Cartel and its Sinaloan confreres. Furthermore, Los Zetas have a few allies and mostly enemies among factions of La Familia enforcer gangs in the state, the venue for cocaine and precursor drug imports and methamphetamine laboratories. The strength of the Sinaloans and their confederates has prevented Los Zetas from gaining a sustained presence in Colima, Nayarit, Sinaloa, Durango, Baja California Sur, Baja California, Sonora, and Chihuahua.

Organization and Resources

Protected witnesses affirm that El Lazca controls Los Zetas with an iron hand. Lieutenants directly under him are or were:[13]

* **Reynosa**: Samuel "El Metro" Flores Borrego;
* **Matamoros**: Flavio "El Amarillo" Méndez Santiago;
* **Coahuila**: Omar Treviño Morales and Jesús Enrigue Rejón Aguilar;

* **Campeche**: Sergio Enrique "El Tlapa" Ruiz Tlapanco;
* **Nuevo Laredo**: Roel "R1 or "El Néctar" Velázquez Caballero and Juan Gerardo "El Kilo" Treviño Chávez;
* **Nuevo León and Coahuila**: Sergio "El Cóncord" Peña Solís/René "El Colosio"/"El Comandante Colosio" Solís Carlos (San Nicolás Garza García), and Sigifredo "El Canicón" Nájera (**Captured March 20, 2009**);
* **Puebla**: Raúl Lucio "Z-16" Hernández Lechuga;
* **Sonora**: Francisco "El 2000" Hernández García;
* **Veracruz and Tamaulipas**: Braulio "El Gonzo" Arellano Domínguez;
* **Quintana Roo**: Javier "El Java" Díaz Ramón (Captured by Army on December 22, 2008); Octavio "El Gori 4" Almanza Morales (**Captured by Army on February 10, 2009**); and
* **D.F. and Mexico State**: "El Tachavo," "El Motos," "El Muro," "El Enfermero," and Jesús Enrique "Z-8" Rejón.

Before their arrests or deaths, Mateo "Comandante Mateo" Díaz López, an original Zeta, ran Veracruz and the southern operations for the Gulf Cartel; Alfredo "El Chicles"/"The Chewing Gum" Rangel Buendía managed affairs in the Federal District and four other states; Rafael del Ángel Vélez Morales (or José Manuel "El Fayo" Figueroa Martínez) took care of business in Cancún; Israel "El Kaibil"/"The Oyster" Nava Cortéz concentrated on Guatemala before seeking to establish beachheads in Aguascalientes and Zacatecas; and Alberto "El Tony" Sánchez Hinojosa (also known as "Comandante Castillo"), oversaw the Tabasco *plaza* before the Army threw him behind bars in September 2008.

Likewise, recent arrests have weakened the paramilitary Zetas but have not brought them to their knees. In addition to the individuals mentioned above, those captured include: Jaime "El Hummer" González Durán in Reynosa on November 7, 2008; and Miguel Ángel Soto Parra, an ex-PJF officer who was a hit man for the organization, on January 7, 2009.

El Lazca usually places second- or third-tier operators in areas that he controls. Five or six small cells compose the state structures. Thus, when authorities captured "El Tony" for receiving six tons of cocaine transported by a semi-submergible vessel off the coast of Oaxaca in mid-2008, they could not destroy Los Zetas' segmented organization.[14]

Los Zetas' Green Beret-style training constitutes their foremost asset. In cooperation with their U.S. counterparts, the Mexican military created the GAFES in the mid-1990s. Foreign specialists, including Americans, French, and Israelis, instructed members of this elite unit in rapid deployment, aerial assaults, marksmanship, ambushes, intelligence collection, counter-surveillance techniques, prisoner rescues, sophisticated communications, and the art of intimidation. It is ironic that loyal GAFES helped to capture kingpins such as Osiel Cárdenas Guillén, whom the renegade GAFES-turned-Zetas had been hired to safeguard.

Los Zetas have pioneered the use of "*narcobanderas*" or "narco-banners" to encourage soldiers to defect. In view of the poor quality of food served to troops, one of the cartel's most effective appeals is that we will not give you "*sopa marucha*"—made from tasteless artificial noodles that convenience stores sell in packages.[15]

The Army apostates have set up at least six camps of their own to train young recruits aged 15 to 18 years old, as well as ex-federal, state, and local police officers. Los Zetas allegedly conduct training at locations southwest of Matamoros, across the border from Brownsville; just north of the Nuevo Laredo airport; near the town of Abasolo, between Matamoros and Ciudad Victoria; and at "Rancho Las Amarillas," near a rural community, China, that is close to the Nuevo Leon-Tamaulipas frontier. To the degree that the Calderón administration achieves more successes, the paramilitary criminals may move their boot camps into the U.S.[16] In March 2009 Guatemalan police discovered a Zeta instructional compound 155 miles north of Guatemala City. The escalating violence at the border prompted Ambassador Garza to close temporarily the United States consulate in Nuevo Laredo.

While not exactly al-Qaeda- or U.S. Marine-style complexes, these converted farms provide a site for instruction in the use of AK-47 assault rifles, AR-15 grenade launchers, and .50-caliber machine guns, as well as for rigorous physical fitness training. Videos posted on the Internet show how instructors have severely punished slackers.

As Alfredo Corchado and Lennox Samuels reported for the *Dallas Morning News* on November 30, 2005:

> [F]our men sit bruised, bloody and bound on the floor before a curtain of black garbage bags. Prodded by an unseen interrogator, they coolly describe how they enforce the rule of Mexico's Gulf cartel: Enemies are kidnapped, tortured and shot in the head, their bodies burned to ashes ... After unseen interrogators question the men, the video ends when a pistol enters the frame and shoots this man in the head.

In addition, the instructional sites provide a venue to dispose of corpses. "Traffickers go to great lengths to prepare themselves for battle," a senior U.S. official said. "Part of that preparation is live firing ranges and combat training courses... And that's not something that we have seen before."[17] Two of the facilities have airstrips.

In addition, Los Zetas have recruited into their ranks ex-troops from Guatemala known as Kaibiles. Reviled as "killing machines," these tough-as-nails jungle warriors and counter-insurgency specialists train in an isolated camp known as "The Hell," 260 miles north of Guatemala City. One reporter compared the Kaibiles to a combination of "U.S. Rangers, British Gurkhas, and Peruvian Commandos." They adhere to the maxim: "If I advance, follow me. If I stop, urge me on. If I retreat, kill me."[18]

Los Zetas' arsenal includes AR-15 and AK-47 assault rifles, MP5 submachine guns, .50 mm machine guns, grenade launchers, ground-to-air missiles, dynamite, bazookas, and helicopters. In November 2008 soldiers on night patrol in Reynosa, a Zeta stronghold, discovered a house containing 540 rifles, 165 grenades, 500,000 rounds of ammunition, and fourteen sticks of dynamite—the largest arms seizure to date.[19] When embarking on operations, the ex-Army troopers wear dark clothing, blacken their faces, drive new, stolen SUVs, and delight in torturing victims before administering the coup de grâce.

Some criminals carry images of mythical narco saint Jesús Malverde. The braggadocio of Zeta Luis Alberto "El Guerrero" Guerrero Reyes led him to wear a hand grenade dangling from a necklace. After he was massacred leaving the Wild West nightclub in May 2004, it took soldiers eight hours to defuse the device before removing it from his bullet-riddled cadaver.[20]

The military defectors also have their favorite *corrido*, "La Escolta Suicida" (The Suicide Escort), which emphasizes pride in defending their "patron":[21]

We are 20 the group of Los Zetas	*Somos 20 el grupo de Los Zetas/*
United as a family/	*unidos como familia/*
We are 20 the force/	*los 20 somos la fuerza/*
With diplomas of suicide/	*con diplomas de suicida/*
Aware that in each action/	*conscientes de que en cada acción/*
We can lose our life....	*podemos perder la vida....*

Many of these young men have received instruction in intelligence, high-powered weaponry and, as mentioned, even trained with their U.S. counterparts.[22] Los Zetas also work with brutal Central American gangs like the Mara Salvatrucha (MS-13) and MS-18 below the Mexican-Guatemalan border, which is as porous as a sieve blasted by buckshot. Guatemalan Police Director Marlene Blanco Lapola indicated the discovery of 500 grenades, six rifles, bulletproof vests, enormous quantities of munitions, three motorcycles, and thirty-seven recruits. The Zetas used those motorcycles "to train their recruits in firing from moving vehicles," said Blanco Lapola, who has been threatened by this killing squad.[23]

Authorities believe that El Lazca works with Guatemala's treacherous Petén-Cobán Cartel composed of ex-Kaibiles, who have established ties with the Mexican paramilitaries in Quintana Roo and Campeche. Guatemala's Civil Aeronautics Agency admits that it cannot control the helicopters that the syndicates use to transport drugs across the 600-mile long border with Mexico. Between 2005 and 2007, their joint operations facilitated imports of 160 tons of cocaine from South America.[24] In April 2008 Guatemala's National Civil Police (PNC) apprehended sixteen suspected Zetas, including the group's second-in-command in the country, "Daniel "El Cachetes"/"Puffed Cheeks" Pérez Rojas. Guatemalan authorities have identified another seventy-eight members of the organization in the northern, northeast, and eastern parts of the country where they seek to "supplant" local narco-traffickers.[25]

Maps found with Pérez Rojas indicated operations in Zacapa, Guatemala, where authorities believe Los Zetas murdered Juan José "El Juancho" León Ardón, who supposedly worked with the Sinaloa Cartel. Other places marked were Sayaxché in Petén Department, Huehuetengo near the Mexican border, and Cobán in the center of the country. According to Cobán residents, heavily armed foreigners with bodyguards began driving through their streets at the end of 2007. "Evidence and reports confirm that Los Zetas are in Cobán and other areas," stated Pedro García Tobar, Guatemala's Secretary of Anti-narcotics Information and Analysis.[26] DEA agents learned of their presence in Quetzaltenango department whose capital, which carries the same name, is the nation's second largest city.

The PNC reported that Los Zetas have made three telephone threats on the life of Álvaro Colom Caballeros, president of Guatemala, a nation teeming with poor, high levels of insecurity, and failed institutions. Secretary García Luna has agreed to respond to any request from Mexico's neighbor to share intelligence or cooperate in other ways.[27] In the wake of twenty-eight drug-related killings in 2008, the Guatemalan government moved Army units to the border where they participated in joint maneuvers with their Mexican counterparts. In March 2009 Guatemala announced the dispatch of 2,000 additional police and Army personnel to the frontier. While asserting that Los Zetas threatened their country from Chiapas, Guatemala's ambassador to Mexico claimed Los Pelones, linked to the Sinaloa Cartel, had developed a zone of influence on his nation's border with El Salvador.[28] El Chapo dominates the drug flow along the Pan-American Highway from Panama to Mexico via El Salvador and

Guatemala, but Los Zetas reportedly have established a parallel corridor from northern Colombia to Mexico, passing through Guatemala.[29]

President Colom's recommendation for a regional force to combat the cartels received a polite but unenthusiastic reception in Mexico City.[30]

Nicola Gratteri, Italy's anti-drug prosecutor, claims that los Zetas have had ties with the Calabrian Mafia, N'drangheta for at least two years. These links spring from the cheaper prices for cocaine offered by Los Zetas and the Gulf Cartel, which the Mexicans delivered for $25,000 per kilogram and the Italians sold to European consumers for $45,000 per kilogram.[31]

In addition to narcotics trafficking, Los Zetas have helped undocumented Cubans reach the United States via Quintana Roo. They charged $2,500 per person in a smuggling operation allegedly run by an ex-member of the Cuban military. This criminality enjoyed the protection of Cancún's police chief, Francisco "El Viking" Velasco Delgado, who was arrested in connection with the slaying of General Tello Quiñones.[32]

Los Zetas have stocked safe houses with grenades, antitank weapons, assault rifles, and other heavy armaments.[33] They reportedly have begun recruiting young Hispanic gangs in Laredo, Texas—the so-called "zetitas"—to broaden their activities in the U.S.[34] The Juárez and Tijuana organizations have allied themselves with the Gulf Cartel against El Chapo's faction of the Sinaloa Cartel, which has moved into northern zones traditionally controlled by the Gulf Cartel. As indicated, except for the Northwest, Los Zetas are believed to operate in most of Mexico, including Mexico City.[35]

Meanwhile, Los Zetas have begun to make common cause with the Beltrán Leyva brothers, the erstwhile comrades of Guzmán Loera. It is said that El Lazca negotiated this pact along with his trusted comrade Miguel "El 40" Treviño Morales, an ex-policeman who unlike most other *jefes* never served in the armed forces. They also reached an understanding with Sergio Villarreal Barragán, a former Durango cop whom the PGR considers the principal operator of the Beltrán Leyvas in Coahuila, Sinaloa, and Durango. Known as "El Grande," the ruthless Villarreal Barragán gained international fame when *El Universal* reported that film stars Salma Hayek and Penélope Cruz stayed at his luxurious ranch for two months during the filming of *Las Bandidas*, a Wild West farce.[36] Héctor "La Burra" Huerta Ríos, operator for the Beltrán Leyva family in Monterrey, purportedly cut a deal with Eleazar "El Chelelo" Medina Rojas of Los Zetas, to divide the Nuevo León *plaza* between the two cartels. The Army apprehended La Burra in late March 2009.[37]

An accord between Los Zetas and the Beltrán Leyvas enhances the latter's ability to revenge the capture of their brother (Alfredo) against El Chapo Guzmán Loera, the Zambada brothers, and Nacho Coronel. Arturo Beltrán Leyva is also believed to have sought assistance from Treviño Morales in importing 23.5 tons of cocaine. The Navy and customs officers found the shipment among containers on a Hong Kong-flagged vessel that had arrived at Manzanillo, Colima, from Buenaventura, Colombia.[38]

Los Zetas intentionally keep their structure muddled to confuse enemies. A second level of leadership falls below Lazcano and his compact team, even as disputes exacerbate the friction between the ex-GAFES and El Coss and Tony Tormenta. In the states where they are active, Los Zetas have a third tier of operators who preside over five or six cells to limit the information that any one member of the organization knows about his associates.

Yet, in addition to commandos, Los Zetas are believed to have several specialized groups:

* "The Veterans" "*El Viejos*" or "*Cobras Viejos*" are the GAFES' deserters who are the ranking members of the organization and, as such, are respectfully referred to as professional—university degree holders ("*los licenciados*") teachers ("*los maestros*") or engineers ("*los ingenieros*");

* The "Ls" or "*Cobras*" serve as weapons porters to Los Zetas for whom they also provide security;

* "The New Zetas" ("*Los Zetas Nuevos*") are constituted by Kaibiles whose training in Guatemala has prepared them to use grenades, rocket-launchers, and other sophisticated weapons; the Ls or Cobras can only fire when Los Zetas Nuevos order them to do so;

* "The Windows" ("*Las Ventanas*") comprise bike-riding youngsters in their mid-teens who whistle to warn of the presence of police and other suspicious individuals near small stores that sell drugs;

* "The Hawks" ("*Los Halcones*") composed of youngsters aged twelve to seventeen. They serve as the eyes and ears of Los Zetas, hanging out on street corners to keep watch over distribution zones; authorities found eighty members, equipped with radio-transmitters, in Matamoros alone;

* "The Cunning Ones" ("*Los Mañosos*") procure arms;

* The Leopards (*Las Leopardos*) are prostitutes who slyly extract information from their clients;

* "The Command" ("*La Dirección*") are approximately twenty communications experts who intercept phone calls, follow and identify suspicious automobiles, and even accomplish kidnappings and executions;[39]

* "The Hidden Ones" ("*Los Tapados*") are poor people, often children, who are recruited with cell phones, school supplies, backpacks, and other items, to hoist banners, chant slogans, and mobilize opposition to the presence of the military and federal police in their states;[40]
* "The Panthers" ("*Las Panteras*") are females concentrated in Nuevo León with *jefas* in most states. Their leader, believed to be Ashly "La Comandante Bombón" Narro López, was captured in Cancún on February 9, 2009, in connection with the murder of General Tello Quiñones. Their task is to negotiate deals with police, politicians, military officers, and others who can assist Los Zetas. Should talks break down, the *pantera* may kill her interlocutor. First identified at a party thrown by El Lazca in mid-December 2006, these women change their make-up and the color and style of their hair according to the assignment they are undertaking;[41]and
* "Military Killers" ("*Los Matamilitares*") form a cell devoted to executing members of the armed forces. This cell, which enjoyed the protection of Cancún Police Chief Velasco Delgado, is believed to have executed Tello Quiñones. Authorities arrested Octavio "El Gori 4" Almanza Morales for the crime, but his brothers Raymundo and Eduardo—also ex-military personnel—are still at large.[42]

Although not identified by a sobriquet, teenagers have helped identify kidnapping victims for Los Zetas in Pachuca, Hidalgo, a *plaza* headed by Alejandro "El Cepillo"/"The Brush" Segura Téllez. There, federal police arrested three youngsters from Nuevo Laredo—Mario "El Yodo" (age 13), Julio "El Fede" (age 14), and Raúl "El Rule" (age 16)—who claimed to be selling clothing.[43] Los Zetas also pay 10,000 pesos for executions to Eduardo "EL Lalito" González Trejo and other young criminals in the Tepito area of Mexico City. The youthful killers belong to such local gangs as El Rey de Tepito or El Vale.[44]

Comandante Sol, whose real name remains a mystery, handles Los Zetas' funds and reports directly to El Lazca, and 18-year-old Cynthia Janet Flores Cepeda was believed to have been a recruiter of females for the outfit before her April 2009 arrest in Fresnillo, Zacatecas, when her confidant and mentor Nava Cortéz died in a shoot-out.[45]

Los Zetas may number between 200 and 300 men and women, most of whom are believed to be in their early to mid-twenties. Although the Army has detailed information about deserters, even key law enforcement agencies must guess at the size and composition of the group, because small-time criminals identify themselves as "Los Zetas" as if it were a brand-name like "McDonald's." This tactic helps elevate the fear of targets and victims. "It's gotten to the point where you get drunk, shoot at some cans and paint your face black, and that makes you a Zeta.... A lot of it is image and myth."[46]

Los Zetas are quick to take revenge against copycats. In May 2008 a 35-year-old man was found in Monterrey. He had been tortured and an ice pick plunged through his thorax, and a note dangled in his hand: "This is one of those who carried out extortions by telephone trying to pass for 'Z'."[47] In February 2009 the brigands executed two "false Zetas" in Reynosa, leaving behind a handwritten note saying "this is what will happen to those who attempt to pass themselves off as Zetas."[48]

The trained assassins employ various means to enhance their esprit de corps. First, they go to great lengths to retrieve the bodies of fallen comrades-in-arms. In what pundits labeled the "invasion of the body snatchers," four armed men broke into the graveyard in Poza Rica, Veracruz, in early March 2007, tied up a security guard, smashed Zeta Roberto Carlos Carmona's gravestone with hammers, and carried off his ornate coffin containing their collaborator's corpse.[49] It is said that you have to murder to get into Los Zetas and die to get out. The syndicate pays benefits to the spouse and children of members who have died in the line of duty.

Second, Los Zetas honor their dead. Three months after authorities killed Guzmán Decenas in late 2002, a funeral wreath and four flower arrangements appeared at his gravesite with the inscription: "We will always keep you in our heart: from your family, Los Zetas." Similarly, they placed a memorial to venerate deceased compatriots in Oaxaca. The inscription read: "Gulf Cartel. God keep in your memory Los Zetas who have died in Oaxaca," as well as "Arturo Guzmán [Decenas] Z1 and all of our fallen brothers in the Oaxaca *plaza*, that you will always remember them and their principles and ideals."[50] The organization has also laid wreaths or *narcocoronas* in public places to warn police and other foes of their presence.[51]

Third, Los Zetas make Herculean attempts to free imprisoned comrades such as already denoted in the May 2009 assault on Zacatecas' Cieneguillas penitentiary. One year earlier, approximately fifty Zetas, dressed as AFI police, entered the grounds of the Dupont-Ostión penal compound in Coatzacoalcos, Veracruz. Once inside the facility, they overpowered the guards and released five of their members. The episode took place twenty-one days after the federal government had undertaken a security initiative in the municipalities of Coatzacoalcos, Cosoleacaque, Minatitlán, and Nanchital. Authorities admitted that correctional officers lacked the weapons to thwart carefully planned and executed raids.

"What can we do in the face of heavily armed groups?" asked the state's director of corrections. "Neither this state nor any other in the Republic has the capacity to confront heavily armed, sophisticated bands, and [thus] we have asked the Federal government to take charge of federal prisoners."[52] Los Zetas ran the Dupont-Ostión prison to the degree that they charged other inmates 2,000 pesos per week to avoid severe beatings and/or to gain access to minor benefits known as *talachas*. Before escaping, they killed at least two prisoners.

Los Zetas' plans sometimes misfire. Authorities frustrated their plot to free El Cachetes Pérez Rojas, arrested in April 2008, from a Guatemala City prison.[53]

Fourth, their accountant keeps meticulous records of transactions. This computerized data enable El Lazca to reward *plaza* chiefs who exceed financial objectives with raises and bonuses (in addition to regular Christmas bonuses). The other side of the coin is that slackers will be moved to a smaller territory or demoted to hit men or couriers.

Finally, Los Zetas retaliate with sadistic savagery against their enemies. Witnesses swear that the paramilitaries set fire to four Nuevo Laredo police officers crammed into barrels filled with diesel fuel. Their remains were buried there the next day.[54]

They also intimidate politicians, many of whom—especially in the Tierra Caliente region—have begun wearing bulletproof vests on a regular basis. In the November 2007 municipal contests in the state, contenders for mayor of Múgica and Nuevo Italia stepped aside after receiving death threats. In Coalcomán, Aguililla, and Tumbiscatío, the paramilitaries barred opponents of their favored standard-bearers from voting. José Vázquez Piedra, the outgoing mayor of Turicato who won a seat in the state legislature, said that the imprimatur of the most powerful cartel in drug-infested areas was crucial to winning a public office.[55] At least one attractive gubernatorial prospect in a north-central state decided not to enter the race in 2009, lest he place his family in jeopardy.

Like other cartels, Los Zetas show the greatest interest in municipal elections because they want politicians who will protect—or close their eyes to—local commercial routes and storage facilities. Should they back a candidate for the Chamber of Deputies, it represents an investment more than the hope of a proximate pay-off; that is, the cartels are counting on the deputy's returning to his state as a prosecutor, secretary of government, mayor, or governor—positions important to their industry.

In early 2009 the PFP captured Miguel Ángel Almaraz Maldonado, president of the PRD in Tamaulipas and contender for the mayoralty of Río Bravo, for enjoying Los Zetas' protection as he sold stolen PEMEX gasoline in the United States. Almaraz had been one of the state's politicians who vocally opposed military operations in Tamaulipas. In 2007 Juan Antonio Guajardo Anzaldúa, himself seeking office in Río Bravo, accused Almaraz of criminal behavior. These charges precipitated death threats against Guajardo, who was killed on December 8, 2007.[56]

The Mexican Government vs. Los Zetas

Major Operations

Los Zetas most notable strikes over the past several years include the following:

* May 16, 2009: Attacked the Cieneguillas prison in Zacatecas and released fifty-three inmates;
* Early March 2009: Organized poor people to demonstrate against the presence of the Army in Nuevo León and other northern states;
* February 3, 2009: Tortured Tello Quiñones, before executing him. Authorities discovered his mangled corpse two days after the mayor of Cancún hired the retired general to form a SWAT team to fight criminals in the vacation Mecca;
* June 2-3, 2007: Robbed casinos in the states of Nuevo Leon, Torreón, Guerrero, Veracruz, Coahuila, and Baja California in a move to gain a share of these businesses;
* May 13, 2007: Kidnapped and later murdered Jacinto Pablo Granda, a Mexican infantry captain near Chilpancingo, Guerrero;
* April 7, 2007: Gunned down local police chief, Ernesto Gutiérrez Moreno, as he dined at a restaurant with his wife and son in Chilpancingo;
* March 6, 2007: Believed to have attempted to murder the secretary of public safety in Tabasco, General Fernández Solís;
* February 6, 2007: Dressed in military uniforms, disarmed and massacred five police officers and two secretaries in Acapulco;
* March 21, 2006: Forced the resignation of Nuevo Laredo police chief, Omar Pimentel, after eight months in office. He stepped down hours after police found three charred bodies dumped by the side of a road leading into the border city;
* June 8, 2005: Killed Alejandro Domínguez Coello, police chief of Nuevo Laredo; and
* January 5, 2004: Efrain Teodoro "Zeta 14" Torres and Gustavo González Castro freed 25 fellow narco-traffickers from a prison in Apatzingán, Michoacán.

Major Government Successes

President Calderón, who compares Los Zetas to al-Qaeda, has made combating the drug mafias his highest law enforcement goal. Some of his successes and those of his predecessor, Vicente Fox, include:

* June 28 (beginning February 4): in six operations the Federal Police and the Army captured 124 individuals who belonged to five cells of Los Zetas in Hidalgo;
* June 27, 2009: The Army and federal and state police killed twelve narco-criminals and captured a dozen more in a battle in Apaseo el Alto, Guanajuato. At least six of the culprits were Zetas;
* May 16, 2009: The Army and federal and state police captured five presumed Zetas who had a formidable arsenal of grenades, assault weapons, pistols, and bulletproof vests in Tapachula, Chiapas;
* May 14, 2009: Federal Police captured seven Zetas, including two female minors; linked to ten acts of extortion and the murder of police in Puebla. The arrests took place in Hidalgo and Veracruz;
* May 8, 2009: Army captured Rafael del Ángel Vélez or José Manuel "Fayo" Figueroa Martínez in Mexico City;
* May 5, 2009: The PGR announced the capture of twelve Army deserters and six Aguascalientes municipal police who had collaborated with Los Zetas;
* April 29, 2009: Police captured suspected Zeta leader Gregorio "El Goyo" Sauceda Gamboa in Matamoros, Tamaulipas;
* April 9, 2009: Federal police killed Israel "El Kaibil"/"The Oyster" Nava Cortéz in a confrontation in Fresnillo, Zacatecas. Captured at the same time was Cynthia Janet Flores Cepeda, who allegedly recruited women for the organization;
* March 9, 2009: Federal Police captured Sergio Peña Mendoza (or Arturo Sánchez Fuentes), alias "El Cóncord," in Reynosa, Tamaulipas;
* March 23, 2009: Army captured Sigifredo "El Canicón" Nájera Talamantes, key Zeta in Coahuila and Nuevo León as well as the possible leader of the attack on U.S. consular offices in Monterrey in October 2008;
* March 4, 2009: Army captured Antelmo "El Chamoy" Lázaro Rodríguez, a Zeta chief in Cancún;
* February 10, 2009: Army captured Octavio "El Gori 4" Almanza Morales, who was believed to have masterminded the February 3 murder of Tello Quiñones;
* January 29, 2009: Army captured five suspected members of Los Zetas in Monterrey, along with a cache of weapons and ammunitions and several vehicles;
* January 6, 2009: Elements of the 25th Military Zone took control of an operations center in San Pablo Xochimehuacan, Puebla, although the local Zeta leader, Manuel "Z-16" Antele Velasco, escaped;
* December 24, 2008: Army captured Javier "El Java" Díaz Ramón, who operated in Cancún;
* December 13, 2008: Enemies executed two Zeta gunmen (Leonel Sandoval Jaramillo and José Ambrosio Navarro García) inside the Mazatlán prison;
* November 7, 2008: Federal police captured of Jaime "El Hummer" González Durán, erstwhile bodyguard of Cárdenas Guillén, in Reynosa;

* September 7, 2008: Army captured Alberto "El Tony"/"El Comandante Castillo" Sánchez Hinojosa, reportedly the organization's chief in Tabasco who also oversaw operations in other southern states;
* August 15, 2008: Federal police captured seven members of Los Zetas' cell in Mexico City, including Alfredo "El Chicles" Rangel Buendía, who coordinated drug trafficking, kidnappings, assassinations, and extortion in the capital and in four other states;
* April 2, 2008: Secretary of Public Security García Luna reported that his agency had spearheaded the capture of José Alberto Martínez Medrano and four accomplices, who had had $6 million in their possession, in Nuevo Laredo; the following day, the Ministry of National Defense issued a communiqué indicating that the 5th Motorized Cavalry Regiment had accomplished the April 2 arrest and that the amount seized was $6,110,950 (Defense Secretary Guillermo Galván Galván's dislike of García Luna sparks such turf battles and impedes cohesion within Calderón's Security Cabinet);
* March 21, 2008: The Army and the PGR captured Raúl "El Dutchman 1" Hernández Barrón, believed to be a founder of Los Zetas who controlled the Gulf Cartel's drug trafficking in northern Veracruz;
* February 11, 2008: Military forces discovered a weapons cache in Cerralvo, near Nuevo Laredo, that included bulletproof vests and eight military uniforms used as disguises;
* February 7, 2008: Soldiers raided the "El Mezquito" ranch west of Reynosa and found one of the largest illegal arsenals in recent memory: eighty-nine assault rifles, 83,355 rounds of ammunition, and plastic explosives capable of demolishing buildings;
* January 27, 2008: The Ministry of Public Security announced the capture of former municipal police director Héctor "El Teto" Izar Castro in San Luis Potosí, where he is believed to have been a leader of the local cell of Los Zetas. His cache of supplies included an AR-180 rifle, three handguns, 100 cartridges, sixty-five packages of cocaine, and three paddles bearing the letter "Z," which were used to beat foes;
* January 13, 2008: The SSP reported the capture of eleven people, most of whom were former military men, in San Pedro de las Colonias, Coahuila. Los Zetas had been using an auto workshop to dismantle stolen cars. The federal police also arrested the town's police commander and four police officers, while seizing twenty-three walkie-talkies, seventeen cell phones, nine cars, one motorbike, twenty-eight kilograms of marijuana, and weapons, including five semi-automatic rifles, one shotgun, one revolver and one rifle;
* April 20, 2007: The Navy captured six Zetas in Pánuco, in northern Veracruz near its boundary with Tamaulipas;
* April 21, 2007: The Attorney General's Office announced the capture of Eleazar "El Chelelo" Medina Rojas and nine other Zetas in Nuevo Laredo. Identified as a top killer and kidnapper for the Gulf Cartel, Medina Rojas had a stash of weapons, including an AR-15, a Colt .223,

a Belgian-made PS90, a Beretta, and various cartridges, as well as cell phones, radios, bulletproof vests, and a collection of vehicles;

* April 19, 2007: Authorities captured Nabor "El Debora" Vargas García, a founder of Los Zetas, and twenty allies after a shootout in Ciudad del Carmen, Campeche. The government claims that Vargas García, who admitted having served in the Presidential Guard's assault battalion, ran Los *Zetas* in Tabasco, Campeche, and Chiapas;

* February 2, 2007: The Attorney General's Office captured José Ramón "El Cholo" Dávila López, a six-year veteran of the GAFES and close ally of Zeta leader Lazcano, in Ciudad Victoria, Tamaulipas;

* September 12, 2006: The Army captured three former Guatemalan *Kaibiles* and five presumed Zetas in Aguililla, Michoacán. They found in their possession 12 assault rifles AK-47 and AR-15; one 9 mm pistol, and 3,000 rounds of ammunition; three fragmentation grenades, black fatigues, tactical vests and ten Kevlar ballistic helmets; and

* March 14, 2003: Captured Víctor Manuel "El Flander II" Hernández Barrón, along with Cárdenas Guillén.

The Government Response

President Calderón has pledged to pursue all of Mexico's criminal organizations. To this end, he has dispatched tens of thousands of soldiers, sailors, marines, and federal police to more than a dozen states and cities. Limited resources mean that he will have to set priorities. Although the Sinaloa Cartel remains an important enemy of the state, it is less violent than its Gulf/Zeta counterpart and has a limited paramilitary capability. Moreover, even with the dramatic successes against Los Zetas, the ex-GAFES continue to pose a serious threat to citizens on both sides of the border.

Many of the commandoes have homes north of the Rio Grande where they seek safe haven and where they attempt to lure young Americans into their clutches.

Their drug distribution routes run through the United States. The U.S. Justice Department bulletin has warned that: "The violence will spill over the Mexican border into the United States and law enforcement agencies in Texas, Arizona and Southern California can expect to encounter Los Zetas in the coming months." In March 2008 the Justice Department said the Los Zetas were involved "in multiple assaults and are believed to have hired criminal gangs" in the Dallas area for contract killings.[57] The paramilitaries are believed to have carried out executions in Texas and other American states. The Dallas police have launched a search for Máximo García Carrillo, a suspected Zeta who owns a house in the Oak Cliff suburb of the city and is alleged to have killed police officer

Mark Nix. Known as a "second-generation" Zeta, the thirty-four-year-old García Carrillo travels with bodyguards armed with automatic weapons and grenade launchers. Los Zetas, who consider Dallas a key point for the transportation and distribution of drugs, also pursue their criminality in Houston, San Antonio, Brownsville, Laredo, and Del Rio. The big but unpleasant question is: How many U.S. officials have they and other cartels intimidated or bribed into cooperating with them?

Moreover, the FBI has reported that Los Zetas control such U.S.-based gangs as the Mexican Mafia, the Texas Syndicate, MS-13, and the Hermanos Pistoleros Latinos.[58]

The armed forces, with which the U.S. enjoys unprecedented cooperation, are especially eager to track down Los Zetas because of the embarrassment they represent to their institution. The Defense Ministry has requested that the Mexican Congress authorize both the trial in military courts of deserters who cast their lot with cartels and the imposition of prison sentence of up to sixty years for such Benedict Arnolds.[59]

As indicated earlier, Los Zetas are involved in myriad criminal activities. They have branched out into kidnappings, murder-for-hire, assassinations, auto theft, extortion, money-laundering, human smuggling, loan-sharking, and even the sale of videos, DVDs, and other contraband. In Tamaulipas, the organization ordered vendors to sell only merchandise provided by Los Zetas by December 1, 2008; such items carry a small sticker showing a Hummer SUV on the upper right-hand side of packages. In addition, they have compelled movie theater managers to allow the copying of first-run films in order to duplicate them for sale.

To the south in Veracruz, Los Zetas call themselves "La Compañía." As in Tamaulipas, they have employed savagery to take control of most illicit activities in the state. They tortured and executed leaders of street vendors who denounced their activities. As a result, informal sellers in Acauyucan, Xalapa, Coatzacoalcos, Minatitlán, and the port of Veracruz only handle DVDs, videos, and other black-market articles provided by La Compañía. Moreover, the brigands have hijacked tractor-trailers and livestock trucks even as they sell protection to table-dance cafes, brothels, bars, and discothèques. "Veracruz is like Chicago in the 1920s," reported *Reforma*.

In San Luis Potosí, a conservative city in the North, street merchants of entertainment and electronic goods have switched to selling vegetables and fruits rather than incur the wrath of Los Zetas or the opprobrium of customers for working with criminals.

Los Zetas also refer to themselves as La Compañía in Oaxaca, where they have taken over *plazas* in the Isthmus of Tehuantepec once dominated by local cartel boss Pedro Díaz Parada, whom authorities captured in January 2007.

For the right price, these bloodthirsty mercenaries might be willing to launch terrorist attacks on vulnerable targets in Texas and throughout the United States. Authorities on both sides of the border have assigned a high priority to eliminating these cutthroats, who incurred a glancing blow when the government rounded up twenty-seven officials in Michoacán in late May 2009, a foray examined in the next section.

La Familia

Although organized several years earlier, La Familia Michoacana—or La Familia—burst into the limelight on September 6, 2006, when gunmen crashed into the seedy Sol y Sombra nightclub in Uruapan, Michoacán, fired shots into the air, ordered revelers to lie down, ripped open a plastic bag, and lobbed five human heads onto the black and white dance floor. The desperadoes left behind a note hailing their act as "divine justice," adding that: "The Family doesn't kill for money; it doesn't kill women; it doesn't kill innocent people; only those who deserve to die. Everyone should know … this is divine justice."[60] Table 1.1 in the first chapter suggests the relationship between the type of execution and the message that the murderer seeks to convey.

The day before the macabre pyrotechnics in Uruapan, the killers seized their victims from a mechanic's shop and hacked off their heads with bowie knives while the men writhed in pain. "You don't do something like that unless you want to send a big message," said a U.S. law enforcement official, speaking on condition of anonymity about an act of human depravity that would "cast a pall over the darkest nooks of hell."[61]

La Familia deposited a similarly self-righteous message at the foot of a black cross in Apatzingán. This city lies at the heart of the Tierra Caliente that embraces thirty-two municipalities at the intersection of Michoacán, Guerrero, and Mexico State—with Apatzingán, Uruapan, Tumbiscatío, and Morelia representing important *plazas* along with other municipalities cited in this section. In this highly productive, mountainous zone, La Familia, Los Zetas, the Jalisco Cartel, and the Milenio Cartel of the Valencia family engage in bloody warfare for control of growing areas and transit routes.[62] Also attractive to the syndicates is mushrooming local narcotics consumption. Of Michoacán's 4.7 million residents, 224,270 young people, ages twelve to twenty-five, are addicts—with cocaine being the substance of choice. There are at least 2,100 points of sale for drugs in the state.[63]

In addition, Michoacán finds the several criminal organizations fighting for the cocaine and precursor chemicals for methamphetamines that arrive either through Lázaro Cárdenas or remote entry points tucked into scores of nearby coves. This port also served as the gateway for chemical imports by multi-millionaire Chinese-Mexican Ye Gon, whose exploits have been described.

The importance of Lázaro Cárdenas derives from its strategic location: Half of Mexico's population lives within a radius of 186 miles of this coastal city, and in 2008 it accounted for more cargo (22,128,000 tons) than any of the country's other twenty-one ports. In 2007, 774 cargo ships arrived—a figure that rose to 1,046 in 2008. By 2015 the portal will handle six million containers annually.[64]

Origins

Various currents have flowed into the heterogeneous organization, which emerged in 2006 with the stated "mission" to eradicate trafficking in methamphetamines and other narcotics, kidnappings, extortion, murder-for-hire, highway assaults, and robberies, according to one of its founders, Nazario "El Más Loco"/"The Most Crazy" Moreno González (also known as "El Chayo").[65]

La Familia evolved from La Empresa, a criminal organization led by Moreno González, José de Jesús "El Chango" Méndez Vargas, and Carlos "El Tísico"/"The Consumptive" Rosales Mendoza. Formerly a member of the Michoacán-based Milenio Cartel (Los Valencias), El Tísico switched his loyalty to the Gulf Cartel, and La Empresa sought to thwart the importation, manufacture, and transport of methamphetamines by Los Valencias, allies of Sinaloa's Guzmán Loera.

In response to his new ally's request, Gulf boss Osiel Cárdenas Guillén dispatched Los Zetas—led by Efraín Teodoro "El Efra" Torres, or "Zeta 14," and Gustavo "The Erotic One" González Castro—to help Rosales Mendoza protect his *plaza* at La Unión, a municipality in Guerrero near Petacalco and Lázaro Cárdenas. Another especially violent Gulf Cartel accomplice was Carlos "La Chata" Pinto Rodríguez, a native of Huerta de Gámbara in the Tierra Caliente who became even more dangerous after his son died in a shoot-out. After Rosales Mendoza participated in an unsuccessful attempt to free Cárdenas Guillén from La Palma, the Army captured him at his attractive residence in the Colonia Lomas de Santa María, Morelia, on October 24, 2004. El Tísico offered a huge bribe if his captors would release him.[66] In 2006 La Empresa severed ties with Los Zetas over the allocation of *plazas* and morphed into La Familia.

In reaction to Los Zetas' incursion, Juan José "The Uncle" Farías, leader of the local *Guardias Rurales*, or Rural Guards, a uniformed Mexican Army auxiliary associated with the 43rd Military Zone in Apatzingán, took the offensive. He sought to expel the intruders from his region as if he were an agent of the French Resistance hammering the Nazis. Meanwhile, he was suspected of being a major narco-trafficker in the region. Farías is believed to have worked with the previously mentioned Rubén "El Mencho" Oseguera Cervantes, also called Nemesio. Nemesio is the cousin of Abigail and José Mendoza Valencia, relatives of Armando Valencia Cornelio, chief of the Milenio Cartel until his imprisonment in La Palma.[67] In retaliation for Farías' opposition, Los Zetas decapitated cheese maker Raúl Farías Alejandres, a relative of The Uncle, on September 4, 2006. A note next to the corpse warned: "One by one you go falling. Greetings to 'The Uncle.' The Family sends you its best. So long, dudes." Four more beheadings followed.[68]

The Uncle, an intrepid Zeta fighter who owns restaurants, hotels, and orchards, has disappeared, perhaps because the Attorney General's Office is investigating his possible connections with Ye Gon. He and his followers, "Los Farías," are allied with the Valencias and the Sinaloa Cartel.

In 2007 Uriel "El Paisa"/"The Confidant" Farías Álvarez, The Uncle's brother and a PRI stalwart, won a landslide victory for the mayoralty of Tepalcatepec, which—along with Aguililla, Apatzingán, and Buenavista Tomatlán—graces a drug-smuggling corridor that connects the Tierra Caliente with Jalisco. He dismissed the idea that he or his relatives had ties to the underworld: "My brother only kept a lookout on orders of the Army. And as a result they said he was a narco."[69] Federal forces took El Paisa into custody, along with nine other mayors, on May 26, 2009.

There is a slight chance that another contingent of La Familia has links to the New Jerusalem millenarian movement, which took root in the Michoacán municipality of Turicato in 1973 under the tutelage of defrocked Catholic priest Nabor "Papa Nabor" Cárdenas, who died at age 98 in early 2008. Members of the sect endeavor to avoid the fiery apocalypse by obeying their ecclesiastical hierarchy, attending up to four religious services daily, performing a day of communal work each week, spurning drugs and alcohol, and requiring women to wear ankle-length costumes that blend medieval garb with traditional Indian dress.[70]

Goals

Handwritten, poorly spelled enigmatic missives showed up next to the decapitated heads in Uruapan as part of La Familia's intense propaganda campaign designed to intimidate foes, terrorize the local population, and inhibit action by the government. Like Los Zetas, La Familia disseminates news of its ghastly deeds nationally through conventional media as well as by Internet videos and carefully placed banners.

On the heels of the Uruapan nightclub deviltry, the gang took out a half-page advertisement in newspapers. The sadists claimed to be crime busters determined to cleanse Michoacán of methamphetamines, kidnappings, extortion, and other criminal deeds. *El Sol de Morelia*, located in the capital of Michoacán that lies 135 miles west of Mexico City, confirmed that it published the half-page on September 22, 2006. *La Voz de Michoacán* also ran the group's manifesto, which appears at the end of this section.

La Familia has also committed itself to maintaining the colonial character of downtown Morelia. In fact, it has even beaten up and, possibly, executed delinquents who have spray-painted graffiti on historic buildings. Such expressions of civic virtue aside, eighteen of the thirty-two police officers in the Tepalcatepec area, near the border with Jalisco, resigned after receiving death threats, while local newspapers exercise self-censorship concerning the sinister band.[71]

La Familia continually asserts its commitment to ridding the state of malefactors. On August 18, 2006, the organization decapitated Jesús Rodríguez Valencia, a member of the Milenio Cartel, placing the following message next to his cadaver: "All that rises falls of its own weight, it would be like this, La Familia greets you, so long dude." Three months later, the police discovered two bodies on the Zamora-La Barca highway, next to which was a note that said: "For those who sell ice [methamphetamines]. This is divine justice. Sincerely, La Familia."[72]

"Divine justice. No to the meth makers, La Familia," was the text discovered alongside a corpse found on the Jacona-Los Reyes highway. The message was scrawled on a green card, reflecting the color that La Familia uses on its emblems, placards, and communications.

Authorities attributed seventeen decapitations to La Familia in 2006 alone. Between the murder of Rodríguez Valencia earlier that year and December 31, 2008, the syndicate killed scores, if not hundreds, of people. In 2008 there were 233 executions in Michoacán and an additional 255 slayings during the first seven months of 2009. Most of the victims belonged to one narco-band or another. Amid rampant bloodshed that instills fear in the population, social scientists like Carlos Antonio Flores Pérez, an analyst formerly with CISEN, say that La Familia's public condemnations of certain ills have helped it gain ground through what is effectively "psychological warfare," and win social legitimacy in a state plagued by violence. "[La Familia] is instituting its own actions to build social roots," said Flores Pérez. "It's a strategy to win over the goodwill of the people in areas in which it operates." At least some *michoacanos* have bought into La Familia's message that the troublemakers, the killers, and the bad guys are outsiders—not locals, or heaven forbid, La Familia itself. "I applaud the emergence of La Familia Michoacana," wrote one Morelia resident on his blog, adding that he thought the group's presence would result in a 70 percent drop in extortion, drug dealing and kidnapping—another crime that La Familia publicly frowns upon, but is said to be responsible for.[73]

What may have begun as a small group of armed men on the prowl to protect their children from methamphetamines has turned into a major criminal outfit, which is just as well-armed and organized as any top drawer drug smuggling organization in Mexico. The Attorney General's Office claims that it is developing a distribution route to the U.S. border that snakes through territory traditionally in the hands of the Sinaloa Cartel. To this end, they have established safe houses as refuges for their traffickers at strategic points along the corridor northward.

Elements of organization dominate narcotics sales in many of the seventy-seven of the 113 municipalities of their home state. La Familia appears to have the strongest presence in Apatzingán, Lázaro Cárdenas, Pátzcuaro, Uruapan, Zinapécuaro, Tiquicheo, Tanhuato, Ocampo, Jacona, San Juan Nuevo, Tancitaro, and Morelia.[74]

Until his capture on December 31, 2008, the chief operative for Morelia was Alberto "La Fresa"/"The Strawberry" Espinoza Barrón, who spearheaded drug trafficking, extortion, and kidnapping in the state capital, as well as cocaine and precursor drugs entering Mexico through Lázaro Cárdenas. La Fresa relied heavily on spies or *puntas* to keep an eye out for the Army, police, and other enemies.[75]

In late April 2009, authorities arrested La Fresa's successor, Rafael "El Cede" Cedeño Hernández, along with forty-three other members of La Familia, who were attending a baptism at the drab Hotel Mesón Tarasco near Morelia. Among those seized with Cedeño Hernández was Francisco Javier "The Camel" Torres Mora, who specialized in killing and kidnapping elements of Los Zetas and the Beltrán Leyva brothers in Guerrero.[76]

In addition to impeding the entry of Los Zetas into Michoacán from Zihuatenejo, Guerrero, El Cede discharged other functions: he oversaw the transport of drugs from Central America; managed the importation of pseudoephedrine from Asia and Europe through Lázaro Cárdenas; extracted payments from bars and night spots where high-school aged prostitutes plied their trade; participated in indoctrinating new Family members; and organized protests against the military's presence in the state. La Familia unfurled banners that warned: "The people are tired of this military invasion. We are living in a state of siege." At the time of his capture, El Cede carried a credential that identified him as a "permanent observer" of the State Commission on Human Rights.[77]

After El Cede was taken into custody, his brother, Daniel Cedeño Hernández, stepped down as a federal deputy candidate in the mid-July election. He had been nominated by the small Mexico Green Ecological Party, which is renowned for irregular practices.

While originating in Michoacán, La Familia has extended its reach into Mexico State, where it controls or has conducted operations in Coacalco, Ecatepec, Lerma, Huixhuilucan, Xonacatlán, Valle de México, Toluca, Tejupilco, Tultitlán, Tultepec, Ixtapaluca, Valle de Bravo, Toluca, Tenango, Zincantepec, Chalco, and other municipalities. In Mexico State, it must compete with the Los Zetas, the Sinaloa Cartel, and the Beltrán Leyva brothers, who, in the D.F.'s western suburb of Huixquilucan, cooperate with the Colombian North Valley Cartel (The Beltrán Leyvas employ Los Pelones to collect payment from small drug dealers and have safe houses in Huixquilucan, Naucalpan, and the Valle de Bravo).[78]

La Familia has corrupted and or intimidated law enforcement personnel. In early November 2008, 100 local police in Chalco, just outside Mexico City, demanded the dismissal of their chief Carlos Adulfo Palafox, whom they accused of having ties with the deadly organization.[79] Mexico State's Attorney General Alberto Bazbaz also cited Jesús García Carrasco, commander of the state's judicial police, as a possible collaborator after he reportedly received 70,000 pesos per month to provide information to La Familia.[80]

On August 21, 2008, a drug distributor in the Valle de Toluca accused José Manzur Ocaña, the well-connected former PGR delegate in the state, of providing protection to Los Zetas and La Familia. Although placed in a witness-protection program, the informant named "Noë" was among those executed in La Marquesa Park bloodbath, which was discussed in Chapter 5.[81]

The rival syndicates soon struck back. In August 2008 three bodies, their hands and feet bound and bearing grotesque torture scars, turned up in San Pablito in the Tultepec municipality. The narco-message at the scene stated: "All of the Michoacán Family will die, but I leave [these bodies] so that you believe me."[82] In September 2008, enemies discharged eighteen bullets into José Luis "El Jaguar" Carranza Galván, whom the PGR identified as a principal operator of La Familia.[83]

In mid-August 2008, "El Chicles" Rangel Buendía, a member of Los Zetas, confessed to Mexico City authorities that he had been ordered to assassinate two leaders of La Familia, José de Jesús "El Chango" Méndez Vargas and Nazario "El Chayo" Moreno González. Apparently Rangel Buendía was not instructed to kill such other presumed Familia big shots as Antonio "El Toñón" Arcos, Servando "El Profe" Gómez Martínez, and Dionisio "The Uncle" Loya Plancarte.[84]

In early July 2009, the Federal Police captured Arnoldo "La Minsa" Rueda Medina, who was believed to be number-three in the organization's pecking order. As the virtual "coordinator of coordinators," La Minsa designated *plaza* chiefs in Aguascalientes, Colima, Guanajuato, Jalisco, Mexico State, Michoacán, San Luis Potosí, and part of Guerrero. In addition, he was responsible for locating and executing members of the Milenio Cartel (Los Valencias). He also handled international contacts, facilitating the importation of precursor drugs through the Ports of Lázaro Cárdenas and Manzanillo. In reaction to Rueda Medina's arrest, La Familia staged four days of attacks (July 11-14) against Federal Police and Army installations in more than a dozen municipalities in Michoacán and Guanajuato, forcing the federal government to dispatch more than 5,500 elements to the region because of the unreliability of state law enforcement agencies. Next to the cadavers of three victims, La Familia left a threatening message, which was signed "The Resistance C3"—the first time the criminal organization has used this name.

Although often intimidated or bribed by La Familia, not all local police have kowtowed to the wishes of the cartel. After law enforcement agents took into custody Miguel "The King" Carvajal in the Valle de Bravo in January 2008, they received a telephoned threat against "touching" their prisoner. In a similar vein, The King told the police: "don't hit me [for] I come in the spirit of peace; my chiefs are now talking with your commanders to strike a deal." Despite this bravado, the extortionist and hit man for La Familia remained behind bars.[85]

On September 2, 2008, in the Nicolás Romero municipality authorities captured Lázaro "El Indio" Bustos Abarca, who commanded a band of twenty kidnappers linked to La Familia.[86]

Ten days later, the PGR announced the murder of twenty-four people in La Marquesa Park in Mexico State. Officials hypothesized that the murders arose from a clash between La Familia and the Beltrán Leyva brothers over control of Huixquilucan, a strategic *plaza* for drug shipments. In mid-November, federal police jailed Pedro Jaime Chávez Rosales, former director of public safety for the municipality, who was believed to be involved in the multiple executions. And in two late May 2009 operations, Federal Police took into custody Javier "El Arqui" Ortiz Chávez, a former policeman in Michoacán who purportedly ran La Familia's operations in the Mexico State municipalities of Coacalco, Tultepec, Tultitlán, and Ecatepec. They also apprehended eleven other syndicate members who stand accused of kidnapping.[87]

 The presence of narco-violence in Mexico State is especially infuriating to Governor Enrique Peña Nieto, a cardinal in the PRI's secular church who is the early favorite to become the PRI's presidential standard-bearer in 2012. Cartels carried out 360 executions in 2008, up from 111 the year before—with 207 murders tallied between January and early August 2009.

 La Familia also has effected operations in Mexico City. On July 31, 2008, a body was found in the trunk of a Chevrolet Corsica parked in the capital's southern borough of Coyoacán. A note attached to the corpse said: "For not paying. Sincerely, La Familia."[88] The western boroughs of Miguel Hidalgo and Cuajimalpa (along the nearby Mexico State municipalities of Huixquilucan and Naucalpan) have become a zone for money laundering and drug transit, exciting a raging conflict among Colombian traffickers, Los Zetas, and La Familia. The competitors dispatch their foes with high-powered weapons, decapitations, and asphyxiation with plastic bags. Next to three bodies discovered in September 2008 lay the message: "I was victim of a kidnapping by those who call themselves La Familia Michoacana; thus, I am carrying out justice by my own hand...."[89]

September 15, 2008, Grenade Attack in Morelia

 The PGR initially accused La Familia of fomenting the September 15, 2008, grenade attack in Morelia's Melchor Ocampo Plaza. Authorities advanced the theory that the fanatical band sought to attract a greater contingent of federal police and military to the state in order to thwart Los Zetas from consolidating their trafficking routes.[90]

 In response to such allegations, La Familia immediately revved up its public relations apparatus. It dispatched a text message to local reporters and residents denying participation in the tragedy and placing the blame on Los Zetas. The Gulf syndicate responded with its own communiqués in the form of banners draped in prominent spots in Puebla, Reynosa, Cancún, Oaxaca, and Nuevo Laredo. The cartel proffered a $5 million reward in dollars, euros, or another currency to anyone who could help capture members of the La Familia that it alleged produced the mayhem: "The Gulf cartel energetically condemns the September 15 attack against the Mexican people. We offer our aid for the arrest of the leaders who call themselves 'La Familia'."[91] The *narcomantas* specifically mentioned Moreno González, Jesús Méndez Vargas, and Enrique "El Kike" Tla-caltepetl—big shots within their nemesis.[92]

The Gulf organization followed up this challenge by placing a red ice chest in the center of Lázaro Cárdenas. The head of a member of its sworn enemies was packed inside the container next to which a green poster proclaimed: "Greetings Chayo, Rogaciano and Chango [reference to La Familia's leaders]. This is for the collection of queers who support the terrorists of La Familia; we do not kill innocent people; we kill terrorists like this one … [illegible] we don't kidnap and we want neither to work with you nor to have contact with you and those you rely on … thanks for those who are supporting us. Sincerely: Gulf Cartel 100%."[93]

Not to be outdone, the Sinaloa Cartel castigated both Los Zetas and La Familia, claiming that "we have never killed innocent people, much less in public events." The syndicate's e-mail communiqué went on to say that the "Sinaloans have always defended the people, we have respected the families of capos and small drug couriers, we have re-spected the government, [and] we have respected women and children." The message, signed by Mayo Zambada and El Chapo, also expressed a determination "to retake the Michoacán *plaza* and kill all who have offended the Sinaloa family."[94]

Journalists for *Proceso* reported that the police received an anonymous tip indicating the whereabouts of the alleged perpetrators of the violence. After meeting with members of La Familia near the Cuitzeo security barracks, authorities seized, blindfolded, handcuffed, and arrested three Zetas for the tragedy. Family members of the prisoners claimed that they were subjected to physical and psychological torture. In the words of a sister and wife:

> They asked him [one suspect] why he had thrown the grenades. After he repeatedly denied the charges, they tied his hands with packing tape and beat him with boards. Next they dragged him to a river and left him alone all night. He also said that they kept him blindfolded with his arms raised all day.[95]

Reforma had indicated that La Familia began to sign-up workers to establish a presence in Guanajuato in mid-2007, and operatives had ar-rived in the town of Salvatierra during February 2008. There they met with "The Lawyer," who sought to broker arrangements with municipal authorities in Salvatierra, Coroneo, Moroleón, and Uriangato, as well as with AFI agents in Uriangato and Salamanca. By offering attractive salaries, The Lawyer has recruited local lookouts, known as "*puntas*," who alert La Familia to military and police movements. In March 2008 Salvatierra's police captured four alleged narco-traffickers, thus thwarting their bid to commence operations in their municipality. However, their arrest unleashed a wave of executions that totaled sixty-one in 2008 and thirty-seven during the first two months of 2009.[96]

For its part, *Milenio* cited the appearance of La Familia in León, Irapuato, Salamanca, Guanajuato City, and Celaya as well as the municipalities of Huanimaro, Pénjamo, Acámbaro, Valle de Santiago, and Dolores Hidalgo.[97] They have even been reported in San Miguel de Allende, a picturesque colonial town that UNESCO has designated a World Heritage Site and that has become a Mecca for American and Canadian retirees, artists, and students. In several of these municipalities, La Familia emulates the Italian Mafia by controlling the small outlets that sell cocaine and marijuana to individuals. When a local distributor refused to cooperate, he was killed. In the past, "El Azul" Esparragoza Moreno, an ally of El Chapo, controlled Guanajuato. In a negotiation between capos, El Azul relinquished the *plaza* to La Familia, thus avoiding a lethal confrontation. Dominance in Guanajuato helps La Familia impede its rivals' access to Michoacán.[98]

Organization and Resources

Proceso magazine journalist Richard Ravelo asserts that the 4,000 members of La Familia were born and raised in Michoacán, that they earn between $1,500 and $2,000 per month, and that they are well connected with state and local officials. He has found that they attend church regularly, carry Bibles, and distribute the Good Book in local government offices.[99] They even justify executions as "orders from the Lord." *El Milenio* has reported La Familia uses the works of evangelical John Eldredge to instruct and motivate their recruits. Unlike La Familia, Eldredge, a graduate of the Los Angeles drug subculture who founded and directs the Ransomed Heart Ministries in Colorado Springs, Colorado, does not espouse violence. Instead, the "big message" of his "small ministry" is "to set men and women free to live from the heart as God's intimate allies … That's what we are devoted to—seeing men and women come fully alive as the image-bearers of a breathtaking God."[100]

La Familia boasts that it enjoys grassroots' support because it provides assistance to campesinos, constructs schools, donates books, prevents the sale of adulterated wine, and employs "extremely strong strategies" to bring order to the Tierra Caliente.[101] Thus, they furnish a contrast to the Milenio Cartel, which has recruited outsiders called "*Antizetas*."[102]

La Familia acquires resources by selling protection to merchants, contraband hucksters, loggers, hotels, local gangs, and small-scale drug sellers. Rather than speak in terms of extortion, the cartel maintains that it "protects" its clients.[103] When vendors of pirated diskettes in the Valle de Bravo, Mexico State, informed authorities of La Familia's extortion, members of the criminal organization returned to advise them: "For complaining to the police, the monthly quota that you must pay this time is 30,000 pesos and [an additional] 10,000 pesos per month." When arrested, the brigands told law enforcement agents: "We come in a peaceful manner. We are neither kidnappers nor gangsters (*rateros*). We come to restore order and help those whom you cannot."[104]

Like the Zetas, activists in the organization sometimes wear uniforms, carry arms, and drive vehicles similar to those of the AFI. This allows them greater freedom to move around their areas of interest.[105] Moreover, leaders of the group have become so brazen that they have designed their own outfits to mark their identity and distinguish their members from adversaries. They treat informants with grotesque cruelty. In April 2009 they murdered at least fourteen people in Lázaro Cárdenas. Authorities found the bullet-riddled body of a 35-year-old man whose hands had been tied behind his back and a black plastic bag wrapped and taped over his head. A note next to his corpse warned: "This is what happens to informants of the Z [Zetas], sincerely, La Familia."[106]

Reports indicate the fragmentation of La Familia, whose leadership—known as "Los Sierras"—holds sway in the Tierra Caliente. A Guatemalan prisoner told SIEDO that the leader is known as "Sierra One," the second-in-command as "Sierra Two," etc. up to "Sierra Eleven." Other operators bear sobriquets such as Sierra Jupiter, Sierra Raven, and other fanciful names. Each chief manages a unit of twenty-two to thirty men, who are responsible for patrolling and monitoring movements in the municipalities under La Familia's domain. The journalist Ravelo also reported that the organization has an executive council composed of businessmen and government officials, along with narco-traffickers from regional and municipal cells.[107]

These factions include:

* "The Historic Ones" ("*Los Históricos*"), who have links with Los Zetas;
* "The Extortionists" ("*Los Extorsionistas*"), composed of businessmen and growers who concentrate on extorting money from anyone from surgeons to municipal mayors to priests;
* "Debt Collectors" ("*Los Cobradores de Deudas*"), who are allied with the Milenio and Sinaloa cartels and who traffic in methamphetamines;
* An unnamed group that concentrates on selling pirated films, DVDs, computer software, and video games;[108] and
* "*Los Yonqueros*," who carry out kidnappings in Mexico State and the D.F.[109]

Loya Plancarte, an ex-Zeta now presents himself as the spokesman for La Familia. The 53-year-old Michoacán native, who manages press and public relations for the organization, contends that through kidnappings and executions the cartel is ensuring "a peaceful climate for law-abiding citizens." In addition, he cited as his cartel's principal targets El Chapo Guzmán and the Beltrán Leyva brothers because they were responsible for methamphetamine addiction in Michoacán communities."[110]

Pressure from Mexico City forced the February 2009 resignation of Citlallí Fernández González as Michoacán's secretary of public safety because of her lack of success against cartels and, possibly, because her boyfriend (who may have been Loya Plancarte) was linked to La Familia. She then became an adviser to PRD governor Leonel Godoy Rangel. On May 26, 2009, federal authorities arrested Fernández González as part of a stunning thrust against twenty-seven public officials in Michoacán, including the ten mayors whose names appear in Table 8.2.

In addition to Fernández González and the mayors, the federal forces took into custody various municipal security directors (Arteaga and Tumbiscatío), ranking law enforcement personnel (Lázaro Cárdenas, Morelia, and Zitácuaro) as well as state public servants (chief of advisers to the attorney general, the economic development director, police agents, and the head of police training). A PGR spokesman, who eschewed the idea of political motivation, stressed that the strike was nonpartisan and derived from intelligence amassed by SIEDO. In provincial areas, there are few secrets about the conduct of public figures. The focus was on Lázaro Cárdenas and trafficking routes from the port. Even though several cartels absorbed hits, preliminary reports indicate that La Familia took the brunt of the assault.[111]

In the aftermath of this venture, the Secretary of Public Security issued a communiqué about the arrest of other La Familia members: Wilibaldo

Table 8.2
Michoacán Mayors Apprehended and Alleged Criminality in their Municipalities

Municipality	Mayor	Political Party	Influential Cartel(s) in municipality	Reported Criminal Activity in municipality	Killings in 2009
Apatzingán	Genaro Guizar Valencia	"For a Better Michoacán" Coalition of PRD-PT-Convergencia	La Familia, Los Zetas/ Gulf Milenio	Largest meth laboratory in the country	10
Aquila	José Cortéz Ramos*	PRI	Los Zetas/Gulf	In early May, Marines eradicated nine marijuana fields	0
Arteaga	Jairo Germán Rivas Páramo	PRI	La Familia and Los Zetas/ Gulf	A paramilitary attacked the mayor and struck several of his staff	0
Buenavista	Osvaldo Esquival Lucatero*	"For a Better Michoacán" Coalition of PRD-PT-Convergencia	Los Zetas/ Gulf	Police attacked with grenades in town of Razo de Órgano	5
Ciudad Hidalgo	José Luis Ávila Franco	PAN	Los Zetas/ Gulf	None reported	0
Coahuayana	Audel Méndez Chávez*	PRI	Los Zetas/ Gulf	None reported	0
Lázaro Cárdenas	Mariano Ortega Sánchez (Arrested June 29)	"For a Better Michoacán" Coalition of PRD-PT-Convergencia	La Familia, Los Zetas/ Gulf Milenio	Murders and importation of narcotics through this port city	N.A.
Tepalcatepec	Uriel Farías Álvarez	PRI	Los Zetas/ Gulf and Milenio	Mayor's brother Juan José considered a key lieutenant for Los Valencias (Milenio Cartel)	1

Table 8.2 (cont.)

Tumbiscatio	Adán Tafolla Ortiz	PAN-PRI-PVEM	Los Zetas/ Gulf and Milenio	None reported	0
Uruapan	Antonio González Rodríguez	PAN-PANAL	Los Zetas/ Gulf, La Familia, and Milenio	In Aug. 2008, secretary of the municipality kidnapped; still missing	14
Zitácuaro	Juan Antonio Ixtlahuac Orihuela	PRI	Los Zetas/ Gulf	In March, the Army captured eight individuals armed with AK-47s and AR-15s	0

* Released June 29, 2009.
Source: "Ligan a Alcaldes con 'La Familia,'" *Reforma*, May 27, 2009; "Nombres de los 27 Detenidos," *El Universal.com*, May 26, 2008; Attorney General's Office, Press Release 567/09, May 27, 2009; and Azucena Silva and Rafael Rivera, "Cae alcalde de Lázaro Cárdenas, *El Universal*, June 30, 2009.

"El Wili" Correa Alcántara (kidnappings and executions); Nicolás "México" Morales González (*plaza* of Melchor Ocampo municipality); Luis Yarza Solano (western Michoacán); Martín "El Cheyas" Sandoval Gómez (Valle de Bravo, Mexico State); José Ángel "Oliveras" Oliveras Marín (bodyguard of Dionisio Loya Plancarte); and Juan "Juan Serna" Herrera Jiménez (purchase and storing of drugs).[112]

Six months before May 26 foray into the state, federal agents had captured Wenceslao "El Wencho" Álvarez Álvarez, an ally of La Familia who ran an international operation out of Nueva Italia, a Michoacán municipality where, ironically, on November 17, 1938, Lázaro Cárdenas established the first ejido of his administration. The late president had promised that the communal farm would serve as a model of progress for the nation. Like many growers in the Tierra Caliente, El Wencho produced avocados. He claims to have turned to narco-trafficking to revenge the 1999 kidnapping and murder of his father by a vicious gang, Los Arcila. Led by Jorge Álvarez Arcila, a local farmer, and Daniel Farías, the former warden of the Pátzcuaro prison, these brigands enjoyed impunity as they carried out a dozen kidnappings in the Tierra Caliente between 1996 and 2000.

The PGR has connected "El Wencho" to La Familia. His cocaine network allegedly extended from Colombia through Guatemala, Honduras, El Salvador, Venezuela, and the Dominican Republic, as well as to Atlanta and other U.S. cities. The U.S. Drug Enforcement Administration has identified him as a lieutenant of Treviño Morales, a big cheese in Los Zetas. Álvarez Álvarez called the charges against him "false," insisting that he was only a grower of tomatoes, peppers, mangos, and other crops on land rented by his entire family.[113]

In addition to his underworld exploits, El Wencho also owns—or has an interest in—"Los Mapaches" of Nueva Italia, a second division soccer team that he purchased for 1 million pesos.[114] The AFI waited to arrest the narco-aficionado until Los Mapaches completed a match against El América of Coapa, a third division team. The police also took twenty players into temporary custody. The previous October 21, the Mexican Football Federation had disqualified Los Mapaches from league play.[115] Soon after El Wencho's arrest, the PGR issued a communiqué saying that the team owner "operated an organized crime cell dedicated to the purchase, acquisition, transport, and sale of drugs to the United States and [was also involved in] financial transactions and money laundering related to drug trafficking." Still, his team dedicated its next match to Álvarez Álvarez and the announcer asked spectators to hold hands and pray for the accused, even as two Air Force helicopters hovered over the field. A large sign in the stadium proclaimed the team's official sponsors—Empresas Nobaro, Materiales del Río, Hotel Los Arcos, Agroquímicos Cobián, Pinturas Constitución, Mofles Coria, and Importaciones Nobaro—companies believed to be owned by El Wencho.[116]

This complex group known as La Familia bears similarities to Colombia's United Self-Defense Forces (Autodefensas Unidas de Colombia—AUC), an amalgam of right-wing vigilantes, rural self-defense militia, former military and police personnel, who oppose anyone believed to be supportive of the rebels belonging to the Colombian Revolutionary Armed Forces (Fuerzas Armadas Revolucionarias de Colombia—FARC). The religious zeal of La Familia manifests itself in its preference for executions over negotiations. So strong is the organization that it appears to have achieved dominance in Michoacán, eclipsed Los Zetas in Mexico state, crossed swords with the Beltrán Leyvas in Mexico State and Guerrero, and ousted a faction of the Sinaloa cartel from Guanajuato. La Familia, which is extremely volatile because of its diverse components and messianic élan, suffered a notable setback in the May 26 operation in Michoacán. The ultimate success of the round-up depends on the daunting task of recruiting mayors and other public figures who either have no links with La Familia and other cartels, or who have the ability to resist their bribes, blackmail, and well-honed murder skills. If Calderón repeats these strikes in other states, he runs the risk of opening up more fronts than he has the resources to control. Whether or not the foray transforms Michoacán, it sent an emphatic message to governors and mayors throughout the country that they could be the next targets of the military and the Federal Police and the military, which deplores the impunity enjoyed by crooked officials.

Figure 8.1
La Familia Enunciates Its Principles

The Michoacán Family

Who are we?
Common workers from the hot lands region in the state of Michoacán, organized by the need to end the oppression, the humiliation to which we have constantly been subjected by people who have always had power, which in turn allowed them to perpetrate all kinds of dirty tricks and abuses in the state. These include members of the Milenio cartel, those named Valencia, and other gangs, like the Gang of 30, who from the 80s until today have terrorized much of the state, above all the areas of Puruarán, Turicato, Tacámbaro, and Ario de Rosales, and who have carried out kidnappings, extortions, and other crimes that disturb Michoacán´s peace.

Mission:
Eradicate from the state of Michoacán kidnapping, extortion in person and by telephone, paid assassinations, express kidnapping, tractor-trailer and auto theft, home robberies done by people like those mentioned, who have made the state of Michoacán an unsafe place. Our sole motive is that we love our state and are no longer willing to see our people's dignity trampled on.

Perhaps at this time there are people who don't understand us, but we know that in the areas most affected they understand our actions, since now it is possible to ward off these delinquents who come from other states and whom we will not allow to enter Michoacán and continue committing crimes. We are eradicating completely from the state the retail sale of the lethal drug known as ice, as it is one of the worst drugs, one that causes irreversible damage to society. We are going to prohibit the sale of altered wine said to come from Tepito. We know that what comes from there is of poor quality.

Objective:
To maintain the universal values of the people, to which they have full right.

Unfortunately, in order to eradicate the ills we have mentioned, we have had to resort to robust strategies, as we have seen that this is the only way to bring order to the state. We will not allow it to get out of control again.

Why did we form?
When the Michoacán Family organization began, we did not expect that it would be possible to get rid of kidnapping, paid assassination, fraud, and the sale of the drug known as ice. But thanks to the great number of people who have had faith, we are achieving control over this great problem in the state.

The Family as a group of people has grown, such that at this moment we cover the entire state of Michoacán. This organization sprang from the firm commitment to fight the out-of-control crime that existed in our state. The Family has achieved great, important advances by fighting these problems little by little, but we still cannot declare victory. We can say that the state has seen an 80% improvement with regards to these problems. We have also reduced kidnapping by the same percentage.

People who work decently at any activity need not worry. We respect them, but we will not allow people from here or from other states to commit crimes or try to control other types of activities. When we first began to organize and proposed putting an end to the street sale of the drug known as ice, many told us that not even First World countries have been able to get it under control. Nonetheless, we are doing it.

For reflection:
What would you do as a resident of Michoacán? Would you join the family if you saw that we are fighting these crimes? Or would you let them proliferate? Give us your opinion.

You, family man. I ask you: Would you like to see your son out on the streets in danger of getting involved in drugs or crime?

Would you support this organization in its fight against the maladies that attack our state? The media have been responsible and objective in their coverage of events that have occurred. We appreciate their impartiality and thank them for their coverage of our actions.

Other countries have not even seen such organizations formed on the people's behalf, and yet we have already begun.... Success depends on the support and understanding of Michoacán society.

Sincerely,
The Michoacán Family
Prepared by Juan Carlos García Cornejo (Translated by Mark Stevenson, the Associated Press)

Notes

1. Quoted in "Border-town Killing Sends Message," *Los Angeles Times*, June 10, 2005.
2. Quoted in Alfredo Corchado, "Cartel's Enforcers Outpower their Boss," *Dallas Morning News*, June 11, 2007.
3. Quoted in U.S. Department of Justice, *National Drug Threat Assessment 2008* (Washington, D.C.: National Drug Intelligence Center, 2007).
4. "Los Zetas el otro ejército," *Sitio Extra Oficial, Fuerza Aérea Mexicana*, January 20, 2007. *www.extrafam.mforos.com.*

5.   The Mexican Army has several special forces units, including the regular GAFES, who are deployed in the twelve military regions; and the extremely select "High Command Special Forces Airmobile Group," whose cadres report directly to the secretary of defense.

6.   The Mexican Army suffered 99,849 desertions, including 1,023 officers, between 2000 and 2006; see Alberto Najar, "Desertaron 100 mil militares con Fox," *Milenio*, July 20, 2007. Most defections occur during soldiers' first year in uniform.

7.   Marco A. Rodríguez Martinez, "El poder de los 'zetas'" www.monografías.com.

8.   Library of Congress, *Organized Crime and Terrorist Activity in Mexico*, 1999-2002, February 2003.

9.   J. Jesús Blancornelas, "La escuela de Los Zetas," *La Crónica*, December 13, 2005.

10.   Quoted in Corchado, "Cartel's Enforcers Outpower their Boss."

11.   Alejandro Gutiérrez, *Narcotráfico: El gran desafío de Calderón* (Mexico City: Planeta, 2007, Chapters 1 and 5; and Francisco Gómez, Narcoguerra sitia a la capital," *El Universal*, March 31, 2009.

12.   Francisco Gómez, "Narcoguerra sitia a la capital," *El Universal*, March 31, 2009.

13.   "La mitad del país, bajo el mando de Los Zetas," *Milenio.online*, November, 25, 2008.

14.   "Arraigan a líder de 'Zetas' de Tabasco," *El Nuevo Heraldo*, September 9, 2008.

15.   Carlos Heredía Díaz, Interview with author, Mexico City, March 11, 2009.

16.   Alfredo Corchado, "Drug Cartels Operate Training Camps near Texas Border Just inside Mexico," *Dallas Morning News*, April 4, 2008.

17.   Quoted in *Ibid.*

18.   "Los Kaibiles: Las 'maquinas de matar,'" *Terra*, October 2, 2005.

19.   Lacey, "In Drug War, Mexico Fights the Cárteles and Itself."

20.   Brandon M. Case *et al.*, "Officials Develop Clearer Picture of Zetas," *Mexico News* (*El Universal*), March 21, 2005.

21.   "Ex militares sirven de sicarios a cárteles mexicanos, SeguRed.com, July 25, 2006. http://www.segured.com/index.php?od=9&link=7765.

22.   Council on Hemispheric Affairs, "Mexican Drug Policy: Internal Corruption in an Externalized War," Press Release, June 26, 2007. *www.coha.org*.

23.   "Hallan guarida de 'Zetas' en Guatemala," *Reforma*, March 28, 2009.

24.   Lemic Madrid, "Los Zetas pasan de ser brazo armado a cabeza," *Excelsior*, September 9, 2008; and José Méndez, "Narco pasa frontera sur en helicopters, revelan," *El Universal*, December 19, 2008.

25.   "Cae otro presunto Zeta en Guatemala con arsenal," *El Universal*, December 19, 2008.

26.   Luis Ángel Sas, "'Los Zetas' buscan el control del narco Cobán," *El Periódico*, September 4, 2008.

27.   "Acusan amenazas de 'Zetas' contra Colom," *Reforma*, March 1, 2009; and Juan Veledíaz and María de la Luz González, "México ofrece ayuda a Colom por amenazas," *El Universal*, March 3, 2009.

28.   Antonio Baranda, "Preocupa el narco a Guatemala," *Reforma*, April 8, 2009.

29.   Alejandro Medellín, "Cárteles del país abren nuevas rutas en CA," *El Universal*, March 29, 2009.

30.   Roberto del Solar, "Guatemala Militariza Frontera con México," *Nuevo Excelsior*, January 8, 2009.

31.   Irene Savio, "Confirman nexo 'Zetas' e italianos," *Reforma*, September 19, 2008.

32. The source of this information is "Pitufo," an ex-Zeta now in a witness protection program; see "Tenía ex militar negocio con 'Zetas,'" *Reforma*, April 5, 2009.
33. Roig-Franzia, "Drug Trade Tyranny on the Border," p. A16.
34. "Polarización en el SNTE," *El Universal* ("Bajo Reserva"), July 28, 2007.
35. Alfredo Corchado, "Cartel's Enforcers Outpower their Boss," *Dallas Morning News*, June 11, 2007.
36. Darío Dávila, "Un capo y dos 'bandidas'," *El Universal*, June 10, 2008.
37. Jorge Alejandro Medellín, "La Burra había pactado con los Zetas: SIEDO," *El Universal*, March 25, 2009.
38. "Investigan pactos de Beltrán con 'Zetas'," *Reforma*, November 25, 2008.
39. Alejandro Suverza, "Los Zetas, una pesadilla para el cartel del Golfo," *El Universal*, January 12, 2008, p. 1; Rodríguez Martínez, "El poder de los 'zetas'"; and Francisco Gómez, "'Los Zetas' por dentro," *El Universal*, December 31, 2008.
40. Juan Alberto Cedillo, "Pandillas al servicios del narco," *El Universal*, March 3, 2009.
41. "Reclutan Zetas a mujeres," *El Norte*, March 27, 2009.
42. Jorge Alejandro Medellín, "Cae célula 'zeta' de 'matamilitares,'" *El Universal*, February 12, 2009.
43. "Extorsionaban Zetas en Hidalgo.—PF," *Reforma*, March 5, 2009; and "Caen 3 niños 'Zeta'," *Reforma*, March 6, 2009.
44. "Banda que ejecutó a Moneda Rangel, trabajaba para los Zetas," *Milenio*, March 18, 2009.
45. "Confirman muerte de cabecilla de 'Los Zetas,'" *El Diario*, April 11, 2009.
46. Quoted in Corchado, "Cartel's Enforcers Outpower their Boss."
47. "Dan 'Zetas' narcoconsejo," *Reforma*, May 4, 2008.
48. César Peralta González, "Ejecutan a falsos 'Zetas' en Reynosa, tenían un narco-mensaje," *Milenio*, February 28, 2009.
49. "Invasion of the Body-Snatchers," *Reuters*, March 9, 2007.
50. "Aparecen 'Zetas' en panteón," *Reforma*, November 2, 2008.
51. Marcelo Beyliss, "Amenanzan con narcoflores a la policía de Sonora," *El Universal*, November 24, 2008.
52. Zeferino Tejeda Uscanga quoted in Lev García, "Rescata comando a Zetas …¡de penal!," *Reforma*, May 17, 2008.
53. "Advierten que 'Zetas' prevén rescatar a líder en Guatemala," *El Porvenir*, September 5, 2008.
54. Alfredo Corchado, "Drug Cartels Operate Training Camps near Texas Border Just inside Mexico," *Dallas Morning News*, April 4, 2008.
55. Pablo César Carrillo, "Elección con tufo a narco," *EXonline*, November 17, 2007.
56. "Siempre bajo sospecha," *Reforma*, April 1, 2009.
57. Corchado, "Drug Cartels Operate Training Camps near Texas Border Just inside Mexico."
58. Ruben Mosso, "FBI: Los Zetas problema de seguridad nacional para EU," *Milenio. com*, January 9, 2008.
59. Abel Barajas, "Soldiers Face 60 for Aiding Traffickers," *Laredo Morning Times-Reforma News Service*, October 2, 2006.
60. The five decapitated men may have been involved in the murder of a waitress/prostitute who worked in the bar and had been impregnated by a member of La Familia. A few days before the ghastly incident, she refused to have sex with these men, who waited for her when the bar closed, and raped and killed her. La Familia began its own investigation and found these individuals guilty. This may explain why the death note indicated that they "do not kill women."

61. James C. McKinley Jr., "Mexican Drug War Turns Barbaric, Grisly," *New York Times*, October 26, 2006.
62. Alejandro Suverza, "El poder de 'La Familia Michoacana,'" December 4, 2006, *El Universal*.
63. "Mil 200 negocios pagan renta al narco en Morelia," *Milenio.com*, September 24, 2008.
64. Rafael Rivera, "'Boom' carguero en Lázaro Cárdenas," *El Universal*, December 29, 2008.
65. "Toma 'La Familia' ley en Michoacán," *Reforma*, November 24, 2006; there is an undated, photocopied training document, "Pensamientos de la Familia," which contains preachments signed by "El Loco," Nazario Moreno González.
66. Iván González, "Rosales estaba ligado a Osiel Cárdenas: PGR," *EsMas*, *www. esmas.com/noticierotelevisa/mexico*; and "Ofrece 'El Tísico' soborno a captores," *Reforma*, November 3, 2004.
67. "La SIEDO ya investiga sobre los decapitados y narcorrecados," *MiMorelia.com*, August 22, 2008 *www.mimorelio.com*.
68. Pablo César Carrillo, "Acusación de narco me da risa," *Excelsior*, November 13, 2007.
69. Quoted in Carrillo, "Acusación de narco me da risa."
70. "Like a Church on a Hill," *News-Press* (Ft. Myers), September 26, 1999.
71. Will Weissert, "Michoacán ensagretada por decapitaciones de los narcos," *La Voz*, October 23, 2006.
72. "Toma 'La Familia' ley en Michoacán."
73. Quotations in this paragraph came from "La Familia: Society's Saviours or Sociopaths," September 25, 2008. *http://cyanide257.wordpress.com/2008/09/25//*.
74. Francisco Gómez, "'La Familia,' imagen y ritos del narco," *El Universal*, January 1, 2009.
75. Ignacio Alzaga, "'La Fresa' sí era el jefe de la Familia, confirma Sedena," Ignacio Alzaga, *Milenio*, December 30, 2008.
76. "Cae presunto jefe de La Familia Michoacana," *Noroeste.com*, April 22, 2009.
77. "Exigió Rafael Cedeño en febrero de 2008 el regreso de soldados a sus cárteles, *El Norte*, April 21, 2009.
78. "Disputan 4 cárteles el estado de México," *Reforma*, November 14, 2008.
79. "Policías de Chalco vinculan a su jefe con 'La Familia Michoacana,'" *Notisistema Informa*, November 7, 2008 *www.notisistema.com*.
80. "Seguridad," *Terra*, October 17, 2008. *www.terra.com.mx/*.
81. "Acusan nexus con narco de ex delegado en Edomex," *Reforma*, September 19, 2008.
82. "'Va a morir toda La Familia michoacana, sino me creen allí les dejo esto'; tres ejecutados," *Alerta Periodista*, August 19, 2008. *www.alertaperiodistica.com.mx*.
83. "Multiplica 'Familia' violencia en Edomex, *Reforma*, September 14, 2008.
84. "Mexico: Army Arrests La Familia Leader in Raid," *Stratfor*, December 30, 2008; and Gustavo Castillo García, "Líderes religiosos, los principales jefes de *La Familia* michoacana." *La Jornada*, March 27, 2009.
85. Francisco Gómez, "Dominar al país, plan de 'La Familia'", *El Universal*, August 1, 2008.
86. Alejandro Jiménez, "Alentados en Morelia: un año de golpes para frenar poderío," *El Universal*, September 18, 2008.
87. "Capturan a operador de 'La Familia' en Edomex," *W Radio*, May 26, 2009.
88. "La Familia: Society's Saviours or Sociopaths."
89. Arturo Sierra, "Mata narco a 21 al Poniente del DF," *Reforma*, September 20, 2008.

90. Alfredo Méndez, "Todo apunta a que La Familia es culpable, según la Procuraduría," *La Jornada*, September 19, 2008.
91. "'Cartel del Golfo': recompense por captura de autores de atentado en Morelia," *Milenio.com*, October 4, 2008.
92. Carlos Figueroa, "Aparecen narcomantas en dos estados; ofrecen recompensas por líderes de La Familia, *La Jornada de Oriente*, October 6, 2008.
93. "Dejan cabeza con narcomensaje en hielera en Michoacán," *La Opción de Chihuahua*, October 24, 2008.
94. "El Chapo and Zambada: Vamos por Los Zetas y La Familia," *Proceso*, September 23, 2008.
95. Jorge Carrasco Araizago and Francisco Castellanos J., "Caso Morelia: confesiones 'bajo tortura,'" *Proceso*, October 2008.
96. "Reclutan sicarios para Guanajuato," *Reforma*, February 1, 2009.
97. "Se adueña La Familia de plaza de Guanajuato," *Milenio*, November 8, 2008.
98. *Ibid.*
99. "La Familia: Society's Saviours or Sociopaths."
100. Ransomed Heart Ministries, "Ransomed Heart is a small ministry devoted to a big message" *www.ransomedheart.com/ministry/who-we-are.aspx.*
101. Luis Astorga, *Seguridad, traficantes y militares* (Mexico City: Tusquets Editorial, 2007): 190.
102. "Pelean Michoacán Zetas y La Familia," *Reforma*, September 18, 2008.
103. "Mexico's Hydra," *Security in Latin America networkedintelligence.wordpress. com/tag./la-familia/.*
104. "Paga o muere: tradición de 'La Familia,'" *El Universal*, February 22, 2009.
105. "Dominar al país, plan de la Familia," *www.deyaboo.forumcommunity.net.*
106. "Ejecutan a un hombre en Lázaro Cárdenas, Michoacán, dejan narcomensaje," *Milenio.com*, April 18, 2009.
107. "Bajo control de 'Los Sierras': El organigrama del grupo," *El Universal*, January 1, 2009.
108. "El Cártel La Familia, sospechose del narcoatentado en Michoacán, *E-Consulta*, September 18, 2008. *www.e-consulta.com.*
109. "Dan prisión a cómplices de 'La Familia,'" *Reforma*, January 30, 2009.
110. Alejandro Jiménez, "Atentados en Morelia Investigan ligas entre alcaldías y 'Familia,'" *El Universal*, September 19, 2008; and Sam Logan and Kate Kairies, "U.S. Drug Habit Migrates to Mexico," *Americas Policy Program Special Report*, February 7, 2007. *www.americas.irc-online.org.*
111. "Ligan a Alcaldes con 'La Familia,'" *Reforma.com*, May 27, 2009.
112. "Capturan a seis presuntos integrantes de La familia michoacana," *Milenio.com*, June 12, 2009.
113. "Entra 'Wencho' al narco en busca de revancha," *Reforma*, November 12, 2008; and María de la Luz González, "Mapaches 'lavaron' en siete países," *El Universal*, October 15, 2008.
114. "Paga 'El Wencho' $1 millón por equipo," *Reforma*, November 14, 2008.
115. Raúl Ochoa, "Narcofutbolistas, Nueva modalidad de los capos," *Proceso*, October 9, 2008.
116. F. Castellanos and Raúl Ochoa, "Oran y marchan en defense de narcoequipo," *Proceso*, October 13, 2008.

9

U.S.-Mexican Narcotics Policy:
The Mérida Initiative and Beyond

On February 7, 1985, five armed men hustled DEA agent Enrique "Kiki" Camarena into a car in broad daylight near the U.S. Consulate-General in Guadalajara, and co-workers never saw him alive again. The incident reflected both the drug kingpins' arrogance and the grotesque failure of corrupt Mexican officials to conduct a legitimate investigation. Indeed, the episode converted narcotics smuggling, at least from Washington's perspective, from a law enforcement issue to one of national security. After intense political hardball demanding his return, on March 5, 1985, authorities discovered the tortured, bruised, and decomposing bodies of Camarena and his Mexican pilot buried in plastic bags in a shallow grave seventy miles south of Guadalajara. Prosecutors believed the murders constituted retaliation for a series of drug raids that had cost the capos billions of dollars.[1] Camarena was working on "Operation Godfather," investigating Miguel Ángel "The Godfather" Félix Gallardo, the Sinaloa drug boss who supplied heroin and cocaine to southern California and other areas of the Sun Belt.

The kingpin generated upwards of $30 million a month, which paid for a lot of favors, as well as expanding his activities throughout Mexico and the United States. Félix Gallardo was closely allied with fellow Sinaloan Rafael Caro Quintero, whose Sonora cartel stretched from the Andes to major U.S. cities; he shipped a ton and a half to two tons of cocaine each month, which put him on a par with Medellín's and Cali's infamous racketeers.[2]

A high-school football star, ex-Marine, and former police officer, Camarena infiltrated trafficking gangs even as he kept his face off TV screens. Nevertheless, he incurred the wrath of top dogs Félix Gallardo and Caro Quintero by exposing a 12-kilometer square, sophisticated irrigated marijuana farm and drying sheds. This enterprise had flourished as an agricultural oasis known as *el Búfalo* in the Chihuahua desert with blatant connivance of federal and local police.

Foot-dragging by Mexican officials investigating the execution infuriated the overwhelmingly Mexican-American population of Camarena's hometown of Calexico, California. Along the major highway, local citizens erected a billboard that proclaimed: "Warning: Not Safe to Travel to Guadalajara, Mexico."

The death of the 37-year-old agent, who left behind a wife and three young sons, stirred a media maelstrom, including a *Time* magazine cover story on May 7, 1988. As *Time* reported: "Parents who had come together in local coalitions to fight the drug problem took Kiki as their model, embracing his belief that one person can make a difference, and adopting his symbol—the red ribbon—as their own. They began the continuing tradition of wearing and displaying red ribbons as a symbol of intolerance toward the use of drugs." A mini-series, *Drug Wars: The Camarena Story*—captured an Emmy award. Congressman Duncan Hunter and teacher David Dhillon launched "Camarena Clubs" in California high schools and in 1986 club members presented a proclamation to the First Lady. The following year members of parent teacher organizations in California, Illinois, and Virginia wore red ribbons during late October. In 1988 Congress proclaimed the first National Red Ribbon Week, which Nancy Reagan chaired.[3]

U.S. Customs agents vented their fury at Mexico's inaction by meticulously searching vehicles at the frontier, virtually paralyzing border traffic for several days.[4] American officials accused their Mexican counterparts of allowing Camarena's killers to escape. In response, some Mexican law enforcement agents alleged that the torture of the DEA professional indicated his connivance with drug barons whom he had double-crossed. They also claimed that the DEA, whose reputation paled in comparison with that of the FBI and CIA, was inventing a hero to burnish its image.

Meanwhile, Senator Jesse Helms and the DEA administrator lambasted Mexican politicians not only for their involvement in narcotics trafficking, but also for other forms of venality. The feisty Helms even asserted that Miguel de la Madrid's election in 1982 was fraudulent and that the PRI had falsified the 1985 voting tallies by keeping two sets of returns, "one public, one private." The North Carolina curmudgeon said that the PRI "is to a great extent tied directly into the system of graft and corruption" and has been preserved through "socialist methods of economic control to direct graft and corruption to the ruling circles."[5]

Caro Quintero was found in Costa Rica and, in 1989, sentenced to forty years in prison for the murder of the American who became a drug-war martyr. When lawyers employed a technicality to overturn this conviction, the Mexican Attorney General's Office insisted that Caro Quintero would not be freed because he was already behind bars for another crime. In the unlikely event that Caro Quintero gained release from his Mexican sentences, there was a longstanding request on file for his arrest and extradition to the United States, according to a U.S. Justice Department official, who spoke on condition of anonymity.

News of possible legal machinations angered Camarena's former fellow agents. "Kiki's killing symbolized corruption at its worst in Mexico," said Phil Jordan, a retired DEA special agent in Dallas and former director of the organization's El Paso Intelligence Center. "We know why Kiki was taken from us—because the [Mexican] government was working in complicity with the godfathers of the drug trade ...."[6] A survey conducted by Louis Harris and Associates in 1986 found that 63 percent of Americans believed its inability to curb the heavy drug trafficking indicated that something was seriously wrong with Mexico's regime.[7]

Camarena's execution reverberated throughout Washington and poisoned U.S.-Mexican relations for years. The DEA's forcible abduction from Guadalajara of a Mexican physician believed to have been involved in the Camarena affair intensified bilateral tensions.

The Certification Process

In reaction to the Camarena imbroglio, U.S. legislators passed the Anti-Drug Abuse Act of 1986, which required the president to make a determination—and report to Congress—on the progress of drug producing and/or drug transit countries to eliminate the drug threat. The chief executive had until March 1 to certify that countries were cooperating fully with U.S. policies or that they had taken adequate steps on their own to reduce drug proliferation. He could waive sanctions if it were in the United States' national interest.

As part of the certification process, the U.S. Department of State's Bureau of International Narcotics and Law Enforcement Affairs (INLE) presented findings on drug strategies and actions. It also analyzed drug commerce and abuse in every country and categorized them as a major producing and/or transit countries, precursor chemical source countries, or money laundering countries. In theory, this report provided an objective basis for determining compliance with the U.S. statute and, at the same time, publicized the status of the nations evaluated. In practice, ambiguous terminology and lack of specific administrative guidelines gave the president substantial flexibility in determining whether a country had taken "adequate steps" or what constituted "vital national interest." Congress could hold public hearings and, if it disagreed with the White House's judgment, overturn certification within thirty days. Any such legislation would be subject to a presidential veto, which Congress can override only with a two-thirds vote in both houses.

Among the sanctions that could be applied to decertified countries were:

* Suspension of most foreign assistance and financing of military sales, with the exception of counter-narcotics and humanitarian aid;
* Opposition by U.S. representatives to loans by multinational development banks; and
* Increased tariffs and denial of preferential trade benefits, at the president's discretion.

Legislators introduced resolutions to disapprove Mexico's certification in five years (1987, 1988, 1997, 1998, and 1999). Both houses passed attenuated resolutions in 1997, and the following year a Senate resolution met defeat on the floor. Even with certification, the scheme exposed Mexico to virulent criticism. In light of the ubiquity of drug activity in Mexico, Republican Senator Paul Coverdell, chairman of the Senate subcommittee on western hemisphere affairs, said that to label Mexico cooperative "would make whatever credibility the process had a total hypocrisy."[8]

In response to this invective, Mexico begrudgingly—and sometimes superficially—sought to highlight its commitment to fighting drugs. In reality, it viewed the certification ordeal as an imperial attack, an affront to its sovereignty, and myopia about the reasons for the demand. Within Mexico, certification constituted a diplomatic version of poking a sharp stick in the eye of a neighbor. President Ernesto Zedillo (1994-2000), a vocal opponent of the law even suggested that U.S. should be subjected to the same review for their guilt on the consumption front. Nevertheless, decertification of Colombia signaled that the practice should be taken seriously and that the consequences were real.

After fifteen years of the program, drugs became cheaper and more widespread than before. According to a table prepared for the White House Office on National Drug Control Policy by the RAND Corporation, the price per pure gram of cocaine dropped from $300 to just over $150 in 2001 (in 2002 U.S. dollars).

Figure 9.1
U.S. Wholesale and Retail Prices of Cocaine, 1981-2003

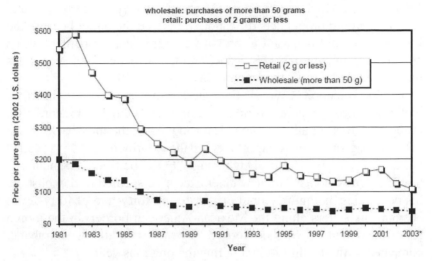

wholesale: purchases of more than 50 grams
retail: purchases of 2 grams or less

*2003 figures are based on data for January-June only.
Source: Prepared for ONDCP by the RAND Corporation.

Among others, Senator Charles Grassley, chairman of the Senate's Caucus on International Narcotics Control, believed that certification served an important function. In his own plan, the State Department would review countries with historically poor track records, while sparing nations like Mexico an annual critique. This proposal recognized that one broad standard could not succeed throughout the world. Grassley's recommendation would have retained accountability linked to certification only for nations where scrutiny would prove useful.[9] While the oversight stratagem complicated cooperation, the immediate effect was positive in the view of columnist Sergio Sarmiento, who argued that it "generates pressure and helps to remind governments in Latin America that they have to make an effort."

In contrast, Rep. Silvestre Reyes insisted that the certification process had "outlived its usefulness and should be eliminated or dramatically changed." He argued for concentrating on reducing the demand in our own neighborhoods by establishing more effective prevention and treatment programs. In terms of foreign policy, he advocated cooperation with Mexico to reform their police, legal framework, and judiciary.

Several highly publicized captures of well-known traffickers did take place before the March 1 deadline: Mexican authorities apprehended the

Gulf Cartel's Juan García Abrego on January 14, 1996; and they arrested General Gutiérrez Rebollo two weeks before the Clinton administration's 1997 decision. Mexican officialdom had feared that the Gutiérrez Rebollo brouhaha would propel decertification. It dodged the bullet because the United States did not want to provoke an unproductive battle with its neighbor. Moreover, the U.S. leader and ten of his cabinet secretaries were scheduled to visit that country in early May 1997.

The 2000 election of Vicente Fox Quesada drew rave reviews in Washington and throughout the world and initially strengthened bilateral ties. It appeared that, finally, someone had vanquished the mossbacks in the PRI. U.S. legislators were eager to reward the "Marlboro Man"—so called because of his 6-foot 5-inch height, huge "FOX" belt-buckle, and hand-tooled cowboy boots. The new chief executive seemed to demonstrate his bona fides; he quickly fired or transferred forty-five of forty-seven customs inspectors along the Mexican-American border. In the month following this move, Mexico stopped 150 trucks containing contraband, compared with just thirty-eight during the previous year.

According to some observers, Mexico was even poised to tackle the thorny issues of corruption and extradition of drug barons. They insisted that key foreign policy matters were neglected because certification complicated the bilateral agenda. Instead of working with Mexico in other mutually beneficial areas, debates over certification captured the attention of both nations.[10]

As a former envoy observed: "The annual narcotics certification drama dominated U.S.-Mexican relations for years, causing untold grief for successive ambassadors and always roiling the bilateral waters. By 1998 certification was an idea that had outlived whatever usefulness it might have ever had."[11] Although Mexico was never blacklisted, Colombia—paralyzed by the rise and consolidation of the Medellín and Cali cartels—was twice sanctioned (1996 and 1997). That nation's president, Ernesto Samper, retaliated by suspending eradication flights over coca and poppy growing zones. A New York Times editorial concluded: "Certification is a clumsy tool. ... The annual review process, now required by law, forces Washington into difficult choices between papering over problems or offending an otherwise friendly country. It should be eliminated."[12]

On the eve of George W. Bush's mid-February 2001 meeting with Vicente Fox in Mexico, the Senate passed a resolution urging the chief executive to, among other things, "review the current illicit drug certification process, and ... seek to be open to consideration of other evaluation mechanisms that would promote increased cooperation and effectiveness in combating the illicit drug trade." When President Fox addressed the U.S. Congress seven months later, he advocated suspending certification, emphasizing that "trust requires that one partner not be judged unilaterally by the other."[13]

Beginning in 2000, members of Congress including Senators Christopher Dodd, Kay Bailey Hutchinson, Barbara Boxer, and Grassley along with Representatives Jim Kolbe and Reyes, introduced bills to modify the certification strictures. In the end, Congress passed a one-year waiver in 2001 and a modification in 2002, virtually ending the annual tug-of-war. This measure required only that the president designate and withhold assistance from countries that had "failed demonstrably" to make substantial counternarcotics efforts. This language effectively took Mexico off the hook.[14]

Militarization of Counternarcotics Activities[15]

After Salinas ascended to the presidency in late 1988, Washington officials paid less attention to the military's role because they believed that the dynamic new chief executive would overhaul civilian police forces. He seemed to demonstrate his good faith in early 1989 by jailing the venal chief of the Oil Workers' Union, ousting Elba Esther Gordillo's predecessor as head of the corrupt SNTE, and imprisoning a prominent banker for stock-market manipulation.

Even before Salinas' inauguration, U.S. spies developed information that big traffickers were constructing heavily fortified compounds in the Mexican countryside. Working with the military, the CIA helped form what they envisioned as an elite team of about fifty young soldiers who would strike more effectively and operate more secretively than the police. Mexican law enforcement officials remained in dark about this plan, intelligence analysts told Tim Golden of the *New York Times*.

The team's first operation, targeting a cocaine smuggler's stronghold in Sinaloa, ended when a police agent working for a cartel captured one soldier involved in the operation. The next foray went from bad to worse. On the morning of April 11, 1988, helicopters swung out of the dawn sky near the northwest town of Caborca, a sanctuary of a reputed marijuana smuggler. "The idea was that you could take a well-trained military unit and go in there and boom—take everybody out," a former official stated. The soldiers did pull off the raid, but they did so at what turned out to be a workshop in a residential neighborhood and wound up killing four apprentice welders. As protests flooded the air, Mexican Attorney General Sergio García Ramírez was so mystified that he asked the U.S. Embassy whether its agents had carried out the sortie themselves.

Eventually, the Mexican military issued a terse statement taking responsibility for the attack, but not disclosing the CIA's involvement. After a third bungled incursion against another suspected drug base, the program was shut down for good. When U.S. officials next looked to the Mexican military, it was in 1994, the last year of the six-year presidential term when few decisions are made. U.S. diplomats and, later, General Gordon R. Sullivan, Army chief of staff, broached the idea of greater Mexican military support for the police. Local PGR executives quickly turned thumbs down on the suggestion.

Ernesto Zedillo, who took office on December 1, 1994, had called drug trafficking one of the most serious problems affecting national security. U.S. officials strongly endorsed that viewpoint, and briefed Zedillo's aides on such developments as the use of passenger jets to fly cocaine into Mexico from Colombia. "The military was the only trained, disciplined force that you could use to deal with this situation in the short term," one of the president's closest aides confided: "There was no one else."

The Mexican president first brought in Army commanders to revamp the country's drug-control strategy. He then authorized them to work with the United States in what turned out to be an abortive effort to deploy its aging F-5 fighter jets to chase drug aircraft. Finally, he began allowing military officers to replace federal police agents in several border cities plagued by smugglers—a move discussed earlier.

Washington strongly recommended that the armed forces become the lead agency in Mexico's fight against crime syndicates. "They didn't have anybody to play with on the Mexican end of the drug issue, so they went for the military," a former senior official who was involved in U.S. policy in Mexico said, referring to the Defense Department and the CIA. "They knew the risks, but they thought they could control the situation."[16]

In October 1995 William J. Perry made what the *New York Times* called "the first official visit to Mexico in memory by an U.S. secretary of defense." He sought to convince Defense Secretary Enrique Cervantes Aguirre and the Zedillo administration of both the importance of the military's role in anti-drug operations and the imperative to train forces to conduct the battle more efficiently. James R. Jones, the American ambassador during this period, denied that U.S. officials had encouraged the new role for Mexico's armed forces. "The temporary detailing of military officers to civilian law enforcement was the Mexicans' and Zedillo's decision—we had nothing to do with that," Jones affirmed. "Our efforts to improve the quality and exchange of intelligence information and our training programs for certain military units had nothing to do with their decision."[17]

Soon the first group of Mexican soldiers participated in special thirteen- to fourteen-week counter-drug programs at Fort Bragg, North Carolina. Once they completed training, they were sent as instructors to the Mexican Army's twelve regions and forty zones (there are now 46 zones). Pentagon officials said that the anti-drug curriculum of the trainees—the often-mentioned GAFES—ranged from air-assault operations and military policing to human rights. The Department of Defense also turned over Vietnam-era UH-1H helicopters to ferry troops into combat—with the understanding that the "Hueys" would be deployed only against cartels, not leftist rebels.

Meanwhile, the CIA, determined to remain relevant after the fall of the Berlin Wall had removed one of its reasons for existence, helped instruct, equip, and provide operational support for a special force of the Mexican Army's intelligence section called the Center for Anti-Narcotics Investigations. Composed of ninety carefully selected junior officers, this contingent—referred to by its Spanish initials as CIAN—began to take shape in the 1990s. The *New York Times* reported that: "Several U.S. officials compared the program to the CIA's work in Colombia, where the agency has been credited with critical help in the capture of major drug traffickers. A key difference, they noted, has been Mexico's extreme sensitivity to anything involving the CIA." CIAN supposedly pursued Amado Carrillo Fuentes before he died in mid-1997, and participated in skirmishes with the Arellano Félix Organization. "It could be a time bomb," a former intelligence official observed, "because they have a lot less control over that unit than they think they do."[18]

Washington began to prepare plans to "militarize" the fight against illegal substances. The policy found expression in the National Defense Authorization Act of 1989, which designated the Pentagon as the "single lead agency" for the detection and monitoring of illicit drug shipments into the United States. Soon thereafter, President George H.W. Bush announced the Andean Initiative, a $2.2 billion, five-year plan aimed at halting cocaine trade at its source. U.S. military personnel had been involved in training, equipping, and transporting foreign anti-narcotics personnel since the early 1980s; however, the Andean strategy dramatically enlarged their role and expanded the infusion of U.S. assistance to the police and military forces in the region. Bolivia and Peru, the region's other major coca-producers, also received sharp increases in assistance, but the majority of the drug-war funds went to Colombia.

Congress passed the Anti-Drug Abuse Act of 1988 to create the Office of National Drug Control Policy (ONDCP) within the Executive Branch. The ONDCP would establish policies, priorities, and objectives for the nation's drug-control program, with a view to reducing illicit drug use, manufacturing, trafficking, narcotics-related crime and violence, and drug-induced illnesses.

The Andean Initiative evolved into Plan Colombia, which zeroed in on Colombia, Peru, and Bolivia—with the concentration of Pentagon spending aimed at the Caribbean and the Gulf of Mexico transit zones. The agreement between Colombian President Andrés Pastrana and Clinton gave rise to the Plan in 2000 and changed the dynamics of the drug trade.

In the late 1990s, analysts talked about Colombia as a potential failed state. The U.S. Government General Accountability Office has shown that Plan Colombia has not curbed the production of coca and the transportation of cocaine. Still, the program has diminished violence in major cities and strengthened the Bogota regime's capacity to strike against insurgents, notably the National Liberation Army, the Colombian Revolutionary Armed Forces, and the United Self-Defense Forces. "Colombia, which until recently possessed an under-developed military, has come a long way in eight years and the presence of the central state around the country's territory is stronger than ever before."[19]

The increased surveillance of Caribbean passageways to the U.S. prompted Colombian criminals to divert cocaine and heroin shipments through the Central American isthmus and Pacific Ocean, with both routes spring boarding through Mexico. In the meantime, attacks on the Cali and Medellín operations forced their reorganization into smaller, boutique units to minimize penetration and continue operations. As mentioned earlier, the fragmentation of erstwhile Colombian Leviathans opened the way for ever-wealthier Mexican cartels to take possession of the cocaine destined for American consumers.

In late 1993 President Clinton pledged to move away from the failed supply-side strategy toward "a comprehensive national crusade against drug abuse" and associated violence and law-breaking at home.[20] He shifted the emphasis of military maneuvers away from interdicting cocaine as it passed through transit zones and into the U.S. Instead, the chief executive endeavored to dismantle the so-called "air bridge" that connected coca growers and coca paste manufacturers in Peru and Bolivia with Colombian refiners and distributors. As a result, exporters quickly abandoned air routes in favor of the region's labyrinth of waterways. The

Pentagon responded by supporting programs that targeted the sea routes in both source countries and their neighbors.

Just when bilateral relations seemed to be warming, the Mexican government endured another shock with the revelation of "Operation Casablanca." This was the code name for a three-year undercover investigation in which the U.S. Customs Service investigated major Mexican banks for handling illicit drug profits. Made public in May 1998, the sting led to money-laundering charges against twenty-two high- and middle-level officials from twelve of Mexico's nineteen largest banks. Authorities seized two tons of cocaine, four tons of marijuana, and nearly 11 billion pesos ($100 million) over a three-year period. Law enforcement personnel arrested several of the prominent bankers on a private plane flying from Mexico to a brothel near Mesquite, Arizona.[21] "By infiltrating the highest levels of the international drug trafficking financial infrastructure, Customs was able to crack the elaborate financial schemes the drug traffickers developed to launder the tremendous volumes of cash acquired as proceeds from their deadly trade," U.S. Treasury Secretary Robert Rubin affirmed. Clinton's Attorney General Janet Reno added that: "Operation Casablanca built a road map that tracked the structure of the international drug cartels from the kingpins to the couriers and the bankers in between."[22]

Mexicans fumed that Washington did not notify Los Pinos of the project, which Zedillo decried as a breach of Mexican "sovereignty." Even as the White House defended the raid against the money launderers, it tried to mollify the irate Mexicans. In a phone call to his counterpart, Clinton "expressed regret that better prior consultation had not been possible in this case." U.S. officials said they did not alert the Mexicans because they feared for the safety of the undercover agents. A number of Mexican functionaries were believed to be involved in drug trafficking and a leak might have torpedoed the venture.[23]

After two weeks of bombast directed at Uncle Sam, the PGR admitted it had actually been informed of the covert scheme in January 1996. The notification may have gotten lost in the bowels of the bureaucracy when Zedillo unceremoniously fired his attorney general in early 1997. Of this advisory, respected Colegio de México nationalist historian Lorenzo Meyer said: "It's a trick, a very clever way of claiming it was not a secret investigation when in fact it was secret—'We are going to give you a hint, and when it becomes public we can say but we told you.'"[24]

Mexico and other nations of the hemisphere have taken Washington to task for not cooperating enough in combating the narco-traffickers that dominated the drug flow from the Andes to 230 cities in the fifty United States. After all, Americans consume the lion's share of the illegal substances; provide arms to the criminal syndicates; and suffer far fewer deaths at the hands of the desperadoes than the Mexicans, which have had 167 federal policemen and many more soldiers killed during the two-and-a-half years since Felipe Calderón's inauguration.

In mid-June 2007 Attorney General Medina Mora, a key architect of Mexico's anti-crime strategy, deplored Washington's policy as "cynical with respect to consumption." A conservative product of the private sector and a former executive in his nation's intelligence service, CISEN, the attorney general said that the United States only saw the problem outside its borders and did little to reduce the domestic demand for illegal narcotics. He also excoriated as "absurd" the lax gun-control laws north of the border, where towns are home to some 1,200 gun vendors who sell everything from "fragmentation grenades to rocket launchers." The United Nations, he stressed, estimates that 70 percent of the revenue generated by drug transactions remains in the places where the substances are consumed.[25]

He failed to point out that Mexican cartels now dominate the U.S. illicit drug market, according to reports by the National Drug Intelligence Center (NDIC). It found that Mexican crime organizations use their well-established routes "to transport cocaine, marijuana, methamphetamine, and heroin … throughout the country," even though the Colombians still maintain control over South American cocaine and heroine smuggling and distribution in areas of the East Coast.[26] Mexican syndicates also produce methamphetamines and marijuana north of the Rio Grande. Their favorite sites are federal parks and forests in California. Now they are undertaking production in the Pacific Northwest and, to a lesser extent, the eastern U.S.

The Department of Justice-based NDIC also reported that Mexicans were boosting sales by knitting stronger ties with prison and street gangs, including the Tri-City Bombers, the Hermanos Pistoleros Latinos, the Texas Syndicate, and the Mara Salvatrucha.[27] According to the FBI, these cartels concentrate on wholesale distribution and leave retail sales to local bands. In addition, the Mexicans have been connected to arms trafficking, money smuggling, auto theft, and kidnapping.[28]

The Beltrán Leyvas, the Juárez Cartel, the Sinaloa Cartel, La Familia, and Los Zetas have swarmed across Arizona, which one observer has called "a giant narcotics storage center." Served by Interstate 10, Phoenix has become the nation's "kidnapping capital"—with 370 cases reported in

2008. "We're in the eye of the storm," the city's police chief Andy Anderson told ABC News in explaining the violent crimes and ruthless tactics employed by Mexican criminals. "If it doesn't stop here, if we're not able to fix it here and get it turned around, it will go across the nation," he added.[29]

The cartels have established a specific turf within the U.S., and each is dominant in a geographical area: Houston, Los Angeles (Sinaloa); Houston and other areas of Texas (Gulf); west Texas (Juárez); southern California and west Texas (Tijuana); Dallas (Gulf and Los Zetas); Chicago (Gulf, Sinaloa, and La Familia); Los Angeles (Gulf and Los Zetas); and Atlanta (Gulf, Los Zetas, and La Familia). One law enforcement agent confidentially confided that "Atlanta is like Los Angeles in the 1980s and Miami in the 1990s." From these and other venues, they distribute their product throughout the nation. Table 9.1 indicates the presence of the Mexican Cartels in various states.

George W. Bush's March 2007 Visit to Guatemala and Mexico

When President Bush visited Guatemala City on March 12, 2007, his host, Óscar Berger, expressed alarm over the mounting criminality washing across his country. According to a diplomat present at the conversations between the chief executives and their staffs, the Guatemalan leader said, in effect: "We are a poor country. We lack the resources with which to protect our citizens from the cartels. We need the U.S. military to come in and help us." This lengthy complaint captured Bush's attention. Although he had not arrived with an anti-drug strategy for the region, the visitor and his host agreed that the scope of the challenge argued for considering a multinational venture.

In formal remarks, Bush affirmed that this represents:

[A] serious problem because narco-trafficking destabilizes areas. It's in our interests in our country to promote prosperity and peace and stability. Narco-traffickers promote instability and tensions, which make it hard for the general populace to become prosperous. It also turns out narco-traffickers who oftentimes leave behind the poison as they head to other markets. In other words, the local population can become deeply affected by drugs ... in my judgment, the best way to deal with this problem, and to convince others throughout our country that it makes a lot of sense to commit assets is to think regionally. Because as the President [Berger] mentioned one of the interesting dynamics that's taking place here is that people and goods are moving quite freely across borders. Well, if people and goods are moving quite freely; drug traffickers will be moving quite freely. And there's kind of almost a borderless domain for these people.[30]

Bush agreed to begin work on a collaborative program, and Secretary of Defense Donald H. Rumsfeld made a follow-up visit to reiterate the

Table 9.1
U.S. Cities and States Where Mexican Cartels Reportedly Operate

Cartel(s)*	U.S. Cities and States Where They Reportedly Operate
The Federation (Sinaloa, Milenio, Jalisco, Sonora, and Colima cartels); also included are the Beltrán Leyva brothers who have split with Sinaloans Joaquín Guzmán Loera and Mayel Zambada García	Arizona: Douglas, Glendale, Naco, Nogales, Peoria, Phoenix, Sasabe, Sierra Vista, Tucson, and Yuma. Arkansas: Little Rock. California: Calexico, El Centro, Los Angeles, Oakland, Otay Mesa, Riverside, San Diego, San Francisco, and San Ysidro. Colorado: Colorado Springs and Denver. District of Columbia: Washington. Florida: Miami, Orlando, and Tampa. Georgia: Atlanta. Illinois: Chicago and Joliet. Indiana: Fort Wayne and Indianapolis. Iowa: Des Moines. Kentucky: Lexington. Louisiana: New Orleans and Shreveport. Maryland: Baltimore. Massachusetts: Boston. Michigan: Detroit. Mississippi: Hattiesburg and Jackson. Missouri: St. Louis. Nebraska: Omaha. New Jersey: Atlantic City and Newark. New Mexico: Columbus, Deming, and Las Cruces. New York: New York. North Carolina: Charlotte and Raleigh. Ohio: Akron, Cincinnati, Cleveland, Columbus, Dayton, and Toledo. Oklahoma: Oklahoma City and Tulsa. Oregon: Eugene, Klamath Falls, and Portland. Pennsylvania: Philadelphia and Pittsburgh. Rhode Island: Providence. Tennessee: Memphis and Nashville. Texas: Beaumont, Brownsville, Dallas, El Paso, Fabens, Fort Hancock, Fort Worth, Houston, Laredo, Midway, Rio Grande City, Roma, San Antonio, and Tyler. Virginia: Arlington and Galax.
Gulf and Los Zetas	Arizona: Nogales. Florida: Jacksonville, Lakeland, Miami, Orlando, Tampa, and West Palm Beach. Georgia: Atlanta. Illinois: Chicago and East St. Louis. Kentucky: Louisville. Louisiana: Lafayette and New Orleans. Maryland: Greenbelt. Massachusetts: Boston. Missouri: St. Louis. Nebraska: Omaha. New York: Buffalo and New York.

Table 9.1 (cont.)

	North Carolina: Greensboro, Raleigh, Wilmington, and Wilson. Ohio: Cincinnati. Oklahoma: Oklahoma City. Pennsylvania: Philadelphia. South Carolina: Greenville. South Dakota: Sioux Falls. Tennessee: Knoxville and Memphis. Texas: Brownsville, Corpus Christi, Dallas, Eagle Pass, Edinburg, El Paso, Fort Worth, Houston, Laredo, McAllen, Rio Grande City, Roma, and San Antonio.
Juárez	Arizona: Douglas, Phoenix, and Tucson. Colorado: Aurora, Colorado Springs, and Denver. Georgia: Atlanta. Illinois: Chicago. Indiana: Indianapolis. Kansas: Dodge, Kansas City, Liberal, and Wichita. Massachusetts: Boston. Missouri: Kansas City. Nevada: Las Vegas. New Jersey: Atlantic City and Newark. North Carolina: Charlotte and Raleigh. Ohio: Cincinnati, Hamilton, and Toledo. Oklahoma: Oklahoma City and Ponca City. Oregon: Portland. Pennsylvania: Philadelphia and Pittsburgh. Texas: Alpine, Big Springs, El Paso, Fort Stockton, Hidalgo, Houston, Lubbock, Midland, Mission, Odessa, Pecos, Presidio, Tyler, and Waco. Wyoming: Rock Springs.
Tijuana	Alaska: Anchorage. California: Calexico, Goshen, Los Angeles, Porterville, Sacramento, San Diego, Stockton, and Tulare. Massachusetts: Boston. Minnesota: Minneapolis and St. Paul. Nebraska: Omaha. Nevada: Las Vegas. New Jersey: Camden. New York: New York. Ohio: Cleveland. Pennsylvania: Philadelphia. South Dakota: Sioux Falls. Washington: Seattle.

* Most authorities are still not familiar with La Familia Michoacana

Source: Local, State, and Federal reports compiled by National Drug Intelligence Center, *State of Affairs Report: Cities in Which Mexican DTOs Operate Within the United States*, April 11, 2008 (DTOs refer to "Drug Trafficking Organizations").

president's commitment. The cabinet official announced that the U.S. would lift its ban on military aid to Guatemala because of local efforts to revamp the country's extremely powerful military, which suffered from an unsavory record of atrocities and kidnappings. Between 1960 and 1996, approximately 200,000 people were killed or went missing, the majority being Mayan peasants. "I've been impressed by the reforms that have been undertaken in the armed forces," Rumsfeld said at a joint news conference. "I know it is a difficult thing to do but it's been done with professionalism and transparency." The secretary stressed the relationship among drug trafficking, arms sales, and terrorism in the region.[31]

From Guatemala, the U.S. chief executive flew to Mérida to rendezvous with Felipe Calderón. Here he heard the same discouraging message in even sharper terms. While vowing to fight drug-running in his country, Calderón highlighted Washington's responsibility for widespread consumption because "while there is no reduction in demand in your territory, it will be very difficult to reduce the supply in ours."[32] The Calderón administration had publicly chastised the U.S. government for supplying inadequate assistance to Mexico. The U.S. State Department reported that in fiscal year 2006 Mexico had received almost $40 million for its anti-drug ventures compared with the $600 million allocated to Colombia.[33] The White House had provided an estimated $36.7 million in fiscal year 2007—with the figure for fiscal year 2008 falling to $27.8 million on the grounds that Mexico boasted the world's thirteenth largest economy.[34] After the Mérida Initiative took effect, funding skyrocketed.

Still, several months passed before the White House received a response from Mexico City about a joint venture. In a late May trip to Washington, Mexican Foreign Secretary Patricia Espinosa Castellano flashed the green light, and exploratory talks began under three rubrics: Mexico's priority programs (judicial reform, organization of a national police force, and combating corruption); U.S. priority programs (bulk money smuggling, arms trafficking); and joint priorities (helicopters, creating an information platform, and Gamma ray and X-ray machines for border surveillance). A State Department representative chaired each of the six inter-agency working groups that concentrated on such matters as judicial reform, aviation, informatics/information technology, and non-intrusive inspection equipment.

Meanwhile, the Central Americans, caught in a vortex of shifting electoral cycles within several countries, were hard-pressed to come up with specific proposals. "It was like herding cats," observed a U.S. foreign service officer. As recently as early 2009, Guatemala's Vice President

José Rafael Espada, complained that the venture had proceeded "without much consultation" with governments of Central America. Of course, leaders of these small nations quietly fret that Mexico might attempt to tutor and manipulate them. Just as Mexico regards the United States as the "colossus of the North," Central Americans worry about the ancient Aztec nation's influence in their economic, cultural, political, and military affairs.

The Mérida Initiative made a perilous journey through the legislative labyrinth, and the measure required several iterations as lawmakers went back and forth with both the Bush administration and Calderón government over the human rights issue. Sensitive to concerns on Capitol Hill and cognizant of the growing concerns within Mexico about potential abuses, State Department officials had stressed the importance of including a human rights provision in any accord.

U.S. legislators were reluctant to bestow security aid on a country with a history of corruption and a checkered record of human rights protection. This was one of the reasons that, from the beginning, diplomats stressed to Congress that there would be no money transferred to Mexico. The program would entail only equipment and training that the U.S. government would procure and deliver. Legislators initially demanded that civilian courts, not military tribunals, be invested with the authority to investigate alleged abuses by soldiers, and they demanded that assistance be denied to violating countries. "Ensuring that our tax dollars are spent effectively and in accordance with basic human rights is the least that Congress and the taxpayers have a right to insist on," said Patrick Leahy, a Vermont Democrat who chaired the Senate Appropriations Subcommittee on Foreign Operations.[35]

The original language on human rights cast a pall over the measure, and it languished on life support in early spring. Few inside Mexico, including many deputies and senators harbored any hope that the U.S. Congress would reverse course and strike offending conditions from the bill.

To give impetus to the Mérida Initiative, Mexican and U.S. officials began to underscore and broadcast Mexico's recent successes against traffickers. In late 2007, for example, Navy, police, and customs officers discovered twenty-three tons of cocaine cached in a container vessel at the West Coast port of Manzanillo. U.S. Ambassador Garza called the mega-seizure "further proof of President Calderón's commitment to cripple drug lords and bring them to justice."[36] Authorities also arrested Sandra Ávila Beltrán, 45, who purportedly managed public relations and helped ship cocaine from Colombia to Mexico for the Sinaloa Cartel.

The raven-haired "Queen of the Pacific" and niece of Félix Gallardo, described herself as a housewife who earned her income by renting homes and selling clothes.[37] Mexico's police and military jailed many more suspected narco-merchants.

To show its readiness to cooperate, the Bureau of Alcohol, Tobacco, Firearms, and Explosives (ATF), an agency of the U.S. Department of Justice, unveiled "Project Gunrunner." Under this program, the ATF pledged to deploy resources strategically on the Southwest Border to deny weapons to criminal organizations and to combat firearms-related violence in the area.[38]

The Bureau assigned 200 agents to the project and, in late February 2009, after Congress had approved the Mérida plan, arrested the owner of X-Caliber Guns, a Phoenix arms shop. He allegedly had sold more than 600 weapons, including 515 AK-47 rifles and one .50 caliber rifle, which were smuggled into Mexico. An Arizona court threw out criminal charges on grounds that prosecutors had not demonstrated that the third-party buyers, or "straw purchasers," had misrepresented their identity when acquiring the arms. "There is no proof whatsoever that any prohibited possessor ended up with the firearms," he ruled.[39]

Despite this acquittal, William D. Newell, ATF director for Arizona and New Mexico, said that Operation Gunrunner had increased arrests (450 percent), convictions (300 percent), and investigations (400 percent). He failed to mention the low baseline used by his agency. Newell did emphasize, however, that the cartels had been acquiring more .50 caliber handguns, known as "cop killers," because their ammunition penetrated armored vehicles and bulletproof vests.[40]

Misgivings on Capitol Hill

Earlier the mounting violence below the border cooled the ardor of U.S. legislators for the Mérida gambit. "Our first priority must be to secure our own border and equip our own personnel before we even discuss sending one nickel to the corrupt Mexican government," harrumphed John Culberson, a GOP representative from Houston.[41]

On May 23, 2008, the Senate approved $400 million for Mexico—of which $46 million was for fiscal year 2009 and approximately $350 million for fiscal year 2008. Legislators stipulated that they would withhold up to 15 percent of the funds until the U.S. State Department verified that Mexico was meeting certain human rights criteria. Even as Mexican diplomats in Washington roamed the halls of the Capitol to soften the offending verbiage, *La Jornada* newspaper termed the interventionist language "a grotesque and absurd pretension." At one point, Mexico City's archdioceses urged "rejection" of a plan that it derided as no more than "offensive charity."[42] A near-miracle saved the venture.

Every year the U.S.-Mexico Inter-parliamentary Commission, composed of lawmakers from both countries, holds a meeting that generally wastes the participants' time and Mexican and U.S. taxpayers' money. Yet, at the June 6-7, 2008 sessions in a posh Monterrey neighborhood, Mexican politicians managed to convince many of the eleven U.S. participants that imposing human rights restrictions would constitute a poison pill for any anti-narcotics plan.

The nation's three major parties advanced the same argument typified by remarks by PAN Senate leader Santiago Creel. He argued that predicating "the Mérida Initiative on [Mexico's] unilateral actions would constitute a setback in our bilateral relations—based on confidence and shared responsibility. Whatever conditionality, regardless of its type, would be unacceptable to the Mexican Senate."

Deputy Alejandro Chanona Burquete exhorted the U.S. Congress to "remove all the conditions because in this political game lack of communication is an issue ... [we must] recognize that the water has already sloshed over into both societies through organized crime and narco-trafficking. Either we charge our batteries or this will suffocate us, and the number of deaths that we have already witnessed will continue to escalate."[43] Arturo Sarukhán, the country's ambassador to Washington, had skillfully disseminated the same message throughout the executive and legislative branches of the U.S. government.

Senator Christopher Dodd, who led the U.S. delegation to Mexico, complained about the executive branch's failure to communicate with Congress over the Mérida plan. Truth be told, State Department professionals wanted to brief lawmakers before the president introduced the supplemental budget in October 2007, but the White House would not allow them to do so. As a result, legislators receive only scanty information beforehand. Immediately after submission of the budget bill, diplomats make clear they were at the disposal of congressmen and their staffs. It took a while to drum up interest, specifically from Senator Dodd's office.

In Mexico, however, the Connecticut senator gained an insight into the depth of nationalist sentiment among local policymakers. Upon returning to Washington, he convinced Appropriations Subcommittee Chairman Leahy and other colleagues that any strings attached to the program would amount to a deal breaker.[44] The upshot was that senators and representatives agreed to jettison from the bill most of the nettle-some stipulations protecting human rights. Once Congress passed the measure, the president signed it into law on June 30, 2008, as part of the Iraq supplemental funding bill. "Both administrations proclaimed themselves satisfied with the deal, and Congress hailed a new era in binational cooperation."[45]

Mexicans interpreted this volte-face on conditionality as a "change of attitude" by the United States with respect to combating drugs. In the words of Jorge Montaño Martínez, former Mexican ambassador to Washington and to the UN: "I consider this decision a success inasmuch as it's the first time the United States recognizes that it's not a Mexican, or Central and South American problem, but that it [the U.S.] needs to assume costs and responsibilities."[46]

Package Assembled

The final iteration of the package of $400 million largely reflected the initial version put forward by Bush on October 22, 2007. According to the president's proposal and authorization by the House of Representatives, the entire three-year arrangement could allocate up to $1.4 billion to Mexico and its neighbors for aid to design and carry out counter-narcotics, anti-terrorism, and border security measures. In fiscal year 2008 and succeeding years, the Bureau of International Narcotics and Law Enforcement Affairs coordinated the State Department's support for the Mérida Initiative, a program that provides assistance to Mexico and Central America in three broad areas: counternarcotics, counterterrorism and border security; public security and law enforcement; and institution building and rule of law.

The United States released $197 million as the first tranche of the resources on December 3, 2008. In a flight of hyperbole, Ambassador Garza lauded the disbursement as "the most significant effort ever undertaken" by the two countries to fight drugs. Tables 9.2 and 9.3 indicate how Mérida Initiative funding has soared. Despite the controversy over conditionality, Washington withheld 15 percent of these monies contingent on Mexico's satisfying four requirements: improving the transparency of the nation's police forces; ensuring civilian investigations and prosecutions of police and military personnel credibly accused of violating human rights; engaging in consultations with Mexican human rights groups; and prohibiting the admission in trials of testimony obtained through torture.[47]

Table 9.2
Provisions of the Mérida Initiative for Fiscal Years 2008 and 2009*

Ministry/Agency	FY 2008	FY 2009	Explanation
Army	105,500**	20,200	Transport helicopters, training, maintenance; scanners and inspection devices
Navy	100,000	100,000	Surveillance planes and maintenance
Attorney General's Office	85,387	26,379	Armored vehicles; refurbish surveillance aircraft; forensics equipment; software, etc.
Public Security Ministry	31,950	147,550	Transport helicopters, aircraft; inspection equipment; polygraphs, etc.
Immigration Service	31,287	60,470	Equipment for document verification and software for database
Ministry of Communication & Transportation	25,310	5,872	Equipment and upgrades for mail-service security
Customs Service	31,447	38,400	Inspection equipment—arms trafficking
Intelligence Service (CISEN)	7,933	8,864	Software, equipment, and training
Finance Ministry	5,000	0	Financial intelligence software
Network for Technology Transfer in Addictions	15,157	10,950	Prevention, treatment, and rehabilitation programs
Courts Management	15,000	0	
Prison System	3,000	1,500	
Support for NGOs	6,029	7,315	Culture of lawlessness, bar associations, human rights organizations and training
Program Support	37,000	22,500	
TOTAL	500,000	450,000	

* As presented in Table 9.3, Congress added additional funds in these years.
** Thousands of dollars
Note: Andrew Selee, who prepared Figure 9.1, presented the following clarifying information about what the assistance would cover: (1) non-intrusive inspection equipment such as ion scanners, gamma ray scanners, X-ray vans and canine units for Mexico and Central America; (2) technologies to improve and secure telecommunications systems that collect criminal information in Mexico; (3) technical advice and training to strengthen the institutions of justice, case management software to track investigations through the system, new offices of citizen complaints and professional responsibility, and witness protection programs to Mexico; (4) up to five Bell 412 EP helicopters, two Cessna 208 Caravans, and CASA-235 surveillance airplanes to Mexico; and (5) equipment, training and community action programs in Central American countries to implement anti-gang measures and expand the reach of these measures.

Source: Andrew Selee, "Overview of the Mérida Initiative: May 2008," Woodrow Wilson Center for Scholars.

Table 9.3
U.S. Counternarcotics Assistance to Mexico, 1999 to 2010*

Fiscal Year	(Millions of dollars)
1999	8.0
2000	4.1
2001	10.0
2002	12.0
2003	12.0
2004	37.0
2005	39.7
2006	39.6
2007	36.7
2008 (Supplemental Funds)	352.0
2009 (Bridge Funds)	48.0
2009 (Omnibus Appropriations Bill)	300.0
2009 Supplemental Request	66.0
2009 House Appropriations Committee reported bill	470.0
2010 Requested Funds	450.0

* Since FY2008, counternarcotics funding for Mexico has come from three aid accounts: International Narcotics Control and Law Enforcement Support Assistance (INCLE), Foreign Military Financing (FMF), and Economic Support Funds (ESF).

Source: Mark P. Sullivan and June S. Beittel, Congressional Research Service, *Mexico-U.S. Relations: Issues for Congress,* May 13, 2009.

Obama Administration Announces New Steps to Tackle Drug Cartel Violence

Although Barack Obama had never previously set foot in Mexico, after winning the White House his first session with a foreign head-of-state was with Felipe Calderón in Washington. The president-elect told his visitor:

It has been especially gratifying to me to participate in this meeting because I'm such an admirer of the work that President Calderón has done on behalf of this country. Not only has he shown leadership in the economy but he has shown extraordinary courage and leadership when it comes to the security issues, dealing with drug trafficking, dealing with the violence that has existed as a consequence of the drug trade. So my message today is that my administration is going to be ready on day one to work to build a stronger relationship with Mexico.[48]

Later, in trips to Mexico and in public statements, the president, Secretary of State Hillary Rodham Clinton, and Homeland Security Secretary Janet A. Napolitano reaffirmed the chief executive's determination to fight the cartels in tandem with their southern allies.

During his mid-April 2009 twenty-four-hour stopover in Mexico, Obama called for a "new era" in the U.S.-Mexico partnership. "Something that Calderón and I recognize is that you can't fight this war with just one hand," the American leader said at a news conference, thrusting his hand up in a punching move. "You can't just have Mexico making an effort and the United States not making an effort and the same is true on the other side." He went on to vouchsafe U.S. resources worth billions of dollars over several years as well as stressing his intention to mobilize more American agents on both sides of the border.[49]

A remarkable deployment of Mexican troops, FBI agents, squads of Secret Service agents, and local police assured security for the distinguished guest. The upscale Polanco district where he stayed brought to mind Baghdad's "green zone." The perimeter around his luxury hotel was cordoned off to traffic and pedestrians underwent meticulous searches. "At times the youthful and charismatic president, a 'man of the people' like J.F.K., who engenders a superstar appeal, was restricted to 'bunker-like mobility.'" The chief executive arrived in his official limousine, known affectionately as "the beast," a shiny, impressive version of a military personnel carrier.[50]

In a late March visit, Secretary Clinton acknowledged her nation's responsibility in the narcotics trade. "Our insatiable demand for illegal drugs fuels the drug trade," she said using especially blunt language. "Our ability to prevent weapons from being illegally smuggled across the border to arm these criminals causes the deaths of police officers, soldiers and civilians," she added. The secretary of state promised to seek an additional $80 million from Congress to provide Mexican authorities with three Blackhawk helicopters to held track drug runners. She also announced a new "White House Initiative" to deploy 450 more law enforcement officers at the border and crackdown on the smuggling of guns and drug money into Mexico.[51]

On Tuesday, March 24, 2009, Secretary Napolitano, unveiled a Southwest Border Security Initiative (SBSI) before a Senate subcommittee. She characterized the measure as a broad, interagency effort that will refocus her department's resources on the growing violence along the U.S.-Mexico border. The SBSI endeavors to curtail the violence by focusing on two elements: a redeployment of personnel to the border and increasing resources for screening border traffic. In total, she averred, the Homeland Security Department (DHS) will dispatch more than 360 additional officers and agents to the border and Mexico. She estimated the total cost for the added resources at no more than $184 million, which the department said it could make available by shifting funds within its current budget.

Napolitano also highlighted that:

- The Homeland Security Department will double assignments to the Border Enforcement Security Task Forces (BEST), from ninety-five to 190 personnel, at a cost of $5.7 million. BEST teams, which serve under Immigration and Customs Enforcement (ICE), "have already made more than 2,000 criminal arrests and seized nearly 8,000 pounds of cocaine."
- The department will triple the number of intelligence analysts it has on the southern border, at a cost of $3.3 million.
- ICE plans to increase its attaché personnel that work with the Mexican attorney general by 50 percent, from twenty-four to thirty-six agents, at a cost of $650,000. Since fiscal year 2008, the ICE attaché in Mexico City has reported the seizure of more than $25 million through a partnership with Customs and Border Protection.
- ICE intends to double the personnel in the violent crime-alien departments along the border, adding fifty agents and officers, at a cost of $2.3 million.
- ICE will quadruple the number of border liaison officers, from ten to forty.
- Homeland Security also will send resources to high-volume border crossings to assist in traffic screening with X-ray scanners, license plate readers, and drug- and cash-sniffing dogs. The technology should reduce the volume of drugs, weapons, and currency that crosses the U.S.-Mexican border.[52]

Napolitano stated that monies for the initiative would come from "realigning from less urgent activities, fund balances, and, in some cases, reprogramming."[53]

While many welcomed Obama's outreach to Mexico, some congressmen questioned whether this shift of Department of Homeland Security assets would undermine the ability to enforce the nation's immigration laws. Rep. Lamar Smith (R-Tex.) summed up this widespread frustration, saying: "The administration appears to be using border violence as an excuse to reduce interior enforcement of our immigration laws and enact gun restrictions. ... [W]e must ensure that [this initiative does] not undercut our national security and immigration enforcement responsibilities." Napolitano's proposal raised concerns that these "strategic redeployments" could reduce effectiveness in combating illegal immigration.[54]

In addition, the White House has not indicated how the SBSI materially differs from the Bush-era Mérida Initiative. Is it just a "make-over" of the previous plan for equipping, training, and funding the Mexican government to wage war against drug cartels? The answer may be that DHS and the Pentagon have developed a contingency program to deploy National Guard detachments to the U.S.-Mexican border under a $350 million proposal—separate from Mérida funds—"for counter-narcotics and other activities...." The request, which does not mention troop movements, was tucked away in the supplemental budget sent to Congress in April 2009.

In response to this solicitation, Nita Lowery, a New York Democrat and a senior member of the House Appropriations Committee, said: "Frankly, I'm baffled that an additional $350 million has been requested under the defense appropriation." Also skeptical was Joy Olson, executive director of the pro-human rights Washington Office on Latin America, who observed that the request lacked the accountability provisions embedded in the Mérida Initiative. "They may say that this is for the National Guard, but the way it's written it is really a blank check for the Defense Department to do whatever it wants on counterdrug issues at the border—and it doesn't say which side of the border," Olson said, adding: "When it came to Mérida, Congress scrutinized every dollar. Now the administration is asking Congress to give DOD [Department of Defense] almost as much money for counterdrug activities without any explanation."[55]

No doubt this measure pleased Texas Governor Rick Perry and Arizona Governor Jan Brewer, who were piqued at the Washington's unwillingness to activate the National Guard for the purposes of border security. At the same time, the Pentagon and the DHS found themselves involved in an inter-agency "food fight" over who should direct the use of troop to combat the Mexican cartels. "It should not be that we always rely on the Department of Defense to fulfill some need," stated General Victor E. Renuart Jr., head of the U.S. Northern Command, which is charged with defending the continental United States. Her senior counselor said that Napolitano "feels we have an obligation to do whatever we can do to disrupt those forces that are destroying lives in over 200 American cities. ... It comes down to whether folks want to be as aggressive as we can be against the cartels and take advantage of this historic opportunity" of collaboration between the two countries.[56]

President Obama has signaled that he is open to the movement of 1,500 additional National Guardsmen, but is "not interested in militarizing the border." Congress spent the $250,000 ultimately requested for the proposal on other Department of Justice and DHS border security programs, but indicated that it would revisit the question once the White House reached a firm decision.[57]

The 90 Percent Gun Myth

Staunch defenders of the Second Amendment have raised another concern about U.S. security policy toward Mexico; namely, the methods contemplated by the administration to deter the southward flow of firearms.

That nine out of ten weapons used by Mexican drug cartels come from the United States has become an article of faith—enunciated, affirmed, and reiterated on both sides of the Rio Grande. Obama, Clinton, and Napolitano are among those who have played fast and loose with this figure.

President Calderón has repeatedly excoriated the tsunami of American armaments battering his country. "This [drug] war is being waged with guns purchased not here but in the United States ... more than 90 percent of the guns recovered in Mexico come from the United States, many from gun shops that lay in our shared border." Sarukhán, Mexico's envoy to the United States, asserted that: "Ninety percent of all weapons we are seizing in Mexico ... are coming from across the United States."[58]

Obama agreed during his mid-April visit to Mexico: "This war is being waged with guns purchased not here, but in the United States. More than 90 percent of the guns recovered in Mexico come from the United States, many from gun shops that line our shared border," he affirmed at a joint press conference with his Mexican host.[59]

But Calderón, Sarukhán, Obama, and others have omitted important qualifiers when regurgitating the wildly exaggerated percentage, which originated from the U.S. Bureau of Alcohol, Tobacco, Firearms and Explosives. The federal agency does not have statistics for *all* weapons in Mexico, where gun sales are largely controlled. The 90 percent number derives only from guns that the Mexican government sent to the agency for tracing and that the ATF could successfully track down.[60]

ATF Special Agent Newell reported that in the 2007-2008 time span Mexico submitted 11,000 weapons to his agency to identify. It succeeded in discovering the provenance of 6,000 of these firearms—5,114 of which came from the United States.

Why did the 90 percent figure—sometimes analogized to a "bridge of iron" between the two countries—gain such currency?

Needless to say, misinformation was one factor.

More important was political expediency. Public-opinion polls indicated that Calderón's PAN faced a major challenge from the PRI and its allies in the July 5, 2009 congressional and gubernatorial contests. Although his prudent handing of the spring influenza outbreak and his hard line on narco-traffickers appeared to have enhanced his party's chances, the president's otherwise modest achievements led the PAN to blast the PRI's coziness with drug cartels. At the same time, Los Pinos has taken Uncle Sam to task for the economic recession, the demand for drugs, and the southbound cascade of sophisticated weapons. There are nuggets of truth in these rebukes, but the 90 percent figure for guns is a blue-sky number. On May 6, 2009, Felipe Calderón even floated the possibility that the 2009 spring bout with influenza may have originated in the United States inasmuch as the first case was in California.[61]

For his part, President Obama has shown a willingness to don a hair shirt and intone "mea culpas" for America's perceived and real offenses to its neighbor, which President James K. Polk divested of half its territory in the Mexican-American War.

By ingratiating himself with Mexico, Obama may strengthen his standing with Hispanic-American voters who backed him three-to-one against Republican John McCain in the 2008 race for the White House. It will require a breathtaking effort to deliver a program of legalization for unlawful aliens, which the National Council of La Raza, the Mexican-American Legal Defense and Education Fund, the League of United Latin American Citizens, and other lobbying groups have demanded. The president, who appointed an American of Puerto Rican ancestry to the U.S. Supreme Court, has raised the issue of immigration reform. Nevertheless, the sharp recession means any similar bill will encounter an uphill struggle on Capitol Hill.

In many ways, the debate over the percentage of arms is academic. The crime organizations command the resources to purchase their firepower on the international arms market where the Russians, French, British, Germans, and Chinese are important purveyors.

Between 2000 and 2007, the leading arms merchants were the U.S. ($134.8 billion), Russia ($67.5 billion), France ($32 billion), the United Kingdom ($26.4 billion), Germany ($13.9 billion), China ($12.5 billion), and Italy ($7 billion).[62] The China North Industries Corporation, known as NORICO, has become the leader in producing cheap knockoffs of automatic weapons used by the underworld. Pundits say that Central America is sinking because of the weaponry left from the civil wars of the 1970s and 1980s, and what passes for Mexico's border with Guatemala teems with unguarded entry points.

As a matter of fact, one can buy AK-47s from the Korean mafia at Tepito and other sprawling markets in downtown Mexico City. If a patron cannot afford to purchase a weapon, the Asians will rent him one at a reduced price for, say, a single bank heist. Regrettably, Mexico's police and military personnel are renowned for reselling arsenals of arms that they have captured.[63]

Whatever the figure, converting the iron bridge into an "iron trickle" by curbing American arms shipments to the Midas-rich Mexican cartels would constitute a thorn in their sides—not a 50 mm bullet in their blackened hearts.

President Calderón's Anti-Crime Initiatives

On the heels of Obama's visit, Felipe Calderón crafted a package of national security reforms for Congress. The most far-reaching proposal contemplated the "declaration of the existence of domestic security threat," which would authorize the armed forces to carry out police functions. If approved by lawmakers, the president would activate the legislation if there were an attempted uprising against the state, aggression directed at elements of the National Security Council, or acts that endangered the order, peace, and public security of a municipality, state, or region. Before acting, the chief executive would consult with the National Security Council and Congress' Bicameral National Security Committee.[64]

President Calderón also proposed a new Code of Firearms. This initiative would (1) outlaw bullets such as the so-called "*mata-policías*" that can penetrate protective vests, (2) increase from twenty-four to thirty years the penalty for possessing more than fifty prohibited munitions, (3) imprison cartel members and other convicted defendants who, while not possessing arms, benefited from their use, (4) impose stricter punishment on police and other public employees who violate gun laws, and (5) apply a four- to ten- year prison sentence on those who leak information about federal public security agencies.[65]

Calderón insists that civilian police with take charge of the drug war by the end of his *sexenio*, December 1, 2012. Only a modern Dr. Pangloss would take this affirmation seriously. A medley of programs—the Mérida Initiative, the Southwest Border Security Initiative, the possible dispatch of National Guardsmen to the border, and Calderón's anti-crime legislation—indicate that Mexican and U.S. armed forces are destined to play an ever greater role in confronting the criminal organization that pose security threats to the neighboring nations.

Notes

1. "Mexico and United States; An Undiplomatic Murder," *The Economist*, March 30, 1985, p. 51.
2. Shannon, *Los Desperados*, pp. 115-116.
3. U.S. Drug Enforcement Administration, "Kiki and History of Red Ribbon Week" *www.usdoj.gov/dea/ongoing/red_ribbon/redribbon_history.html.*
4. Jay Matthews, "Murder of Drug Agent Lights Hometown Anger; Friends Warn Travelers of Mexico Danger, *Washington Post*, March 14, 1985.
5. Quoted in Mary Thornton and Joanne Omang, "Mexican Chief's Election Fraudulent, Helms Says," *Washington Post,* June 18, 1986.
6. Anita Snow, "Sentence Overturned for Convicted Killer of U.S. Drug Agent," *Associated Press*, April 25, 1997.
7. Survey conducted between July 18-22, 1986, The Roper Center for Public Opinion Research *www.ropercenter.uconn.edu.proxy.*
8. Quoted in Michael S. Serrill and Tim Padget, "Corrupt but Certified," *Time Magazine,* March 10, 1997.
9. Ken Guggenheim, "Senator Offers U.S.-Mexico Drug Plan," *Star Tribune*, February 15, 2001.
10. K. Larry Storrs, "Drug Certification/Designation Procedures for Illicit Narcotics Producing and Transit Countries," Congressional Research Service Report for Congress.
11. Jeffrey Davidow, *The U.S. and Mexico: The Bear and the Porcupine* (Princeton: Marcus Wiener, 1994): 48.
12. "Mexico's Drug Problem," *New York Times*, March 2, 1998.
13. Dana Wilkie and Joe Cantlupe, "Trust Us, Fox Urges," *San Diego Union-Tribune*, September 7, 2001.
14. This section benefits greatly from K. Larry Storrs, *CRS Report for Congress, Drug Certification/Designation Procedures for Illicit Narcotics Producing and Transit Countries*, September 22, 2003. *www.fas.org/irp/crs/RL32038.pdf.*
15. This section relies heavily on Tim Golden, "Dangerous Allies: U.S. Helps Mexico's Army Take Big Anti-Drug Role," *New York Times*, December 29, 1997.
16. Quoted in *Ibid.*
17. Quoted in *Ibid.*
18. *Ibid.*
19. González, "To Die in Mexico: Rumblings of a Drug War."
20. Quoted in Bruce Michael Bagley, "After San Antonio," Bruce M. Bagley and William O. Walker III (eds), *Drug Trafficking in the Americas* (Coral Gables: University of Miami North-South Center Press, 1996): 69.
21. James C. McKinley Jr. "Mexico Arrests Wanted Figure in Drug Cartel," *New York Times*, February 1, 2005.
22. These quotations are from Don Van Natta, Jr., "U.S. Indicts 26 Mexican Bankers in Laundering of Drug Funds," *New York Times*, May 19, 1998.
23. "Clinton Voices 'Regret' to Mexico," *United Press International*, May 26, 1998.
24. Quoted in James F. Smith, "Mexico, Still Upset, Now Says it Knew of 'Sting' Plan," *Los Angeles Times*, June 5, 1998.

25.   Quoted in Alfredo Méndez, "'Cínica,' la política antidrogas de EU; su ley 'absurda': Medina Mora" *La Jornada*, June 15, 2007.

26.   Colleen W. Cook, Congressional Research Service, *CRS Report for Congress: Mexico's Drug Cartels*, October 16, 2007. *www.fas.org/sgp/crs/row/RL34215.pdf.*

27.   Rolando Herrera, "Pelea narco territorio en México y ... en EU," *Reforma*, October 5, 2008.

28.   Cook, Congressional Research Service, *CRS Report for Congress: Mexico's Drug Cartels.*

29.   J. Jesús Esquivel, "El narco mexicano, imparable, *Proceso*, June 10, 2008; Brian Ross *et al.*, "Kidnapping Capital of the U.S.A.," *ABC News*, February 11, 2009; and Equivel, "Arizona, narcobodega gigante," *Proceso*, June 28, 2009.

30.   Quoted in White House, "Presidents Bush and President Berger of Guatemala Participate in Joint Press Availability," Guatemala City, March 12, 2007. *http://www.whitehouse.gov/news/releases/2007/03/20070312-4.html.*

31.   Ginger Thompson, "U.S. to Lift Ban on Military Aid to Guatemala," *New York Times*, March 25, 2005; and Martín Rodríguez P., "Drogas y terrorismo, prioridad tras reunión," *Prensa Libre.com*, March 27, 2006. *www.prensalibre.com.*

32.   Peter Baker, "Calderón Admonishes Bush on Thorny Issues," *Washington Post*, March 14, 2007, p. A-9.

33.   Hanson, *"Backgrounder: Mexico's Drug War."*

34.   Congressional Research Service, "Mexico's Drug Cartels," October 16, 2007, p. 14. *www.fas.org/sgp/crs/row/rl34215.*

35.   Quoted in Ken Ellingwood, "U.S. Merida Aid Initiative Angers Some in Mexico," *Los Angeles Times,* June 5, 2008.

36.   Quoted in "Mexico Doubles Size of Huge Cocaine Haul," *Reuters*, November 1, 2007. *www.reuters.com.*

37.   "Mexico Arrests Highest-Profile Female Suspected Drug Trafficker," *Associated Press*, September 29, 2007.

38.   U.S. Embassy (Mexico), "Our Continued Efforts Will Deny Firearms to Criminal Organizations and Reduce Gun Violence," statement by Ambassador Antonio O. Garza, January 16, 2008. *www.usembassy-mexico.gov.*

39.   James C. McKinley Jr., "U.S. Is a Vast Arms Bazaar for Mexican Cartels," *New York Times*, February 26, 2009; and Tim Gaynor, "Arizona Judge Dismisses Charges in Gunrunning Case," *Reuters*, March 18, 2009.

40.   "Compra narco más armas antiblindaje.—EU," *Reforma*, February 23, 2009.

41.   Quoted in Richard S. Dunham, Stewart M. Powell, and Dudley Althaus, "GOP Texans Balk at Aid to Mexico," *Houston Chronicle*, May 16, 2008.

42.   Marc Lacey, "Congress Trims Bush's Mexico Drug Plan," *New York Times*, May 23, 2008; and Noemí Gutiérrez and Jorge Alejandro Medellín, "Iniciativa Mérida es limosna: Iglesia," *El Universal*, March 12, 2009.

43.   Both quotations appeared in Roberto Garduño, "Sepultan el Plan Mérida en la interparliamentaria México-U.S.," *La Jornada*, June 8, 2008.

44.   The Dodd-Leahy connection was crucial inasmuch as Rep. Sylvester Reyes and other leader of the Congressional Hispanic Caucus, which endorsed the Mérida scheme, were not key members on either the House or Senate Appropriations Committees.

45.   Laura Carlsen, "A Primer on Plan Mexico," Americas Policy Program Special Report, May 5, 2008. *http://americas.irc-online.org/am/5204.*

46.   Quoted in Jeremy Schwartz, "Mérida Initiative: Behind the Scenes," *Cox Newspapers*, July 1, 2008.

47.   Witness for Peace, "Mérida Initiative 'Plan Mexico' Fact Sheet." *www.witnessforpeace.org/downloads/Mex_Merida%20Initiative%20factsheet%20WFP2.pdf.*

48. Foon Rhee, "Obama Lunches with Mexico's Leader," *Political Intelligence*, January 12, 2009. *www.boston.com/news/politics/political intelligence*.
49. Ioan Grillo, "A War They Can Win?" *GlobalPost*, April 17, 2009. www.globalpost.com.
50. This description benefits greatly from Michael Werbowski, "Obama's House Call," *Worldpres.org*, April 20, 2009.
51. Mark Landler, "Clinton Says U.S. Feeds Mexican Drug Trade," *New York Times*, March 25, 2009.
52. Department of Homeland Security, *Napolitano Press Release*, March 24, 2009.
53. "Napolitano's Senate Testimony," *The Hill*, March 25, 2009.
54. Matthew M. Johnson, "White House Plan for Mexico Border Stirs Questions from Lawmakers," *CQ Quarterly*, March 24, *2009 www.cqpolitics.com/wmspage.cfm?docID=news-000003082814&cpage=2*.
55. These quotations appear in Mary Beth Sheridan and Spencer S. Hsu, "Plan Would Put Troops on US-Mexican Border; Pentagon Initiative Expands Military Role in Drug War," *Boston Globe*, April 25, 2009.
56. Spencer Hsu, "Agencies Clash on Military's Border Role," *The Washington Post*, June 28, 2009.
57. *Ibid.*
58. "More than 90 Percent of the Guns Recovered in Mexico Come from U.S.," *St. Petersburg Times* (Truth-O-Meter), April 16, 2009.
59. "More than 90 Percent of the Guns Recovered in Mexico Come from U.S."
60. *Ibid.*
61. Mayolo López, "No es tiempo de cantar Victoria.—FCH," *Reforma.com*, May 7, 2009.
62. Richard F. Grimmett, "Conventional Arms Transfers to Developing Nations, 2000-2007," *CRS Report for* Congress, October 23, 2008.
63. Mario Torres, "En Tepito, venta y renta de armas de fuego," Televisa, February 4, 2005 *www.esmas.com/noticerostelevisa/investigaciones/423638.html*.
64. Claudia Guerrero, "Blinda iniciativa de FCH a Ejército," *Reforma*, April 23, 2009.
65. Claudia Guerrero, "Pide FCH legislar contra el crimen," *Reforma*, April 23, 2009.

10

Prospect for Mexico's Becoming
a Failed State

Can Felipe Calderón take back his country from the drug cartels and reduce the flow of narcotics into the United States? There are several strategies, in conjunction with the United States, which might be pursued in the battle with criminal syndicates.

1. Continue the War on Drugs

During the first half of 2009, President Calderón's government achieved a record number of arrests, arms and money seizures as well as dismantling narco laboratories, raiding their safe houses, and disrupting their operations centers. Still, the continued reliance on large troop movements will tax the capability of the armed forces, while increasing the odds of corruption within an institution that has long enjoyed public esteem. This strategy will also precipitate more bloodshed. While a significant federal presence can temporarily tamp down violence in one area, the police and Army soon find that they must put out fires elsewhere. The narco-traffickers simply wait for their departure before returning to business-as-usual in what one DEA agent characterized as the "whack-a-mole" effect.[1]

Rather than develop an approach that targets the cartels with pin-point surgery, the president hoped to eradicate this cancerous menace using massive and indiscriminate doses of chemotherapy in the form of large troop and police strikes. While he has undoubtedly eradicated parts of a malignant growth, he has inadvertently triggered the displacement and mitosis of lethal narco-cells throughout the Mexican state. Outbreaks of bloodshed inevitably have erupted when surviving lieutenants competed with each other to succeed any fallen capo, and just as often a rival cartel moved in to fill a power vacuum in the aftermath of "successful" government initiatives.

As noted in Chapter 7, the heavy reliance on interdiction has taxed the military's small number of combat troops, resulted in claims of human rights violations, generated an ever-higher level of fatalities, and accentuated the armed forces' hostility toward corrupt civilians.

The president's readiness to arrest public figures—those subterranean enablers of narco-traffickers—in addition to direct attacks on the criminals themselves will alter the dynamics of the drug war. There is no doubt that a forceful military intervention is still necessary, but a compelling argument can be made for other supporting strategies: (1) continuing the focus on politicians and businessmen in league with gangsters; (2) improving the gathering and analysis of intelligence, as well as infiltrating cartels; (3) forcing an integration and coordination of intelligence gathering organizations—especially where it would narrow the distrust between military and civilian agencies; (4) assigning and arranging to train skilled intelligence personnel to work cooperatively with international agencies that are monitoring the flow of drugs in the global markets; (5) developing and strengthening broad-based support for the initiatives which have begun in the area of judicial reform; (6) devising more secure programs to encourage and protect informants and witnesses as one means to foster higher levels of trust and cooperation from citizens; (7) identifying specific hotspots of drug movement, especially in those specific ports, airports, and train terminals that are currently open sieves; (8) fashioning an electronic monitoring surveillance system, and an air radar network that can cover the country for more than three hours a day as was the case in mid-2009; (9) introducing more systematic forensic accounting systems to reduce the flow of laundered funds; and (10) taking full advantage of the new law that authorizes the seizure of the assets of criminals and their accomplices.

After reviewing the policies of 107 countries, security analyst Edgardo Buscaglia believes that asset seizure is fundamental to fighting the cartels. "The only thing that El Chapo Guzmán [and the other syndicates] … fear is the takeover of their lands, their businesses, their commercial centers, and their stock in various legal enterprises." He insists that the "feudalization" [by criminal organizations] of municipalities in Mexico increased from 63 percent to 72 percent in recent years. He argues that Calderón cannot build an alliance for such a crackdown if he concentrates on states governed by opposition parties while minimizing strikes against PAN-dominated states.[2]

Needless to say, Buscaglia indulges in the hope that there is a critical mass of politicians from across the spectrum who genuinely want reform.

With respect to money laundering, Mexico has long had a tradition of dealing in an underground economy. A historical reliance on smuggled goods—*fayuquero*—gained a stronger foothold during the financial crises of the 1980s and 1990s. In all large cities, it is just as common to purchase goods from street vendors as it is to deal with long-established merchants, who—by the way—are required to pay taxes, acquire business licenses, and submit to inspections. The credit crunch fomented a situation where borrowing rates reached usurious levels, and it made more sense to deal in pesos (or dollars). Now Mexican consumers are more likely to purchase or legally rent most goods and services on a cash basis and not just for small items. Airplanes, helicopters, flight-school instruction, armored vehicles, hotel rooms, buildings, and homes can all be bought without presenting a passport, voting credential or any credible identification. Criminals benefit and take advantage of this "cash-and-carry" culture and tradition.

There must be impediments to diminish this simple way of laundering funds, and U.S. and Mexican governments should require banks and money handlers like Western Union to record and report unusual transactions. To its credit, the U.S. Treasury Department has stepped up investigations of questionable firms. In May 2009 the agency blacklisted and froze the assets of thirteen companies believed to traffic drugs and launder money. Affected by the action was Pedro Antonio "The Architect" Bermúdez Suaza, who had been accused of acting as a key intermediary between Colombian and Mexican crime syndicates.

Mexico's railway transport system, linking Lázaro Cárdenas, Veracruz, Tampico, and other seaports to connections on the U.S. border, also requires greater scrutiny. In 2009 AFI agents removed 800 kilograms from a boxcar bound for Mexicali. Kansas City Southern de México is a subsidiary of Kansas City Southern (KCS), a U.S. conglomerate, which has 2,645 track miles in Mexico. In view of KCS' presence in the North and Central regions of Mexico, Washington must explore security procedures on this and other railroads hauling cargo throughout North America.[3] As noted earlier, the nation's airports—in Mexico City, Monterrey, and a dozen or more other cities—remain cesspools of criminality, and customs officials are notorious for welcoming *mordidas*.

Unless broad support can be cultivated within the full spectrum of political, religious, business, and media sectors, Calderón will have no hope of accomplishing the structural changes to guarantee the rule of law and achieve more than a marginal advance against organized crime—all the more reason he should move against venal politicians.

Corruption so engulfs Mexico that the creation of an honest, professional national police—albeit a sound idea—shimmers like a mirage in the Sonoran desert. The government declared victory when it allowed state and local police to join federal law enforcement agencies in investigating narco-crimes. The rub comes in the vulnerability of such police to succumbing to graft and intimidation. In many cities, local law enforcement officials cover all bases: some are connected to one cartel; their colleagues represent another. In this ambience, it is impossible to know who can be trusted with strategic information.

With enormous resources at their disposal, the cartels and their agents will have little difficulty protecting themselves from the police thanks to the recruitment of Army deserters and veterans. To keep elite GAFES from joining the syndicates, the Mexican military raised the commandoes' salary to $1,100 per month in 2007. In spite of that, cartels promptly doubled the amount as standard pay for their own "troops."[4] "The [Mexican] army can no more control this situation than the Americans and the British can control the situation in Iraq," insisted Mexico's former anti-drug prosecutor Samuel González Ruiz. He explains that "the army can make its presence felt and perhaps limit some of the most extreme expressions of the violence, but the structural causes remain."[5]

Recent reports reveal that cartels are increasingly relying on so-called "gatekeepers," alluded to earlier in the discussion of Zetas in chapter 8, to accomplish the movement of more than 80 percent of the drugs from Mexico into the United States.[6]

It is extremely difficult—probably impossible—to eradicate the cartels. They or their offshoots will fight to hold on to an enterprise that yields Croesus-like fortunes from illegal substances craved by millions of consumers. In addition, the U.S. intelligence community estimates that some 450,000 people work in one or more facets of Mexico's drug sector. Narco-dollars contaminate everyone they touch, including U.S. federal and local law enforcement officers. On March 23, 2009, the PGR offered robust bounties for information leading to the arrest of major capos listed in Table 10.1. One criminal organization may take advantage of the project to affect the capture of a competing lord. There is also the risk that law enforcement agents will turn over incriminating material to friends so that they can cash in and protect themselves from prosecution.

In any auction for information, the cartels could easily outbid the government. After El Chapo Guzmán escaped from prison in January 2001, the DEA promised—to no avail—$5 million to anyone who could assist with his capture.[7] Although supposedly "untouchable" Guzmán

Loera remains at large, the government has shackled at least four of the suspects with prices on their heads, which may indicate that the reward program is succeeding.

On another positive note, disgruntled citizens have become more disposed to report suspicious behavior to the Defense Ministry. The military received 5,734 tips in 2008 and 4,058 calls during the first four months of 2009. In contrast, the SSP registered only 884 similar reports. This demonstrates the confidence garnered by the military 'because the Army's counter-narcotics drives have been much more intense," indicated security expert Javier Oliva Posada.[8]

If lady luck smiles on Calderón and he managed to curb drug activities in Mexico, an international cucaracha effect—or displacement—will probably take place with Asian, Middle Eastern, and Russian suppliers replacing Mexican distributors in the American marketplace. In such an event, Mexican mobsters would likely concentrate on the local market and undertake more kidnappings, murders-for-hire, extortion, human smuggling, contraband commerce, loan-sharking, bank robberies, and the sale of protection. In other words, follow the example of the AFO, Los Zetas, and La Familia. Nevertheless, it would constitute a stunning advance if the Mexican government, in concert with the U.S. and other allies, could narrow the scope of the internal drug industry and limit violence against law abiding residents.

Even though certification was no longer salient, the Calderón regime snared several important actors just a few days before Secretary of State Hilary Rodham Clinton visited Mexico on March 25-26, 2009. Among those apprehended were Octavio Almanza Morales (Los Zetas/February 10), Héctor Huerta Ríos (Beltrán Leyva brothers/March 24), Vicente Zambada Niebla (Sinaloa Cartel/March 21), and Sigifredo Nájera Talamontes (Gulf Cartel/March 20). Since then, the number of arrests—particularly of corrupt politicians and stalwarts of Los Zetas, the Beltrán Leyva family, and La Familia—has soared.

America's top foreign policymaker has praised Mexico's assertiveness. She has admitted that Americans' "insatiable" appetite for narcotics and failure to stanch arms smuggling had contributed to Mexico's Time of Troubles. "We will stand shoulder to shoulder with you," she affirmed in talks with Calderón and Foreign Secretary Espinosa.[9] Obama reiterated this pledge during the August 9-10, 2009 "Three Amigos" summit in Guadalajara.

The PGR has raised the quixotic possibility of relocating Mexico from center stage to the wings of narco-trafficking, by proposing that

Table 10.1
Rewards Offered by Mexican Government for Information
about Major Criminals

Cartel	Capo	Reward*
Gulf-Zetas	Heriberto Lazcano Lazcano, alias "El Lazca"; "Z-3"; "El Verdugo"	30 Million Pesos
	Jorge Eduardo Costilla Sánchez, alias "El Coss"	30 Million Pesos
	Ezequiel Cárdenas Guillén, alias "Tony Tormenta"	30 Million Pesos
	Miguel Angel Treviño Morales, alias "L-40"; "Comandante 40"; "La Mona"	30 Million Pesos
	Omar Treviño Morales, alias "L-42"	30 Million Pesos
	Iván Velázquez Caballero, alias "El Talibán"; "L-50"	30 Million Pesos
	Gregorio Sauceda Gamboa, alias "El Goyo"; "Metro-2"; "Caramuela" **(Apprehended April 28, 2009)**	30 Million Pesos
	Sigifredo Nájera Talamantes, alias "El Canicón" **(Apprehended March 20, 2009)**	15 Million Pesos
	Ricardo Almanza Morales	15 Million Pesos
	Eduardo Almanza Morales	15 Million Pesos
	Raymundo Almanza Morales, alias "El Gori" **(Apprehended May 20, 2009)**	15 Million Pesos
	Flavio Méndez Santiago, alias "El Amarillo"	15 Million Pesos
	Sergio Peña Solís and/or René Solís Carlos, alias "El Cóncord"; "El Colosio"	15 Million Pesos
	Raúl Lucio Fernández Lechuga, alias "El Lucky"	15 Million Pesos
	Sergio Enrique Ruíz Tlapanco, alias "El Tlapa"	15 Million Pesos

Table 10.1

Sinaloa/Pacific ("The Federation" until fissures took place)	Joaquín Guzmán Loera and/or Joaquín Archivaldo Guzmán Loera, alias "El Chapo"	30 Million Pesos
	Ismael Zambada García, alias "El Mayo Zambada"	30 Million Pesos
	Ignacio Coronel Villarreal, alias "Nacho Coronel"	30 Million Pesos
	Juan José Esparragoza Moreno, alias "El Azul"	30 Million Pesos
	Vicente Zambada Niebla, alias "El Vicentillo" **(Apprehended March 19, 2009)**	30 Million Pesos
Beltrán Leyva Brothers	Arturo Beltrán Leyva, alias "El Barbas"	30 Million Pesos
	Mario Alberto Beltrán Leyva y/o Héctor Beltrán Leyva, alias "El General"	30 Million Pesos
	Sergio Villarreal Barragán, alias "El Grande"	30 Million Pesos
	Edgar Valdez Villarreal, alias "La Barbie"	30 Million Pesos
	Francisco Hernández García, alias "El 2000"; "El Panchillo"	15 Million Pesos
	Alberto Pineda Villa, alias "El Borrado" (Believed Apprehended May 5, 2009)	15 Million Pesos
	Marco Antonio Pineda Villa, alias "El MP"	15 Million Pesos
	Héctor Huerta Ríos, alias "La Burra" or "El Junior"	15 Million Pesos
Carrillo Fuentes/ Juárez	Vicente Carrillo Fuentes, alias "El Viceroy" or "El General"	30 Million Pesos
	Vicente Carrillo Leyva **(Apprehended April 2, 2009)**	30 Million Pesos
	Juan Pablo Ledesma and/or Eduardo Ledesma, alias "El JL"	15 Million
La Familia	Nazario Moreno González, alias "El Chayo"	30 Million **Pesos**

Table 10.1 (cont)

	Servando Gómez Martínez, alias "El Profe"; "El Tuta"	30 Million Pesos
	José de Jesús Méndez Vargas, alias "El Chango"	30 Million Pesos
	Dionicio Loya Plancarte, alias "El Tío"	30 Million Pesos
Arellano Félix/ Tijuana	Teodoro García Simental, alias "El Teo" or "El Lalo"; "El 68"; "El K-1"; "El Alamo 6"; "El Tres Letras"	30 Million Pesos
	Fernando Sánchez Arellano, alias "El Ingeniero"	30 Million Pesos

* The peso-dollar exchange rate was 14.4 on March 23, 2009.

Source: "Ofrece PGR hasta 30 mdp por 37 narcos," *Reforma*, March 23, 2009.

three things need to happen: (1) prevent small cocaine-ferrying aircraft from Colombia, Panama, and Venezuela from landing in Mexico, forcing South American producers to circumvent its nation and home in on expanding European demand; (2) speculating that if the United States, which now produces 70 percent of its needs, becomes self-sufficient in marijuana it would reduce the incentive to produce it within Mexico; and (3) encouraging suppliers of precursor chemicals in Asia and Europe to manufacture methamphetamines in their home countries—rather than outsource the production to Mexican laboratories.

2. Reach a Modus Vivendi with the Cartels

In mid-2008 President Fox's former spokesman, Rubén Aguilar, proposed that the government consider negotiating with the local *mafias* to stem the wave of violence plaguing the country. In return for legalizing the sale and consumption of narcotics, the cartels would agree to certain conditions—above all, halting the torture, murder, kidnapping, beheadings, and the sale of drugs to minors. "We must constrain the action of organized crime, obligate them to obey rules of operation and in this context, we would have to accept the possibility of ... legalizing the sale of drugs under certain agreements" he said in an interview with the Tijuana's *Frontera* newspaper.

"It is quite probable that other types of rules of the game will be established among the organized criminal bands. We are not going to eliminate narco-trafficking, [but] we can diminish the violence with which it seeks to enhance its operating spaces," he added.[10]

Politicians from across the spectrum came down like a ton of bricks on Vicente Fox's former communications director. It was as if he had proposed shuttering the Basilica of Guadalupe or prohibiting the feast of the Three Kings. And Felipe Calderón led the charge. "My government," he said "does not negotiate nor will it ever negotiate with criminal organizations, with those that we combat without favoritism [and we] are committed not only to confront them but to defeat them with all of the force of the State."[11]

Senators, deputies, and other nabobs fell all over themselves hurling invective at Aguilar. Senator Felipe González González, chairman of the Public Security Committee, blasted the idea as "crazy." Justiniano González Betancourt, his counterpart in the Chamber of Deputies, also objected: "You cannot cut deals with crooks, least of all with criminal organizations. They are poisoning [our] society and do not merit acquiring legitimacy through an agreement, an accord or a pact."[12]

Such naysayers ignored the fact that there is nothing wrong with negotiation per se. After all, in December Arturo Beltrán Leyva and "El Mayo" Zambada agreed to a two-week truce during the 2008-09 Christmas holiday. Even drug lords relish a reprieve from the deadly hunt. Of course such truces may only delay the inevitable—thirty-seven people died on January 7 on the day after the cease-fire ended. Some law enforcement agents believe the Sinaloa Cartel's inability to dislodge its rivals—the Gulf Cartel and Los Zetas—from Nuevo Laredo explains the decreased violence in Latin America's largest portal, through which 8,500 trucks cross each day. As part of the deal, El Chapo's organization purportedly agreed to pay a transit tax for drugs passing through Tamaulipas. Emerging from the conflict stronger than ever were Los Zetas, whose members continue to operate semi-independently from the Gulf Cartel.[13]

Mexican businessmen have proposed negotiating with narco-traffickers, according to Tello Peón. The drug czar summarily dismissed the idea, saying: "I am absolutely convinced that there is no way this can be done. I was surprised that ... important entrepreneurs came and told me the same as you; I am speaking of reaching a deal with organized crime. There is no way."[14]

The proliferation of criminal syndicates makes bargaining more and more unlikely. When the Sinaloa, Gulf, and a limited number of other organizations ruled the roost, pursuing ad hoc pacts may have been possible. A new generation of ruthless chieftains is springing up around the country amid an ongoing kaleidoscopic shift in alliances. As Sinaloa journalist Javier Valdéz Cárdenas said: "Calderón took a stick and whacked a beehive." Consequently, negotiations appear unfeasible—unless the syndicates were to consolidate into a manageable few. The Colombian experience suggests that they are more likely to evolve into smaller groups—*los cartelitos*—than to consolidate.

3. Focus on Demand Side: Education and Treatment

It is pharisaical of Washington to assign the burden of blame on Mexico for an influx of drugs that satisfies America's proverbial big nose. Only when U.S. officials accept co-responsibility with Mexico by placing as much weight on curtailing consumption as they do on reducing supply will progress take place. Drugs have become an international challenge and as Professor Bruce M. Bagley observed, "the Mexican-U.S. trade is a manifestation—virulent to be sure—of that global trade."[15]

Escalating demand requires much greater attention to prevention, education, and treatment, especially in prisons where small-time drug dealers go behind bars as amateurs only to emerge years later as hardened professionals. Although it varies each year, a disproportionate share of federal War on Drug monies is earmarked for curbing supply rather than reducing demand. The dismal record of this effort argues strongly for a new approach.

4. Thinking about the Unthinkable: Decriminalization

More and more right-wing libertarians and leftist progressives believe that America's draconian drug laws are as outdated as corsets and high-buttoned shoes. In off-the-record conversations, scores of well-known liberal, moderate, and conservative politicians endorse decriminalizing, if not legalizing, the possession of marijuana for personal use by adults. Many believe in treating cocaine and heroin addiction as a health concern—not as criminal behavior—and permitting addicts to obtain controlled substances with doctors' prescriptions. At the same time, they favor actively promoting methadone treatment for heroin addicts. A few have dared to express their private opinions publicly. Former Alaska senator Mike Gravel and maverick wannabe for the 2008 Democratic presidential openly espouses such views—not because he favors narcotics, but due to the abject failure of the supply-side course.

Some elected officials have gone even further. In 1999 New Mexico's Governor Gary Johnson became the nation's highest office-holder to advocate drug legalization. He reasoned that everything from marijuana to heroin ought to be legalized because the U.S. anti-drug effort is an expensive bust. "Control it, regulate it, tax it," the state leader urged with respect to recreational drugs, because "if you legalize it we might actually have a healthier society. He asked why "should you go to jail for just doing drugs?" By one estimate, the U.S. spends $40 billion a year trying to intercept shipments and arrest drug dealers and users. In response to this endeavor, Johnson stated, "I say no. I say you shouldn't."

Arizona Attorney General Terry Goddard, no legalization advocate, has called for revisiting the ban on marijuana. "The most effective way to establish a virtual barrier against the criminal activities is to take the profit out of it [sic]," he told a U.S. Senate subcommittee.[16]

Despite all federal and local law enforcement attempts, only about 5 percent to 15 percent of the illegal substances coming into the United States are actually seized. The rest feed a $200 billion a year illicit business that caters to an estimated 13 million Americans each month.[17] The Rand Corporation reports that treatment of addicts is ten times more effective than interdiction in lowering cocaine use.[18] At the very least, the U.S. should authorize the medicinal use of narcotics so that doctors can prescribe doses to patients who will benefit from ingredients found in them.

In 2006 the Fox administration introduced a bill to decriminalize the possession of small amounts of the most popular illegal drugs. Under his initiative, penalties would be relaxed for possessing 500 milligrams of cocaine, five grams of marijuana, five grams of raw opium, and twenty-five milligrams of heroin, among other substances. "Mexico is trying to make the right choices.... The Mexican legislation will go a long way toward reducing opportunities for police corruption and harassment in their interaction with ordinary citizens," averred Ethan Nadelmann, executive director of the Drug Policy Alliance, a group that favors ending the war on drugs. In contrast, Washington came out swinging against the measure, which the Roman Catholic Church inveighed against and Mexico's Congress ultimately shelved; the bloodshed related to obtaining and holding *plazas* continues unabated.

The majority of Washington's international anti-narcotics spending is directed toward Latin America and the Caribbean. Despite militarization and generous funding for the drug war, illegal substances continue to flood into America. The crackdown in Mexico has driven down cocaine consumption in the U.S. by 15.9 percent even as the price of the drug has fluctuated from $95.4 to $118.61 per ounce and its purity has declined.[19]

There is no silver bullet with respect to the importation, processing, sale, and consumption of drugs. Americans and their leaders should have learned one thing from the Eighteenth Amendment, no matter how well intended are prohibitionists, customers will obtain products they desire. Prohibition represented a repetition of the mythological king seeking to sweep back the sea with a broom.

In a rare display of candor, then candidate Obama indicated that he had used drugs as a younger man. Citing his mother's death from cancer in her early 50s, he compared marijuana to morphine, saying there was little difference between the two. Moreover, Attorney General Eric Holder has pledged to halt raids on distributors of medical marijuana in California, Nevada, Maine, and the other ten states where pot can be obtained for medicinal purposes.[20]

This partisan divide is clear according to columnist Froma Harrop, who has highlighted the president's support for decriminalization earlier in his career and lauded his choice of former Seattle Police Chief Gil Kerlikowske as his drug czar. She pointed out that Kerlikowske "presided over a city that had virtually decriminalized small-scale possession of marijuana," while his predecessor John Walters, was a hard-line law enforcer. The evolution of public attitudes appeared in a survey about the Michael Phelps incident in which the Olympic superstar was photographed smoking cannabis at a party. Sixty percent of Americans still regarded Phelps favorably, but most also thought the Kellogg Company made the right decision in dropping him as a celebrity endorser. In light of other domestic and international issues, Obama may allow states to decide if they want to cross what one activist called "the Reefer Rubicon."[21]

At his "Digital Town Meeting" in March 2009, the new chief executive was deluged with e-mails criticizing the nation's drug statutes. The National Organization for the Reform of Marijuana Laws (NORML)—a pro-legalization group—mobilized thousands of communications—and the outpouring publicized the issue. Sample question: "What are your plans for the failing, 'War on Drugs,' that's sucking money from tax payers and putting non-violent people in prison longer than the violent criminals?"

White House aides did not pick such inquiries for the president, but Obama did acknowledge that the topic was a popular one—and a media buzz accompanied by opinion surveys ensued.

Meanwhile, New York Governor David A. Paterson admitted having used cocaine and smoked marijuana in his youth. He and legislative leaders teamed up to relax 1973 laws enacted during the administration of Governor Nelson A. Rockefeller to fight a drug-related "reign of terror." Critics had long castigated the "Rockefeller drug laws" as racist and punitive, crowding prisons with people who would be better served with treatment. The changes will eliminate mandatory minimum terms for low-level, nonviolent drug felonies, which could slash the prison population by thousands at a time when the Empire State faced a $16 billion deficit and the annual cost for confining an inmate was $45,000.[22]

In February 2009 a state legislator from San Francisco introduced a bill to tax, regulate, and legalize adult consumption of cannabis. This proposal gathered cobwebs until Governor Arnold Schwarzenegger stepped forward. Staring at a potential $21.3 billion budget deficit in 2010, he called for a debate on legalizing and taxing marijuana for recreational use. "I'm always for an open debate on it. And I think we ought to study very carefully what other countries are doing that … [have] legalized marijuana and other drugs. What effect did it have on those countries?" he said on May 5, 2009.

The defeat of a package of belt-tightening referenda questions two weeks later will force the so-called "Gobernator" and his aides to scrutinize even more closely the revision of California's drug policy. A Field Poll showed that 56 percent of the states' voters supported liberalizing California's law. Such a measure could yield $1.3 billion in annual revenues and save another $1 billion on enforcement and incarceration. Other state executives mired in financial woes will watch closely how California proceeds. The United States has about 2.3 million people in prison or jail, up from 1.5 million in 1994—with a ten-fold increase for drug offenders from 50,000 (1980) to 500,000 (2007).[23]

In February 2009 a commission composed of three former Latin American presidents—Mexico's Zedillo, Brazil's Fernando Henrique Cardoso, and Colombia's César Gaviria—lambasted current policies as rooted in "prejudices, fears and ideological visions" that inhibit debate. The leaders called on governments to refocus their programs on treating users, moving toward the decriminalization of marijuana, and investing more resources in education projects. Cardoso emphasized the centrality of U.S. leadership in breaking the cycle of drug-based crime and violence. "It will be almost impossible to solve Mexico's problems and other countries' problems without a more ample, comprehensive set of policies from the U.S. Government," he declared.[24]

Although a majority of Americans continue to adhere to the status quo, the portion of the population favoring legalizing marijuana has climbed from 27 percent in 1973 to 41 percent in 2009—with young people,

Westerners, Democrats, political independents, and college-educated adults evincing the greatest support for change.

U.S. federal, state and local governments have spent hundreds of billions of dollars to keep the country "drug-free." Yet heroin, cocaine, methamphetamine and other illicit substances are more available than ever before. The drug war itself contributes to many of the evils that its paladins decry. So-called "drug-related" crime arises from prohibition's distortion of supply and demand laws, as explained by the late economist Milton Friedman.

In 1990 the Nobel Laureate economist began a letter to U.S. drug czar Bill Bennett by quoting Oliver Cromwell's eloquent words: "I beseech you, in the bowels of Christ, think it is possible [that you and President George W. H. Bush] may be mistaken" in waging the drug war, adding:

> Your mistake is failing to recognize that the very measures you favor are a major source of the evils you deplore. Of course the problem is demand, but it is not only demand, it is demand that must operate through repressed and illegal channels. Illegality creates obscene profits that finance the murderous tactics of the drug lords; illegality leads to the corruption of law enforcement officials; illegality monopolizes the efforts of honest law forces so that they are starved for resources to fight the simpler crimes of robbery, theft and assault.[25]

A staid British magazine reiterated its agreement, arguing that: "By any sensible measure, this 100-year struggle has been illiberal, murderous and pointless. That is why *The Economist* continues to believe that the least bad policy is to legalise drugs."[26]

Zero tolerance statutes that restrict access to clean needles intensify other public health problems like HIV and hepatitis C. What about the drug war as a promoter of "family values?" Rather than strengthening families, this approach places the children of inmates at risk of educational failure, joblessness, addiction, and delinquency. Drug abuse is bad, but the drug war is worse. Few public policies have compromised public health and undermined our fundamental civil liberties for so long and to such a degree as the war on drugs.[27] A medley of factors—the failure of the current strategy, the high cost of incarceration, economic uncertainty, the bloodletting sparked by the drug war in both countries, and evolving U.S. demographics—power the move towards a gradual liberalization of policy, at least on a state-by-state basis. As indicated in Appendix 5 not the least of the considerations is the substantially higher death rate from tobacco and alcohol than from now illicit drugs.

Notes

1.   Quoted in Brands, "Mexico's Narco-Insurgency and U.S. Counterdrug Policy," p. 15.
2.   Jésica Zermeño Núñez, "Un pacto político salvará a México," *Reforma*, June 212, 2009.
3.   "Welcome to Kansas City Southern," 2007 *www.kcsouthern.com/en-us/Pages/default. /aspx/.*
4.   Sam Enriquez and Hector Tobar, "Mexican army faces tough war with drug cartels," *Los Angeles Times*, May 16, 2007.
5.   Quoted in Jo Tuchman, "Narco War Spirals out of Control," June 24, 2007, *Mail&Guardian.on line.*
6.   J. Jesús Esquivel, "Los dueños de la frontera," *Proceso*, August 12, 2007. *www. proceso.com.mx.*
7.   Ricardo Ravelo, "Se buscan soplones…," *Proceso*, April 5, 2009.
8.   Benito Jiménez, "Recibe el Ejército record de denuncias," *Reforma*, May 18, 2009.
9.   Matthew Lee, "Clinton: US Shares Blame for Drug Wars," *Associated Press*, March 26, 2009.
10.   "Sugiere Rubén Aguilar negociar con el narco," *Reforma*, December 18, 2008.
11.   Quoted in Mayolo López, "Descarta Calderón negociar con cárteles," *Reforma*, December 20, 2008.
12.   "Critican propuesta de Rubén Aguilar," *Reforma*, December 19, 2008.
13.   Marc Lacey, "In Mexican City, Drug War Ills Slip into Shadows," *New York Times*, June 13, 2009.
14.   Aline Corpus, "Sugieren empresarios negociar con el narco," *Reforma*, January 24, 2009.
15.   Bagley, "The Manuscript," electronic mail to author.
16.   Quoted in Gray, "We Tried a War Like This Once Before."
17.   "New Mexico Governor Calls for Legalizing Drugs," October 6, 1999. *www.cnn. com.*
18.   C. Peter Rydell and Susan S. Everingham, *Controlling Cocaine: Supply Versus Demand Programs*, Rand Corporation, 1994. *www.rand.org/pubs/monograph_reports/.*
19.   Information from the White House's Office of National Drug Control Policy; see, "Sube en EU el precio de cocaina," *Reforma*, August 12, 2007.
20.   Froma Harrop, "Will President Obama Cross the "Reefer Rubicon?" *Pocono Record*, February 19, 2009.
21.   Bob Engelko, "U.S. to Yield Marijuana Jurisdiction to States," *San Francisco Chronicle*, February 27, 2009.
22.   Jeremy W. Peters, "Albany Reaches Deal to Repeal '70s Drug Laws," *New York Times*, March 25, 2009.
23.   Rebecca Cathcart, "Schwarzenegger Urges a Study on Legalizing Marijuana Use," *New York Times*, May 7, 2009.
24.   Stuart Grudgings, "Latin American Ex-leaders Urge Reform of US Drug War," *Reuters*, February 11, 2009.
25.   Milton Friedman, "An Open Letter to Bill Bennett," *Freedom Daily*, April 1990.
26.   "How to Stop the Drug War," *The Economist*, March 5, 2009.
27.   Drug Policy Alliance Network, "What's Wrong with the War on Drugs," *www. drugpolicy.org/drugwar/.*

Conclusion: A Failed State?

The U.S. Joint Forces Command recommended that Mexico be monitored alongside Pakistan as a "weak and failing" state that could crumble swiftly under relentless assault by violent drug cartels. Retired U.S. Army General Barry R. McCaffrey, the former U.S. drug agency director, wrote in a separate analysis that the Mexican government "is not confronting dangerous criminality—it is fighting for its survival against narco-terrorism" and could lose effective control of large swaths near the U.S. border. Outgoing CIA director Michael V. Hayden listed Mexico with Iran as a possible top challenge for President Obama. And former U.S. House Speaker Newt Gingrich emphasized that Mexico could turn into a surprise crisis for the new president by year's end.[1]

Felipe Calderón bristles at the "failed state" characterization, and the Obama administration has turned summersaults to refute that appellation. Freedom House and other think-tanks that assess "freedom," "democracy," and "failed states" have given Mexico reasonable high marks in recent years; however, in 2009 Freedom House chided "the government's inability to implement an effective response to the power of organized criminal groups that have spread violence and terror through significant parts of the country." Still, this distinguished organization focuses on processes rather than practices—namely the presence of a competitive multiparty political system, universal adult suffrage, regular transparent and fair elections, and access of major political parties to the media and open campaigning.[2]

The Fund for Peace and *Foreign Policy Magazine*, which ranked Mexico 98 (a one implies a Somalia-like collapse) on its 2009 "Failed States Index," concentrate on ethnic conflicts, separatist movements, disputes with neighboring countries, risks of military coups, guerrilla activities, and terrorist organization, and control of territory.[3]

Although helpful, such criteria overlook the chasm between the political elite and grassroots' constituents, breeding in the latter a sense of political helplessness. This situation arises from several factors. These include a constitutional ban on reelecting chief executives and the absence of a run-off if no contender garners 50 percent—plus one vote. President Calderón entered Los Pinos with 33.9 percent of the ballots cast, just a .6 percent lead over Andrés Manuel López Obrador. A second round of voting to achieve a 50 percent mandate would likely have forced parties to negotiate, bargain, and compromise in pursuit of a successful mandate. The crystallization of a winning coalition might have contributed to collaboration in Congress where intolerance between and among parties thrives, and continually leads to deadlock and drift.

Other constitutional and electoral law elements that divorce the establishment from the masses are (1) prohibiting independent candidacies, (2) forbidding civic groups from airing media ads during campaigns, (3) continuing the dominance of party chiefs in selecting nominees and ranking them on proportional representation lists used to select one-fourth the Senate and two-fifths of the Chamber of Deputies, (4) disallowing deputies, senators, governors, state legislators, and mayors to serve consecutive terms in their offices, and (5) failing to forge a coherent, responsible left.

With respect to the last point, López Obrador began his political career as a PRI mover-and-shaker. In 1989 he embraced the newly minted Democratic Revolutionary Party to advance his career. Twenty years later, he broke with the PRD to accept the backing of two small, opportunistic organizations: the Workers Party (PT) and the Convergence party (*Convergencia*). In the 2009-2012 Congress, the self-named "Legitimate President" and his followers will oppose any Calderón initiative even as they cross swords with a moderate New Left faction (los Chuchos) that has disavowed their former candidate and who have come to dominate the PRD. Should one of these groups support a presidential bill on a subject other than higher social spending or monopoly-busting, the other accuses it of selling out to the running dogs of neoliberalism, and increasingly more common—to "neo-fascism."

These considerations combined with the fact that so many lawmakers lack defined constituencies militate against advancing the interest of average men and women. All the while, elected officials line their pockets with generous salaries, hefty fringe benefits, Christmas bonuses, travel funds, free medical care, office expense accounts, pensions, "leaving office" stipends, and many other ways to live the good life. At the same time, the Federal Electoral Institute (IFE), which registers voters, supervises elections, and reports preliminary vote tallies, lavishes monies on political parties (3.6 billion pesos in 2009). No wonder that the late, inordinately powerful politician and PRI dinosaur Carlos Hank González uttered the lapidary phrase: "Show me a politician who is poor and I will show you a poor politician."[4]

Former Sinaloa Governor Juan S. Millán Lizárraga recounts the story of a newly elected deputy who visited an impoverished flyspecked village in the far reaches of his Veracruz district. He told the subsistence-level and dirt-scratching peasants who shuffled into the town square to hear him: "Take a good, long look at my face … because this is the last time you are going to see it in this shit-kicking pueblo. And he kept his word."

The national media shed some light on irresponsible federal officials, but governors tend to rule the roost as caciques in their states. These executives, like archbishops and bishops, reign over dioceses thanks to a compliant press (whose owners fear losing state advertising), close economic bonds to the businessmen (who salivate for government contracts), and blatant manipulation of states legislatures (whose member receive extravagant salaries and benefits in return for rubber-stamping executive initiatives). The thirty-one state governors and Mexico City mayor whom PRI presidents kept on a short leash gained emancipation from central dominance when the opposition swept to power in 2000. Except when they descend on Mexico City during the preparation of the national budget, state executives can thumb their noses at Los Pinos. Of course, the arrest of the Michoacán politicians will make governors more attentive to the president's agenda, lest they become bull's-eyes of the next round-up.

In blatant violation of the existing Constitution, Jalisco's executive Emilio González Márquez forked over ninety million pesos of taxpayers' money to the Roman Catholic Church to construct a Sanctuary for Mexican Martyrs—a contribution that he was later forced to withdraw in light of massive public outrage. The PAN charged Fidel Herrera Beltrán, governor of Veracruz, with earmarking public monies for PRI candidates in his state's 2007 municipal and state legislative races with a view to "burying" the opposition. For decades, governors across the political spectrum have engaged in direct or indirect vote buying.[5]

Mexico State's chief executive and presidential hopeful Enrique Peña Nieto has flouted a formal IFE ban on out-of-season TV commercials by overloading the airways with self-promoting messages throughout the country. On a titillating note, former Morelos Governor Sergio Estrada Cagijal won fame for taking girlfriends on flying trysts in his state's "Helicopter of Love."

Some cronies of politicians act even more cynically. As mentioned earlier, the SNTE teachers' union and its chief Elba Esther Gordillo, whom the late M. Delal Baer described as "Jimmy Hoffa in a dress," have colonized the nation's public schools. Mexico ranks last in reading, science, and mathematics among the 30 members of the OECD, according to the 2006 PISA international exam. Middle class families make whatever sacrifices necessary to enroll their children in private schools.

Meanwhile, the egregiously corrupt STPRM oil workers' union maintains a hammerlock grasp on Petróleos Mexicanos. This impedes efficient operations within a featherbedded monopoly even in the face of plummeting proven reserves and a legislative stalemate over opening the firm to private capital. For example, PEMEX has neither the technology nor expertise to explore and develop deep-water reservoirs. State oil companies from Norway and Brazil are among those interested in developing these deposits under "risk contracts"—namely, the firms would finance their operations in return for a portion of any hydrocarbons recovered. Cuba and every other oil-endowed country in the developing world—except North Korea and Mexico—enter into these kinds of arrangements.

It appears that segments of the PRI and leftist politicians would rather leave the oil under the waters of Gulf of Mexico than authorize risk contracts. And some critics may be missing the big picture if they limit their protests to symbolic and rhetorical complaints about violating Lázaro Cárdenas bold initiative to create a Mexican institution. Such "nationalist complaints" may focus on chanting "The Oil is Ours!" even while American and other multinational corporations, based on U.S. territory and acting legally, employ sophisticated drilling techniques to extract these precious resources from under their noses.

At the same time, corrupt electrical workers abet the theft of enormous amounts of electricity from the state oligopoly: Light and Power of the Center, which serves the D.F. and nearby states, and the Federal Electricity Commission, which powers the rest of the country.

The weakness of the Mexican state also manifests itself in the nation's antiquated, fiscal regime combined with the ineffectiveness of the local version of the Internal Revenue Service. This double whammy means that tax collections, which have fallen during the 2009 recession, approach only 12 percent of GDP—on par with Haiti, an utterly failed state, and one-third of the figure for the United States.

Highly publicized cruelties have sparked fear within the population, but they have also conveyed the idea that wrongdoers can act with impunity. In early 2009 the government admitted the existence of 233 "zones of impunity" where crime runs rampant.[6] Although Mexican officials did specify these areas, they are believed to include (1) the Tierra Caliente, a mountainous region contiguous to Michoacán, Guerrero, and Mexico State, (2) the "Golden Triangle," a drug-growing Mecca where the states of Sinaloa, Chihuahua, and Durango converge in the Sierra Madres, (3) the Isthmus of Tehuantepec in the Southeast, (4) neighborhoods in cities along the U.S. Mexican border where cartel thugs carve up judges, behead police officers, and disappear journalists who incur their wrath, (5) metropolitan areas around Mexico City, and (6) the porous border between southern Chiapas state and Guatemala.

So bad is the situation that, after the mid-2009 torture and slaying of its leader, the Mormon community in Galeana, Chihuahua, prepared to field an armed self-defense force of seventy-seven volunteers. After vacillating, the PRI governor sought to prevent vigilantism—a reaction to profound insecurity—by inviting the young Mormons to train to become state preventative policemen. PAN state legislator Fernando Álvarez Monje rejected this idea, indicating that formation of a community force would mean that citizens were taking justice into their own hands. Meanwhile, continued violence in Monterrey—accentuated by a machine gun-killing in the city's Macroplaza commercial center on July 12—has prompted one citizens' group to organize to defend themselves. Such efforts are likely to spread.

Then there is the ubiquitous street violence exemplified by the unsolved murders and disappearances of hundreds of women in Ciudad Juárez. Such a crisis means that the affluent shell out untold millions of pesos for bodyguards, armored vehicles, and sophisticated electronic security devices. Many Mexican big wigs, including law enforcement personnel, live north of the border with the protection of the U.S. government. As mentioned above, even Mexico City and adjoining states (México, Morelos, Hidalgo, and Puebla) have become magnets for organized crime—with Los Zetas, La Familia, the Beltrán Leyva brothers, and the Sinaloa and Gulf Cartels vying for control. At the same time, prisoners often run penal institutions rather than their keepers.

Citizens can stage huge marches, swarm into the Zócalo central plaza to vent their spleens, taunt deputies and senators as they enter their legislative precincts, but the survey found in Table 1 shows that most people feel impotent with respect to influencing policy and policy makers.

The future? In a report for the University of Miami's Center for Hemispheric Policy, scholar Luis Rubio wrote: "There are regions of the country where all vestiges of a functioning government have simply vanished," while in the rest, "the climate of impunity, extortion, protection money, kidnapping and, in general, crime has become pervasive."

Table 1
Public Confidence in Institutions

	Public Confidence (August 2008)	Public Confidence (March 2007)	Change in Confidence Rating
Federal Electoral Institute	43%	55%	-12
Supreme Court	49	40	-9
Chamber of Deputies	24	34	-10
Senate	24	36	-12
Political Parties	22	27	-5

Source: Based on a survey of 515 households in 32 entities of the country conducted on August 16 and 17, 2008—with a +/-2.5% error of margin at a 95% confidence level; Alejandro Moreno, "Baja apoyo ciudadano," *Reforma*, August 27, 2008.

Only a Cassandra in deep funk could conclude that Mexico will implode as is possible in Afghanistan or Pakistan. There are too many factors—the Mexican armed forces, the Roman Catholic Church, the middle class, the Monterrey business community, the banking system, labor and professional organizations, the U.S. government, and international financial institutions, etc.—to let this happen. Felipe Calderón and his successors must act to prevent ungovernability in cities like Ciudad Juárez and Tijuana, and in states like Guerrero, Durango, Sinaloa, and Michoacán.

They must also be on guard against the emergence—in some cases, the consolidation—of what Crane Brinton in his classic *Anatomy of Revolution* called "dual sovereignty." He referred to leaving the government and other legal entities in control of certain political, economic, social, and cultural areas and abdicating responsibility and dominion of organized crime to others—a danger that the PAN leader warned about in Durango. Although often selected through bullets rather than ballots, the powerful luminaries who dominate the narcotics syndicates may wield greater power and possess more resources than their legitimate competitors. And they do not face term limits unless, of course, they run afoul of foes and authorities who luck out and capture them.

There is a limit on how many dragons any president can confront but Mexico eventually must modernize PEMEX, the state electricity companies, public education, telecommunications, and health and retirement agencies, to mention a few. Structural bottlenecks inhibit the nation's competitiveness in third markets—with the result that China, India, and the Asian Tigers, which are now eating Mexico's lunch—can look forward to devouring its breakfast and dinner.

In the face of Sisyphean obstacles, the PRI's secular church was poised for a comeback. It sought to expand beyond its 106 deputies in the outgoing Congress. Many analysts believed that only a PAN victory in the Nuevo León gubernatorial showdown could keep the chief executive politically alive during the remainder of his tenure. Negative vital signs abounded apart from the cartels' ghastly violence: scary street crime, diminished tax collections, sagging oil revenues, multiple prison escapes, falling remittances from Mexicans abroad, an influenza outbreak that devastated the tourism industry, soaring unemployment, a profound recession, and a struggling U.S. economy. The nation's GDP declined 8.2 percent in the first quarter of 2009—with an officially estimated drop of 5.5 percent for the entire year.[7] Many independent economists have predicted that national income will contract 8 to 9 percent.

Despite Mexico's Job-like afflictions, Felipe Calderón found new life. His approval rating soared to 69 percent in early June 2009 and surpassed that of Barack Obama. Buoying his popularity was his steady handling of affairs and his enhanced reliance on such well-connected veterans as Gómez Mont (Interior), Tello Peón (executive secretary of the National System of Public Safety), and Luis Felipe Bravo Mena (private secretary).

In addition, the chief executive has ignored death threats to fight the cartels hammer and tongs, leading to highly publicized arrests. Despite charges of "over-reacting," he handled the April 2009 health crisis with candor, professionalism, and efficiency, and he immediately showed solidarity with families of the 49 children who died in the early June ABC day-care center fire in Sonora—a tragedy that has cast the spotlight on scores of unscrupulous owners of such government-subsidized facilities.

Domestic issue prevailed, and it is unclear whether he also benefited from new occupants at 1600 Pennsylvania Avenue. On the one hand, Barack Obama and his entourage have recognized the U.S.'s role in the economic slump, drug consumption, and the southbound torrent of arms. On the other hand, the White House and U.S. lawmakers have poured money into equipment and training to combat Mexican criminal organizations, which have not respected international boundaries. In May 2009 El Chapo Guzmán, who insist he avoids unnecessary violence, instructed his associates in the United States to "use their weapons to defend their loads [of drugs] at all costs." He was referring not only to competitors but to U.S. law enforcement agents.[8]

Like a bulldog, PAN president Germán Martínez Cázares unsparingly savaged the revolutionary secular church and its legacy of corruption, criminality, and crookedness. In the process, he reminded some Mexico-watchers of the PRI's similarity to Carlito Brigante, the leading character in Al Pacino's film, *Carlito's Way*.

A life-long criminal, Carlito finds himself with an unexpected second chance. Thanks to a technicality, he is set free after serving only five years of a thirty-year prison sentence. He declares himself reformed, tired of life in the underworld, and determined to go straight. But he found himself trapped in his past and unable to change his behavior.

Like Carlito, the PRI has little credibility as a reformed church, much less one that favors an all-out war against the cartels with which it collaborated and helped prosper for so many years. In the same vein, it chastised Calderón's handling of the economy, even though most mature Mexicans remember the PRI-inspired crises of 1976, 1982, 1988, and 1994. Its cardinals and archbishops also lacked an array of recent legislative accomplishments and did not devise a coherent platform with which to court a cynical electorate.

Martínez Cázares' invective appeared to gain traction in mid-May when former President Miguel de la Madrid, in an interview with *CNN Español* reporter Carmen Arístegui, alleged that the Salinas brothers had stolen enormous sums from the government (Carlos) and had rubbed elbows with narco-criminals (Raúl and the late Enrique). The 75-year-old suddenly had a revelation and retracted his charge. The damage had been done and the PAN featured the ex-chief executive's statement about rampant "immorality" in televisions commercials. Rumors filled Mexico City that authorities would charge one or more PRI notables with narco-trafficking—with former Tamaulipas Governor Tomás Yarrington and Colima gubernatorial candidate Anguiano Moreno, who triumphed on July 5, mentioned among a plethora of potential quarry.

Ricardo Monreal Ávila saved the administration the trouble when the Zacatecas senator vilified Amalia García—his personal nemesis and successor as PRD governor of state—for the May 16, 2009 Cieneguillas prison escape. The PAN had been quietly cooperating with the PRD against the PRI in states where Felipe Calderón's party is weak: Oaxaca, Guerrero, and Zacatecas. Martínez Cázares rushed to the defense of García, who had failed to deploy state police lest her sister, Zazatecas' deputy attorney general for investigations, bear the brunt of the criticism. A few days' later the PGR charged Monreal's family with illegal deeds. To be specific, the Army had confiscated 14.4 tons of marijuana plus scales and processing equipment on the family's Zacatecas farm.[9]

To convey a sense of even-handedness, on May 25 the PGR revealed that a former state police chief had sworn that PAN's ex-governor of Morelos, Estrada Cajigal, had solicited "contributions" from presumed drug *mafiosi*. Next, the president authorized the "non-partisan" sweep of twenty-seven public servants in Michoacán and promised more arrests of local officials even as Federal Police and soldiers arrested ninety law enforcement officers, including ten commanders, accused of colluding with narco-traffickers in Monterrey.

The De la Madrid-Monreal-Morelos-Michoacán blows bumped up the PAN's numbers in June opinion surveys. This gave the chief executive the freedom to spurn direct action against PRI "big fish" in favor the PAN's fomenting leaks and innuendos about its chief foe. The ruling party did suffer an embarrassment in Monterrey's affluent municipality of San Pedro Garza García. A leaked tape recording, which was broadcast nationwide, indicated that Mauricio Fernández Garza, PAN's ultimately successful mayoral nominee, had vetted his public safety plan with the Beltrán Leyvas' representatives.

Instead of parrying the PAN's attacks, the extremely confident party president Beatriz Paredes Rangel, Senator Manlio Fabio Beltrones, and Mexico State governor Enrique Peña Nieto—in concert with the PRI's eighteen state executives—took a different tack. They concentrated on wooing lapsed members, pursuing converts, reaching out to new voters, and revitalizing the edifice of their weather-worn church, which—unlike competitors—enjoys a presence in the 31 states and the DF. In so doing, they sought to take advantage of what promised to be a modest turnout in the mid-2009 contests.

Several factors contribute to this perception: the negativity of advertising, the lack of interest in off-year elections, the contempt for politicos, and the adroit use of the Internet and the media by prestigious intellectuals and civic groups to encourage ballot defacement to punish a system whose officeholders ignore the public's interest and lack accountability.

In the final analysis, anti-PRI charges fell on deaf ears, particularly to those of many young voters who recall the pop music of Michael Jackson, but not the economic debacles of Echeverría, López Portillo, De la Madrid, and Salinas. Martínez Cázares also had to contend with "friendly fire" in the gubernatorial campaign in San Luis Potosí, where local PAN activists resented the nation party's imposition of the nominee. In Querétaro, he had to deal with a self-aggrandizing outgoing governor who had awarded contracts to cronies and had logged more frequent flier miles than a UN secretary-general. In other words, PAN leaders had adopted the same methods that they had lambasted the PRI for employing. Above all, a deepening recession trumped every other consideration.

On Election Day, the PRI (36.8 percent/237 deputies) outpolled the PAN (28 percent/143 deputies), the PRD (12.2 percent/71 deputies), and the PVEM (6.7 percent/22 seats), according to a preliminary IFE report. The revolutionary clerics also garnered five of the six governorships up for grabs, thanks in part to the "Peña Nieto effect"; specifically, the extremely attractive Mexico State governor made successful personal appearances, provided generous resources, and furnished trained cadres to assist prospective PRI bishops and archbishops.

Although 44.8 percent of the 71.5 million eligible voters showed at the polls, the ballot spoilage drive yielded remarkable dividends nationwide (5.4 percent) and in a number of jurisdictions: Mexico City (10.8 percent), Chihuahua (7.5 percent), San Luis Potosí (7.4 percent), Puebla (7.3 percent), and Michoacán (6.7 percent). In 61 percent of the 281 electoral districts, the "*voto nulo*" was greater than the margin between the first- and second-place finishers. Advocates of this strategy plan to institutionalize their effort, which unites sympathizers of all political beliefs (through www.votosnulos.com) in hopes of forcing electoral reforms.

The PRI and its alliance partner, the PVEM, will dominate the Congress, which convened on August 29, 2009. They will bear responsibility for crafting a tight-as-a-tick 2010 budget.

What are the prospects for the PRI's temporal church, which has several aspirants hoping to succeed Calderón? Just as every lieutenant in Napoleon's Army supposedly carried a marshal's baton in his knapsack, many PRI governors have tucked presidential sashes into their briefcases. Peña Nieto's bravura performance in the mid-year races accentuated his status as the early front-runner, and Mexico State's so-called "golden boy" may avoid even token opposition from fellow governors. Still, Beltrones and Paredes have their own agendas for higher office. If its aspirants can avoid a knock-down-drag out clash among themselves, the PRI is well positioned to retake Los Pinos, Mexico's Holy See. Enhancing its prospects is the dearth of prospective PAN competitors (Interior Secretary Fernando Gómez Mont and Deputy Josefina Vázquez Mota have received the most attention), while the probable candidacies of López Obrador (PT and *Convergerncia*) and Mexico City's PRD mayor, Marcelo Ebrard, will fracture the left.

In the interest of promoting harmony, PRI's college of cardinals—key governors, powerful big-city mayors, senators, deputies, powerbrokers such as the ubiquitous Carlos Salinas, and other party luminaries—must unite behind one of their number to choose a potential secular pope. They might do so in a conclave such as the one that Salinas convened to make certain that the PRI won the 1994 presidential election—a lay version of the 2005 session that selected Cardinal Joseph Ratzinger as the new ruler of the Apostolic See.

In accepting his vaunted post, the PRI contender must identify goals beyond clichés about revolutionary nationalism. Skeptics doubt that the unreformed revolutionary church can break its reliance on peasant groups who extort subsidies from the government, papered businessmen who prefer protectionism to free trade, unions like the STPRM that view reform as anathema, nationalists who regard PEMEX as a sacred cow, and other groups in its hidebound congregation.

The PRI could improve the prospects for the next pontiff by working with Calderón and the PRD to legally oust common foes who have impeded the country's development—for example, Elba Esther Gordillo. Many party veterans have no love-lost for the SNTE teachers' boss, but they would have to convince her friends among the governors not to thwart such a venture.

The PRI could cooperate with the PAN to remove Martin Esparza, potentate of the obscenely corrupt and heavily featherbedded Mexican Electricians' Union. SME's employer, the state-operated Luz y Fuerza del Centro, should also be eliminated, with another public company, the Federal Electricity Commission, taking over service in the DF area.

Finally, few observers expect the PRI to undergo an *aggiornamento*. To the contrary, the party's hierarchy, invigorated by its mid-2009 landslide, seems focused more on the thirteen state elections in 2010, including ten gubernatorial contests, instead of prudent economic policy. In particular, PRI spokesmen have urged an expensive emergency economic recovery program along with possible tax cuts. While politically popular, such measures will obviate a critically needed root-and-branch tax overhaul. If the U.S. economy does not rebound sharply, a protracted recession can be blamed on the incumbent chief executive. Nevertheless, Peña Nieto, Beltrones, Paredes, or another stalwart, if successful in reaching the presidency, may inherit a failed economy and, along with it, a loss of legitimacy and an exodus of believers.

Of course, the PRI might not gain entry to the Promised Land should Calderón—in the quest of shaking up a dysfuntional political system and ensuring himself a prominent place in his nation's history—complement his anti-drug drive with an all-out battle against the impunity relished by public officials, including those in his own party.

Notes

1.   Schumacher-Matos, "In Mexico, Faltering, Not Failed."
2.   Arch Puddington, "Freedom in the World 2009: Setbacks and Resilience," Freedom House. *www.freedomhouse.org.*
3.   Fund for Peace, "The Failed State Index 2009," *Foreign Policy*, June 29, 2009.
4.   George W. Grayson, "Mexican Officials Feather their Nests while Decrying U.S. Immigration Policy," *Background*er, Center for Immigration Studies, April 2006.
5.   "Dirigió elecciones Fidel Herrera," *Reforma*, May 28, 2009.
6.   The government claimed the 233 zones of impunity were down sharply from 2,204 such zones the year before; see, Lacey, "In Drug War, Mexico Fights the Cartels and Itself."
7.   "Mexico, Politics and Policy," *Zemi Communications*, May 19-25, 2009.
8.   Josh Meyer, "Sinaloa cartel may resort to deadly force in U.S.," *Los Angeles Times*, May 6, 2009.
9.   María de la Luz González, "Cándido Monreal, indiciado," *El Universal*, May 22, 2009.

Appendix 1
Selected Figures in Narco-Trafficking

Aguirre, Galindo, Manuel "El Caballo" (Tijuana Cartel).

Alcides Magaña, Ramón "El Metro" (Juárez Cartel/Cancún area); arrested June 12, 2001.

Alonso, Villarreal, Édgar (Gulf Cartel)

Arellano Domínguez, Braulio "El Gonzo"/"El Z-20 (Los Zetas); at large.

Amezcua Contreras, Adán; born 1969; (Colima Cartel); arrested November 10, 1997 and May 3, 2007 in Zapopan.

Amezcua Contreras, José; born 1965 (Colima Cartel); arrested June 1, 1998.

Amezcua Contreras, Luis; born 1964 (Colima Cartel); arrested June 1, 1998.

Amezcua Contreras, Patricia (Colima Cartel); at large.

Amezcua Contreras, Martha (Colima Cartel); at large.

Amezcua Contreras, Emma (Colima Cartel); at large.

Arellano, Bernardo Cristóbal "El Morete" (Tijuana Cartel/El Teo faction); arrested June 5, 2009

Arellano Félix, Benjamín "El Min": born March 12, 1952, Sinaloa (Tijuana Cartel); arrested March 9, 2002.

Arellano Félix, Carlos; born August 20, 1955 (Tijuana Cartel); arrested and served his term.

Arellano Félix, Eduardo "The Doctor"; born Oct. 11, 1956, Culiacán, Sinaloa (Tijuana Cartel); captured by Army in Tijuana, October 26, 2008; at large.

Arellano Félix, Francisco Javier "Little Tiger"; born December 11, 1969, Sinaloa (Tijuana Cartel); arrested August 16, 2006.

Arellano Félix, Francisco Rafael; born October 24, 1949, Sinaloa (Tijuana Cartel); arrested Aug. 7, 1980; extradited to U.S. September 2006; released March 4, 2008.

Arellano Félix, Eduardo Ramón; born November 10, 1956 or August 31, 1964, Culiacán, Sinaloa (Tijuana Cartel); killed February 10, 2002.

Armas, Quito "La Cobra" (La Familia); at large.

Arizmendi López, Daniel "El Mochaoregas" (The Ear Cutter); born July 22, 1958, Miacatlán, Morelos; arrested August 17, 1998.

Avila Beltrán, Sandra "Queen of the Pacific"; born 1962, Tijuana (niece of Miguel Ángel Félix Gallardo); arrested Sept. 28, 2007.

Avilés Pérez, Pedro "The Mountain Lion"; born 1940, Sinaloa (Sinaloa Cartel); killed September 9, 1978.

Barajas Landa, Oscar "El Perro"; born 1982/83 (La Familia); arrested in Guerrero, 2009.

Barrera Medrano, Nicario "El Nica" (La Familia); at large.

Beltrán Leyva, Alfredo "El Mochomo" (Stinging Red Ant); born February 15, 1951; Sinaloa (Beltrán Leyva brothers); arrested January, 21, 2008.

Beltrán Leyva, (Marcos) Arturo "El Barbas" (The Beard); born September 27, 1961 or September 21, 1961 or June 5, 1962 or February 5, 1958, Culiacán or Badriguato (Beltrán Leyva brothers)—at large.

Beltrán Leyva, Carlos; born Badiraguato, Sinaloa (Beltrán Leyva brothers); at large.

Beltrán Leyva, Mario Alberto "El General"; born Badiraguato, Sinaloa (Beltrán Leyva brothers); at large.

Beltrán Leyva, Héctor "El H"; born Sinaloa (Beltrán Leyva brothers); at large.

Beltrán Uriate, Jesús Raúl; born Badiraguato, Sinaloa (Milenio Cartel); arrested December 2006.

Buendía Gutiérrez, Delia Patricia "Ma Baker" (Neza Cartel/DF); arrested on August 20, 2002.

Briceño, José Juan "El Cholo" (Tijuana Cartel); at large.

Bursiaga Armenta, Isaac "El Teco" (Beltrán Leyva brothers); arrested in Sonora in late June 2009.

Camacho Pérez, Félix or José Hernández González "El Boti" (Los Zetas/Gulf Cartel); Army seized him in Cancún, May 28, 2009.

Cárdenas Guillen, Osiel "The Friend Killer"; born May 18, 1967, Matamoros (Gulf Cartel); arrested March 14, 2003 and extradited to the U.S. January 20, 2007.

Cárdenas Guillén, Antonio Ezequiel "Tony Tormenta" (Gulf Cartel); at large

Caro Quintero, Rafael; born October 24, 1954, Badriguato, Sinaloa (Guadalajara/Sonora Cartel); arrested April 5, 1985.

Caro Quintero, Miguel Ángel; born 1963, Caborca, Sonora (Sonora Cartel); arrested December 20, 2001.

Carrillo Fuentes, Amado, "Lord of the Skies"; born 1956, Guamuchilito, Sinaloa (Juárez Cartel); died July 3, 1997, D.F.

Carrillo Fuentes, Rodolfo; (Juárez Cartel); executed in Culiacán, September 11, 2004.

Carrillo Fuentes, Vicente "El Viceroy"; born Oct. 16, 1962, Guamachilito, Sinaloa, (Juárez Cartel); at large.

Carrillo Leyva, Víctor "The Engineer"; born July 19, 1976, D.F. (Juárez Cartel); arrested in D.F., April 3, 2009.

Castañeda Chávez, Ramiro (La Familia); at large.

Castrejón Peña, Víctor Nazario (Los Zetas); at large.

Cázares Salazar, Blanca Margarita "La Emperatriz"; (Sinaloa Cartel); at large.

Cedeño Hernández, Rafael "El Cede" (La Familia); arrested near Morelia, April 19, 2009.

Contreras González, Ofelia (Sinaloa Cartel); arrested in 2002.

Coronel Villarreal, Ignacio "Nacho"; born February 1, 1954, Veracruz (Jalisco Cartel); at large.

Correa Alcántara, Wilibaldo "El Willi"; born 1974/75 (La Familia); arrested in June 2009.

Costilla Sánchez, Jorge Eduardo "El Coss" (Gulf Cartel); at large.

Dávila López, José Ramón "El Cholo" (Los Zetas); arrested by Tamaulipas Police in Ciudad Victoria, Tamaulipas, February 9, 2007.

Díaz López, Mateo "El Comandante Mateo" (Los Zetas); arrested by local police in Cunduacán, Tabasco, July 15, 2007.

Díaz Parada, Pedro; (Oaxaca Cartel); arrested by federal police and Army, Oaxaca, January 14, 2007.

Díaz Ramón, Javier "El Java" (Gulf Cartel/Los Zetas); arrested in Veracruz, December 23/24, 2008.

Escárrega Rodríguez, César Alberto (Beltrán Leyva brothers); arrested in Sonora, late June 2009.

Escribano, Jerezano Gonzalo "El Z-18" (Los Zetas); at large.

Esparragoza Moreno, Juan José "El Azul" (The Blue); born Feb. 1, 1954, Chuicopa, Sinaloa (Sinaloa Cartel); at large.

Espinosa Barrón, Alberto (or Alberto Espinosa Loya) "La Fresa" (The Strawberry); (La Familia); arrested by Army in Michoacán, December 29, 2008.

Favela Escobar, Jorge

Félix Gallardo, Miguel Ángel; born January 8, 1946, Badriguato, Sinaloa (Guadalajara/Sinaloa Cartels); arrested April 8, 1989.

Flores Cepeda, Cynthia Janet; born 1991 (Los Zetas); arrested in Fresnillo, Zacatecas, April 9, 2009.

Fonseca Carrillo, Ernesto "Don Neto"; born 1931 or 1942, Santiago de los Caballeros, Sinaloa (Guadalajara/Sinaloa Cartel); arrested April 10, 1985.

Fonseca Núñez, Ofelia (Sinaloa Cartel); arrested January 1999.

Galarza Coronado, Antonio "El Amarillo"; born 1960/61 (Los Zetas); arrested in Nuevo León, late October 2008.

García Abrego, Juan "The Doll"; born September 13, 1944, La Paloma, TX or Matamoros (Gulf Cartel); arrested January 14, 1996, and turned over to FBI.

García Azuara, Cantlicia "La Canti" (Gulf Cartel); arrested in Tamaulipas, April 17, 2007.

García Simental, Eduardo "El Teo"; born in mid- to late-1970s (Tijuana Cartel/El Teo faction; allied with Sinaloa Cartel); at large.

García Urquiza, Ricardo "The Doctor"; (Juárez Cartel); federal agents arrested him in D.F, November 11, 2005.

Garza Azuara, Juan Óscar "El Barbas" (Gulf Cartel/Los Zetas); arrested in Tamaulipas, April 17, 2007.

Godoy Castro, Issac Manuel "Dani"/"Martín" (Tijuana Cartel); Army arrested him in Tijuana, April 22, 2009.

González Castro, Gustavo "El Erótico" (Los Zetas); at large.

González Durán, Jaime "El Hummer" (Los Zetas); federal police arrested him in Reynosa, November 7, 2008.

González Pizaña, Rogelio "El Kelín" (Los Zetas); arrested in Matamoros, October 2004.

Gómez Martínez, Servando "La Tuta" (La Familia); at large.

Guerra Alvarado, Julio César "El Gastón" (Gulf Cartel/Los Zetas); arrested in Cancún, late May 2009.

Guerra Ramírez, Rogelio "El Guerra" (Los Zetas); at large.
Guerrero Silva, Óscar Eduardo "El Winnie Pooh" (Los Zetas); committed suicide in Guadalupe, NL, February 1, 2001.
Guerrero Reyes, Luis Alberto "El Guerrero" (Los Zetas); killed in Matamoros, May 10, 2003.
Gutiérrez Azueres, José Damasio "El Chito"; born 1985/86 (Beltrán Leyva brothers); arrested late June 2009.
Guzmán Loera, Joaquín "El Chapo" ("Shorty"); born April 4, 1954 or 1957, Badiraguato, Sin. (Gulf Cartel); arrested June 11, 1993, and escaped January 1, 2001; at large.
Guzmán Quintaniila, Benjamín "El Benji"; (Tijuana Cartel/El Teo faction); arrested in Baja California, April 7, 2009.
Hernández Barrón, Raúl "The Dutchman" (Los Zetas); arrested in Coatzintla, Veracruz, March 21, 2008.
Hernández Barrón, Víctor Manuel "The Dutchman II" (Los Zetas); Army arrested him in Matamoros, March 14, 2003.
Hernández García, Francisco "Dos Mil" (Two Thousand); (linked to Gulf Cartel/active in Sonora); at large.
Hernández Garza, Rodolfo (or Héctor Fernández Garza) "El Popo" (Los Zetas); arrested Pachuca, April 25, 2009.
Hernández Lechuga, Raul Lucio "El Lucky"/"El Z-16" (Los Zetas); at large.
Herrera Jiménez, Juan "Juan Serna"; born 1973/74, Benito Juárez, Michoacán (La Familia); arrested in 2009.
Higuera Guerrero, Gilberto; born April 15, 1952 (Tijuana Cartel/Sinaloa); arrested August 22, 2004.
Higuera Guerrero, Ismael "El Mayel"; born March 17, 1961 (Tijuana Cartel); arrested May 3, 2000.
Ibarra, Elio (La Familia); at large.
Ibarra Lozano, Omar "El 34" (Beltrán Leyva brothers); arrested by Army in San Pedro Garza García, NL, June 26, 2009.
Ibarra Piedra, Martín (La Familia); at large.
Ibarra Yepis, Prisciliano (Los Zetas); at large.
Izar Castro, Héctor "El Teto" (Los Zetas); arrested in Ciudad Fernández, San Luis Potosí, January 2008.
Labra Avilés, Jesús "El Chuy"; born 1945 (Sinaloa Cartel); arrested March 11, 2000.
Lazcano Lazcano, Heriberto "The Executioner"; (Los Zetas); at large.
Lechuga Licona, Alfonso "El Z-27" (Los Zetas); at large.
López Ibarra, Rodolfo "El Nito"; born in 1976 or 1977, Guayamas, Sonora (Beltrán Leyva brothers); arrested by Army in Apodaca, NL, May 2009.
López López, Edith "Queen of the South"; arrested in Querétaro, early December 2008.
Lorméndez Pitalúa, Omar "El Z-10"/"El Chavita" (Los Zetas); arrested in Lázaro Cárdenas, September 21, 2005.
López, Jorge "El Chuta" (Los Zetas); at large.
López Lara, Isidro "El Colchón" (Los Zetas); arrested in Ciudad Victoria, Tamaulipas, September 11, 2005.

López Lara, Eduardo Salvador "El Z-48"/"El Chavita" (Los Zetas); captured and sentenced to twenty years in prison, February 2008.

Loya Plancarte, Dionisio "El Tío" (La Familia); at large.

Márquez Aguilar, Daniel Enrique "El Chocotorro" (Los Zetas); at large.

Mellado Cruz, Galindo "El Z-9"/"El Mellado" (Los Zetas); at large.

Méndez, Alfredo "El Inge" (La Familia); at large.

Méndez Santiago, Flavio "El Z-10"/"El Amarillo" (Los Zetas); at large.

Méndez Vargas, José de Jesús "El Chango" (La Familia); at large.

Morales González, Nicolás "Mexico"; born 1963/64 (La Familia); arrested in June 2009.

Moreno González, Nazario "El Chayo"/"El Más Loco" (La Familia); at large.

Narro López, Ashly "La Comandante Bombón" (Los Zetas); arrested in Cancún, February 9, 2009.

Nava Cortéz, Israel "El Kaibil"/"The Oyster" (Los Zetas); killed in Fresnillo, Zacatecas, April 2009.

Niño García, César (Beltrán Leyva brothers); arrested by Army in San Pedro Garza, June 26, 2009.

Oliveras Marín, José Ángel "Olivares"; born 1978/79, Benito Juárez, Michoacán (La Familia); arrested in June 2009.

Ortiz Chávez, Javier "El Arqui" (La Familia); arrested in Morelia, May 25, 2009.

Ortega, Jorge "La Gaviota" (La Familia); at large.

Palma, Héctor Luis "El Güero"; born April 29, 1960 or Aug. 25, 1962 or Aug. 26, 1962, Sinaloa (Sinaloa Cartel); arrested June 23 1995 and extradited to U.S. January 19, 2007.

Parra Ramos, José Filberto "La Perra" (The Bitch); (Tijuana Cartel); arrested by Army and Navy personnel in Tijuana, June 6, 2009.

Peña Mendoza, Sergio (Arturo Sánchez Fuentes) "El Cóncord" (Los Zetas/Gulf Cartel); arrested in Reynosa, March 2009.

Peñaloza Soberanes, Alfredo (La Familia); at large.

Peñaloza Soberanes, Antonio (La Familia); at large.

Pérez Rojas, Daniel "El Cachetes" (Los Zetas); arrested in by police in Guatemala, March 24, 2008.

Pineda Villa, Alberto "El Borrador" (Beltrán Leyva brothers); arrested by PFP in Cuernavaca, May 5, 2009.

Pinto Rodríguez, Carlos "La Chata"; (Gulf Cartel); at large.

Porras Cisneros, Vicente Antonio "El Rambo"; born 1973/74; arrested in Oaxaca, April 2008.

Rangel Buendía, Alfredo "L-46"; born 1965/66 (Los Zetas); arrested in D.F. in mid-August 2008.

Raydel Rosalio Lopez "Las Muletas"/"The Crutches" (Tijuana Cartel/El Teo); at large.

Retamoza, Eduardo "The Little Wolf" (Guadalajara/Sinaloa Cartel); executed.

Rejón Aguilar, Jesús Enrique "Z-28"/"El Mamito" (Los Zetas); at large.

Reyes Enríquez, Luis "Z-12" (Los Zetas); arrested June 25, 2008.

Rivera García, Adrián "El Primo Rivera" born Tlapa de Comonfort, Guerrero (Beltrán Leyva brothers); Army captured him in Guerrero, January 8, 2009.

Rivera García Sánchez, Dionisio "El Chacho"; (Los Chachos); killed, May 13, 2002.

Rodríguez Mata, María Antonieta "La Tony" (Los Zetas/Gulf Cartel); arrested February 2004 and extradited to the U.S, October 5, 2007.

Rosales Mendoza, Carlos "El Tísico" (The Consumptive); born February 12, 1963, La Unión, Guerrero (Gulf Cartel); Army arrested him in Morelia, October 24, 2004.

Ruiz Tlapanco, Sergio Enrique "El Tlapa" (Los Zetas); at large.

Salcido Uzeta, Manuel "Crazy Pig"; born Sinaloa (Guadalajara/Sinaloa Cartels); killed October 10, 1991.

Sánchez Arellano, Luis Fernando "El Alineador" (Tijuana Cartel); at large.

Sandoval Gómez, Martín "El Cheyes"; born 1983/84; Fresno, Michoacán; arrested in 2009.

Santillán Tabares, Heriberto "The Engineer" (Juárez Cartel); at large.

Salcedo Gamboa, Gregorio "El Caramuela" or "El Goyo" (Los Zetas); arrested in Matamoros, April 30, 2009.

Solís, Saúl "El Lince" (La Familia); at large.

Soto Parra, Miguel Ángel "El Parra"; AFI arrested him in D.F., January 2, 2009.

Soto Vega, Ivonne (Tijuana Cartel); Army arrested her in Tijuana, 2003.

Sunderland López, Beatriz (Sinaloa Cartel); arrested in Mexico City, November 8, 2007.

Torres Sánchez, Juvenal "El Juve" (Los Chachos).

Torres, Efraín Teodoro "El Z-14"/"El Efra" (Los Zetas); killed in Villarín, Veracruz, March 3, 2007.

Trejo Benavides, Raúl Alberto "El Z-6"/"El Alvin" (Los Zetas); died in May 2002

Treviño Morales, Miguel "El 40" (Los Zetas); at large.

Valencia Cornelio, Armando "Juanito"; born (Milenio Cartel); arrested August 15, 2003.

Valencia Gutiérrez, Baltazar "R" (La Familia); arrested in Ixtapalapa, June 16, 2009.

Valencia Valencia, Luis; (Milenio Cartel); at large.

Vargas García, Nabor "El Debora" (Los Zetas); arrested in Ciudad Carmen, Campeche, April 18, 2007.

Vázquez Mireles, Manuel "El Memeloco" (Gulf Cartel); arrested in Veracruz, March 28, 2003.

Velázquez Cabala, Iván "El Talibán" (Los Zetas); at large.

Vera Calva, Carlos "El Z-7"/"El Vera" (Los Zetas); at large.

Villanueva Madrid, Mario Governor "El Checo" (The Crooked One); born July 2, 1948, Chetumal, Quintana Roo (Juárez Cartel); arrested May 24, 2001.

Villarreal Barragán, Sergio "El Grande" (Beltrán Leyva brothers); at large.

Villarreal Valdez, Édgar "La Barbie"; born August 11, 1973, Laredo, TX (Sinaloa Cartel); at large.

Yarza Solano, Luis; born 1972/1973 (La Familia); arrested in June 2009.

Zambada, Ismael "El Mayo"; born 1948, Sinaloa (Sinaloa Cartel); at large.

Zambada, Reynaldo "El Rey"; born Sinaloa (Sinaloa Cartel); at large.
Zatarain Beliz, Ernesto "El Traca" (Los Zetas); at large.
Zúñiega Huizar, Laura "Miss Sinaloa of 2008" (Juárez Cartel); tortured and executed by Los Zetas, December 2008.

Appendix 2

Ex-GAFES Involved in Drug Trafficking

Original Zetas	Military Ties	Specialty and Area of Operations	Status
Arellano Domínguez, Braulio "El Gonzo" or "El Z- 20"	Joined the Army February 22, 1993; deserted June 21, 1999	Sharpshooter; in charge of the main *plazas* in Quintana Roo and Veracruz	At large
Castrejón Peña, Víctor Nazario	Joined the Army on September 1, 1988; On September 30, 1999; he resigned from active duty	Assassinations; hit man for Cárdenas Guillén	At large
Jerezano Escribano, Gonzalo "El Z-18" or "El Cuije"	Joined the Army on April 25, 1992; deserted on May 11, 2000		At large
Dávila López, José Ramón "El Cholo" Alias: Antonio Torres Hernández and David Rubio Conde	Joined Army on April 16, 1995; reached rank of sergeant in GAFES; on February 16, 2001, resigned from active duty and entered the reserves; former member of the Panamerican Protection Service	Excellent marksman; suspect in the kidnapping of a married couple, Ricardo González and Nelly Peña; worked directly under Omar Lorméndez Pitalúa and Heriberto Lazcano Lazcano	Tamaulipas police captured him in Ciudad Victoria, Tamaulipas, on February 9, 2007
Díaz López, Mateo "Comandante Mateo"	In 1996 joined the Army's XV Motorized Cavalry Regiment and then the GAFES; deserted on September 20, 1998	Recruiting and training; graduated from the Conalep in Tabasco in electro-mechanics; in charge of Nuevo León *plaza* until being moved to Cunducacán, Tabasco at the beginning of 2006; in his new post, he killed members of the competing Flores Torruco and Guízar Valencia families; known as the most bloodthirsty of Los Zetas	Local police captured him in Cunduacán, Tabasco, on July 15, 2007
González Castro, Gustavo "El Erótico"	Joined the infantry on March 22, 1990; promoted to corporal in 1995; resigned from the army and joined the reserves on August 1, 1998; and served in the Ministry of National Defense (SEDENA)	Trained in assault operations during seven years in the military; extremely dangerous; helped free 25 fellow narco-traffickers from a prison in Apatzingán, Michoacán	At large

González Dúran, Jaime "El Hummer"	Joined Air Force Nov. 15, 1991; deserted February 24, 1999	Accused of killing popular entertainer Valentín Elizalde in November 2006 after the so-called "Gallo de Oro" had sung "*A Mis Enemigos*" (To my enemies), which Los Zetas considered a warning to them from El Chapo; also wanted in the U.S. for conspiracy, importation and distribution of cocaine and marijuana as well as money laundering; extremely violent; active in plazas in Nuevo León, Tabasco, Michoacán, Tamaulipas (Reynosa and MiguelAlemán), D.F, and Mexico State; extremely dangerous	Federal police captured him in Reynosa on November 7, 2008
Guerrero Silva, Óscar Eduardo "El Winnie Pooh"	Joined 70th Infantry Battalion on January 28, 1992; ex-member of General Services Group EMP; promoted to corporal in 1993; deserted on November 26, 1999	Lieutenant of Cárdenas Guillén	Committed suicide by shooting himself in the head with a 9 mm pistol in Guadalupe, NL, on February 1, 2001
Guerrero Reyes, Luis Alberto "El Guerrero"	Joined 70th Infantry Battalion on March 1, 1987; promoted to corporal on November 1, 1990; became member of Brigada de Fusileros Paracaidistas (BFP), the elite unit before formation of the GAFES, on June 17, 1988; promoted to sergeant on March 1, 1992; left Army Jan. 4, 1999; expert in explosives, martial arts, and grenade launchers	Matamoros *plaza*	Killed in by four hit men riding in a white taxi and possible members of a rival cartel in Matamoros on May 10, 2003
Guerra Ramírez, Rogelio "El Guerra"	Joined the Army on August 25, 1989; resigned on April 18, 1999		At large

Hernández Barrón, Raúl "The Dutchman I" or "Flander I" or "Flandes"	Enlisted in the Army on September 1, 1993; left active duty on September 1, 1999, and joined the reserves	Trafficking drug shipments into the U.S. through the northern region of Veracruz state; likely involved in the assassination of Valentín Elizalde	Elements of the Army and PGR captured him in Coatzintla, Veracruz, on March 21, 2008
Hernández Barrón, Víctor Manuel "El Flander II"			Army special forces captured him in Matamoros on March 14, 2003; sentenced to 29 years in prison
Hernández Lechuga, Raúl Lucio "El Lucky" or "Z-16" or "El Luki"	Joined the Army on September 6, 1996; resigned on October 24, 1997	Chief of Los Zetas in Puebla	At large
Ibarra Yepis, Prisciliano			At large
Lazcano Lazcano, Heriberto "El Lazca" or "The Executioner" or "El Z-3" or "El Verdugo"	Joined the Army on June 5, 1991 at the age of 28; promoted to corporal on July 5, 1993; selected to join GAFES; resigned on March 27, 1998	Leader of Los Zetas; ex-policeman; believed to have killed Francisco Ortiz Franco; co-editor of the Tijuana weekly, *Zeta* (No relation to paramilitaries); current leader of Los Zetas; trained by GAFE in combat, intelligence, and counter-insurgency	At large
Lechuga Licona, Alfonso "El Z- 27" or "El Canitas"	Joined the Army on December 1, 1991; deserted on August 19, 1994	Kidnapping; frontier region of Tamaulipas	Captured by state police in San Luis Potosí on May 25, 2006
Lorméndez Pitalúa, Omar "El Z 10" or "El Chavita" or "El Pita"		Controled the Nuevo Laredo *plaza* along with Iván Velásquez Caballero, Mateo Díaz López, Hector Sauceda Gamboa y Miguel Ángel Treviño; one of top four commanders at time of his arrest	Thanks to an anonymous tip, police captured him in Lázaro Cárdenos on September 21, 2005
López, Jorge "El Chuta"	Joined the Army on October 1, 1979; Deserted on September 17, 1981	Martial arts, explosives, ambushes, guerrilla tactics; instructs new Zetas; reportedly trained in the U.S.	At large

López Lara, Isidro "El Colchón" or "Adrián Rodríguez Alarcón" or "Isidro Lara Flores" or "El Interno" or "El Colchas"	Enlisted in the Army on August 16, 1996; on May 16, 2001, resigned from active duty and joined the reserves	Specialist in kidnappings and murders	Captured in Ciudad Victoria, Tamaulipas, on September 11, 2005
López Lara, Eduardo Salvador "El Chavita" or "El Z-48"		Helped free Ramón "El Cholo" Dávila López from the Matamoros police; faciliated the landing of cocaine shipments at a clandestine airfield in "Las Amarillas" ranch in China, Nuevo León (now a Zeta training camp); and participated in murders and kidnappings	Captured and sentenced to twenty years in prison in late February 2008
Márquez Aguilar, Daniel Enrique "El Chocotorro"	No information is found for Aguilar in SEDENA's online information		At large
Mellado Cruz, Galindo "El Mellado" or "El Z-9"	Joined the Army on Sept. 1, 1992; Resigned on May 1, 1999		At large
Méndez Santiago, Flavio "El Amarillo" or "El Z-10"	Joined the Army on Oct. 16, 1993; resigned on July 4, 1997	Drug trafficking	At large
Pérez Rojas, Daniel "El Cachetes"	Joined the Army on May 23, 1997; Deserted on November 26, 1999; also trained by the U.S.	Second in command, and responsible for the turf battles with rival cartels throughout the country; also helped run Los Zeta operations in Guatemala	Captured by Guatemalan police in Guatemala on April 8, 2008
Rejón Aguilar, Jesús Enrique "El Mamito" or "El Z-28"	Joined the Army on April 5, 1993; deserted November 26, 1999; another version indicates that he joined infantry on Aug. 1991; promoted to corporal in 1993; deserted on Sept. 13, 1998	Expert in explosives; sharp-shooter; in charge of two Tamaulipas plazas with Efraín Teodoro Torres; active in Quintana Roo, Veracruz, and Tamaulipas (Ciudad Miguel Alemán and Ciudad Camargo)	At large
Ruíz Tlapanco, Sergio Enrique "El Tlapa"	Joined the Army on March 6, 1988; Resigned on November 16, 1999	Mountain operations, survival techniques, and counterinsurgency operation; active in municipality of Cárdenas, Tabasco, and, possibly, Campeche	At large

Soto Parra, Miguel Ángel "El Parra"	Joined the Army on May 2, 1994; Resigned on May 1, 1999; head of the Federal Judicial Police in Tamaulipas	Former head of the Federal Judicial Police in Tamaulipas Assisted Osiel Cárdenas Guillén in drug trafficking as a dirty cop in Tamaulipas	AFI arrested him in Coyoacán in southern D.F. on January 2, 2009
Torres, Efraín Teodoro "El Efra" or "El Z-14"	Joined the infantry division on August 1, 1991; promoted to corporal in 1993; deserted September 13, 1998	Controlled two *plazas* in Tamaulipas with Jesús Enrique Rejón Aguilar (Ciudad Miguel Alemán and Ciudad Camargo)	Shot in dispute over winner of a clandestine horse race in rural Villarín, Veracruz, on March 3, 2007
Trejo Benavides, Raúl Alberto "El Alvin" or "El Z-6"	Joined the Army on May 3, 1991; Resigned on March 16, 1999	Accused of participating with Raúl Hernández Barrón in the murder of singer Valentín Elizalde	Shot by rivals and abandoned by his own men; for lack of medical attention, he died in a run-down Matamoros hotel in May 2002; the La Paz funeral home returned his remains to his native Villahermosa
Vargas García, Nabor "El Debora"	Joined the Army on June 28, 1995; On July 1, 1999 he resigned from active duty (and the Presidential Guard's assault battalion) and joined the reserves	Ran a Zeta unit in Tabasco, Campeche, and Chiapas	Captured with twenty of his henchmen after a gunfight in Ciudad del Carmen, Campeche, on April 18, 2007
Vera Calva, Carlos "El Vera" or "El Z-7"	Enlisted in Army Oct. 11, 1989; deserted on Nov. 16, 1999		At large
Zatarain Beliz, Ernesto "El Traca"	Joined the Army on May 1, 1993; On February 16, 1998 he resigned from active duty and joined the reserves	Communications and radio interceptions	At large

Source: "Problema de seguridad nacional en México, los 'Zetas' (desertores del Ejército Mexicano)" "*Soluciones de Seguridad Global*, Belt Ibérica www.belt.es; "El poder de los 'zetas'," Presidencia de la República, "Suma cártel del golfo 5 golpes en su contra," October 30, 2004; "Acorralan a 'Los Zetas,'" *Zeta* weekly No. 1689; Miguel Ángel Pérez López, "Asesinos de Policías de Victoria quedan arraigados, *HoyTamaulipas*, September 15, 2005; "Dictan 20 años de prisión contra el 'Z-48,'" *¡Ehui!*, February 23, 2008; various articles by veteran journalist Miguel Ángel Granados Chapa; and PGR bulletins. Mexican authorities first spoke of thirty-one original Zetas; however, the number in this cast of characters has varied from report to report. Gabriela Regina Arias assisted in preparing this appendix.

Appendix 3

Women and Narco-Trafficking

Scholars have paid scant attention to the role of women in narco-trafficking, mainly because it has traditionally been viewed as a male occupation. In the case of Mexico, the existence of a "macho" culture also may have contributed to a lack of examination. But, one must also consider that there is a relatively small body of academic literature on narco-trafficking in general, and the proliferation of material is a recent phenomenon. The murder, capture, and flight of drug lords have amplified the prominence of women as narco-empires are bequeathed to them. Below are several generalizations about the role of women:

1. Many have come from or married into narco-trafficking families.
2. Some assumed leadership roles after the death or incarceration of family members. For example, Patricia, Martha, and Emma Amezcua Contreras allegedly have struggled to operate the greatly debilitated Colima Cartel now that key male relatives languish behind bars. The media attribute a major role to accountant Enedina Arellano Félix within the AFO or Tijuana Cartel; however, neither law enforcement officials in Mexico nor the United States give credence to this characterization. Members within the AFO reportedly dismiss the idea that she exerts influence within this syndicate, now dominated by her nephew and son who are under attack by Teodoro "El Teo" García Simental.
3. Women are increasingly accused of planning and carrying out kidnappings and executions; for example, the *Zeta* weekly reported that three women who forged documents—Perla and María del Carmen Cervantes and Nadia Teresa de Jesús—used a chainsaw to execute Sergio "El Tantán" Espinoza Flores for failing to turn over a $7,000 check received from a client.
4. Their imprisonment rates are increasing. There used to be one female for every for every four males charged in Tijuana; now the ratio is three-to-one. Below is the number of women imprisoned for drug-related crimes in Tijuana in recent years:
    a. 100 (2003)
    b. 98 (2004)
    c. 109 (2005)
    d. 127 (2006) [Tripp, *"Mujeres en el crimen."*]

The chief of the Special Forces Unit in Sinaloa noted that 15 percent of the 326 suspects apprehended in 2005 were women; the following year females constituted one-quarter of the 247 individuals captured. [Pedro Miguel, "Algo sobre las narcas," *Navegaciones*, October 3, 2007 *www.navegaciones. blogspot.com/2007/10/algo-sobre-las-narcas.html.*]

5. There are several categories of women involved in the drug underground:

a. Cartel leaders such as Delia Patricia "Ma Baker" Buendía Gutiérrez, who concentrated on retail drug sales;

b. Empowered women who gain near mythic fame through their family ties, beauty, derring-do, and conniving such as Sandra Ávila Beltrán about whom *corridos* have been composed. Below is *La fiesta en la sierra* by *Los Tucanes* de Tijuana:
"The party was starting/ and the band was warmed up/ no one else was expected/ everyone had arrived at the party/ but then a rumble was heard/ and a helicopter landed/ the big boss gave the order to lower weapons// A beautiful lady stepped out/ with her AK-47 and camouflaged fatigues/ and the celebration began/ they knew who she was/ she was the famous Queen of the Pacific and all its beaches/ the great business woman/ a big-shot lady" (rough translation by James Creechan);

c. Family members (by birth or marriage) aspire to important roles such as running businesses and money laundering;

d. Spies, who use seductive charms to gain information from law-enforcement agents or capos of other cartels; as described in the table below, Los Zetas use "The Panthers" (*Las Panteras*) to negotiate with the police, Army officers, mayors, and other public officials. If the parlays break down, the Panther is authorized to kill her interlocutor;

e. "Mules," or *muleras,* who transport drugs across the border, including a Colombian woman who had two pounds of cocaine surgically implanted in her buttocks. There is an interesting study of this along the Chihuahua-Texas frontier by Howard Campbell ["Female Drug Smugglers on the U.S.-Mexico Border: Gender, Crime, and Empowerment," *Anthropological Quarterly* 81, no. 1 (2008): 233-67];

f. "Lovers" such as El Chapo's prison girlfriend, Zulema Hernández Ramírez, who was later executed in Ecatepec, Mexico State by Los Zetas on December 17, 2008; and

g. "Trophy Women" and beauty queens who are voluptuous and beautiful recipients of expensive jewelry, automobiles, clothing, and apartments from drug barons, exhibit them at public functions. A prime example is Laura Elena Zúñiga Huizar, Miss Sinaloa 2008, who was arrested on Dec 22, 2008. As in Colombia, some Mexican mothers groom their daughters to be girlfriends of drug barons as described in a novel, later made into a television series, by Gustavo Bolívar Moreno, *Sin Tetas no Hay Paraíso* (Bogotá: Quintero Editores, 2007).

Alleged Female Narco-Trafficker or "Queenpins"	Date and Place of Birth	Cartel	Specialty	Status
Amezcua Contreras, Patricia, Martha and Emma*	Sisters of imprisoned Amezcua Contreras brothers, Jesús and Adán	Colima	Impotent in light of the imprisonment of Jesús and Adán	At large
Arellano Félix, Enedina	Sister of Benjamín, Ramón, and other siblings of the Arellano Félix clan	Arellano Félix Organization (AFO or Tijuana)	Although undoubtedly aware of AFO activities, law enforcement agencies have no arrest warrant for her and doubt that she is engaged in criminal pursuits	No arrest warrants pending
Ávila Beltrán, Sandra "La Reina del Pacífico"	Born in 1961, Baja Calif; third generation in narco-affairs (her uncle Miguel Ángel Félix Gallardo); girl friend of El Mayo Zambada and Nacho Coronel; and her husband is Colombian dealer, Juan Diego "El Tigre" Espinosa Ramírez	Sinaloa (Beltrán Leyva brothers)	Used her seductive powers (enhanced by plastic surgery and hair color) to obtain allies, seal business deals, and deceive the police; as a result, she became an important financial operative and money-launderer***	Captured in D.F. on September 28, 2007; imprisoned in Santa Martha de Acatitla (D.F.)
Buendia Gutiérrez, Delia Patricia "Ma Baker"****		Neza Cartel Based in D.F. suburb, Nezahualcóyotle	Headed, along with Carlos "El Águila" Morales Correo, the sale in the Tepito market of "surplus" cocaine from several cartels controlled sales from small sellers Ecatepec, Texcoco, Chalco, Coacalco, Nezahualcóyotle, and other municipalities in the D.F. area; also accused of killing	Arrested by federal police on Aug. 20, 2002; La Palma prison

				several police officers
Cázares Salazar, Blanca Margarita "La Emperatriz"+	Her husband Arturo Meza Gaspar (who may be dead) and her children (Arturo, Gipsy, and Lizbeth) are wanted in U.S. for money laundering	Sinaloa Cartel with links to Colombia's Cártel del Valle	Believed to launder money through five cells of the Sinaloa Cartel, which is tied to Colombia's Cártel del Valle	At large
Contreras González, Ofelia		Sinaloa Cartel	Stored arms	Imprisoned in 2002
Fonseca Núñez, Ofelia +	Daughter of Ernesto Fonseca Carrillo	Here father was a top leader of the Guadalajara Cartel		Arrested in January 1999; imprisoned in Almoloya de Juárez
Cynthia Janet Flores Cepeda	18-year-old close friend of Zeta leader Israel "El Kaibil"/"The Oyster" Nava Cortéz	Los Zetas	Reportedly, a recruiter of females, but she may have served only as a companion to Nava Cortéz	Arrested in Fresnillo, Zacatecas, With Nava Cortéz on April 9, 2009 ++
García Azuara, Cantlicia "La Canti"	Sister of Josué "El Barbas" Garza	Gulf Cartel	Financial operations; money-laundering	Arrested in Tamaulipas on April 17, 2007
López López, Edith "Queen of the South"	Ex-wife of Raul "El Vaquero"/"The Cowboy" Núñez Morales, who ran cells of small drug sellers in Querétaro		Drug dealer in Querétaro	Captured in Querétaro in early December 2008
Monje Aguirre, Ana Cristina or Linda Pánuco Olson "La Cristina" or "La Escarlet"		Tijuana Cartel		
Narro López, Ashly "La Comandante Bombón"/"Candy"		Los Zetas	Leader of "*Las Panteras,*" a female unit whose primary task is to negotiate accords	Army captured her in connection with the murder of General Tello

			with military officers, the police, mayors, and other authorities. If talks break down, Las Panteras are trained to kill their interlocutors	Quiñones in Cancún on February 9, 2009 +++
Rodríguez Mata, María Antonieta "La Tony"++++	Former police officer in Tamaulipas	Gulf Cartel	Transported more than five tons of cocaine from Guatemala to Texas	Arrested February 2004; extradited to U.S. on October 5, 2007
Soto Vega, Ivonne "La Pantera"	Enjoyed close relationship with Arellano Félix brothers; and a "*compadrazgo*" relation with "El Chuy" Labra Áviles and "El Mayel" Higuera Guerrero	Tijuana Cartel	Money-laundering via money-exchanges, enabling her to launder $120 million in three years. She used funds to purchase real estate +++++	Arrested by Army in 2003 in Tijuana
Sunderland López, Beatriz ++++++	Girlfriend of Petro "El Peri" Barraza Urtusuástegui, who transferred money from various money-exchanges (*casas de cambio*) in Puebla and the D.F. to Chicago's Harris Bank, where a $2.7 million account had been frozen	Sinaloa Cartel	Participated in financial operations via *casas de cambio* in Puebla and the D.F. allegedly to finance drug sales between Colombians and the Sinaloa Cartel	Arrested November 8, 2007 in Mexico City
Tomoy Mars Yu	Wife of Zhenli Ye Gon		Her husband worked with cartels in Michoacán, the entry point for pre-cursor drugs that he used to produce methamphetamines	Arrested in 2007
Zúñiga Huizar, Laura Elena; "Miss Sinaloa of 2008" and "HispanoAmerican Queen of 2008"	Born January 3, 1985, Culiacán, Sinaloa		Juárez Cartel in which her boyfriend Ángel Orlando García Urquiza is a leader	Arrested on Dec. 22, 2008; subsequently released for lack of evidence

*   Hernández Tripp, "Mujeres en el crimen."

**   Daniel Blancas Madrigal, "La Reina del Pacífico y Enedina Arellano Félix: una seductora, violenta y amante de las fiestas; la otra, conservadora y discreta; conozca a las mujeres del narco," *La Crónica*, September 30, 2007.

***   Madrigal, "La Reina del Pacífico y Endedina Arellano Félix."

****   Library of Congress, *Criminality and Terrorist Activity in Mexico*, 1999-2002 www.loc.gov/. *R*eportedly, the following relatives worked with her: María Tiburcia Cázares Pérez, Blanca Armida Aguirre Sánchez, Lizbeth Mesa Cázares, and Gipsy Meza Cázares; see, Gustavo Castillo García, "Aumenta el número de mujeres enredadas en el mundo del narco," *La Jornada*, December 28, 2008; Dirección de Comunicación Social, *Nezahualcóyotl*, May 27, 2004; and Martín Moreno, "Los Cázares," *Excelsior*, December 18, 2007.

+   Procuraduría General de la República, "Ofilia Fonseca Núñez, daughter of Ernesto Fonseca Carrillo, to close to 16 years in jail," Press Release 394/00, July 27, 2000 www.pgr.gob.mx.

++   "Matan a un Kaibil en tiroteo en Zacatecas," *El Universal*, April 10, 2009.

+++   "Reclutan 'Zetas' mujeres para integrar célula: 'Las Panteras,'" *Terra*, March 3, 2009.

++++   Castillo García, "Aumenta el número de mujeres enredadas en el mundo del narco."

+++++   Hernández Tripp, "Mujeres en crimen."

++++++   "Cae operador financiero del 'Cártel del Pacífico,'" *Terra*, November 8, 2007.

Appendix 4

Mexican Police, Anti-Drug, and Intelligence Services

Period	Police/Crime	Anti-Drugs	Intelligence Service(s)
Porfiriato (1876-1911)			
Porfirio Díaz (1876-1911)	**Rurales**		**Reestablished Special Corps of the General Staff**
	Federal Public Prosecutor (MPF) established under Ministry of Justice and Public Education (Secretaría de Justicia e Instrucción Pública-- SJIP)		**Presidential General Staff or Estado Mayor Presidencial—EMP** (created May 7, 1895)
Revolution (1911-20)			
Francisco I. Madero (1911-1913)			**EMP** (authorized on December 11, 1911, as part of reorganization of the Army)
First Chief of Constitutionalist Army, **Venustiano Carranza**	**In 1917 Constitution, the MPF was given responsibility for "penal actions" and the Judicial Police; creation of the Attorney General's Office (PGR)**		**First Section of Army** created in 1915 to spy on foes for control of Mexico
			Carranza reorganized the general staffs of the Constitutional Army into **EMP** (June 26, 1916)
			Investigative Service created in Carranza's Interior Ministry (1918)
Post-Revolution (1920-2000)			
Plutarco Elías Calles (1924-28 and de facto chief executive from 1928 to 1934.	Attorney General's Office (**PGR**), which controlled the Federal Judicial Police (**PJF**)	Department of Public Health (**Departamento de Salubridad-- DSP**) created in 1924 under Ministry of Health	**Presidential Aides-de-Camp** (Ayudantía de la Presidencia)
1930s	**Federal Highway Police (PFC)** under Ministry of Communications and Public Workers (SCOP), which was changed to Ministry of Communications and Transport (SCT) in 1959		Confidential Department (**DC**) Office of Social and Political Information (**OIPS**)
WWII	**PGR**, which controlled the Federal Judicial Police (**PJF**)	**DSP**	Office of Political Information—**OPI** (Under Secretary of Government);
	PFC (SCOP)		
Manuel Ávila Camacho (1940-46)			Converted **Ayudantía de la Presidencial into EMP (S-2)**
			Army (**S-2**)
Miguel Alemán Valdés (1946-52) ; Ruiz Cortines (1952-58); and Adolfo	**PGR**, which controlled the Federal Judicial Police (**PJF**)	**DFS** (**See** column to left)	**DFS**
	PFC (SCOP)	**DSP**	**EMP (S-2)**
			Army (**S-2**)

López Mateos (1958-64)	**Federal Security Directorate (DFS)**, which was created in early 1987 under the control of the presidency; Ruiz Cortines placed **DFS** under Interior Ministry **PFC (SCT)**		
Gustavo Diaz Ordaz (1964-70); **Luis Echeverría** (1970-76); and **José López Portillo** (1976-82)	Secret Service of the Federal District (**SSDF**) **PGR, PJF, and DFS** **Brigada Blanca** and **Los Halcones** Fernando "Don Fernando" Gutiérrez Barrios (FGB) headed **DFS** from 1964 to 1976; in 1977 López Portillo named Javier García Paniagua to head the **DFS**, with FGB becoming sub-secretary of Interior; Paniagua was followed by by Nazar Haro in 1981; José Antonio Zorrilla Pérez, served from 1982 to 1986 **PFC (SCT)**	**DFS** (Interior); see column to left **General Direction of Social and Political Investigations (DGIPS)**	**DFS** **EMP (S-2)** **Army (S-2)** **Naval Force of the Pacific collects intelligence in concert with S-2**
Miguel de la Madrid (1982-88)	**PGR (PJF)** **PFC (SCT)**	**DFS** Disbanded November 29, 1985 in the aftermath of the Tlatelolco massacre, Camarena affair, the Brigada Blanca, los Halcones, and other embarrassments, including spying on de la Madrid; **DFS** replaced by the Directorate of Investigation and National Security (**DISEN**), headed by Pedro Vázquez Colmenares, under the Interior Ministry; this weak institution and the **DGIPS** evolved into **CISEN** **National Coordination of National Security (NCNS)** established under Interior Ministry	**DFS** (See comment in middle column) **DISEN** **NCNS** **Army (S-2)** **EMP (S-2)** **Naval Force of the Pacific collects intelligence in concert with S-2**
Carlos Salinas (1988-94)	**PGR (PJF)** **PFC (SCT)** **Special Anti-Organized Crime Unit (UEDO)** created under **PGR** in February 1994	Col. Jorge Carrillo Olea and Jorge Tello Peón created the **Center for Planning for Drug Control (CENDRO)** In March 1993 Attorney General Jorge Carpizo MacGregor established the **National Institute for Combating Drugs (INCD)** **NCNS**	**Financial Intelligence Unit (Unidad de Inteligencia Financiera** or **UIF** (Finance Ministry) **Center for Research and National Security Nacional (CISEN)** created in February 1989— with Col. Jorge Carrillo Olea as its first director; in a rebuke to FGB, Salinas removed the spy agency from the purview of the Interior Ministry before dismissing FGB in January 1993[1] **Army (S-2)** **EMP (S-2)** **Naval Force of the Pacific collects intelligence in concert with S-2**

UIF (Finance Ministry)

Zedillo (1994-2000)	PGR **Federal Preventative Police (PFP)** formed in 1999 from the Third Military Police Brigade, the Federal Immigration Police, the Federal Highway Police (**PFC**), as well as the small Federal Fiscal Police, the Federal Immigration Police, and some Navy personnel. **National Public Security System (SNSP)** created in 1995 under the Interior Ministry to coordinate anti-crime measures between the federal government and states	In 1997 Zedillo abolished the **INCD** in the wake of the Gutiérrez Rebollo scandal; he then created the **Special Prosecutor for Crimes Against Health (FEADS)** under the direction of a civilian, Mariano Herrán Salvatti.[2] Under **FEADS** were the Border Rapid Response Groups (**GRRF**) and the Special Anti-Money Laundering Unit (**UECLD**)	CISEN EMP (S-2) Army (S-2) **Naval Force of the Pacific collects intelligence in concert with S-2** UIF (Finance Ministry)
Post PRI **Fox** (2000-06)	**Ministry of Public Security (SSP)** authorized in 1999 and created in 2000[3] **Subsecretaría de Estrategía e Inteligencia Policial (SSP/PFP)** **National Council of Public Security** to help formulate over-all security policy On November 2001, the **PJF** was succeeded by the **Federal Investigative Agency (AFI)**	In January 2003, Attorney General (AG) Macedo de la Concha abolished **FEADS**, which he described as a "dung heap" of corruption. In June 2003 the AG merged remnants of **FEADS** with the PGR's **UEDO to form** the **Specialized Unit to Investigate Organized Crime (SIEDO)** within the **PGR** under José Luis Santiago Vasconcelos Also created was the **National Center for the Planning, Analysis, and Information for Combating Crime (CENAPI)** to integrate information about organized crime and collect intelligence about narco-activities, money-laundering, and arms trafficking.	CISEN Fox cut the budget of **CISEN**, believing that it was a political tool of the PRI; the agency lost resources and personnel to the SSP, AFI, and PFP; for instance, General García Luna took the **Anti-terrorism Group (GAT)** to the **PFP**. EMP (S-2) Army (S-2) **Naval Force of the Pacific collects intelligence in concert with S-2** SSP (PFP's General Coordination of Intelligence) PGR (General Coordination of Planning, SIEDO, and CENAPI) UIF (Finance Ministry)
Calderón (2006-)	PGR (SIEDO and CENAPI) **National Council of Public Security** SSP/ Subsecretaría de Estrategía e Inteligencia Política (SSP/PFP) **President sought to merge the PFP and AFI into the Federal Police** On May 30/ June 2, 2009, the president abolished the **AFI** and **PFP** In their places, he established **Federal Ministerial Police (PFM)**—with former AFI chief Nicandra Castro Escarpulli as the first director; Facundo Rosas Rosas, who was named general commissioner of the new **Federal Police,** will report to his ally, the secretary of SSP	SIEDO In 2008 former director Noë Ramírez Mandujano was imprisoned for accepting bribes from the Beltrán Leyva brothers; in September 2009, Marisela Morales Ibáñez became head of **SIEDO**.	CISEN Calderón (1) named confidant Guillermo Valdés Castellanos as director (2) greatly increased the agency budget and staff; and (3) established a training facility for spies EMP (S-2) Army (S-2)—with a staff of 272 in mid-2007 **Naval Force of the Pacific collects intelligence in concert with S-2** SSP (PFP's General Coordination of Intelligence) PGR (General Coordination of Planning, SIEDO, and CENAPI) UIF (Finance Ministry)

Sources: Sergio Aguayo, *La Charola: Una historia de los servicios de inteligencia en México* (Mexico City: Grijalbo, 2001); Benjamin Reames, "Police Forces in Mexico: A Profile," USMEX 2003-04 Working Paper Series, originally presented at the Center for U.S.-Mexican Studies, May 15-17, 2003; Presidencia de la República, Estado Mayor Presidencial" *www.emp.fox.presidencia.gob.mx/sintesis.html*; "Los servicios de inteligencia en méxico, "Coparmex, November 21, 2001; Jorge Luis Sierra, "Fallas de la Inteligencia militar," *El Universal*, July 20, 2007; "Desaparece la AFI; nace la Policía Federal Ministerial, *El Universal*, May 29, 2009; excellent articles and academic papers by Raúl Benítez Manaut, various interviews with Juan Gabriel Valencia Benavides; off-the-record conversations with U.S. and Mexican intelligence personnel; and documents provided by Lic. Fred Álvarez Palafox.

1.   Other director-generals of CISEN were Alejandro Alegre Robiela (1990-94), Jorge Tello Peón (1994-99), Eduardo Medina Mora (2000-04), Jaime Domingo López Buitrón (2005-06), and Guillermo Valdés Castellanos (2006-present).
2.   On January 24, 2009, the Chiapas state government arrested the former federal drug tsar for embezzlement, with additional accusations ranging from links to drug cartels to torture of political prisoners; see, Óscar Gutiérrez, "Encarcelan a Herrán Salvatti en Chiapas," *El Universal*, January 26, 2009.
3.   Its directors have been Alejandro Gertz Manero (2000-2004), Ramón Martín Huerta (2004-05), Eduardo Medina Mora (2005-06); and Genaro García Luna (2006-present)

Appendix 5

Annual Causes of Death in the United States

Tobacco	435,000[1]
Poor Diet and Physical Inactivity	365,000[1]
Alcohol	85,000[1]
Microbial Agents	75,000[1]
Toxic Agents	55,000[1]
Adverse Reactions to Prescription Drugs	32,000[2]
Suicide	30,622[3]
Incidents Involving Firearms	29,000[1]
Motor Vehicle Crashes	26,347[1]
Homicide	20,308[4]
Sexual Behaviors	20,000[1]
All Illicit Drug Use, Direct and Indirect	17,000[1, 5] [13]
Non-Steroidal Anti-Inflammatory Drugs Such As Aspirin	7,600[6]
Marijuana	0[7]

1. (2000): "The leading causes of death in 2000 were tobacco (435,000 deaths; 18.1% of total US deaths), poor diet and physical inactivity (400,000 deaths; 16.6%), and alcohol consumption (85,000 deaths; 3.5%). Other actual causes of death were microbial agents (75,000), toxic agents (55,000), motor vehicle crashes (43,000), incidents involving firearms (29,000), sexual behaviors (20,000), and illicit use of drugs (17,000)." (Note: According to a correction published by the Journal on Jan. 19, 2005, "On page 1240, in Table 2, '400,000 (16.6)' deaths for 'poor diet and physical inactivity' in 2000 should be '365,000 (15.2).' A dagger symbol should be added to 'alcohol consumption' in the body of the table and a dagger footnote should be added with 'in 1990 data, deaths from alcohol-related crashes are included in alcohol consumption deaths, but not in motor vehicle deaths. In 2000 data, 16,653 deaths from alcohol-related crashes are included in both alcohol consumption and motor vehicle death categories." Source: *Journal of the American Medical Association*, Jan. 19, 2005, Vol. 293, No. 3, p. 298.)
   Source:
   Mokdad, Ali H., PhD, James S. Marks, MD, MPH, Donna F. Stroup, PhD, MSc, Julie L. Gerberding, MD, MPH, "Actual Causes of Death in the United States, 2000," *Journal of the American Medical Association*, March 10, 2004, Vol. 291, No. 10, pp. 1238, 1241.

2.   (2000): "Illicit drug use is associated with suicide, homicide, motor-vehicle injury, HIV infection, pneumonia, violence, mental illness, and hepatitis. An estimated 3 million individuals in the United States have serious drug problems. Several studies have reported an undercount of the number of deaths attributed to drugs by vital statistics; however, improved medical treatments have reduced mortality from many diseases associated with illicit drug use. In keeping with the report by McGinnis and Foege, we included deaths caused indirectly by illicit drug use in this category. We used attributable fractions to compute the number of deaths due to illicit drug use. Overall, we estimate that illicit drug use resulted in approximately 17000 deaths in 2000, a reduction of 3000 deaths from the 1990 report."
Source: Mokdad, Ali H., PhD, James S. Marks, MD, MPH, Donna F. Stroup, PhD, MSc, Julie L. Gerberding, MD, MPH, "Actual Causes of Death in the United States, 2000," *Journal of the American Medical Association*, March 10, 2004, Vol. 291, No. 10, p. 1242.

3.   (2003): The US Centers for Disease Control reports that in 2003, there were a total of 31,484 deaths from suicide in the US.
Source: Hoyert, Donna L., PhD, Heron, Melonie P., PhD, Murphy, Sherry L., BS, Kung, Hsiang-Ching, PhD; Division of Vital Statistics, "Deaths: Final Data for 2003," *National Vital Statistics Reports*, Vol. 54, No. 13 (Hyattsville, MD: National Center for Health Statistics, April 19, 2006), p. 5, Table C.

4.   (2003): The US Centers for Disease Control reports that in 2003, there were a total of 17,732 deaths from homicide in the US.
Source: Hoyert, Donna L., PhD, Heron, Melonie P., PhD, Murphy, Sherry L., BS, Kung, Hsiang-Ching, PhD; Division of Vital Statistics, "Deaths: Final Data for 2003," *National Vital Statistics Reports*, Vol. 54, No. 13 (Hyattsville, MD: National Center for Health Statistics, April 19, 2006), p. 5, Table C.

5.   (2003): "In 2003, a total of 28,723 persons died of drug-induced causes in the United States (Tables 21 and 22). The category 'drug-induced causes' includes not only deaths from dependent and nondependent use of drugs (legal and illegal use), but also poisoning from medically prescribed and other drugs. It excludes unintentional injuries, homicides, and other causes indirectly related to drug use. Also excluded are newborn deaths due to mother's drug use."
Source: Hoyert, Donna L., PhD, Heron, Melonie P., PhD, Murphy, Sherry L., BS, Kung, Hsiang-Ching, PhD; Division of Vital Statistics, "Deaths: Final Data for 2003," *National Vital Statistics Reports*, Vol. 54, No. 13 (Hyattsville, MD: National Center for Health Statistics, April 19, 2006), p. 10.

6.   (2003): "In 2003, a total of 20,687 persons died of alcohol-induced causes in the United States (Tables 23 and 24). The category 'alcohol-induced causes' includes not only deaths from dependent and nondependent use of alcohol, but also accidental poisoning by alcohol. It excludes unintentional injuries, homicides, and other causes indirectly related to alcohol use as well as deaths due to fetal alcohol syndrome."
Source: Hoyert, Donna L., PhD, Heron, Melonie P., PhD, Murphy, Sherry L., BS, Kung, Hsiang-Ching, PhD; Division of Vital Statistics, "Deaths: Final Data for 2003," *National Vital Statistics Reports*, Vol. 54, No. 13 (Hyattsville, MD: National Center for Health Statistics, April 19, 2006), p. 10.

7.   (1996): "Each year, use of NSAIDs (Non-Steroidal Anti-Inflammatory Drugs) accounts for an estimated 7,600 deaths and 76,000 hospitalizations in the United States." (NSAIDs include aspirin, ibuprofen, naproxen, diclofenac, ketoprofen, and tiaprofenic acid.)
Source: Robyn Tamblyn, PhD; Laeora Berkson, MD, MHPE, FRCPC; W. Dale Jauphinee, MD, FRCPC; David Gayton, MD, PhD, FRCPC; Roland Grad, MD,

MSc; Allen Huang, MD, FRCPC; Lisa Isaac, PhD; Peter McLeod, MD, FRCPC; and Linda Snell, MD, MHPE, FRCPC, "Unnecessary Prescribing of NSAIDs and the Management of NSAID-Related Gastropathy in Medical Practice," *Annals of Internal Medicine* (Washington, DC: American College of Physicians, 1997), September 15, 1997, 127:429-438, from the web at http://www.acponline. org/journals/annals/15sep97/nsaid.htm [16], last accessed Feb. 14, 2001, citing Fries, JF, "Assessing and understanding patient risk," *Scandinavian Journal of Rheumatology Supplement*, 1992; 92:21-4.

8.   (Average 1982-1998): According to Canadian researchers, approximately 32,000 hospitalized patients (and possibly as many as 106,000) in the USA die each year because of adverse reactions to their prescribed medications.
Source: AMA, 1998), Nov. 25, 1998, Vol. 280, No. 20, from the web at http://jama. ama-assn.org/issues/v280n20/ffull/jlt1125-1.html [17], last accessed Feb. 12, 2001.

9.   An exhaustive search of the literature finds no credible reports of deaths induced by marijuana. The US Drug Abuse Warning Network (DAWN) records instances of drug mentions in medical examiners' reports, and though marijuana is mentioned, it is usually in combination with alcohol or other drugs. Marijuana alone has not been shown to cause an overdose death.
Source: National Academy Press, 1999, available on the web at http://www.nap. edu/html/marimed/; [18] and US Department of Justice, Drug Enforcement Administration, "In the Matter of Marijuana Rescheduling Petition" (Docket #86-22), September 6, 1988, p. 57.

10.   The Centers for Disease Control reported that in 2003, HIV disease was the 22nd leading cause of death in the US for whites, the 9th leading cause of death for blacks, and the 13th leading cause of death for Hispanics.
Source: Heron, Melonie P., PhD, Smith, Betty L., BsED, Division of Vital Statistics, "Deaths: Leading Causes for 2003," *National Vital Statistics Reports*, Vol. 55, No. 10 (Hyattsville, MD: National Center for Health Statistics, CDC, March 15, 2007), p. 10, Table E, and p. 12, Table F.

Glossary of Terms

Acostar—To die

Amparos—Injunction-like decrees issued by Mexican courts

AFI—Mexico's Federal Investigations Agency

Alivianar—To provide assistance

Amordazado—Gagged person

Amphetamina—Amphetamines

Apodo—Nickname

Atorar—To arrest

AUC—United Self-Defense Forces in Colombia

BND—U.S. Bureau of Narcotic Drugs

Burrero—Drug mule

Cachorros—"Puppies" or high-living children of drug barons

Cajuela—Car trunk where bodies are often stuffed

Caleta—Hiding place for drug stash

Cañonazos—Large bribes

Cartelitos—Small cartels

Cartucho—Package of marijuana cigarettes

CNDH—Mexico's Human Rights Commission

Cholo—Street guy

CISEN—Center of Investigation and National Security (Mexico's version of the CIA)

Clavo—Vehicle with secret compartment in which to hide drugs or guns

Cocaine Alley—Main trafficking route across Arizona border controlled by Juárez Cartel

Coliflor Tosteo—Marijuana

"Cooperas o cuello"—"Cooperate or face death" (The threat that Mexican-Chinese chemical importer Zheli Ye Gon claimed to have received from Mexican officials)

Corridos—Ballads that often extol the virtues of major drug lords

Crema de Seda—Shiny fabric for flashy shirts worn by some drug dealers

Cuernos de chivo—Goat horns as AK-47 rifles are called

DEA—-Drug Enforcement Administration

Derecho—A treasonous person

Derecho de piso—A payment made to cross a plaza controlled by a cartel or to operate a business free from harm

Despachar—To kill someone

Diabólito—a cigarette that contains some combination of crack cocaine, marijuana, heroin, and PCPs

DTO—Drug trafficking organization

El Dedo—A gossip

El Otro Lado—The United States

ELN—National Liberation Army of Colombia guerrillas

Encapuchado—Hooded criminal or guerrilla

Encobijado—Assassinated person wrapped in a blanket

Enteipado—A person tied up with a rope

Entambado—Someone in prison

Extorsión Telefónica—Extortion by telephone

FARC—Revolutionary Armed Forces of Colombia

FDS—Mexico's Federal Security Directorate, founded in 1946 to help combat narcotics activities

FEADS—Federal Government Anti-Drug Agency or Fiscalía Especializada en Atención de Delitos Contra la Salud, which was closed in 1993 because of corruption

Feria—Money

GAFES—Airmobile Special Forces Groups

Gomeros—Men and women who convert opium poppies into paste

Guardianes—Individuals or "gatekeepers" used by the cartels to smuggle drugs across the border

Jale—Work

Jefe de Jefes—Big boss like a *Capo de capos*

Jugar Chueco—To betray

Kaibiles—Lethal Guatemalan commandos

La Familia—A violent organization centered in Michoacán whose leaders are religious fanatics

La Linea—Hit men for the Juárez Cartel

Levatón—Abduction

Limpiemos México—Caldeón's slogan: "Let's Clean up Mexico"

Loquear—To take drugs

Los Guëros—Assassins in Sonora believed to be in the pay of the Beltrán Leyva brothers

Los Peones—Assassins in Guerrero believed to be in the pay of the Beltrán Leyva brothers

Los Zetas—Paramilitary arm of the Gulf Cartel that is increasingly independent

Los Narcos—DEA agents

Macho—Men seeking to demonstrate their manliness

Macha—Women seeking to demonstrate their toughness

Mafiosi—Cartel leaders

Malandrine—Person of dubious character

Matón—Thug or bully.

Maxiproceso—Trial involving a large number of defendants

Mordidas—Bribes

Morras—Girlfriends of drug traffickers

Mota—Marijuana

Movida—Closing a deal

Mujeres-trofeo—Trophy women upon whom male narco-traffickers lavish expensive jewelry, clothing, and automobiles

Narcas—Female narco traffickers

Narcoaviones—Planes used to transport drugs

Narcoabogados—Lawyers who defend drug dealers

Narcoaficionado—Drug baron who is a sports fan

Narcoasesinatos—Drug-related killings

Narcobalancera—Gun battle involving narco-traffickers

Narcobodega—Storage place for drugs

Narcobondades—Benefits that nacco-traffickers confer on their communities such as roads, electricity, and church repairs

Narcobautismo—Baptism of the child of a cartel leader

Narcoboda—The elaborate marriage ceremony of a capo such as when Joaquín Guzmán Loera wed for the third time on September 2, 2007

Narcocandidatos—Aspirants for political office who are in thrall to cartels

Narcocañonazo—Large bribes to police

Narcocasas—Homes of cartel members

Narcocacique—Local political boss involved in drug trafficking

Narcoeconomía—Economic activities generated by drug-trafficking

Narcocementerios—Burial areas for cartel victims

Narcocolumnistas—Newspaper columnists who either fail to criticize or praise the cartels

Narcoconcursos de misses—Beauty contests sponsored by capos

Narcoconquista—The concept of cartels taking over a region

Narcoconsejo—Message sent by drug traffickers

Narcocoronas—Funeral wreaths that Los Zetas leave in front of establishment to threaten their foes

Narcocristianos—Christian involved in narco-trafficking

Narcocumbre—Meeting of high-level drug lords

Narcodiplomáticos—Diplomats enmeshed in drug activities

Narcodiputados—Deputies believed to linked to cartels

Narcoemisarios—Emissaries of drug barons

Narcoequipo—Sports team linked to a cartel

Narcoespías—Former narco-traffickers who provide intelligence to the government

Narcoestado—Country in thrall to drug dealers

Narcofiestas—Wild parties thrown by narcotics barons

Narcofosas—A grave where cartels bury their victims

Narcofunctionario—"Public servant" involved in illegal drug activities

Narcofútbol—Soccer teams owned by drug lords such as Los Mapaches of Nuevo Italia, Michoacán

Narcogranja—Farm on which drugs are grown

Narcoguerra—Warfare ignited by drug cartels as in Ciudad Juárez

Narcolaboratorios—Labs for producing methamphetamines and other synthetic drugs

Narcolista—A list of names of contacts or police who have been corrupted

Narcomansión—Large residence of narco-traffickers

Narcomantas—Large posters used by Los Zetas to attract members to their ranks

Narcomascotas—Exotic animals collected by drug dealers

Narcomensajes—Brutal acts through which cartels send messages to their foes

Narcomenudistas—Small-time drug dealers

Narcomilitares—Members of the armed forces who have deserted to the cartels

Narcoministros—Cabinet members who have cast their lot with cartels

Narcomonjas—Religious sister involved in the drug trade

Narconiños—Minors arrested for violating drug laws

Narcopalenque—A cockfighting pit where narco-barons gamble

Narconovelas—Soap operas that focus on drug traffickers

Narcoperiodistas—Newspaper reporters who play down cartel activities

Narcoplantíos—Farms or ranches on which drugs are grown

Narcopolicías—Police officers suborned by drug cartels

Narcopolíticos—Politicians in thrall to underworld figures

Narcoprestanombres—False names used by narco-traffickers

Narcorecados—Notes left by criminals, often at the side of a cadaver

Narcorescate—The rescue of a drug dealer from prison

Narcosacerdotes—Priests who perform marriages and other rites for narco-traffickers

Narcosubmarino—Small, low-lying boats, used to bring drugs ashore from larger vessels

Narcotelevangelistas—TV evangelists with ties to drug dealers

Narcoturismo—Narco tourism

Narcovíctmas—Women exploited by narco-criminals

Operación hormiga—Many people transporting drugs or other illegal items

PAN—National Action Party

Panga—High-speed boat to ferry drugs

Paniqueado—Scared person

Papelito—A wrapper for one gram of cocaine

Pasamojados—Smugglers of illegal immigrants

Pelear—To retreat or escape

Pelctón— Smallest division of the Mexican Army (11 soldiers)

PF—Federal Police

PFM—Federal Ministerial Police

PFP—Mexico's Federal Preventative Police

PGR—Attorney General's Office

Piedra colombiano—Cocaine in paste form

Pitazo—A warning or "*un aviso*"

Pisto—Alcoholic drink

Plan Mexico Seguro—"Safe Mexico Plan" initiated by President Fox late in his administration

Plataforma México—Databases on wanted persons, stolen and lost travel documents and stolen motor vehicles available to Interpol and to Mexican police agencies

Plato o plomo—Accept a bribe or face death

Plazas—Strategic areas for the production, storing, and shipping of drugs

Plomazo—Bullet wound

PRD—Democratic Revolutionary Party

Prestanombre—Pseudonym

PRI—Institutional Revolutionary Party

Project Gunrunner—Plan by the U.S. Bureau of Alcohol, Tobacco, Firearms, and Explosives to curb the flow of guns from the U.S. into Mexico

Puchadores—Small-time drug vendors

Puntas—Lookouts for the cartels

Queenpins—Female drug lords

Rafagazo—Shooting

Rajado—A coward

Rolex—High-grade cocaine

Sicarias—Thugs or hit-women

Sicarios—Thugs or hit-men

SIEDO—Mexico's version of the CIA

Sinaloa Cowboys—Thugs who protect leaders of the Sinaloa Cartel

Sinsemillas— High-quality marijuana produced without seeds

Soplón—Police informant

Tiro de gracia—Shot to the head

Topos—Literally "moles," the nickname for Mexicans who borrowed into collapsed buildings to find victims of the 1985 earthquakes in Mexico City

Un Valiente—A brave man who is greatly admired in Mexican culture

Un/Una Jaladora—Crack whore (male or female)

Yeyo—Cocaine

Zetitas—Members of Hispanic gangs in Laredo, Texas, recruited by Los Zetas

Zetización—Widespread activities by paramilitary groups

For invaluable assistance with this glossary, I am indebted to Professor James Creechan and his students in Sociology 4200 at the University of Guelph. Diego Camacho and Jorge Ibarra, graduate students in the Faculty of International Studies and Public Policy at the Autonomous University of Sinaloa in Culiacán, also made especially important contributions.

Selected Bibliography

Books

Aguayo Quezada, Sergio. *La Charola: Una historia de los servicios de inteligencia en México*. Mexico City: Grijalbo, 2001.

Anaya, Martha. *1988: El año que calló el sistema*. Mexico City: Debate, 2008.

Astorga Almanza, Luís Alejandro. *El siglo de las drogas*. Mexico City: Planeta, 1996.

————. *Seguridad, traficantes y militares*. Mexico City: Tusquets Editorial, 2007.

Bagley, Bruce Michael. *Mexico in Search of Security*. Coral Gables, FL North-South Center (University of Miami), 2004.

Bailey, John J. and Roy Godson (eds.). *Organized Crime and Democratic Governability: Mexico & the U.S. Borderlands*. Pittsburgh: University of Pittsburgh Press, 2000.

Bolívar Moreno, Gustavo. *Sin tetas no hay paraíso*. Bogotá: Quintero Editores, 2007.

Booth, Catherine. *Strong Drink Versus Christianity*. London: S.W. Partridge and Co., 1879.

Brandenburg, Frank. *The Making of Modern Mexico*. Englewood Cliffs, N.J.: Prentice-Hall, 1964.

Camp, Roderic Ai. *Politics in Mexico: the Democratic Consolidation*. New York: Oxford University Press, 2007.

————. *Mexico's Military on the Democratic Stage*. Westport, CT: Praeger and CSIS, 2005.

————. Mexico's Mandarins: *Crafting a Power Elite for the Twenty-First Century*. Berkley, CA: University of California Press, 2002.

Carpenter, Ted Galen. *Bad Neighbor Policy: Washington's Futile War on Drugs in Latin America*. New York: Palgrave Macmillan, 2003.

Centeno, Miguel Ángel. *Democracy within Reason: Technocratic Revolution in Mexico*. University Park, PA: Pennsylvania State University Press, 1994.

Davidow, Jeffrey. *The U.S. and Mexico: The Bear and the Porcupine*. Princeton: Marcus Wiener, 1994.

González, Francisco E. *Dual Transitions from Authoritarian Rule: Institutionalized Regimes in Chile and Mexico, 1970-2000.* Baltimore: Johns Hopkins University Press, 2008.

Grayson, George W. *Mexico's Struggle with Drugs and Thugs.* New York: Foreign Policy Association, 2009.

_____. *Mexican Messiah: Andrés Manuel López Obrador.* University Park, PA: Pennsylvania State University Press, 2007.

_____. *The Mexico-U.S. Business Committee: Catalyst for the North American Free Trade Agreement.* Rockville, MD: Montross Press, 2007.

_____. Mexico: *From Corporatism to Pluralism?* Ft. Worth, TX: Harcourt Press, 1988.

_____. *The United States and Mexico: Patterns of Influence.* New York: Praeger, 1984.

Gutiérrez, Alejandro. *Narcotráfico: El gran desafío de Calderón.* Mexico City: Planeta, 2007.

Kamstra, Jerry. *Weed: Adventures of a Dope Smuggler.* Santa Barbara, CA: Ross-Eirkson, 1983.

Kandel, Jonathan. *La Capital: The Biography of Mexico City.* New York: Random House, 1988.

Liddy, G. Gordon. *Will: The Autobiography of G. Gordon Liddy.* New York: St. Martin's Press, 1980.

Loret de Mola. *Escenarios. Mexico City*: Editorial Oceana de México, 2006.

Malmström, Vincent H. *Land of the Fifth Sun: Mexico in Space and Time.* Hanover, NH: An E-Book in Historical Geography, 2002. *http://www.dartmouth.edu.*

Meyer, Lorenzo. *El presidencialismo mexicano: Del Populismo al neoliberalismo.*

Monsiváis, Carlos, and Julio Scherer. *Parte de guerra: Tlatelolco 1968.* México City: Aguilar, 1999.

Musto, David F. *The American Disease.* New York: Yale University Press, 1973.

Oppenheimer, Andrés. *Bordering on Chaos: Guerrillas, Stockbrokers, Politicians, and Mexico's Road to Prosperity.* Boston: Little Brown and Co., 1996: 298.

Padgett, L. Vincent. *The Mexican Political System, Second Edition.* Boston: Houghton Mifflin, 1976.

Pegram, Thomas R. *Battling Demon Rum: The Struggle for a Dry America, 1800-1933.* Chicago: Ivan R. Dee, 1998.

Poppa, Terrence E. *Drug Lord: The Life and Death of a Mexican Kingpin.* Seattle: Demand Publications, rev. ed. 1998.

Riding, Alan. *Distant Neighbor: A Portrait of the Mexicans.* New York: Alfred A. Knopf, 1985.

Russell, Philip L. *Mexico under Salinas.* Austin, TX: Mexican Resource Center, 1994.

Scherer García, Julio. *La Reina del Pacífico: es la hora de contar.* Mexico City: Grijalbo, 2008.

Scott, Peter Dale and Jonathan Marshall, *Cocaine Politics: Drugs, Armies, and the CIA in Central America*. Berkeley and Los Angeles: University of California Press, 1998.

Scott, Robert E. *Mexican Government in Transition*. Urbana, IL: University of Illinois Press, rev. ed. 1971.

Shannon, Elaine. *Desperados: Latin Drug Lords, U.S. Lawmen, and the War America Can't Win*. New York: Viking, 1988.

Velling, Menno (ed.). *The Political Economy of the Drug Industry: Latin America and the International System*. Gainesville, FL: University of Florida Press, 2004.

Walker III, William O. (ed). *Drugs in the Western Hemisphere: An Odyssey of Cultures in Conflict*. Wilmington, DE: Scholarly Resources, 1996.

Book Chapters

Bagley, Bruce Michael, and William O. Walker III (eds.) "After San Antonio." *Drug Trafficking in the Americas*. Coral Gables: University of Miami North-South Center Press, 1996.

Journal and Magazine Articles

Aguilar Camín, Héctor. "Narco Historias extraordinarias." *Nexos*, May 2007. *www.nexos.mx.com*.

Bailey, John and Matthew M. Taylor, "Evade, Corrupt, or Confront? Organized Crime and the State in Brazil and Mexico." *Journal of Politics in Latin America*, 1, no. 2/2009: 3-29.

Bowden, Charles. "The Sicario: A Juárez Hit Man Speaks." *Harpers*, No. 1908, May 2009: 44-53.

_____"We Bring Fear," *Mother Jones*, July/August 2009: 29-43.

Campbell, Howard. "Female Drug Smugglers on the U.S.-Mexico Border: Gender, Crime, and Empowerment." *Anthropological Quarterly* 80, no. 4 (fall 2007): 233-267.

Fukuyama, Francis. "The Imperative of State-Building." *Journal of Democracy* 15, no. 2 (2004): 17-31.

González, Francisco E. "To Die in Mexico: Rumblings of a Drug War." *Current History*. February 2009.

Leroy, Christophe. "Mexican Intelligence at a Crossroad." *SAIS Review*, XXIV (Winter–Spring 2004).

Musto, David F. "Opium, Cocaine and Marijuana in American History." *Scientific American*, July 1991: 20-27.

O'Neil, Shannon. "The Real War in Mexico: How Democracy Can Defeat Drug Cartels." *Foreign Affairs* 88. no. 4 July/August 2009: 63-77.

Purcell, Susan Kaufman and John F.H. Purcell. "State and Society in Mexico: Must a Stable Polity be Institutionalized?" *World Politics* 32, January 1980: 200.

Government, Think-Tank, Corporate, and Cartel Documents

Anslinger, Harry. "U.S.-Mexican Cross-Border Marijuana Traffic." *Illegal Economy. www.illegaleconomy.com/drugs/us-mexico.*

Astorga, Luis. "Drug Trafficking in Mexico: A First General Assessment." Discussion Paper no. 36. January 22, 2009 *www.unesco.org/shs/most.*

Beittel, June S. "Mexico's Drug-Related Violence." Congressional Research Service, May 27, 2009 *www.fas.org/sgp/crs/row/R40582.pdf.*

Brands, Hal. *Mexico's Narco-Insurgency and U.S. Counterdrug Policy.* Strategic Studies Institute, U.S. Army War College, May 7, 2009 *www.strategic-studiesinstitute.army.mil.*

Congressional Research Service. "Mexico's Drug Cartels." October 16, 2007 *www.fas.org/sgp/crs/row/rl34215.*

Cook, Colleen W. *CRS Report for Congress: Mexico's Drug Cartels.* Congressional Research Service, October 16, 2007 *www.fas.org/sgp/crs/row/RL34215.pdf.*

Council on Hemispheric Affairs. "COHA's Report on Mexico's Prison system: Yet Another Blemished Aspect of Fox's Failed Presidency." May 1, 2006. *www.coha.org.*

——————. "Mexican Drug Policy: Internal Corruption in an Externalized War." Press Release, June 26, 2007. *www.coha.org.*

Drug Enforcement Administration: 1975-80. January 22, 2009 *www.dea.gov/pubs/history/1995-1980.html.*

Drug Policy Alliance Network. "What's Wrong with the War on Drugs." *www.drugpolicy.org/drugwar/.*

Everingham, Susan S., and C. Peter Rydell. *Controlling Cocaine: Supply Versus Demand Programs.* Santa Monica, CA: Rand Corporation, 1994. *www.rand.org/pubs/monograph_reports/.*

Federal Bureau of Investigation. "Wanted: Ignacio Coronel Villareal." *http://www.fbi.gov/wanted/fugitives/cei/villareal_ic.htm.*

Garza. Antonio O. "Our Continued Efforts Will Deny Firearms to Criminal Organizations and Reduce Gun Violence." Released by the U.S. Embassy (Mexico), January 16, 2008. *www.usembassy-mexico.gov.*

Gobierno de México. *Segundo Informe*, September 1, 2008. *www.presidencia.gob.mx/.*

Grayson, George W. "Mexican Officials Feather their Nests while Decrying U.S. Immigration Policy. *Backgrounder*, Center for Immigration Studies, April 2006. *www.cis.org.*

Hanson, Stephanie. *Backgrounder: Mexico's Drug War.* Council on Foreign Relations, June 28, 2007. *www.cfr.org/publications.*

Kairies, Kate, and Sam Logan. "U.S. Drug Habit Migrates to Mexico." Americas Program, Center for International Policy, February 7, 2007. *http://americas.irc-online.org.*

Eskridge, Chris. "Mexican Cartels and Their Integration into Mexican Socio-Political Culture." An earlier version of the paper was presented at the International Conference on Organized Crime: Myth, Power, Profit, October 1999, Lausanne, Switzerland.

Library of Congress. *Organized Crime and Terrorist Activity in Mexico, 1999-2002.* February 2003.

Military Balance. Vol. 107 London: Institute for Strategic Studies, 2007.

Moreno González, Nazario "El Loco." "Pensamientos de la Familia," photocopied and undated.

National Drug Intelligence Center. S*tate of* Af*fairs Report: Cities in Which Mexican DTOs Operate Within the United States,* April, 11, 2008 www. usdoj.gov/ndic/pubs27/27986/index.htm#Contents.

Olson, Joy. Testimony before the Subcommittee on State, Foreign Operations and Related Programs of the U.S. House of Representatives Appropriations Committee, March 10, 2009. *www.appropriations.house.gov/Witness_testimony/SFOPS/Joy_Olson_03_10_09.pdf.*

Puddington, Arch. "Freedom in the World 2009: Setbacks and Resilience," Freedom House. *www.freedomhouse.org/template.cfm?page=1.*

"President Bush and President Berger of Guatemala Participate in Joint Press Availability." White House News Release, March 12, 2007. *http://www.whitehouse.gov/news/releases/2007/03/20070312-4.html.*

Procuraduría General de la República. "Mario Villanueva Madrid Case." August 18, 2007, Press release 400/07.

The Roper Center for Public Opinion Research. Survey conducted between July 18-22, 1986. *www.ropercenter.uconn.edu.proxy.*

Storrs, K. Larry. "Drug Certification/Designation Procedures for Illicit Narcotics Producing and Transit countries." Congressional Research Service Report for Congress, September 22, 2003. *www.fas.org/irp/crs/RL32038.pdf.*

Turbiville Jr., Graham H. "Law Enforcement and the Mexican Armed Forces: New Security Mission Challenges the Military." Foreign Military Studies Office. *http://fmso.leavenworth.army.mil/documents/mxcoparm.htm.*

United Nations Office on Drugs and Crime. *World Drug Report 2009.* New York: UN, 2009 *www.unodc.org/unodc/en/data-and-analysis/WDR-2009. html.*

U.S. Department of Justice. *National Drug Threat Assessment 2008.* Washington, D.C.: National Drug Intelligence Center, 2007 *www.usdoj.gov/dea/concern/18862/2008.pdf.*

U.S. Government Accountability Office. *Firearms Trafficking: U.S. Efforts to Combat Arms Trafficking to Mexico Face Planning and Coordination challenges.* GAO-09-709, June 2009.

"Welcome to Kansas City Southern." 2007 *www.kcsouthern.com/en-us/Pages/default./aspx/.*

Interviews and Electronic Mail

Castejón Díez, Jaime. Interview with author. Mexico City, January 8, 2009.

Flores Velasco, Guillermo. Telephone interview with author. May 23, 2009.

Heredia Diáz, Carlos. Interview with author. Mexico City, March 11, 2009.

Millán Lazárraga, Juan Sigfrido. Telephone interview with author. July 3, 2008.

Núñez, Peter K. Telephone interview with author, May 28, 2009.

Peschard Svedrup, Armand. Telephone interview with author, May 23, 2009.
Valencia, Juan Gabriel. Interview with author. Mexico City, March 10, 2009,
    July 6, 2008, January 13, 2008, August 4, 2007.

Newspapers, Magazines, Electronic Media, and Blog Articles

"Acusan nexus con narco de ex delegado en Edomex." *Reforma*, September
    19, 2008.
Aguilar, Luis F. "En busca del Estado." *Reforma*, August 13, 2008.
Althaus, Dudley, and Marion Lloyd. "Calderón Unveils Anti-Drug Initiative."
    Houston Chronicle, July 3, 2007. *www.chron.com.*
Althaus, Dudley, Richard S. Dunham, and Stewart M. Powell. "GOP Texans
    Balk at Aid to Mexico." *Houston Chronicle*, May 16, 2008.
Álvarez P., Fred. "Fue sedena, no SSP." April 5, 2008. *www.fredalvarez.blogspot.
    com/2008/04/fue-sedena-no-ssp.html.*
Ambriz, Agustín, "Arévalo Gardoqui: la sobra del narco," *Proceso*, May 7,
    2000.
Anderson, John Ward. "After Death, Kingpin's Life Is an Open Book." *Wash-
    ington Post*, November 25, 1997, A-1.
Aranda, Jesús, and Claudia Herrera. "Lealtad contra la delincuencia, pide Calde-
    rón a la tropa; les aumenta $500." *La Jornada*, February 20, 2008.
"Arellano Corp." *Proceso*, September 3, 2006.
"Arraigan a líder de 'Zetas' de Tabasco." *El Nuevo Heraldo*, September 9,
    2008.
"Aspiran niños a ser sicarios." *Reforma*, July 29, 2007.
"Bajo control de 'Los Sierras': El organigrama del grupo." *El Universal*, Janu-
    ary 1, 2009.
Baker, Peter. "Calderón Admonishes Bush on Thorny Issues." *Washington Post*,
    March 14, 2007: A-9.
Barajas, Abel. "Soldiers Face 60 for Aiding Traffickers." *Laredo Morning Times-
    Reforma News Service*, October 2, 2006.
Barnet, Jeff, and Ana Maria Ruiz-Brown. "Top Drug Lord Reported Dead;
    Juárez Cartel Changes Hands." *www.nmsu.edu/~frontera/old_1997/
    aug97/897amado.html/.*
Beaubien, Jason. "Economy, Drug Wars Hurt Cross-Border Business." *Morning
    Edition*, National Public Radio, December 4, 2008.
Bergman, Jake. "The Place Mexico's Drug Kingpins Call Home." PBS Drug
    Wars. *www.pbs.org/wgbh/pages/frontline/shows/drugs/business/place.
    html.*
Beyliss, Marcelo. "Amenanzan con narcoflores a la policía de Sonora." *El Uni-
    versal*, November 24, 2008.
Booth, William. "Kidnap Consultant Taken in Mexico." *Washington Post*, De-
    cember 16, 2008: A-15.
————. "Mexico Kidnapping Death Stokes Outrage." *Washington Post*,
    December 14, 2008.
"Border-town Killing Sends Message." *Los Angeles Times*, June 10, 2005.
Bourdeaux, Richard. "Mexico's Master of Elusion." *Los Angeles Times*, July
    5, 2005.

————————. "Since his Escape, Drug Cartel Chief Joaquín 'Shorty' Guzmán has Expanded his Empire, Waged War on Rivals, and Become a Legend." *Los Angeles Times*, July 5, 2005.

Brito, Luis. "Refuerzan PFP con otro General." *Reforma*, December 19, 2008.

————————. "Matan nueve agentes en una semana." *Reforma*, May 10, 2008.

Burton, Fred, and Scott Stewart. "Mexico: Examining Cartel War Violence through a Protective Intelligence Lens." *Stratfor*, May 14, 2008.

Cabrera, Javier. "Urgen reviser operativo policíaco." *El Universal*, November 30, 2008.

"Cae otro presunto Zeta en Guatemala con arsenal." *El Universal*, December 19, 2008.

Camacho, Carlos. "Las adicciones han crecido entre 15 y 20 por ciento anual, dice Medina Mora." *La Jornada*, August 3, 2007.

"Can Calderón Win Mexico's Drug War?" *Newsweek International*, May 28, 2007.

Cano, Luis Carlos. "ONG protestan contra las acciones militares." *El Universal*, November 30, 2008.

Carlsen, Laura. "A Primer on Plan Mexico." *Americas Policy Program Special Report*, May 5, 2008. *http://americas.irc-online.org/am/5204*.

Carrasco Araizago, Jorge, and Francisco Castellanos J. "Caso Morelia: confesiones 'bajo tortura.'" *Proceso*, October 2008.

"'Cartel del Golfo': recompense por captura de autores de atentado en Morelia." *Milenio.com*, October 4, 2008.

Case, Brandon M., Alfredo Corchado, and Laurence Iliff. "Officials Develop Clearer Picture of Zetas." *El Universal (Mexico News)*, March 21, 2005.

Castañeda, Jorge. "Mexico Goes to War: Calderon's drug crusade is winning fans, but can he win the fight?" *Newsweek International*, May 28, 2007.

Castillo García, Gustavo. "Guerras internas del narco; la más cruenta, en el cártel del Golfo." *La Jornada*, February 18, 2007.

César Carrillo, Pablo. "Elección con tufo a narco." *EXonline*, November 17, 2007.

————————. "Acusación de narco me da risa." *Excelsior*, November 13, 2007.

"Clinton voices 'regret' to Mexico." *United Press International*, May 26, 1998.

"Cobra el hampa 38 vidas en 7 estados; 19, solo en Tijuana." *La Jornada*, December 1, 2008.

Corchado, Alfredo. "Cartel's Enforcers Outpower their Boss." *Dallas Morning News*, June 11, 2007.

————————. "Drug Cartels Operate Training Camps near Texas Border Just inside Mexico." *Dallas Morning News*, April 4, 2008.

Corchado, Alfredo, and Tracey Eaton. "Mexico Intensifies Hunt for Drug Lord." *Dallas Morning News*, April 13, 2005.

"Crece aprobación." *Reforma,* June 1, 2007.

"Critican propuesta de Rubén Aguilar." *Reforma*, December 19, 2008.

"Da juez 47 años de cárcel a 'El Metro.'" *El Diario*, June 21, 2007.

"Dan 'Zetas' narcoconsejo." *Reforma*, May 4, 2008.

Dávila, Darío. "Un capo y dos 'bandidas.'" *El Universal*, June 10, 2008.

Dávila, Patricia. "La boda del Capo Mayor." *Proceso*, September 1, 2007.

Diaz, Lizbeth. "Mexico Death Industry Thrives on Drug War Killings." *Reuters*, November 1, 2008. http//wap.alertnet.org/thenews/newsdesk/N01349201. htm.

De la Luz González, María. "Mapaches 'lavaron' en siete países." *El Universal*, October 15, 2008.

"Dejan cabeza con narcomensaje en hielera en Michoacán." *La Opción de Chihuahua*, October 24, 2008.

"Denuncian ayuda de Procampo a narcos." *El Siglo de Torreón*, October 28, 2008.

"Descarta DEA cambiar agentes por infiltración del narco en Embajada." *El Universal*, October 27, 2008.

"Detenido el jefe de Interpol México en el marco de la 'operación Limpieza.'" *El Periódico.com/Internaciona*l, November 18, 2008.

Dillon, Sam, and Craig Pyres. "Court Files Say Drug Baron Used Mexican Military." *New York Times*, May 24, 1997.

"Dominar al país, plan de la Familia." *www.deyaboo.forumcommunity.net.*

"Drug Cartels: the Growing Violence in Mexico." *Stratfor*, October 2006.

Duggan, Paul, and Ernesto Londoño. "Not Your Average Drug Bust; Suspect Wanted in Mexico Found in Wheaton Restaurant." *Washington Post*, July 25, 2007.

"El Cartel La Familia, sospechose del narcoatentado en Michoacán." *E-Consulta*, September 18, 2008. *www.e-consulta.com.*

Ellingwood, Ken. "U.S. Merida Aid Initiative Angers Some in Mexico." *Los Angeles Times,* June 5, 2008.

Enriquez, Sam, and Hector Tobar. "Mexican army faces tough war with drug cartels." *Los Angeles Times*, May 16, 2007.

"Entra 'Wencho' al narco en busca de revancha." *Reforma*, November 12, 2008.

Esquivel, J. Jesús. "El narco mexicano, imparable." *Proceso*, June 10, 2008.

————. "Los dueños de la frontera." *Proceso*, August 12, 2007.

"Ex militares sirven de sicarios a cárteles mexicanos." *SeguRed.com*, July 25, 2006. *http://www.segured.com/index.php?od=9&link=7765.*

Fedarka, Kevin, et al. "The Capture of Mexico's Most Wanted." *Time*, January 29, 1996.

Fernández Menéndez, Jorge. "La verdadera historia de los Arellano Félix." *Arcana*, March 1, 2002. *www.drogasmexico.org.*

Figueroa, Carlos. "Aparecen narcomantas en dos estados; ofrecen recompensas por líderes de La Familia." *La Jornada de Oriente*, October 6, 2008.

"Fox: Drug Trafficking Reached Presidency." *UPI*, February 8, 2005.

Friedman, Milton. "An Open Letter to Bill Bennett" *Freedom Daily*, April 1990. *www.fff.org/freedom/0490e.asp.*

Garduño, Roberto. "Sepultan el Plan Mérida en la interparliamentaria México-U.S." *La Jornada*, June 8, 2008.

Garduño, Silvia. "Crece con Calderón la migración a EU." *Reforma*, September 21, 2008.

Golden, Tim. "U.S. Officials Say Mexican Military Aids Drug Traffic." *New York Times*, March 26, 1998.

—————. "Dangerous Allies: U.S. Helps Mexico's Army Take Big Anti-Drug Role." *The New York Times*, December 29, 1997.

Gómez, Francisco. "'Los Zetas' por dentro." *El Universal*, December 31, 2008.

—————. "'La Familia,' imagen y ritos del narco." *El Universal*, January 1, 2009.

—————. "Dominar al país, plan de 'La Familia.'" *El Universal*, August 1, 2008.

—————. "El cártel del Golfo y su disfraz de altruismo." *El Universal*, January 7, 2008.

González, Iván. "Rosales estaba ligado a Osiel Cárdenas: PGR." *EsMas. www. esmas.com/noticierotelevisa/mexico.*

Guggenheim, Ken. "Senator Offers U.S.-Mexico Drug Plan." *Star Tribune*, February 15, 2001.

Heath, Edward. "Drug Wars," PBS Frontline, 2000.

Herrera, Rolando. "Pelea narco territorio en México y … en EU." Reforma, October 5, 2008.

Hurtado, Javier. "México secuestrado." *Reforma*, August 14, 2008.

Inter-American Dialogue. *Latin American Advisor.* March 13, 2008.

International Pen. "Mexico: Editor Abducted and Shot Dead." October 15, 2008. *www.internationalpen.org.uk.*

"Invasion of the Body-Snatchers." *Reuters*, March 9, 2007.

"Investigan pactos de Beltrán con 'Zetas.'" *Reforma*, November 25, 2008.

"The Jazz Age: the American 1920s." *Digital History*. January 20, 2009. *http:// www.digitalhistory.uh.edu/database/article_display.*

Jiménez, Alejandro. "Alentados en Morelia: un año de golpes para frenar poderío." *El Universal*, September 19, 2008.

Jiménez, Benito. "Identifica el Ejército tres rutas de cárteles." *Reforma*, June 14, 2007. *www.reforma.com.*

Kurtz-Phelan, Daniel "The Long War of Genaro García Luna." *New York Times Magazine*, July 13, 2008.

"La Familia: Society's Saviours or Sociopaths." *http://cyanide257.wordpress. com/2008/09/25/La-Familia.*

"La mitad del país, bajo el mando de Los Zetas." *Milenio*, November 25, 2008.

"La SIEDO ya investiga sobre los decapitados y narcorecados." *MiMorelia.com*, August 22, 2008. *www.mimorelia.com.*

Lacey, Marc. "Mexico's Unsuccessful Drug War, Painfully Preserved and Hidden." *New York Times*, November 27, 2008.

—————. "Congress Trims Bush's Mexico Drug Plan." *New York Times*, May 23, 2008.

—————. "Drug Killings Haunt Mexican School Children." *New York Times*, October 19, 2008.

Lakshmanan, Indira A.R. "Drug-related Violence Moves into Acapulco." *Boston Globe*, July 30, 2006.

Lauría, Carlos, and José Simón. "Mexican President Must Protect Freedom of Expression." *San Francisco Chronicle,* July 23, 2007.

León, Rodrigo, and Alejandro Moreno. "Encuesta/Destacan el crimen." *Reforma,* January 1, 2009.

"Like a Church on a Hill." *News-Press* (Ft. Myers), September 26, 1999.

Logan, Samuel. "Mexico's Internal War." *Power and Interest News Report,* August 14, 2006. http: //www.pinr.com.

"Los Zetas el otro ejército." *Sitio Extra Oficial, Fuerza Aérea Mexicana,* January 20, 2007. *www.extrafam.mforos.com.*

Madrid, Lemic. "Los Zetas pasan de ser brazo armado a cabeza." *Excelsior,* September 9, 2008.

Marosi, Richard. "Mystery Man Blamed for Gruesome Tijuana Deaths." *Los Angeles Times,* December 18, 2008.

—————. "A Tijuana Blood Bath." *Los Angeles Times,* October 6, 2008.

Martínez, Fernando. "Ubican 4 mil puntos donde venden droga." *El Universal,* July 7, 2007: C3.

Martínez, Julieta. "Asesino de novia de 'capo' avivó la violencia." *El Universal,* December 2, 2008.

Matthews, Jay. "Murder of Drug Agent Lights Hometown Anger; Friends Warn Travelers of Mexico Danger." *Washington Post,* March 14, 1985.

McCombs, Brady. "Es Nogales el premio de guerra entre cárteles." *Arizona Daily Star,* September 19, 2008.

McKinley Jr., James C. "Mexican Drug War Turns Barbaric, Grisly." *New York Times,* October 26, 2006. *www.nytimes.com.*

—————. "Mexico Sends 4 Kingpins to Face Trial in the U.S." *New York Times,* January 21, 2007: 15.

—————. "Mexico Arrests Wanted Figure in Drug Cartel." *New York Times,* February 1, 2005.

Méndez, Alfredo. "Todo apunta a que La Familia es culpable, según la Procuraduría." *La Jornada,* September 19, 2008.

—————. "'Cínica,' la política antidrogas de EU; su ley 'absurda': Medina Mora." *La Jornada,* June 15, 2007.

Méndez, José. "Narco pasa frontera sur en helicópteros, revelan." *El Universal,* December 19, 2008.

Mendoza Aguilar, Gardenia. "Indagan mal uso de programas oficiales." *La Opinión,* October 31, 2008.

"Mexican Military Special Forces Arrest Alfredo Beltrán Leyva, One of the Main Leaders of the Sinaloa Cartel. Cash, Firearms, and 3 Others Arrested." *Narcotic News,* January 21, 2008. *www.narcoticnews.com/Cocaine/2008/ Jan/Cocaine_2008_Jan_21_Culiacan_Sinaloa.*

"México and United States; An Undiplomatic Murder." *The Economist,* March 30, 1985: 51.

"México Arrests Highest-Profile Female Suspected Drug Trafficker." *Associated Press,* September 29, 2007.

"México Doubles Size of Huge Cocaine Haul." *Reuters,* November 1, 2007. *www.reuters.com.*

"México indaga 'invitación' a militares a unirse a narcos." *La voz.com*, April 14, 2008.

"México Pledges to Help U.S. Fight Terror." CNN.com./U.S.

"Mexico Says More U.S. Drug Aid Expected by January." *Associated Press*, December 17, 2008.

"Mexico to Try 19 Soldiers in Civilian Shootings." *Reuters*, June 11, 2007.

"Mexico's Drug Problem." *New York Times*, March 2, 1998.

"México's Hydra." *Security in Latin America.* networkedintelligence.wordpress. com/tag./la-familia/.

"Mil 200 negocios pagan renta al narco en Morelia." *Milenio.com*, September 24, 2008.

Millán González, Omar. "Funeral Homes See Big Rise in Business." *San Diego Union-Tribune*, November 16, 2008.

Miller Llana, Sara. "Setbacks in Mexico's War on Corruption." *Christian Science Monitor*, December, 30, 2008.

————. "As Mexico's Drug War Rages, Military Takes over for Police." *Christian Science Monitor*, December 5, 2008.

Mosso, Ruben. "FBI: Los Zetas problema de seguridad nacional para EU." January 9, 2008.

"Multiplica 'Familia' violencia en Edomex." *Reforma*, September 14, 2008.

"'Nacho' se expande mientras cárteles riñen." El Universal, October 9, 2008.

Najar, Alberto. "Desertaron 100 mil militares con Fox." *Milenio,* July 20, 2007.

"New Mexico Governor Calls for Legalizing Drugs." *CNN*, October 6, 1999.

"Nos persiguen por 'estigma': Carrillo Fuentes." *Noroeste*, December 12, 2008.

"Ofrece 'El Tísico' soborno a captores." *Reforma*, November 3, 2004.

Omang, Joanne, and Mary Thornton. "Mexican Chief's Election Fraudulent, Helms Says." *Washington Post,* June 18, 1986.

"Over 150,000 March in Mexico against Crime." *Reuters*, August 31, 2008.

Padget, Tim, and Michael S. Serrill. "Corrupt but Certified." *Time*, March 10, 1997.

"Paga 'El Wencho' $1 millón por equipo." *Reforma*, November 14, 2008.

"Pelean Michoacán Zetas y La Familia." *Reforma*, September 18, 2008.

Peirce, Neal. "Bush Has a Faculty Prescription for Mexican Drug Violence." *Richmond Times Dispatch*, May 25, 2008.

Piñeyro, José Luis. "México: ¿seguro?" *El Universal*, April 14, 2007.

"Por qué se fue Alejandro Junco." *Reporte Indigo*, September 12, 2008.

"Polarización en el SNTE." *El Universal* (Bajo Reserva Column), July 28, 2007.

"Policías de Chalco vinculan a su jefe con 'La Familia Michoacana'." *Notisistema Informa*, November 7, 2008. www.notisistema.com.

Preston, Julia. "Drug Corruption Links Mexican Military to Spate of Abductions." *New York Times*, March 9, 1997.

"¿Quiere saber dónde se producen las células rojas?" *Milenio*, April 17, 2007.

Ravelo, Ricardo. "El cártel de Juárez: poder creciente." *Proceso*, July 10, 2005.

"Report Ties Ex-official to Juárez Cartel." *The Herald* (*El Universal*), January 21, 2006.

"Responde hampa con violencia." *Reforma* (Enfoque), November 30, 2008.

Rivera, Rafael. "'Boom' carguero en Lázaro Cárdenas." *El Universal*, December 29, 2008.

Rodríguez, Martín P. "Drogas y terrorismo, prioridad tras reunión." *Prensa Libre.com*, March 27, 2006. *www.prensalibre.com.*

Rodríguez, Olga R. "Mexican Senate Approves Judicial Reform." *Associated Press*, March 7, 2008.

—————. "Mexico Denies Drug Suspect Paid for Party." *Boston Globe*, April 30, 2006.

Rodriguez Martínez, Marco A. "El poder de los 'zetas.'" *www.monografías.com.*

Roig-Franzia, Manuel. "Drug Trade Tyranny on the Border." *The Washington Post,* March 16, 2008, A-16.

Rose, David. "The House of Death." *The Observer*, December 3, 2006.

Rubio, Luis. "Violencia." *Reforma*, June 8, 2008.

San Pedro, Emilio. "In the Shadow of the Cartels." *BBC World Service. www.bbc.co.uk/worldservice/news/2008.*

Schwartz, Jeremy. "Mérida Initiative: Behind the Scenes." *Cox Newspapers*, July 1, 2008.

"Se adueña La Familia de plaza de Guanajuato." *Milenio*, November 8, 2008.

"Se suma nueve ejecuciones a la ola de violencia en todo el país." *El Universal*, April 18, 2007.

"Secuestran a dos personas al día en promedio: PGR." *El Imparcial,* September 15, 2008.

"Seguridad." *Terra*, October 17, 2008.

Serrano, Mónica. "The Parallel Economy." *BBC World News Service,* January 22, 2009.

Shimer, Katie. "Coke: From Where it Grows... To Your Nose." *Portland Mercury*, May 22, 2003.

"Shocking Culture of Impunity and Violence." *freemedia.at/cms/ipi/statements_detail.html?ctxid=CH0055&...&year=2008.*

Sierra, Arturo. "Mata narco a 21 al Poniente del DF." *Reforma*, September 20, 2008.

Smith, James F. "Mexico, Still Upset, Now Says it Knew of 'Sting' Plan." *Los Angeles Times*, June 5, 1998.

Snow, Anita. "Sentence Overturned for Convicted Killer of U.S. Drug Agent." *Associated Press*, April 25, 1997.

Solutions Abroad. "Kidnappings in Mexico." *www.solutionsabroad.com/en./security.*

Stevenson, Mark. "Mexico Outraged over Corrupt Police, Kidnappings." *Associated Press*, August 21, 2008.

"Sube en EU el precio de cocaína." *Reforma*, August 12, 2007.

Suverza. Alejandro. "Los Zetas, una pesadilla para el cartel del Golfo." *El Universal*, January 12, 2008: 1.

—————. "El poder de 'La Familia Michoacana'." *El Universal*, December 4, 2006.

"Templo Mayor." *Reforma*, December 28, 2008.

Thompson, Barnard R. "Kidnappings are out of Control in Mexico." *Mexidata Info*, June 14, 2004. *www.mexidata.info.*

Thompson, Ginger. "U.S. to Lift Ban on Military Aid to Guatemala." *New York Times*, March 25, 2005.

Tobar, Héctor. "Drug Kingpin Extraditions Will Likely Help Calderón." *Los Angeles Times*, January 22, 2007.

"Toma 'La Familia' ley en Michoacán." *Reforma*, November 24, 2006.

Tuckman, Jo. "Drug Wars Cast a Long Shadow over Acapulco's Future." *The Guardian,* February 10, 2007.

—————. "Narco War Spirals out of Control." June 24, 2007, *Mail & Guardian Online.*

"Un país inseguro." *El Siglo de Torreón*, August 30, 2008.

"U.S. Releases First Part of Drug Aid for Mexico." *Associated Press*, December 4, 2008.

"'Va a morir toda La Familia michoacana, sino me creen allí les dejo esto'; tres ejecutados." *Alerta Periodista*, August 19, 2008. *www.alertaperiodistica. com.mx.*

Van Natta, Jr. Don. "U.S. Indicts 26 Mexican Bankers in Laundering of Drug Funds." *New York Times*, May 19, 1998.

Villalpando, Rubén. "La violencia en Ciudad Juárez provoca éxodo de 3 mil familias." *La Jornada*, November 17, 2008.

Weiner, Tim. "Mexico Imprisons Two Generals, Longtime Suspects in Drug Cases." *New York Times*, September 2, 2000.

Weissert, Will. "Michoacán ensagretada por decapitaciones de los narcos." *La Voz*, October 23, 2006.

Wilkinson, Tracy. "Mexican Drug Lord Seems Everywhere—and Nowhere." *Richmond Times-Dispatch*, November 5, 2008: A-28.

Zemi Communications. "Mexico, Politics and Policy." September 2008 through May 2009.

"'Zetas' y Beltrán crean megacártel." *El Universal*, May 19, 2008.

Index